J. L. Wilkinson and the
Kansas City Monarchs

Also by William A. Young

John Tortes "Chief" Meyers: A Baseball Biography
(McFarland, 2012)

J. L. Wilkinson and the Kansas City Monarchs
Trailblazers in Black Baseball

WILLIAM A. YOUNG

McFarland & Company, Inc., Publishers
Jefferson, North Carolina

LIBRARY OF CONGRESS CATALOGUING-IN-PUBLICATION DATA

Names: Young, William A., 1945– author.
Title: J. L. Wilkinson and the Kansas City Monarchs : trailblazers in Black baseball / William A. Young.
Description: Jefferson, North Carolina : McFarland & Company, Inc., Publishers, 2016. | Includes bibliographical references and index.
Identifiers: LCCN 2016044895 | ISBN 9781476662992 (softcover : acid free paper) ∞
Subjects: LCSH: Wilkinson, J. L., 1878–1964. | Baseball team owners—United States—Biography. | Kansas City Monarchs (Baseball team)—History. | African American baseball players—History. | Negro leagues—History. | Baseball—United States—History.
Classification: LCC GV865.W476 Y68 2016 | DDC 796.357092 [B]—dc23
LC record available at https://lccn.loc.gov/2016044895

BRITISH LIBRARY CATALOGUING DATA ARE AVAILABLE

ISBN (print) 978-1-4766-6299-2
ISBN (ebook) 978-1-4766-2614-7

© 2016 William A. Young. All rights reserved

No part of this book may be reproduced or transmitted in any form or by any means, electronic or mechanical, including photocopying or recording, or by any information storage and retrieval system, without permission in writing from the publisher.

On the cover: J. L. Wilkinson standing beside Kansas City Monarchs players at the 1924 Negro Leagues World Series (National Baseball Hall of Fame Library, Cooperstown, New York)

Printed in the United States of America

McFarland & Company, Inc., Publishers
Box 611, Jefferson, North Carolina 28640
www.mcfarlandpub.com

Table of Contents

Preface and Acknowledgments	1
Prologue: "A Thrilling and Fascinating Epic"	4
1. Early Life and a Start in Baseball (1878–1911)	7
2. Breaking New Ground—The All-Nations Team (1912–1919)	13
3. Founding the Monarchs and the Negro National League (1920–1923)	23
4. Negro National League and World Champions (1924–1929)	44
5. The Innovator—Night Baseball and Barnstorming (1930–1936)	68
6. Joining the Negro American League (1937–1938)	98
7. J. L. Wilkinson and the Rebirth of Satchel Paige (1938–1939)	106
8. The "Black Yankees"—The Monarchs Reach Their Peak (1940–1945)	118
9. J. L. Wilkinson, Jackie Robinson and the Integration of Baseball (1945)	139
10. Final Years for Wilkinson and the Monarchs (1946–1964)	157
Epilogue: The Long Road to Cooperstown	186
Appendix: Kansas City Monarchs Rosters and Records During the J. L. Wilkinson Era (1920–1948)	191
Chapter Notes	206
Bibliography	223
Index	227

Preface and Acknowledgments

As I walked out of the exhibit area at the Negro Leagues Baseball Museum in Kansas City, Missouri, my head was spinning. The magnificently displayed narrative of the many contributions of African Americans not only to baseball but also to the struggle for equality and democracy in the United States had overwhelmed me. What an incredible story! It is a must-see not only for baseball fans, but for all who value the ongoing fight for human dignity.

I had entered the museum's displays knowing a little about the role of blacks in baseball. Like most baseball fans, I was familiar with stars like Jackie Robinson, Satchel Paige, and Josh Gibson. Thanks to Ken Burns' excellent PBS documentary in 1994, I was also aware of the player, manager, and coach who had become the ambassador for black baseball, John "Buck" O'Neil.

I came out of the exhibits with a much deeper and richer appreciation of those who fought during the days of segregation to establish and maintain successful black teams and the Negro Leagues. For nearly a half-century they provided opportunities for African American baseball players to develop and flourish. Those opportunities, of course, existed because others did not. An insidious "gentleman's agreement" among major league owners denied black athletes the opportunity to compete on equal playing fields with white athletes.

Then, in 1947, standing on the shoulders of the African American ballplayers of the segregated era, Jackie Robinson opened the door for future generations of stars.

One picture in the museum exhibits particularly caught my eye. It was a photograph of the two teams that played in the first Negro Leagues World Series in 1924. The Kansas City Monarchs, champions of the Negro National League, and the Hilldale Club, winners of the pennant in the Eastern Colored League, were standing in one long line with team officials. All the faces were black except one. Next to the Monarchs players there was a short white man wearing a suit and tie and a fedora hat. The picture's caption indicated that he was J. L. Wilkinson, founder and owner of the Kansas City Monarchs and one of the organizers of the Negro National League. It would be interesting to learn more about J. L. Wilkinson, I thought, as I walked on to the next exhibits.

Emerging from the displays, I saw a group gathered around a distinguished looking older gentleman. He was nattily attired in a beige, pinstriped suit and gold tie. As I came closer, I recognized him as John "Buck" O'Neil. A museum guide told me Mr. O'Neil often came to the museum, which he had been instrumental in founding, to chat with visitors. Among my most prized possessions are the baseball and the book Buck O'Neil signed for me that day. At a brief ceremony, attended by a few other veterans of the Negro

Leagues, my wife and I heard Mr. O'Neil speak about his love for the game. It was hard to believe he was in his nineties; he appeared to have the energy and enthusiasm to play a few innings that very afternoon.

Visiting the museum and meeting Buck O'Neil inspired me to delve more deeply into the history of African American baseball and, in particular, to learn more about J. L. Wilkinson. Reading his engaging autobiography,[1] I learned that as a young boy looking at the same 1924 World Series picture, Buck O'Neil had also wondered, "What is that white man doing there?"

First, however, I had another project to complete, a biography of one of the first Native Americans to reach stardom in the major leagues—John Tortes Meyers. He was Christy Mathewson's catcher for John McGraw's New York Giants, and had played in four World Series for the Giants (1911–1913) and Brooklyn Dodgers (1916). When *John Tortes "Chief" Meyers: A Baseball Biography* was published, I was ready to tackle another important, but neglected, baseball story.

Reading about the history of black baseball in general and the Negro Leagues in particular, I soon discovered the central role J. L. Wilkinson played. His many contributions were recognized in 2006 when he received, posthumously, the highest honor in the game, induction into the National Baseball Hall of Fame at Cooperstown, New York. But to my surprise, no book-length biography of J. L. Wilkinson had yet been written.

Were there enough resources for such a work, I wondered? All of the histories of the Negro Leagues I consulted mentioned Wilkinson and how respected he was by his players and other owners, but it was obvious he was a modest, discreet man who avoided controversy and the public spotlight. Where to begin?

As I had with the Meyers biography, I reached out to my subject's family and was able to locate J. L. Wilkinson's grandson, Ed Catron, who put me in contact with his cousins, Diane Pond and Sharon Brescian. All three Wilkinson grandchildren graciously shared memories of their grandfather and his wife, Bessie, with me.

I also was able to listen to interviews with Diane and Sharon's late father, J. L.'s son, Dick, and Ed's late mother and Wilkinson's daughter, Gladys Wilkinson Catron. Historian Janet Bruce Vaughn recorded both during her research for the foundational study of the Kansas City Monarchs, *The Kansas City Monarchs: Champions of Black Baseball*.[2] She generously contributed tapes of these interviews and a number with Kansas City Monarchs players to the State Historical Society of Missouri. I was able to listen to these interviews at the society's research center on the campus of the University of Missouri in Columbia.

I also drew on the thorough, well-researched histories of the Negro Leagues that have been published in recent decades. Particularly helpful were works by Dick Clark, Phil Dixon, Leslie Heaphy, Lawrence Hogan, John Holway, Neil Lanctot, Larry Lester, and Robert Peterson.

When I reached out to the National Baseball Hall of Fame Library in Cooperstown, New York, the Library's efficient staff quickly scanned their entire Wilkinson file and sent it to me. It contained some very valuable material, particularly relating to Wilkinson's induction into the Hall of Fame. I am especially grateful to photo archives assistant Ken Roussey for his help in locating appropriate photographs in the Hall's collection.

The staff of the Kenneth Spencer Research Library at the University of Kansas in Lawrence was helpful in my review of the files of Monarchs co-owner T. Y. Baird. My wife and I spent some very productive hours reading through the Baird Collection. Kathy

A. Lafferty, a public services and reference librarian, was particularly helpful in providing access to photographs in the collection.

I would also like to express my appreciation to Nancy Sherbert, curator of photographs and acquisitions coordinator, at the Kansas State Historical Society, and Larry Lester, owner of NoirTech Research, Inc., for their assistance in finding photographs.

To obtain the books and articles not locally available, I relied on Cindy Schoolcraft, then a resource sharing assistant at Westminster College's Reeves Library, and Daniel Boone Regional Library's excellent interlibrary loan service.

The principal primary resource for this project was the *Kansas City Call*, the African American weekly newspaper that began publication in 1919 and continues to this day. Fortunately, the *Call* was available to me on microfilm at the State Historical Society of Missouri Research Center in Columbia. The center's staff was most helpful, teaching me how to use the latest generation of microfilm readers. As I began to read through the hundreds of articles in the *Call* relevant to my research, the story of J. L. Wilkinson, baseball pioneer, and the team he founded and lovingly guided for nearly three decades, came to life and took shape. At a time when the major daily newspapers mostly ignored the Kansas City Monarchs and other black teams, African American weeklies like the *Call* provide the documentation essential to reconstructing their histories. Donna Stewart, the current publisher and managing editor of the *Kansas City Call*, was gracious in her support of my research.

Finally, I am deeply grateful for the love and support of my family—my children Rachel and Matthew, their spouses Gabe and Carrie, my grandchildren Noah and Sadie, and my wife and tireless editor Sue—without whom my enthusiasm for what turned into a several-year project would likely have faded.

Prologue:
"A Thrilling and Fascinating Epic"

In 1945 Wendell Smith (1914–1972), renowned sports editor of the African American weekly the *Pittsburgh Courier,* penned the following tribute to J. L. Wilkinson[1]:

> One of those who has made a definite contribution to black baseball is J. L. Wilkinson, the silver-thatched, soft-spoken owner of the fabulous Kansas City Monarchs. Wilkinson has been in Negro baseball for more than twenty years, and during that time he has not only invested his money, but his very heart and soul. He has stayed in the game through storm and strife because he has loved it, not because he had to. There is no owner in the country—white or Negro—who has operated more honestly, sincerely, or painstakingly. His baseball history is an epic as thrilling and fascinating as any sports story ever written.

Smith had already earned the right to have his opinion respected. For more than a decade he had played a central role in promoting the integration of major league baseball. He was to become a key figure in Branch Rickey's selection of Jackie Robinson (who was playing for the Monarchs in 1945) as the first Black to play in the modern major leagues (see Chapter 9). In 1994, in recognition of his many contributions to baseball, Smith was posthumously voted the winner of the prestigious Spink Award.

It took 61 years, but Cooperstown finally agreed with Smith's assessment. In February 2006, a special committee of Negro Leagues and pre–Negro Leagues baseball historians included J. L. Wilkinson in a group of 12 players and five executives selected for induction into the Hall of Fame. On July 30, 2006, Wilkinson's son, Dick, his grandchildren Sharon Brescian, Ed Catron, and Diane Pond and other family members were present for the induction ceremony. Dick read from the plaque honoring his father[2]:

> J. LESLIE WILKINSON "J. L." "WILKIE"
> KANSAS CITY MONARCHS, 1920–1948
>
> AN INNOVATIVE AND GENEROUS OWNER WHO FOUNDED AND OPERATED THE KANSAS CITY MONARCHS FROM 1920–1948. RESPECTED FOR HONESTY AND FAIRNESS WITH HIS PLAYERS. HIS MONARCHS DOMINATED BLACK BASEBALL, WINNING THE MOST LEAGUE TITLES AND TWO NEGRO LEAGUE WORLD SERIES CHAMPIONSHIPS. CREATED MULTI-RACIAL ALL-NATIONS BARNSTORMING TEAM THAT FLOURISHED FROM 1912–1918, THEN HELPED FOUND THE NEGRO NATIONAL LEAGUE IN 1920. DEVISED PORTABLE LIGHTING SYSTEM WHICH ALLOWED TEAMS TO PLAY NIGHT GAMES AND SURVIVE THE GREAT DEPRESSION. SENT MORE PLAYERS, INCLUDING JACKIE ROBINSON, TO MAJOR LEAGUES THAN ANY OTHER NEGRO LEAGUES OWNER.

By the time he was inducted into the Hall of Fame, J. L. Wilkinson had long since faded from the pages of most histories of baseball. He was remembered only by his family, a handful of historians who had painstakingly worked for several decades to bring to life the fascinating story of black baseball, and the few surviving players from the Kansas City Monarchs who had played on the team when Wilkinson was principal owner.

Without exception those who knew J. L. Wilkinson had deep respect for him. Legendary Monarch player and manager John "Buck" O'Neil (1911–2006) called him "an innovator, a man ahead of his time"[3] and said he had known only two men in his life who were not prejudiced. One was his father. The other was J. L. Wilkinson. "I was from the South, mind you," O'Neil wrote in his autobiography, "so I was unaccustomed to meeting a white man who treated me the way he would his own son. If a hotel was short of rooms, Wilkie [the nickname by which he was known to his players and close associates] thought nothing of bunking with the manager or me. He never missed a payroll, which is saying something, and he often gave players advances on their next season's salary." O'Neil wanted people to understand, "once you got to know Mr. Wilkinson, you didn't even think twice about what color he was. You only knew he was a genius…. [He] took black baseball into new territory."[4]

Clifford "Connie" Johnson (1922–2004), a Monarch pitcher who went on to play in the major leagues with the Chicago White Sox and Baltimore Orioles, said: "You don't find many people like J. L. Wilkinson in this world. He had no conception of discrimination. Everyone was the same to him. All the players liked him. He was for real. No doubt about that. A fine fellow."[5]

Wilkinson was also a smart businessman. "[Y]ou got to keep your ball players satisfied," he said. "If you underpay a man, he's not satisfied. He's not going to give his best." Following his own advice, Wilkinson would buy a tourist bus for his players so they could sleep on the road if suitable rooms were not available and cook their own meals when restaurants would not serve them. He knew that looking after the welfare of his players improved their odds of winning.[6]

J. L. Wilkinson also knew the importance of presenting a positive image to the public. He insisted his players "be dressed nice and act nice," remembered Byron "Mex" Johnson (1911–2005), who played for Wilkinson from 1937–1940. "You didn't hear any cussing or see us look raggedy and dirty. We represented the Monarchs."[7]

Dick Wilkinson expressed the attitude all in his family share about his father. "I never knew a ball player or person that didn't like my dad," he said. "He was very calm, a quiet type of person. He never showed much emotion. Always the professional! Never saw him without a suit and tie and hat on. Never drank, never smoked. Just a fine person."[8]

Leo Durocher, the fiery major league manager, is remembered for saying, "Nice guys finish last!" It can also be said that nice guys usually don't get much ink. So it was with J. L. Wilkinson. He shunned the spotlight, preferring to see his players and associates receive the accolades.

However, long before major leagues owners Bill Veeck and Charlie Finley achieved fame as promotional geniuses, J. L. Wilkinson blazed the trail. Negro Leagues historian Larry Lester has called Wilkinson "baseball's original drum major." In the mid-1920s, he introduced "Kid's Day" or "Knothole Day" (kids 15 and under, free) and "Ladies Day" or "Fannettes Day" (all ladies free). In 1922 he hired female ushers to attract women to games and to tone down men's behavior at the park. In 1930 he developed an innovative portable lighting system that enabled workers to come out to see games at night. The system allowed the Monarchs to schedule both day and night games during the barnstorming tours that kept black baseball alive during the Great Depression. Wilkinson also scheduled special attractions, such as exhibitions by Olympic track champion Jesse Owens and bathing beauty contests. Working with his longtime business manager, Quincy J. Gilmore, the Monarchs owner created one of the first and most successful booster clubs in baseball history. A deeply religious man himself, Wilkinson reached out to churches in the black community, hosting special ministers days at the ballpark. In return, some pastors ended Sunday services early so parishioners could make it to the stadium for the first pitch of Sunday doubleheaders. Long before giveaway attractions became commonplace, Wilkinson handed out prizes provided by local merchants.[9]

During World War II, J. L. Wilkinson said, "We know that baseball is essential, and we're going to play for the war workers, both day and night games and on Sundays and weekdays." He gave free admission to soldiers in uniform and adjusted the time of games to accommodate defense workers' swing shifts.[10]

According to noted baseball analyst and historian Bill James, J. L. Wilkinson was among a small group of Negro Leagues owners, which included Rube Foster, Cum Posey, Gus Greenlee, and Abe and Effa Manley, who were "financial wizards." With the exception of Wilkinson, all were black. Each was adept at finding and nurturing the best black athletes in the country. To boost enthusiasm for the game, they developed an annual East-West All-Star Game that attracted large throngs. In the worst of financial times, they sustained their teams by traveling throughout the United States, Canada, and Mexico, playing games in small towns. James has written that Wilkinson and the others "set the stage for Jackie Robinson. By the time integration arrived, baseball was more ready for it than almost any other segment of American society." In the opinion of James, as well as that of most other knowledgeable experts, Wilkinson's Kansas City Monarchs were the very best team in all the Negro Leagues.[11]

J. L. Wilkinson certainly won the respect of his fellow Negro Leagues owners. For example, Ed Bolden, the African American owner of the Hilldale Daisies, called him "the most fair-minded, square shooting white man I have ever met who is interested in Negro baseball."[12]

Although white daily newspapers rarely mentioned Wilkinson and the Monarchs, African American weeklies like the *Pittsburgh Courier, Chicago Defender, Baltimore Afro-American,* and especially the *Kansas City Call,* covered them extensively. Serendipitously, in 1919, just a year before Wilkinson founded the Monarchs, the *Call* began publication. The *Call* recognized early on the importance of Wilkinson and the Monarchs to the black community of Kansas City. In 1922 the paper noted[13]:

> From a sociological point of view, the Monarchs have done more than any other single agent to break the damnable outrage of prejudice that exists in this city. White fans, the thinking class at least, cannot have watched the orderly crowds at Association Park ... and not concede that we are humans at least, and worthy of consideration as such.

In his study of the Negro Leagues, Bruce Chadwick captured well the essence of the mystique and appeal of the Monarchs' saga: "If a writer sat down to pen a novel about baseball that tied together every myth and legend of the game—from the start of *Field of Dreams* to the finale of *The Natural* with a touch of *The Boys of Summer* thrown in— he or she would eventually write the story of the real-life Kansas City Monarchs."[14]

And without J. L. Wilkinson there would be no Kansas City Monarchs story to tell.

Chapter 1

Early Life and a Start in Baseball (1878–1911)

One of the first in-depth studies of the Negro Leagues called black ballplayers of the pre–Jackie Robinson era "invisible men," because they were largely unknown to all but the most dedicated scholars and devoted fans.[1]

One researcher has aptly coined the phrase "the invisible man among invisible men" to describe J. L. Wilkinson.[2] Until recent years, Wilkinson's many accomplishments were largely forgotten, and some of the most basic facts published about him were incorrect. For example, a common error over the years has been replacing his actual last name "Wilkinson" with "Wilkerson." As early as 1922, the *Kansas City Call* identified the Monarchs owner as "Wilkerson."[3] At times, in the same article, he was called both "Wilkinson" and "Wilkerson."

Other mistakes made about Wilkinson have included giving an incorrect date and place of his birth and assigning him a first name he did not have. All three errors are found in the entry on J. L. Wilkinson in the respected *Biographical Encyclopedia of the Negro Baseball Leagues*. It reads in part "Wilkinson, James Leslie (J. L.). Born: 1874, Perry, Ia. Died: Aug. 21, 1964, Kansas City, Mo."[4]

In point of fact, Wilkinson was born on May 14, 1878, and not in Perry, but Algona, Iowa.[5] The front page of the May 15, 1878, *Algona Republican* carried the note: "Born, on Tuesday, May 14th to Mr. and Mrs. J. J. Wilkinson of Algona, a son."[6] His parents named their son J. Leslie, leaving him to choose later in life what the "J." stood for.[7] He never made that decision. The first names "James" and "John" were the inventions of associates, ballplayers and sportswriters who assumed the "J." must have stood for something.[8] This error appeared as recently as the announcement of Wilkinson's nomination for induction into the Baseball Hall of Fame in 2006, when a February 24, 2006, press release from Cooperstown identified him as "James Leslie 'J. L.' Wilkinson."[9] There is no evidence Wilkinson ever bothered to correct these errors when they were made about him during his lifetime.

Wilkinson himself preferred to be known as "J. L." Early on, he was given the nickname those who knew him best frequently used—"Wilkie."[10]

J. L. Wilkinson's parents were born in Michigan. His father, J. J., attended a business college in Detroit, Michigan. He married Myrta "Mertie" Harper before the two moved to Algona, Iowa, seat of Kossuth County, where J. J. taught, served as superintendent of schools, sold insurance, and participated in local politics. J. L. was the oldest of the Wilkinson children.[11]

The 1885 Iowa Census lists John J. Wilkinson (33), Myrtia [sic] D. Wilkinson (28), J. Leslie (6), George H. (4), and Stanley (2) as residents of Algona. J. J. was named president of the new Northern Iowa Normal School when the college moved to Algona in 1886.[12] According to two writers who interviewed Wilkinson in 1950, he "grew up in a liberal atmosphere," which may help explain his lifelong acceptance of people of all races at a time when prejudice was common.[13]

Ralph J. Christian has done the most extensive research on J. L. Wilkinson's early life in Iowa and start in baseball. His excellent 2006 article in *Iowa Heritage Illustrated*[14] provides the basis for the following overview of the formative period in the baseball pioneer's life.

Wilkinson would spend nearly 37 years in his native Iowa before moving to Kansas City. By 1892 his family had relocated to Jefferson, Iowa; then to Omaha, Nebraska, where J. L. "became an accomplished pitcher and likely graduated from high school"; and finally to Des Moines, Iowa. There he worked for his father, who had become a manager at Iowa National Life Insurance.

Wilkinson attended Highland Park Normal College in Des Moines, where he played baseball, becoming "one of the premier hurlers of Des Moines and central Iowa." He also played professional and semi-pro baseball, often using the pseudonym "Joe Green" so as not to jeopardize his amateur status, or perhaps "lest he incur the wrath of his father."

During the 1895 season "Green" was a pitcher for several Des Moines teams, including the Turners, Cycling Club, and Clippers. In a game in which he pitched the Cycling Club to a 4–3 victory over Iowa Agricultural College in Ames, he gave up only five hits and struck out ten. In the next several years, as Wilkinson refined his pitching skills, he averaged nine strikeouts per game and was known for his coolness under fire. He played for additional teams in Winterset and Brooklyn, Iowa—the latter the source of a statement he liked to repeat: "Did you know I played for Brooklyn?"

In 1899 Wilkinson pitched for the Des Moines Stars, a semi-pro team established ten years earlier by future Hall of Fame executive Ed Barrow. The team was composed mostly of newsboys and carriers who were 18 to 21 years old, so it is possible Wilkinson hawked newspapers and magazines while playing for the Stars.

The 1900 census records that the 22-year-old J. L. (called Leslie J. on the form) was still living with his father, John J. (46) and mother, identified on the form as Myrtel W. (42). J. L.'s listed occupation on the census form was "clerk" at Chase Brothers, a Des Moines grocer that fielded a semi-pro team on which Wilkinson likely pitched.[15] He was being heralded by *Iowa State Register* sportswriters for his "wonderful pitching," when a broken wrist brought his dreams of being a professional moundsman to a sudden halt. Wilkinson's son Dick recalled years later that his father, a right-handed pitcher, broke his wrist sliding into second base.[16]

After Wilkinson suffered the injury that cut short his pitching career, his father gave him work in his real estate and contracting firms. Though his future prospects as a baseball player were limited, Wilkinson continued to play the sport. In 1904 he joined a new semi-pro team that had been organized by Hopkins Brothers Sporting Goods of Des Moines. By this time Wilkinson had moved to the shortstop position. The club rarely played in Des Moines. Instead, it traveled to towns that could be reached by train, with a return trip the same day, because the players had other jobs in Des Moines and could not be gone long. Some turned down opportunities to play on professional minor league teams. The Hopkins Brothers team played for a purse of $50–$100, plus 60 percent of

1. Early Life and a Start in Baseball (1878–1911)

J. L. Wilkinson (front row, left) played shortstop for and managed the semi-pro Hopkins Brothers Sporting Goods team in Des Moines, Iowa, from 1904–1908 (Ed Catron).

the gate if they won or 40 percent if they lost. Sometimes they pooled money to place side bets on the game, ranging from $25 to $150. Playing against college, amateur, semi-pro, and even professional clubs, they drew well, and the team was so successful they began to have trouble booking games with teams who feared losing to them. As the sports section of the *Des Moines Register and Leader* headlined, "HARD TO GET GAMES. HOPKINS BROS. HAVE AMATEUR TEAMS FRIGHTENED BY THEIR PROWESS." In search of teams willing to play them, Wilkinson and his teammates took a two-week road trip into northwestern Iowa.

Hopkins Brothers concluded the 1904 season with a doubleheader against an all-black team, the Buxton Wonders. Buxton was a coal-mining town in southeastern Iowa with a majority African American population. Virtually the whole town turned out, as 700 watched Hopkins Brothers take the first game, then saw their Wonders (augmented by several black players from Chicago) win the second contest. The *Register Leader* called the doubleheader "two first class exhibitions of the national game."

In 1905 Wilkinson became captain and manager of the Hopkins Brothers team. A *Register and Leader* sportswriter called him a "good shortstop" who "plays with his head." However, "he is unfortunate in not being able to hit." The same year Wilkinson had his first experience in the organization of a league, as H. H. Polk of the Interurban Railroad Company took the initiative in creating what he called the Interurban League. His company provided free transportation and uniforms, and teams could choose between a guarantee of expenses and a 60–40 split of gate receipts. Reflecting another issue Wilkinson would later face in the Negro Leagues, competitive balance proved a problem. Hopkins Brothers had the most talent, and the *Register and Leader* reported that efforts were being made to help weaker teams.

One widely circulated, but hard to confirm, story is that Wilkinson moved into baseball management when "the manager of his semi-pro team took off with all the money" and his teammates decided their shortstop would be a better manager than player.[17] Another possibility is that the manager of the team simply left, and his teammates voted for Wilkinson to take over running the club.[18]

Wilkinson planned another, more extended, road trip for the Hopkins Brothers team, this time into northern Iowa, Minnesota, and the Dakotas. He decided to take only his best players and jeopardized the Interurban League's future by scheduling non-league games and forfeiting some previously scheduled league contests. Wilkinson astutely sensed that the future for Hopkins Brothers was in touring independently; the Interurban League folded by June.

Hopkins Brothers slumped in 1907, losing to Marshalltown, Oskaloosa, Boone, Fort Dodge and even two games to the team at Iowa's premier liberal arts college, Grinnell. The Hopkins Brothers team limped home with a 2–13 record, but their losses made them more attractive opponents.

Wilkinson's skills as a promoter began to be evident in 1907 as he scheduled several games to coincide with fairs, carnivals, festivals and even reunions. In Garner, Iowa, for example, the Baseball Tournament and Street Carnival offered a $750 purse. It did not escape the young entrepreneur's notice that fans were abuzz about the person calling balls and strikes—"Miss Amanda Clement, the only lady professional baseball umpire in the world."

In 1908 Hopkins Brothers returned to its winning ways, emerging victorious in 31 of 33 games in one stretch, often by large margins. Victory may have been too sweet, and finding competitors was likely proving more difficult. In any event, Wilkinson disbanded the team in September.

In addition to taking on the Buxton Wonders in 1904, Wilkinson may have played against a black team that had organized around the turn of the century in his hometown—the famed Algona Brownies. Regardless, Wilkinson surely was aware of and influenced by the exciting type of baseball the Brownies and other all-black teams of the era were playing.

In an intriguing coincidence, the young Wilkinson may have at least briefly crossed paths with a 21-year-old rookie catcher named Branch Rickey, who in 1903 was making his professional debut with the Le Mars, Iowa, team in the short-lived South Dakota-Iowa League.[19] Over four decades later, J. L. Wilkinson would be a principal player in the drama that led to Branch Rickey's signing of Jackie Robinson to play in the Brooklyn Dodgers organization, and the breaking of the color barrier in major league baseball (see Chapter 9).

In another example of his entrepreneurial vision, Wilkinson decided in 1908 to organize the Hopkins Brothers Champion Lady Baseball Club.[20] "Bloomer Girls" or simply "Bloomer" teams were named after a style of loose-fitting trousers developed by a woman named Amelia Bloomer, making it easier for women and girls to play various sports, including baseball. By the first decade of the twentieth century, female teams were becoming popular, and J. L. Wilkinson was not one to pass up a new promotional opportunity.

Advertised as "Ladies Clubs," the teams typically had a few men among their players. Hall of Famer Rogers Hornsby, for example, got his start in professional baseball as a 17-year-old by donning a wig and bloomers and playing for a "girls" team in Texas. Several bloomers teams had been touring successfully since the late 19th century, playing men's amateur and semi-professional teams. Hundreds of bloomer teams were organized and some continued touring into the 1930s.

Beginning in 1902, one of the most famous women's clubs, the Boston Bloomer Girls, had been playing in Des Moines and barnstorming across Iowa, spurring the development of other bloomer teams. According to women's baseball historian Debra A. Shattuck, "the Bloomer Girls teams relied on sideshow style appeal to draw fans and, not surprisingly, the bottom line was money."[21] That combination clearly appealed to J. L. Wilkinson.

Although he was willing to rely on gimmicks to make a profit, Wilkinson realized early that unless he put a quality product on the field, fans would not be impressed. During the spring of 1909 he went on a scouting trip and returned with some excellent players: Celia Brown at first base; Mary Fey, second base; and outfielders Alice Burke, Edith Ryan, and Kittie Hisey. Others he recruited were a Miss Kroll, a pitcher, probably the best player in the group, and May Arbaugh, who played under the name "Carrie Nation," the famous, ax-wielding temperance activist and suffragette. Wilkinson lured Arbaugh away from the Boston Bloomer Girls, where she had earned the reputation as "to women ball players what Honus Wagner is to the men." Promotional material put out by Wilkinson stressed that these were "Girls Who Can Really Play the Great National Game." He promised "an aggregation of the World's Greatest Lady athletes ... making sensational catches and daring slides."

To supplement the women, Wilkinson penciled himself into the lineup and added a catcher named Ben Reeves, an Iowa farm boy known as the "Rocky Mountain Wrestler," because he had allegedly trained for three months in Denver. As an added attraction to the baseball games, Wilkinson advertised that Reeves was ready to take on all comers in wrestling matches.

J. L. Wilkinson delivered on his promise of quality baseball. His Hopkins Brothers Champion Lady Baseball Club won its first game, 6–3, against Seevers, one of the best men's semi-professional teams in Iowa. The team's winning record convinced a *Register and Leader* sportswriter that "baseball is a woman's as well as a man's game." "The girls," the writer continued, "play a high class article of ball, fielding, hitting, throwing, and running the bases remarkably well." Kroll's pitches included "a line of slants and benders that would make the best of league twirlers set up and take notice." Foreshadowing another feature of Wilkinson's teams throughout his career, the women displayed "fine conduct on the field" that made "a decided hit with the crowd."

Another aspect of Wilkinson's managerial style already evident with the Hopkins Brothers Champion Lady Baseball Club was taking care of his players on the road. For a planned western barnstorming tour, Wilkinson leased a Pullman Palace Car. He christened the dark green railroad car, with six staterooms, a dining room, kitchen and baggage room the Marathon. The team pulled out of Des Moines on June 7, 1909, with its luxury accommodations, accompanied by their mascot, a brown bulldog named Buster.

J. L. Wilkinson the innovator was also already at work. He had built what was in effect a portable ball park—a 14-foot-high, canvas fence, 1,200 feet long, and a canopy-covered grandstand that could hold as many as 2,000.[22]

The young entrepreneur had found a moneymaker. He left the real estate partnership he had entered with his father, purchased a stylish residence in an upper middle-class area of Des Moines, and reinvested profits in the team. In 1910 he recruited a second wrestler, Gus Poppas, as a back-up to Reeves, who had reportedly taken to the ring with 300 opponents. Joining the team was a "Miss Murphy, most likely 17-year-old Lizzie Murphy, who was on her way to becoming the 'Queen of Baseball,' the best woman player in the country." She may have been on loan from the Boston All-Stars, a semi-pro team that barnstormed throughout New England and Canada.[23] Wilkinson rewarded his team's success by leasing a larger Pullman car.

The 1910 census records J. L. Wilkinson's occupation as "Commercial Agent & Phonographs." His father and mother's birthplaces are listed as Michigan. Their children are identified as J. Leslie (32), Harriett (20), and Lee N. (13). J. L.'s wife Bessie M. Wilkinson (29) is also included on the census form.[24]

Wilkinson's daughter, Gladys Wilkinson Catron, said her mother, Bessie, met her father when he was playing baseball. "She was at a game," Gladys recalled, "when he slid into the base, and they laughed over the years because Mom was disgusted, and said, 'Look how dirty he is!' She didn't know the first thing about baseball then. He got her a rulebook so she would know what was happening. Mom and Dad married in 1908." Bessie grew to love the game and at times traveled with her husband and his teams on barnstorming trips. According to Gladys, Bessie's parents were not pleased their daughter had taken up with a "baseball man." "They were Methodists. Sunday baseball was a plain sin." Gladys said that her father's parents also opposed Sunday baseball, but they never objected to their son's owning a Negro team.[25]

Baseball historians herald Wilkinson's innovative creation of a portable lighting system for his Kansas City Monarchs traveling team in 1930 (see Chapter 5), but that was 20 years after his first experiment with night baseball. The *Register and Leader* reported that in May of 1910, Wilkinson's team played a night game in Stratford, Iowa, calling the well-attended contest, "[a] very novel and interesting game." The paper also noted the team later played "in Chicago to 5,000 fans by daylight and a crowd of the same size at night." At this point Wilkinson may have been trying out a system using acetylene gas. It was apparently not very successful, because he soon gave up the idea.

By 1912 Wilkie's career path was set. The Des Moines city directory that year listed him as "Wilkinson, Jas. L., Ballplayer, Res., 1239 10th."[26] "James," or course, was not quite correct, but for the rest of his life baseball would be not only his vocation but also his passion.

CHAPTER 2

Breaking New Ground— The All-Nations Team (1912–1919)

The success of his Bloomers team over several seasons made J. L. Wilkinson even more ambitious. In addition to barnstorming ladies clubs, touring teams made up entirely of a particular national or ethnic group—African Americans, Native Americans, Europeans, Chinese, Japanese, or Hawaiians—were increasingly popular in the early twentieth century. Wilkinson exploited the concept but added a twist no one else had tried. He decided to create a team composed of a mix of nationalities and ethnicities. However, as with the Ladies team, he knew that his multinational, ethnically diverse team would have to play quality baseball in order to attract and maintain crowds.[1]

It took Wilkinson several years to put together the team he had in mind—made up ideally of Native Americans, Japanese, Hawaiians, Canadians, Scots, Germans, Frenchmen, Turks, Cubans, Mexicans, Chinese, Filipinos, Jews, African Americans, and Caucasian Americans. He chose the fitting name All Nations. The team was at first sponsored by Hopkins Brothers Sporting Goods and later Goldsmith Hardware Store.[2]

Wilkinson did not find players from all the backgrounds he envisioned, but the team he put together was quite diverse.

When All Nations debuted on May 5, 1912, in Des Moines before an enthusiastic crowd of 1,000, they won the seven-inning game, 3–0, against the Moose Lodge team, then a powerhouse of the Des Moines City League. Impressed with the pitcher for Wilkinson's team, the *Des Moines Capital* reported, "The lanky colored twirler of the All-Nations team was the sensation of the day in his way of pitching. He had a variety of curves that fairly dazzled the Moose team and [only one] reached first."

The hurler was John Donaldson (1891–1970), a Glasgow, Missouri, native whose mother was black and father was white. Donaldson had been pitching for the Tennessee Rats, a black barnstorming team, when Wilkinson lured him away. Another Wilkinson attribute that would serve him well over the years was evident in the signing of Donaldson—his uncanny ability to find and recruit talented baseball players. The Missouri pitcher had reportedly struck out 21 batters in a 14-inning game and two days later, 24 in a 16-inning game.

Donaldson had a good fastball and change-up and excellent control. According to Buck O'Neil, many who saw both Satchel Paige and John Donaldson pitch said, "Donaldson was just as good. A hard throwing lefty, Donaldson threw a slider before anyone

In 1912 J. L. Wilkinson organized a multi-ethnic, barnstorming team he called All Nations, claiming on the roster were Cuban, Filipino, Hawaiian, Japanese, European-American and Native American players. This picture includes John Donaldson (third from left) José Méndez (seventh from the left) and, perhaps, Goro Mikami (who went by "Jap Mikado") (far right). In this version of the photograph, the name of the All Nations' sponsor, Goldsmith Hardware Store, is clearly shown on the uniforms (courtesy NoirTech Research, Inc.).

knew you could throw a hard curve."[3] As retired major league baseball scout Bill Clark has put it, "[John Donaldson] was Satchel Paige before there was a Satchel Paige."[4]

On May 6, 1912, the All Nations club, with their canvas fence and portable grandstands borrowed from the Bloomers, left Des Moines in its $25,000 Pullman car (called "Loretta") on a barnstorming tour that likely extended all the way to California and the Pacific Northwest before returning through the Dakotas and Minnesota to Iowa. After a game against the Fort Dodge, Iowa, town team, Dodgers outfielder Red Sanders said of Donaldson, this "negro has more 'stuff' than 'Rube' Marquard [a star pitcher for the New York Giants] or other big leaguers."[5]

When the talented hurler took the mound he was sometimes "jeered and otherwise abused" by locals in the small towns in which All Nations played. However, Donaldson accepted "the abuse with a gracious smile," and responded by striking out the players on the local team and, more often than not, recording shutouts.[6]

According to Wilkinson's daughter, Gladys Wilkinson Catron, "[m]y dad said if he had been in the major leagues, [Donaldson] would have topped all the men that ever pitched ... that it wasn't appreciated how outstanding he was."[7] As soon as he was able to climb up the stairs of the Pullman car, Wilkinson's son Dick traveled with All Nations in the summers for a couple of years. He claimed Donaldson "had a great curve ball. I heard Dad say he was one of the best."[8] Opposing batters described Donaldson as "a wonder." During his years with the All Nations team he pitched against major leaguers like

Hal Chase and Earl Smith, who "marveled at his burning speed, remarkable control and baffling curves."[9]

In 1913 John Donaldson threw three consecutive no-hitters. He was pitching three to four complete games a week, and the southpaw kept up that pace for four years. In 1915 Donaldson struck out 133 batters in his first full month of play. By season's end he was striking out an average of 18–20 a game. Toward the end of the 1915 season, All Nations played seven games against the Chicago Union Giants, a black team, all on neutral fields. It matched the Union Giants' legendary Dick Whitworth, who had finesse and poise, against Donaldson's speed and control.[10]

A *Chicago Defender* reporter claimed that in 1916 Donaldson struck out 240 men in twelve games. In an 18-inning game in Sioux Falls, Iowa, he was credited with 35 strikeouts, then 27 in 12 innings a few days later.[11] It was likely during the 1916 season, when he recorded more than 500 strikeouts for the second year in a row, that Donaldson's arm suddenly went numb, and "soon he was struggling to pitch more than once a week." It would take several years of limited pitching for his left arm to recover fully.[12] As would become his pattern with players struggling with injury, Wilkinson showed patience, keeping Donaldson on his teams as an outfielder, allowing him time to recover his full arm strength.

John Donaldson joined Wilkinson's Kansas City Monarchs when the team began play in 1920 and stayed with them until 1923. After leaving the Monarchs he made a living playing for a series of small towns in the northern Midwest and Canada. In July 1925, Donaldson pitched a perfect game for the Radford, Saskatchewan, club.[13]

Donaldson returned to the Kansas City Monarchs in 1931. He retired after the 1938 season and worked for the post office in Chicago until he signed on as a White Sox scout in the late 1940s. Peter Gorton, who operates the Donaldson Network, a group of over 400 researchers committed to telling John Donaldson's story, has claimed, "[w]e've been able to document over 350 victories and account for nearly 100 more. We have logged more than 4,000 strikeouts."[14] Donaldson recorded a career ERA of 1.37 and had at least six no-hitters. John McGraw said of him, "If Donaldson were a white man or if the unwritten law of baseball didn't bar negroes from the major leagues, I would give $50,000 for him and think I was getting a bargain."[15] By playing for local teams who paid him cash, Donaldson is credited with clearing the way for other black players in the northern states.[16]

J. L. Wilkinson and John Donaldson remained close over the years. Both were deeply religious, coming from Methodist backgrounds, and both were known for their rock solid moral values. Donaldson often visited the Wilkinsons and made the trip from his home in Chicago to Kansas City for his friend's funeral in 1964. Despite his superb record and his longevity, Donaldson has not yet been inducted into the National Baseball Hall of Fame at Cooperstown. Many, including Peter Gorton and the other researchers in the Donaldson Network, think the honor is long overdue.

The other All Nations pitching ace, José Méndez (1887–1928), had already established himself as a premier hurler. During exhibition games in Cuba, "*El Diamente Negro*" ("The Black Diamond") had bested major league star twirler Eddie Plank and legendary pitcher Christy Mathewson (earning him another sobriquet, "The Black Mathewson"). Méndez demonstrated great control, superb fielding, and excellent speed though he was only about 5'8" and 155 pounds.

John McGraw claimed that if Méndez were white he would also draw $50,000 from

BASE BALL!!
FEDERAL LEAGUE PARK
SEPTEMBER 24-5-6
ORIGINAL A. B. C.'s
VS.
WORLD'S ALL NATIONS

Heralding the First Appearance of The World's All Nations
The Great Donaldson will Positively Pitch 1 of These Games

Composed of Hawaiians, Japanese, Cubans, Filipinos, Indians, Chinese, direct from their native countries

JOHN DONALDSON
The Greatest Colored Pitcher in the World. Donaldson pitched 65 games last season, winning 60 of them.

JOSE MENDEZ
The Crack Cuban Pitcher, who defeated the Detroit Tigers, "American League Champions," 1-0, 10 innings, fanning Ty Cobb and Sam Crawford.

BLUKOI---The Giant Hawaiian, considered by critics to be the best 2nd baseman outside of Organized Base Ball.

PRIETO---The Sensational Cuban Pitcher, who won every game he pitched at Havana, Cuba, in 1915.

Traveling in Their Own Private Hotel Car
WILKINSON & GAUL, Sole Owners

ALL NATION TEAM DOING GREAT WORK

Shows That All Races Can Play Ball Together Regardless of Color

The All Nations baseball team besides playing the A. B. C.'s of Indianapolis off their feet and winning one game from the champion American Giants, have demonstrated to the world one thing in particular—that it is possible for black and white to play professional baseball in harmony on one team. This fact more than anything else has pleased the thousands of fans who turned out to see them play.

No doubt this was in the true minds of many spectators and those of whom are the most keen observers of the national pastime.

Yes, Sunday's game showed the big magnates that it is their fault that pennants do not come to them and that it is "colorphobia" that kept the Cubs and Sox out of the pennant. With such men as Hill, Barber, Petway, Lloyd, Gans and Grant, either club would have bolstered its percentage.

We know that the Sox could have used Petway when Schalk was injured. Lloyd would have easily made good at short and Hill or Barber would have covered about the center garden like a calf in a pasture. Felsh never could have duplicated Hill's feat Sunday.

Whithworth or Donaldson is far better than any pitcher on either the north or south side.

Yet with all this the fans go back to sit another winter to figure out why no world's series came to Chicago. The truth is in a few words. Color of a man's skin did it.

John McGraw some years ago signed a clever second baseman named Grant. Nobody objected till the New York team won a few games from Chicago. Then a big-headed Irishman named Pop Anson, then manager of the west side team, howled like a stuck pig. They sought the ruling of the National commission and finally had a rule made barring men of color.

Anson said the public objected. Far from it. The All Nations make him out a candidate for the Ananias club.

Mr. Gaul, their manager, told me that they play to crowded parks in every town, many of the smaller places suspending business during the afternoon of the game.

Two men were enough—John Donaldson and Mendez. Neither are white. It certainly seems as though the men with the money would break down the barriers and let these men through, give them a chance to earn a living and fight it out on an even basis.

It is not up to the white players—at least it should not be. The magnates should give the public what they demand—a winning ball club, not a club of white men, but a club of all men like the All Nations, regardless of color or creed, a team with ability.

According to many who saw them play, and as this *Chicago Defender* headline suggests, the All Nations demonstrated that race should not be a factor in determining who should be allowed to play baseball professionally. The article appeared more than three decades before the breaking of major league baseball's color barrier (*Chicago Defender*, October 7, 1916).

a major league club. McGraw called him "sort of Walter Johnson and Grover Alexander rolled into one"[17] and said at times he wondered if Méndez might be a better pitcher than Mathewson.

By the time Méndez signed with All Nations after the team's first season, the Cuban pitcher had a sore arm, but Wilkinson decided to take a chance on him, having him play

Opposite: Federal League Park in Indianapolis was the home of the Hoosiers of the short-lived Federal League (1913–15), a rival to the National and American Leagues. The park was rented to the Indianapolis A.B.C.'s, one of the premier African American teams of the era, who played at the park against Wilkinson's All-Nations team. In this version of the photograph, the name of the team's early sponsor (Goldsmith Hardware) is obscured (National Baseball Hall of Fame Library, Cooperstown, New York).

shortstop and pitch occasionally. He joined the Kansas City Monarchs in 1920 playing every position at one time or another and serving as a player/manager—winning pennants in 1923 and 1925 and guiding the Monarchs to victory in the first Negro Leagues World Series in 1924.[18]

José Méndez would join Wilkinson as an inductee into the National Baseball Hall of Fame in 2006.

In addition to Donaldson and Méndez, the All Nations' roster included other groundbreaking players. Outfielder Goro Mikami was from Japan and went under the pseudonym "Jap Mikado" when he joined All Nations. Seven decades later, *Des Moines Register* sportswriter Maury White received a letter from a Tanabe, Japan, sportswriter. Kazuo Sayama was seeking information on a traveling baseball team once based in Des Moines called the All Nations team to confirm that one of the players was named Jap Mikado. Professional baseball did not start in Japan until 1936, and if there were such a player on All Nations, he would be the first professional Japanese baseball player. White had never heard of All Nations and could find no clippings about the team in the *Des Moines Register* archives.

It took several more years, but the mystery of Goro Mikami (also known as "Jap Jacobs") was solved. Mikami was born in Kofu, near Mount Fuji, Japan, on November 6, 1889, and graduated from Waseda University, a leading Japanese private school. He came to the United States to pursue graduate studies. J. L. Wilkinson discovered Mikami when the left fielder played against some Iowa colleges in May 1911. He may have been a student at Knox College in Galesburg, Illinois, at the time.[19] After going home to Japan, Mikami returned to join Wilkinson's All Nations team in May 1912, so he was indeed the first Japanese professional baseball player. It would be more than a half-century before the major leagues signed a Japanese player, Masanori Murakami, who joined the San Francisco Giants in 1964.[20]

Bill "Plunk" Drake (1895–1977), an African American member of All Nations, was a right-handed pitcher who was an emery ball specialist. Drake would put sandpaper on his

Called in his native Cuba "*El Diamente Negro*" ("The Black Diamond") and compared with major league greats like Christy Mathewson, pitcher José Méndez (1887–1928) was signed by J. L. Wilkinson to pitch for his All Nations team. He later played for and managed the Kansas City Monarchs (1920–1926). He was posthumously inducted with Wilkinson into the National Baseball Hall of Fame in 2006 (National Baseball Hall of Fame Library, Cooperstown, New York).

belt, cutting the ball when he hitched up his pants, to give it movement. According to Drake, "[y]ou could break an emery ball four different ways." He was also a notorious "beanballer" (hence his nickname).[21] After a season with the Tennessee Rats, Drake joined All Nations in 1915–1916. Later he played for Wilkinson's Kansas City Monarchs (1922–1925).

Drake delighted in saying, "I used to make Wilkinson so doggone mad." As an example, "Plunk" said that Wilkinson once told him one of the fellows on the local team All Nations was playing was a good hitter. "If he's so good, what's he doing out there?" Drake retorted. "He's a white boy. I've *got* to be out there, there's nowhere else I can go. But if he's that good, he'd be in the big leagues. What's he doing out there?" Regardless, Drake always said he had fond memories of his days with All Nations and later with the Monarchs. "We just had a dandy good time," he said, recalling sleeping in tents and fishing in the evening, and remembering Wilkinson as "an awful good man."

According to Drake, All Nations only had two pitchers. "You had to pitch; you had to win in those days. I was the right-hander. John Donaldson was the left-hander." According to Drake, when he started with All Nations, "you could get the best room in town for $2.50 a week. You could get a T-bone steak for 25 cents, and if you ate what you call soul food, black-eye peas and that kind of stuff, it was 15 cents, hash was 15 or 20 cents with biscuits.... I was getting a hundred dollars a month, why, that was a fortune according to what a dollar was worth back in those days."[22]

Other key players on the 1912 All Nations team included third baseman Sam Crow, a Cherokee Indian, and second baseman and utility man Frank Blattner. Blattner was from Oskaloosa, Iowa, but to add to the All Nations' diversity, he played under the name "Blukoi" and was identified as "Hawaiian" or a "full-blooded American Indian."

Another player who went on to a stellar career was the great Cuban left-handed hitter, base stealer, and center fielder Cristóbal Torriente, who was also inducted with Wilkinson in 2006 into the National Baseball Hall of Fame. He joined All Nations in 1916 and the Monarchs in 1926.[23]

Other stalwarts on All Nations included Virgil Barnes, who later was with the New York Giants; Art Smith, who played for the Kansas City Blues of the American Association; Art Dunbar, who played with the Chicago White Sox; and Rollo Yendez.

Another key All Nations player was Clarence "Pops" Coleman, an African American catcher. "Pops" Steno Gatto was listed as an Italian, along with Couteau (French), Pedros (Filipino), Schaumburg (German), and Figarolo (Cuban).[24] Other players found on All Nations rosters were Frank Evans (outfield/ third base), Ricardo "Chico" Hernández, Hurley McNair (outfield), B. Turner (first base), and Wesley Wilkins (pitcher). Wilkinson may have also penciled himself in at times.[25]

During the spring of 1913, J. L. Wilkinson's All Nations team trained in Des Moines, probably at Des Moines University, located near the Wilkinson family residences. Some All Nations players likely boarded with the Wilkinson family. After finishing their training, the team took to the road for their games. Wilkinson's wife Bessie and young son Dick accompanied him in the Pullman coach on some of the trips.

Advertising All Nations as "direct from their native countries, Hawaiians, Japanese, Cubans, Filipinos, Indians and Chinese," Wilkinson later recalled, "[w]e all ate, slept and played together. There was never any trouble. We were a happy family." They got around Jim Crow laws where they existed by traveling in their specially built Pullman car.[26]

As testament to Wilkinson's emphasis on quality, the team won 119, lost 17, and tied two in 1913. The budding entrepreneur also demonstrated his promotional mastery by covering all the bases. With two wrestlers and an orchestra, All Nations contests always featured a wrestling match, a ball game, and then a dance.[27] All Nations team members were expected not only to play baseball but also to compete with the wrestlers or play with the dance band. José Méndez is reputed to have been a hit as a guitarist and cornet player.[28]

For J. L. Wilkinson, the "rainbow of nationalities" was "the proverbial melting pot of gold." Billed as a "recreation" team, All Nations in fact "had some of the finest players in the game." The combination of good advertising, promotional gimmicks and quality baseball brought out the crowds.

In 1914 the team went on a western tour before returning to Iowa and surrounding states, where their games often overlapped with local fairs and festivals. It is likely that about this time J. E. Gaul became a partner in the team, bringing much-needed capital and relieving Wilkinson as field manager. Wilkinson put his extra time to good use, promoting and publicizing the team. Increased newspaper coverage enabled him to highlight two new pitchers—an African American named Jess "Cannonball" Jackson and an 18-year-old Chippewa Indian pitcher, Joe Graves. The legendary Philadelphia Athletics manager Connie Mack, who had already signed another Chippewa pitcher, Hall of Famer Albert "Chief" Bender, optioned Graves to All Nations to give him more experience. John Donaldson continued his spectacular work on the mound, pitching 41 straight innings without surrendering a base hit and 81 innings giving up only two.

Wilkinson's second attempt at night baseball occurred with the All Nations team in 1914. Games under the 50,000-candlepower lights were played in New Ulm, Owatonna, and Austin, Minnesota. According to an Austin newspaper, "The All-Nations management carries a special lighting system for the night games and offers to refund the admission if the fans cannot see every play. This is a novelty and ought to pack the stands."[29]

In 1915 Wilkinson continued to list Des Moines as his residence, but spring training for All Nations occurred elsewhere, most likely in Kansas City. The team was gaining national recognition. In a matchup of powerhouses, All Nations fell to one of the premier African American teams of the era, Rube Foster's Chicago American Giants, who were barnstorming through Iowa in the summer of 1915. The game was played at the Sibley, Iowa, Carnival and Street Fair before a crowd of 3,000.

As baseball historian Larry Tye has noted, with his All Nations team "J. L. Wilkinson made Rube Foster squirm." On the one hand, All Nations was "a model for diversity," but in 1915 "it was a provocation to the Foster-Booker T. Washington school of black advancement," which emphasized separate, black-owned and run institutions. Baseball was at the center, but, as we have noted, the All Nations' act also included a sideshow, and Foster did not have much use for such gimmickry. On the other hand, as Foster began to organize a black professional baseball league he had little choice but to include a white owner. The obvious selection would be Wilkinson (see Chapter 3). Foster knew Wilkinson had the baseball know-how and cash, and within a few years he would have a team and access to a stadium. At some level Foster must have also known Wilkinson was "not just the only choice but the right one." He had a passion for baseball and a determination to succeed.[30] Moreover, Rube Foster likely overcame his initial reluctance, because, with his All Nations club, J. L. Wilkinson had respected the barnstorming territory of Chicago's African American teams. That may be why All Nations played only four games in Des Moines and avoided central Iowa and other parts of the Midwest.

2. Breaking New Ground (1912–1919)

Soon after the 1915 season ended, Wilkinson moved his family and the All Nations operation to Kansas City, because, as historian Janet Bruce Vaughn has noted, Kansas City "had both the black population and the access to large cities Des Moines lacked."[31] It was a good move as All Nations flourished with Kansas City as its base during the 1916 season. The club replaced the black Kansas City Union Giants as the most popular baseball team in the area.[32] All Nations swept a doubleheader (9–5 and 5–2) and tied a game (5–5), then lost one (5–1) against C. I. Taylor's Indianapolis A.B.C.'s, considered by many to be the dominant black club before World War I.[33] *Sporting Life* reported that All Nations was "strong enough to give any major league club a nip-and-tuck battle."[34]

During the 1917 season the All Nations team was decimated when five of its 14 players were drafted into the armed services, among them John Donaldson, who served in France with the U.S. Army's 365th Infantry. As Wilkinson later observed, "Well, we were playing out in Casper, Wyoming, and the first draft of the war caught five of our fourteen All-Nation players. That only left us with NINE players. But we still had a 35 game schedule before us.... We played every one of those games, and won every one save one. That we lost by a score of 1 to nothing."[35]

While on furlough in 1917 from the 25th Infantry team, where he was starring as a diminutive but powerful pitcher, five-foot, seven-inch Charles Wilber "Bullet Joe" Rogan (1893–1967) was scheduled to pitch against John Donaldson and the All Nations team in Kansas City. That game was rained out, but Wilkinson was so impressed by Rogan as both a pitcher and a hitter that he asked him to remain with All Nations for the rest of the 1917 season. Rogan suited up for a doubleheader against Guy Green's Nebraska Indians on May 5, 1917. He watched as Donaldson struck out a dozen and allowed only four hits in an All Nations win. On May 6 Wilkinson put Rogan in left field, and his only hit drove in a key run. He also stole home in a 5–4 win. When All Nations went on the road, Rogan was with the team.

On that 1917 All-Nations squad were three future Hall of Fame inductees: Cristóbal Torriente, José Méndez, and Rogan. Back in Kansas City, Wilkinson sent Rogan to the mound against the St. Louis Giants. Apparently soon thereafter, Rogan returned to the 25th Infantry, because his name is not found on box scores for the rest of the 1917 season.[36]

Despite having moved the All Nations' base of operations to Kansas City, Wilkinson apparently still called Des Moines home in 1918. When he registered with his draft board on September 2, 1918, he did so as "J." Leslie Wilkinson. He listed his occupation as Business Manager of Advance Specialty Company (207 Observatory Blvd., Des Moines) and his residence as 1503 11th Street in Des Moines. He identified his eye color as "gray-blue" and his hair as "light."[37]

Wilkinson disbanded the original All Nations in 1918 (after a 34–1 record), briefly revived the team in 1919 as a local Kansas City club,[38] and the next year turned his attention to organizing his new team, the Kansas City Monarchs. Black All Nations players would form the core of the Monarchs' entry into the new Negro National League, including pitcher/shortstop José Méndez, infielder Frank Blukoi, outfielder Hurley McNair, and pitchers "Plunk" Drake and "Bullet Joe" Rogan.

In 1920 and 1921, and from 1923–1925, J. L. Wilkinson maintained All Nations as a "farm team" for the Monarchs, basing the club in Omaha. Future Monarchs Newt Allen and Willie Bobo spent their rookie years with All Nations, and veteran Monarchs were sometimes assigned to the traveling team, their names still a draw in the small towns where All Nations played. It could also be a disciplinary destination as Monarchs manager Sam Crawford sent some players who misbehaved to the All Nations team to finish out their season.[39] The All Nations team closed the 1923 season with 117 wins and 14 losses.[40] John Donaldson was the All Nations' manager in 1923–24.[41]

In 1923, when he was 15, Chet Brewer, who would play for the Monarchs from 1925–1935, saw the All Nations squad pass through his hometown of Des Moines. He was impressed that the team "had Negroes, whites, Cubans, a Chinese, even two girls."[42]

Games with the All Nations team were huge events in midwestern communities. The *Kansas City Call* reported on June 1, 1928, that All Nations was on the road in Watertown, South Dakota, falling to a semi-pro team, 4–3. The team had "Indians, Whites, and Negroes." The *Bismarck Tribune* noted, "men of any race who can play baseball well are accepted on the [All-Nations] team."[43]

The status of All Nations is unclear during the early years of the Great Depression, but an All Nations team based in Des Moines was active during the 1936 season. "Players of all races are eligible including Negro, Indian, Japanese, Philippine and Chinese," a release published on May 1, 1936, in the *Kansas City Call* announced.

As Timothy Gay has observed in his study of interracial baseball before Jackie Robinson, "[f]ew social experiments in the early twentieth century were carried out with the panache of James [sic] Leslie Wilkinson's All-Nations team." With a band for dances after games, wrestling matches, a portable grandstand, a private Pullman car, and even, for a time, a primitive lighting system for night games, Wilkinson was indeed an innovative promoter well ahead of his time. More importantly, in an era when people were flocking to see D. W. Griffith's *The Birth of a Nation* (released in 1915), in which "heroic" Ku Klux Klansmen were shown rescuing white Southern belles from monstrous black soldiers, the All Nations team was proving not only that blacks and members of other racial minorities could perform as well as white major leaguers in the national pastime, but that it was possible for blacks and whites to play together as teammates.[44]

CHAPTER 3

Founding the Monarchs and the Negro National League (1920–1923)

In 1878 an African American player named John W. "Bud" Fowler broke the color line in professional baseball when he pitched three games for a previously all-white Lynn, Massachusetts, team. Other blacks soon followed and in 1884 two brothers, Welday and Moses Fleetwood Walker, were on the roster of the Toledo, Ohio, Blue Stockings of the American Association, one of three major leagues that year.[1]

As African American participation on previously all-white teams peaked, the tide turned. In July 1887, Moses Walker was playing for the Newark Little Giants of the International League. Cap Anson, one of the star white players of the era and captain of the National League Chicago White Stockings, refused to allow his team to play an exhibition game against the Newark club as long as a black player was on the roster. Sol White, author of the first history of black baseball, was a 19-year-old when Anson stomped off the field.[2] White later observed, "[w]ith his great popularity and power" Anson's opposition "hastened the exclusion to the black man from the white leagues."[3] The same day, the International League owners voted that teams would not be allowed to offer future contracts to black players.

Since he already had a contract to play, Moses Walker remained in the International League, enduring more encounters with the bigoted Anson. In August 1889, when the two major leagues, the American Association and the National League, effectively banned black players, the era of exclusion of blacks from the top white professional teams (the so-called "gentleman's agreement") had begun. It would last until 1945, when Branch Rickey signed Jackie Robinson, who was playing for J. L. Wilkinson's Kansas City Monarchs at the time, to a contract with the Brooklyn Dodgers organization (see Chapter 9). The "Bible of baseball," the *Sporting News*, which later challenged the signing of Jackie Robinson, noted somberly on March 23, 1889, that "[r]ace prejudice exists in professional baseball ranks to a marked degree, and the unfortunate son of Africa who makes his living as a member of a team of white professionals has a rocky road to travel."[4]

Denied the opportunity to play on integrated professional teams, African Americans focused on following the example of the first all-black team, the Philadelphia Pythians, who had begun play in 1867. In 1885 waiters at the Argyle Hotel on Long Island, New York, formed a team to provide entertainment for the hotel's guests. Most on the Argyle team would turn professional as the Cuban Giants, considered by many to be the first great black team in history. The Cuban Giants played games against white major leaguers over the years and filled out their schedule with minor league and semi-pro teams, mostly in the Midwest and East. During the winters they typically played in Cuba.

Sol White claimed the name "Cuban" was chosen to convince fans the team was foreign, not black. He said players often spoke gibberish on the field so it would sound like a foreign language. According to Buck O'Neil, "Giants" was understood in the African American community as code for "a black team." White newspapers would not publish stories or photos of black teams, so if knowledgeable fans saw an ad for the "Miami Giants," for example, they knew it was a black club.[5]

The U.S. Supreme Court's decision in Plessy v. Ferguson (1896) allowed segregationist Jim Crow practices to flourish and convinced black leaders that they should establish black schools, businesses, newspapers, churches, and sports teams. Numerous black organizations, including baseball teams, formed to promote racial pride, and, by shortly after the turn of the twentieth century, 20,000 African American businesses had opened. By 1914 there were 40,000. The African American periodical *Half Century* noted in 1919, "[a]s time moves on the Colored race is waking up to the fact that it is folly to depend upon any race except its own to assist it in molding itself to the fabric of American life."[6]

Despite repeated, failed attempts to form professional African American baseball leagues, a number of independent African American teams organized. These included, among others, the Leland Giants, the Kansas City Giants, the Baltimore Black Sox, and the Algona Brownies. In late August 1909, Rube Foster (1879–1930) and the heralded Chicago Leland Giants reputedly played the Kansas City Giants in a three-game series to decide the Negro World Championship. Indeed, in the first two decades of the twentieth century there were a number of series claiming to crown a black baseball champion.[7]

Foster had won the nickname "Rube" by out-pitching white major league star Rube Waddell in an exhibition game in 1902. Having excelled as one of the best black pitchers in the first decade of the century and as a player/

Andrew "Rube" Foster (1879–1930), shown here in the uniform of his beloved Chicago American Giants, whom he played for and managed, is best known as the driving force behind the formation of the Negro National League (NNL) in 1920. In recognition of his pioneering role as a baseball executive, he was inducted into the National Baseball Hall of Fame in 1981 (National Baseball Hall of Fame Library, Cooperstown, New York).

manager in the second, Foster was on the verge of earning a reputation as "black baseball's first great impresario." The Texas-born Foster was genial, calling everyone "darlin' in a southern drawl." He did not drink and was a good husband and father, but he carried a revolver and was a tough-as-nails negotiator with the white owners whose ballparks were the venues for black clubs when the white teams were on the road.[8]

In 1911 Foster took control of the Leland Giants, renaming the team the Chicago American Giants. He served not only as owner but also as player/manager. Foster's American Giants would be the premier professional African American baseball team until a decade later, when J. L. Wilkinson's Kansas City Monarchs challenged them for that honor.

Foster and other owners of African American teams believed that if they could establish their own league, jobs would open up not only for players but also scouts, umpires, clerks, ticket sellers, secretaries, bus drivers, and others. The businesses in the black neighborhoods where teams played would also get a boost. As early as April 16, 1910, Foster had proclaimed in a column published in the *Indianapolis Freeman*, "the time is now at hand when the formation of colored leagues would receive much consideration" if financial support could be found. "Now will our businessmen and friends of the profession make an effort to help us reach the coveted goal of complete success or will they stand by and see us fail?" he asked. "Which shall it be!" Foster knew that if black players wanted recognition from the white major leagues they needed to be organized, with enforced schedules, contracts, and regular pay.[9]

In 1919 race riots broke out in 26 cities across the United States. The worst was in Chicago, where "the violence started [in July] when a black youth dozing on a rubber raft floated too near a white beach and was stoned to death."[10] Fifteen whites and 23 blacks died, and over 500 people were injured. Whole neighborhoods were burned and looted.

As the rioting raged, J. L. Wilkinson approached fellow Kansas Citian Charles Dillon "Casey" Stengel (1890–1975), who was playing for the Pittsburgh Pirates of the National League, with the idea of a white major league all-star team holding a series with the black Chicago American Giants. Stengel agreed and recruited a team of major leaguers including Missouri native, and former teammate, Zack Wheat of the Brooklyn Dodgers.

A new African American determination and self-reliance emerged out of the 1919 riots. The African American weekly, *Chicago Whip*, led the way in condemning segregation and calling for new black leaders who would "love their race and country and know no superior" and be "grounded in truth, love, and service."

Rube Foster was positioned to lead the response to the challenge. The Chicago riots had dashed Foster's hope that white owners might wake up to the absurdity of racial separation in baseball. Consequently, he was more determined then ever that blacks should start their own league. On letterhead proudly proclaiming *American Giants Base Ball Club, The Greatest Aggregation of Colored Base Ball Players in the World*, he announced there would be a new black professional league by the next baseball season.[11] Foster's goal was to "keep Colored baseball from the control of the whites, and do something concrete for the loyalty of the race."[12]

On November 29, 1919, the first in a series of columns Foster wrote for the *Chicago Defender* enumerated the problems facing independent black teams and stressed the benefits of an organized league. There was mutual distrust between players and owners, he claimed, because of the practice of players jumping teams and owners raiding players.

Foster asserted club owners would have to agree not to tamper with other teams' players, and players would need to be assured that their incomes were based on actual gate receipts. He believed that to be successful, each team in a black league would need access to a ballpark, and there must be parity among clubs. Foster castigated other owners of black teams, saying "the majority do not know a ball player when they see one," and called for a meeting of owners for the purpose of drafting a constitution black baseball leaders could accept. Those committed to this goal would need to show their good faith and commitment by depositing $500.

Foster foresaw a plan that would be patterned after white organized ball, with the Eastern and Western winners meeting in a "real world's championship." That, he hoped, would some day lead to an encounter with the champion of the white major leagues. "Only in uniform strength is there permanent success," Foster asserted.

In the column published on January 3, 1920, he contrasted the raiding of players among black clubs with the reserve clause in major league baseball that bound a player to a team until it released or traded him. Black players feared organization because they thought it would reduce their salaries, but Foster claimed forming leagues would have the opposite result. There were black investors ready to put money into Negro Leagues baseball, but Foster warned they would not wait forever for clubs to organize on the model of the white major leagues. Foster was convinced his call for organization would be "the salvation of baseball."

In May 1919, a new African American weekly newspaper, the *Kansas City Call,* began publication.[13] Its founder was Chester Arthur ("C. A.") Franklin (1880–1955). Members of the Paseo Y.M.C.A. volleyball team, on which Franklin played, were among the paper's first subscribers. The *Call* would grow to become one of the six largest black weeklies in the country and continues publication to this day.

Franklin was born in Denison, Texas, to a barber and a teacher at a time when African Americans were leaving Texas in search of better educational opportunities for their children. In 1887 Franklin and his family moved to Omaha, where his father started a newspaper, the *Omaha Enterprise.* C. A. attended the University of Nebraska for two years, but when his father became ill he had to leave school to take over the role of editor of the *Enterprise.* To improve his father's health, the Franklins migrated to Colorado in 1898 and bought another newspaper, eventually called the *Star.*

In 1913, C. A. Franklin moved to Kansas City, and six years later started the *Kansas City Call.* The paper began as a four-page sheet, with a weekly run of 2,000. As soon became obvious in his weekly editorials, Franklin was a strong advocate of black self-reliance and endorsed the ideas of W. E. B. Dubois. For example, in the January 14, 1922, edition of the *Call,* under the headline "The Manhood of Kansas City Negroes is Challenged," Franklin decried the manipulation of blacks in Kansas City politics, concluding: "We are not underlings because other men say we are, we are masters of our fate. Strong men, just men of every race, will applaud the day when we cease to be measured by the scorn of our contemners, and offer our own proved merit."

By 1928 the circulation of the *Kansas City Call* had grown to 18,000. Nearly every African American home in Kansas City was receiving a copy of the paper from a carrier. At the same time, mail circulation throughout the state of Missouri and the states to the southwest was growing. The *Call* was on the way to becoming one of the largest black businesses in the region. By mid-century the *Call* had expanded to 32 pages with 40,000 copies sold a week.

3. Founding the Monarchs and the Negro National League (1920–1923)

From its first issues, under Franklin's leadership, the *Call* promoted the rights and interests of the black community of Kansas City and African Americans throughout the country. In the 1920s and 1930s the newspaper covered fully the campaigns to expand the right to vote for African Americans and for equal opportunities for Blacks in employment, education, and housing. One of the *Call's* first victories in Kansas City was breaking the ban against African Americans serving on juries. It also fought for decent housing in the city for blacks and their right to live where they pleased—at personal risk to Franklin and the Rev. D. A. Holmes, who joined him in the struggle. The paper strongly endorsed the struggle against segregation in the armed forces and the fight for non-discriminatory hiring in government agencies.

Nor did the *Call* shy away from addressing the most highly charged national issues facing African Americans. It ran frequent front-page stories on the scourge of lynching and kept yearly track of the numbers of lynching victims state by state.

From its beginnings the *Call* also published regular articles about African American baseball teams in the city. Serendipitously, one of Franklin's friends was J. L. Wilkinson, who the same year the *Call* began publication was hard at work organizing the Kansas City Monarchs. For nearly three decades Franklin and Wilkinson would enjoy a close working relationship, and the *Kansas City Call* would be the major source of press coverage of the Monarchs throughout the history of the team.

On February 7, 1920, the *Chicago Defender* announced that the long-anticipated meeting of blackball magnates to form a new black league would occur the following week in Kansas City, Missouri.[14] The decision to hold the meeting in Kansas City strongly suggests that J. L. Wilkinson, owner of the newly organized Kansas City Monarchs, was intimately involved in pre-planning the gathering. In addition to Wilkinson, the following owners or representatives were scheduled to attend: C. I. Taylor, Indianapolis A.B.C.'s; John Matthews, Dayton Marcos; John "Tenny" Blount, Detroit Stars; Charlie Mills, St. Louis Giants; Joe Green, Chicago Giants; and Rube Foster, Chicago American Giants. Foster had also been given the proxy for the Cuban Stars. Two of the teams, it was announced before the meeting, the Cuban Stars and Chicago Giants, would be exclusively traveling teams in the new league.

Several leading black sportswriters were also invited to the gathering, among them David Wyatt of the *Indianapolis Ledger*, Charles Marshall of the *Indianapolis Freeman*, A. D. Williams of the *Indianapolis Ledger*, and Cary B. Lewis of the *Chicago Defender*. With the exception of Wilkinson, all the owners and writers at the meeting were African Americans.

The first session took place on Friday, February 13, 1920, in the Y.M.C.A. at 18th and Paseo in the heart of Kansas City's famed jazz district. Also present were other black leaders: W. A. Kelly of Washington, D.C; attorney Elisha Scott of Topeka, Kansas (renowned civil rights lawyer, whose sons worked on the famed 1954 Brown v. Board of Education case that led to the integration of public schools); and Elwood C. Knox of the *Freeman*. The other owners chose Rube Foster to be "temporary president" and Lewis as secretary. Taylor was named vice-president.

Foster announced he had already obtained a charter for what he called the National Negro Baseball League (NNL), then produced the document. According to the *Kansas City Call*, the others present were dumbfounded but pleased to learn Foster had already incorporated the new league in Illinois, Michigan, Ohio, Pennsylvania, New York, and Maryland.

All contentious issues, such as the allocation of players and drafting of a constitution, were turned over to Scott and the journalists present. Wyatt, Knox, Lewis and Scott then worked into the early morning hours of Saturday, February 14, to shape a "baseball bill of rights" for the new league. By noon they were ready to present the preamble and constitution. League rules were established to control the behavior of managers and players. For example, managers could be fined and players who jumped their contracts could be suspended. Players were not to swear or fight. Teams were not to protest umpires' calls by leaving the field. Wilkinson almost certainly played a role in the emphasis on clean play. He always insisted that his teams play hard but fair. As one *Kansas City Call* writer suggested two years after the NNL was founded, Wilkinson's slogan for his team's play against opponents had proven to be "treat him right, but beat him."[15]

The journalists also developed balanced player rosters for the NNL. Foster showed his good faith by allowing his premier player, future Hall of Fame outfielder Oscar Charleston, and submarine pitcher William "Dizzy" Dismukes (who would later join the Monarchs) to be sent to the Indianapolis A.B.C.'s. The Chicago Giants received pitcher Walter Bell and slugger John Beckwith. Five players (Pete Hill, Bruce Petway, Ed Wesley, Dick Whitworth and Jimmie Lyons) went to the Detroit Stars. Wilkinson and the Monarchs took All Nations stars José Méndez and John Donaldson. For his willingness to break up his own team, Dave Wyatt of the *Defender* gave Foster the moniker the "King of Baseball."

The major differences between the new African American league and the white majors were that in the NNL barnstorming games were allowed during the season, ballparks were leased not owned, umpires were provided by individual teams, and players usually received their cut of the profits of a game before owners did. In addition, booking agents were essential to filling out a team's schedule.

The original league constitution also included associate membership status for the Hilldale Club from Darby, Pennsylvania, near Philadelphia; the Atlantic City Bacharach Giants; and the eastern Cuban Stars. Associate members could have some games scheduled by the league, but games between full and associate members would not count in the NNL standings.

The owners present agreed not to start NNL play until April 1921, to allow teams time to secure rights to ballparks. Each owner present signed the constitution and purportedly submitted a $500 deposit. Foster may have posted the amount for several of the owners unable to raise it. The February 27 edition of the *Call* proclaimed, "[i]t was the first time in the history of a baseball meeting that there was exhibited so much harmony and good spirit."

Within two weeks of the Kansas City meeting, an eight-team NNL was in place and the decision had been made to move up the starting date for league play from April 1921 to May 1, 1920. Charles Marshall wrote in the *Freeman* there would be salary caps, a playing schedule, and posted admission prices. He insisted fans could expect "professional major league ball playing and not outlaw or semi-professional pastime." The smartest move, in Marshall's view, was the election of Foster as permanent president. "Give us more men like C. I. Taylor, 'Tenny' [sic], Blount, Foster and Wilkinson who urge the playing of clean ball," he wrote.

In the end, why did Rube Foster allow J. L. Wilkinson to join the NNL as the only visible white owner? It may have been that Foster's effort to find a suitable black owner to field a Kansas City team had failed. Dr. Howard Smith, superintendent of Kansas City's

3. Founding the Monarchs and the Negro National League (1920–1923)

black hospital, was a potential owner, but he lacked baseball knowledge and the finances needed for a team. Furthermore, he had no lease for a suitable baseball stadium.[16]

According to Buck O'Neil, Foster overcame his initial reluctance to consider Wilkinson because the Monarchs' owner had already earned the respect of both the black and white communities in Kansas City. Furthermore, Foster knew Kansas City was a prime location and, as O'Neil noted, "Wilkie held the lease to the [white Kansas City Blues'] ballpark." According to O'Neil, "[t]he other owners prevailed upon Rube to change his mind."[17] Moreover, by the time of the organization of the Monarchs, Wilkinson had won the endorsement of a major black weekly, the *Freeman* of Indianapolis.[18]

It was certainly not wealth that attracted the other owners to J. L. Wilkinson. He had no inherited fortune or lucrative business he could draw on to fund the Monarchs. Wilkinson's son, Dick, remembered, "[e]very year he'd mortgage the house before the season, then come home that fall and pay it off. He never missed a season or a payroll but, boy, he came close a lot of times."[19]

Whatever Rube Foster's reasons, he forged a close relationship and business alliance with J. L. Wilkinson. Dick remembered, "as a kid that Foster ... would call my father for advice. They were extremely close friends."[20]

Why did Wilkinson choose to organize an all-black professional baseball team and join an all-black league? According to his son Dick, "the reason Dad started the Monarchs was that he wanted the best, and he couldn't afford to be a major league owner; otherwise he might have gone into the [white] major leagues. But he wanted to have the best; and the Monarchs were the best."[21]

There is uncertainty about the make-up of the original 1920 Kansas City roster. Two of Wilkinson's All Nations players, John Donaldson and José Méndez, had played for the Detroit Stars in 1919. As part of the agreement to balance team strength, the owner of the Stars, Tenny Blount, allowed Méndez and Donaldson to join the Monarchs. From the All Nations team Wilkinson also tapped Frank Blukoi. In addition, he recruited Rube Currie and Hurley McNair of Gilkerson's Union Giants, Rube Tyree of the Kansas City Allies, and two Missourians, Hugh Blackburn of Knobnoster and Otto "Jay Bird" Ray of Lexington. Letters were also sent to two infielders, George "Tank" Carr and Edgar "Blue" Washington in Los Angeles.

In his search for players, Wilkinson drew on the advice of his friend Casey Stengel, whose white all-star team had lost a series to the all-black 25th Infantry regimental team at Fort Stephen Little in Nogales, Arizona. Stengel called the army team "the Wreckers" and recommended to Wilkinson five of their outstanding players: pitcher and outfielder Wilber "Bullet Joe" Rogan (whom Wilkinson already knew), shortstop Walter "Dobie" Moore, power-hitting outfielder Oscar "Heavy" Johnson, crafty southpaw Andy Cooper, and talented first baseman Lemuel "Hawk" Hawkins.

The experience of Carroll "Dink" Mothell (1897–1980) provides insight into Wilkinson's hardnosed negotiating style and his persistence. In March 1920, Mothell, who was playing with the Topeka Giants, wrote Wilkinson to inquire about joining the Monarchs. Weeks later he received a reply from the Monarchs' owner, offering him $120 a month. In addition to playing on the semi-pro Giants, Mothell had a good job in construction and was disappointed at Wilkinson's offer. "Dink" went to Kansas City and asked Wilkinson for a higher salary, but the Monarchs' owner told him that since he had not yet made the ballclub, $120 was all he could offer him. Mothell packed his bags and returned to Topeka. For the next few years, "Dink" was in and out of baseball. All the while Wilkinson

When the Negro National League (NNL) formed in 1920, J. L. Wilkinson's Kansas City Monarchs were among the founding teams, remaining with the first NNL until 1931. The 1920 Monarchs included the following players: front row, from left—José Méndez, unidentified, Bartolo Portuando, Walter "Dobie" Moore, Otto "Jaybird" Ray, Hurley McNair; back row, from left—John Donaldson, Sam Crawford, Rube Currie, Vicente "José" Rodríguez, Zack "Hooks" Foreman, unidentified, George "Tank" Carr, Wilber "Bullet Joe" Rogan (courtesy NoirTech Research, Inc.).

kept his eye on Mothell, waiting for the right time to sign him. That moment came in 1924. "Dink" Mothell would remain with the Monarchs for ten years, earning a reputation as an outstanding utility player.[22]

Wilkinson also signed Frank Floyd as the team's trainer. Floyd, who was known by the nickname "Jew Baby," was the only black chiropractor in Kansas City. He served as Monarchs trainer for 30 years, traveling with the team, giving rubdowns and also dispensing a range of advice, including guidance on romantic matters, to players.[23]

One debated question about the founding of the Monarchs is the precise role played by Thomas Younger (T. Y., Tom) Baird from Kansas City, Kansas, a former baseball player and, by 1919, a successful businessman. Baird was born on January 27, 1885, in Madison County, Arkansas. He moved with his parents to Kansas City in the early 1900s.

As a young man Baird played semi-pro baseball. However, his baseball career was cut short in 1918 when he fractured his right leg in two places while working in White City, Kansas, as a brakeman for the Rock Island Railroad.[24] The break did not heal properly, and Baird, who spent two months in the hospital, had a limp for the rest of his life.

After leaving the railroad, Baird opened the first of a number of billiard halls and bowling alleys he would own. Although he could no longer play the game himself, Baird remained involved in the local baseball scene as a manager and promoter.[25] One of his

3. Founding the Monarchs and the Negro National League (1920–1923)

semi-pro teams was called the "T. Y. Bairds." It was in that context that he likely first met J. L. Wilkinson, who recruited him to join in organizing the Monarchs. As one commentator observed in 1950, looking back on the early years of the Monarchs, "Wilkinson wanted a good 'gate guardian' and induced Baird to join him."[26]

According to Baird's daughter, Harriet Baird Wickstrom, her father and Wilkinson were from the outset equal partners in owning the Monarchs.[27] However, if that were the case, Baird was largely a silent partner who stayed behind the scenes even more than Wilkinson. In the early days of the Monarchs, Baird and Wilkinson were rarely seen together.[28] Wilkinson's son Dick said he did not even know Baird was an owner of the team until he was 14. He would see Baird at the ballpark and didn't know what his role was.[29]

According to historian Tim Rives, the empathetic Wilkinson served in the role of general manager and built close bonds with the players. By contrast, "[t]all, lean Tom Baird, whose austere mien did not suggest easy intimacy, covered the business end of the operation, booking games and making deals. Baird spent so much time behind the scenes that some early Monarchs players never knew he owned part of the club."[30]

The apocryphal story circulated that Baird was Wilkinson's son-in-law, and some Monarchs players were still telling the tale when Janet Bruce Vaughn interviewed them in the late 1970s. According to Quincy (Q. J.) Gilmore's wife, Alberta, Baird's leg injury also kept him from traveling with the Monarchs in the early years.[31]

From the formation of the Monarchs through 1935, Wilkinson worked closely with and placed considerable trust in Gilmore, a Kansas City undertaker hired to serve as the Monarchs' traveling secretary. Q. J. Gilmore was indeed "an unrecognized force behind the organization of Negro professional baseball" and, after Wilkinson and Baird, "the third most important figure in the Monarchs management." He filled whatever assignment Wilkinson asked of him. For example, when Wilkinson suffered a bout of appendicitis in Chicago in 1921, he had Gilmore take over running the team on the road until he recovered.

One of Gilmore's principal responsibilities was writing promotional articles for the Monarchs that appeared in the sports section of the *Kansas City Call* and other African American papers. In particular, he submitted advanced articles printed before games to encourage attendance, offering perpetually optimistic assessments of the Monarchs' prospects.

Secretary Gilmore and Monarchs player "Bullet Joe" Rogan operated the team headquarters out of their shared business, the Monarchs Billiard Room, located across from the famous Street Hotel on 18th Street.

Gilmore also served as the Negro National League's secretary and treasurer in 1928, and in 1929 left Kansas City for Dallas to become president of the fledgling Texas-Oklahoma-Louisiana League. When that league failed, he returned to the Monarchs for a few more years.[32]

Roy "Bubba" Johnson was playing for the Kansas City Tigers in 1919, when Tom Baird spotted him and asked if he would like to join a traveling club. Johnson told Janet Bruce Vaughn in a 1981 interview that he played in 1919 with All Nations. He joined the Monarchs the next year. As he recalled, the gate at exhibition games was split (60 percent to the winners and 40 percent to the losers). Johnson said "Wilkerson [sic] and Baird" would each take about $50 and give the rest to the players. His contract was for $125 a month. Fed up with the poor travel conditions and the racial prejudice he experienced,

Johnson left the Monarchs after the 1922 season to take a police job. Johnson remembered the controversy over whether Wilkinson and Baird should be allowed to own a black club, since they were white. He said that Wilkinson treated the players fine, and all accepted him, calling him "Wilkie." After Johnson left the Monarchs, Wilkinson and Baird gave him a pass to attend games every year.[33]

Beginning with the 1920 season, Wilkinson maintained sandlot and semi-pro teams, many representing local black businesses; they became training grounds for the Monarchs club. Before they began traveling south for spring training in the mid-1920s, the Monarchs (sometimes called "Wilkinson's Warriors") worked out at Paradeway Park at 17th and the Paseo, in the heart of the black community, playing against the reconstituted All Nations team, local semi-pro teams, and even a squad from the federal penitentiary at Leavenworth, Kansas. Wilkinson was always on the lookout for talent. Typically, he had recruits play in exhibition games to evaluate their ability. He then would sign them for the Monarchs, assign them to the All Nations team or a semi-pro team, or give them a railroad ticket home.

Wilkinson's determination to remain behind the scenes is evident from the origins of the team. He sent Quincy Gilmore and another Kansas City black leader, Dr. Howard Smith, who, as noted above, had first been considered as owner of an NNL team in the city, to public functions in the black community to represent the team. At the Opening Day of the inaugural 1920 season, Wilkinson did not ride in the owners' car in the parade, placing Gilmore there instead. Among black leaders in Kansas City, Wilkinson had a "good reputation for being diplomatic, unassuming, and easygoing." One black leader, Robert Sweeney, said, "Wilkie ... had a good image in the Negro community—all over the country." Wilkinson also gained the support of local leaders in the Kansas City chapter of the National Association for the Advancement of Colored People (NAACP) because of his fair treatment of his players and others who worked for him.[34]

Although players had to provide their own shoes and gloves, Wilkinson supplied uniforms—usually three sets. In a variety of colors (white with maroon trim for home games) the uniforms usually had "Monarchs" across the chest and "KC" on the sleeves.[35]

In a 1948 interview, J. L. Wilkinson claimed John Donaldson came up with the name Monarchs "when we were feeling around for a name to give to a reorganization of the All-Nations team." One suggestion, preferred initially by Wilkinson, was the Kansas City Browns, but when Donaldson proposed Monarchs, "[r]ight away," Wilkinson remembered, "the name sounded good and we adopted it."[36] It would not take long before the team proved, as the *Kansas City Call* proclaimed, that they were, paraphrasing eighteenth century poet William Cowper, "MONARCHS OF ALL THEY SURVEY."[37]

Only 82 days after the NNL constitution was drafted and approved, the first league game was played on May 2, 1920, in Indianapolis. The Indianapolis A.B.C.'s beat the Chicago Giants, 4–2, before a crowd of at least 6,000.

Wilkinson chose All Nations star José Méndez as the first field manager for the Monarchs. It would not be an easy job. During the first two months of the 1920 season, three of the Monarchs' regulars went down with injuries and, though Wilkinson claimed to have recruited new players, relief was slow to arrive. The Monarchs limped along.

Help finally appeared when two former 25th Infantry players, Wilber "Bullet Joe" Rogan and Walter "Dobie" Moore, arrived for the game on July 4, 1920. Rogan was in left field and Moore at shortstop. The next day Rogan pitched his first NNL game against

3. Founding the Monarchs and the Negro National League (1920–1923)   33

the American Giants. The *Chicago Defender* noted Rogan had arrived in Kansas City after a three-night train ride and "gave an exhibition of hurling that had 10,000 fans yelping, and the American Giants standing on their heads." He allowed only one hit and struck out 11.[38]

The Monarchs traveled to Detroit where, in his second start, Rogan dispatched the Stars, 4–1. At the plate he had his first extra-base hit, a double. In Indianapolis on July 18, "Bullet Joe" won his third game when the Monarchs defeated the A.B.C.'s. Returning to Kansas City, the Kaysees (as the Monarchs were also called) played several non-league games, then took on their rivals, Rube Foster's American Giants. The two powerhouse teams locked horns in an historic six-game series at Association Park, home of the all-white Kansas City Blues of the American Association, which Wilkinson leased for Monarchs games. The first game attracted 2,000 enthusiastic fans who cheered the home team with cowbells and whistles. When John Donaldson collided with American Giants first baseman Leroy Grant, the two started throwing punches. Fifty fans came out of the stands and had to be restrained by gun-toting police officers. The *Kansas City Journal* called the fight "a near riot." The American Giants took the game, 9–7.[39]

Tickets could not be printed fast enough for the second game. A crowd of 20,000 reportedly squeezed into Association Park. Rogan went to the mound, striking out 13 and matching pitches with Chicago's Tom Williams for 11 innings before winning the game himself with a double in the 12th. The Monarchs would go on to win four of the six games.

Newt Allen, a long-time Monarch who saw both "Bullet Joe" Rogan and Satchel Paige pitch, said, "Rogan was better than Paige because Rogan was smarter. Satchel was just a stuff pitcher; he had stuff, but Rogan had the brains. I give Rogan the edge, because he knew how to pitch." Chet Brewer called him "the best pitcher I ever saw in my life." Not only was Rogan a premier

Wilber "Bullet Joe" Rogan (1893–1967) was playing on the famed all-black U.S. Army 25th Infantry team when Kansas City native Casey Stengel saw him and recommended him to J. L. Wilkinson. Rogan starred, both as a pitcher and hard-hitting outfielder, for All Nations (1917) and the Monarchs (1920–1938), including serving as manager (1926–1934, 1936). He was inducted into the National Baseball Hall of Fame in 1998 (National Baseball Hall of Fame Library, Cooperstown, New York).

pitcher, he also could hit and field better than most position players.[40] Monarchs co-owner Tom Baird called Rogan the best player who had ever played for the team.[41]

Led by Rogan's heroics as a hurler and a power hitter, the Monarchs finished the 1920 season with a 42-34-2 record in NNL play. They drew more than 125,000 spectators to Association Park. Combining league and exhibition contests, the Monarchs played an estimated 114 games during the team's first season.[42]

It had been difficult to schedule games, and Rube Foster fell short of his goal of having each NNL team play 100 contests during the 1920 season. There was also a significant disparity in the number of league games each team played. Still, all eight teams survived the first season, supplementing league games with exhibition contests, and turning a profit.[43]

On December 3, 1920, the NNL had its second meeting, this time at a Y.M.C.A. in Indianapolis. Foster was unanimously re-elected president. The Hilldale Daisies and the Atlantic City Bacharachs were formally admitted to the league as associate members, and the Dayton franchise moved to Columbus, with Sol White in charge. An amended constitution mandated the fining of managers or owners guilty of "ungentlemanly actions which hurt the game." A reserve clause was henceforth to be included in player contracts, so that they could not "jump" to other teams. Teams were authorized to refuse to play teams outside the NNL that had "pirated" players. According to an article in the *Pittsburgh Competitor*, Dr. H. M. Smith and Harry St. Clair, another Kansas City black business leader, joined Wilkinson in representing the Monarchs at the meeting. Foster reported to his fellow owners that all NNL teams had made money during the 1920 season, and the eight clubs had drawn more than 660,000 fans.[44]

Despite the success of the initial season, the "ship" that was the NNL was not sailing on calm waters. Under the headline "Will Colored Baseball Survive the Acid Test?" which appeared in the January 20, 1921, edition of the *Kansas City Sun,* Foster ominously warned that the coming 1921 season would either "permanently secure baseball among us or will destroy the good that has been accomplished." He reiterated that with the cooperation of owners and players, he would make the NNL "the ship, all other opposition the sea," a phrase he borrowed from an 1869 speech by the famed abolitionist, Frederick Douglass. The NNL would be a place, Foster assured readers, where "your children will want to seek employment and you will be proud to see them."[45]

Principal contenders for the 1921 NNL pennant were the Chicago American Giants and the Kansas City Monarchs. Wilkinson had the stronger line-up, with the exception of Chicago's Cristóbal Torriente. Four Monarchs topped .350 for the season—Moore, Johnson, Rogan, and first baseman George "Tank" Carr. In a tradition that continued through the team's storied history, Wilkinson stocked the Monarchs with excellent pitchers. In addition to Rogan there were veteran Sam Crawford, youngster and Kansas City native Rube Currie, and lefty John Donaldson.

In search of a catcher, Wilkinson eventually traded first baseman Lemuel "Hawk" Hawkins, catcher "Jay Bird" Ray and a thousand dollars to the Chicago Giants for Frank Duncan, who, though not a great hitter, was a superb catcher with a gun for an arm. He once threw out six American Giants runners in the same game.

Though the American Giants did not have the power hitting of the Monarchs, they had and utilized blinding speed. With Foster directing their every move, the team made its own breaks through exquisite bat control—bunting and placement hitting. He also employed the element of surprise. "We do," he said, "what the other fellow does not expect us to do." Combined with precision pitching and solid defense, the American Giants held their own against the more talented Monarchs.[46] After frustrating losses, especially against Foster's team, the Monarchs would gather in the clubhouse and rehash the game for hours in what they called "skull sessions."

The fierce rivalry between the Monarchs and American Giants was a major draw. Some data has surfaced on Wilkinson's share of gate receipts in 1921. On June 12, in a game against the Cincinnati Cubans, Wilkinson received $2,101.76. He collected $2,600.08 when the Monarchs beat the Detroit Stars in Kansas City in July and $1,720.46 in a September game against the American Giants.

With the team's income based solely on gate receipts, "Wilkinson scheduled as many games as he could jam into six months of baseball." Virtually every small town had a team, and they all wanted to play the vaunted Monarchs.[47] In Missouri, Kansas, Nebraska, Iowa, Arkansas, Oklahoma, Texas, and beyond, the Monarchs played mostly white amateur teams. Games in rural communities often drew 2,000 or more fans.

During one barnstorming game in a small town, a fan bet "Tank" Carr he could not get a ninth-inning, two-out hit that would give the Monarchs a comeback win. Carr homered, and the fan handed over a big bay horse. Wilkinson bought the horse from Carr, paying him in liberty bonds.[48]

The Monarchs completed their 1921 barnstorming tour with a well-attended game at Richmond, Missouri, located in a county that was only five percent African American. They ended the 1921 NNL season in third place, behind the Chicago American Giants and St. Louis Giants.

In a series to determine the professional baseball champions of Kansas City for 1921, the Monarchs faced off against the Kansas City Blues of the American Association, the top-rated team in the white minor leagues. The Blues took the series, 5–1. The Monarchs would get their revenge the next year.

In December 1921, Rube Foster wrote four essays for the *Chicago Defender* assessing the problems he thought still afflicted black baseball. They included ignorance of baseball among the "respectable and class-conscious," players breaking contracts, a lack of "race" umpires hired by the league, and a need for more financial investments in the game from middle-class and wealthy individuals.[49]

Despite the ongoing challenges Foster identified, the NNL was the first black league not only to survive two seasons but also to do well enough financially to have hopes of continuing well into the future.[50]

According to Secretary Gilmore, the future of the Monarchs was bright. "You can rest assured," he wrote, "that the Monarchs of 1922 will be much stronger than the team of 1921.... J. L. Wilkerson [sic] the owner of the Monarchs will ... spend money to secure the best on the market."[51]

After the 1922 winter meeting, the NNL announced that the Cincinnati and Columbus clubs would be replaced by teams in Cleveland and Pittsburgh. The league teams would include the St. Louis Giants, Pittsburgh Keystones, Kansas City Monarchs, Indianapolis A.B.C.'s, Chicago American Giants, Cleveland Tate Stars, and Detroit Stars. The Cuban Stars would be strictly a traveling club.[52]

Another example of Wilkinson's business acumen is evident in his incorporation of the team during the 1922 season as the Kansas City Monarchs Baseball and Entertainment Company, with $20,000 in capital stock. The move served to give him personal financial protection in the event of a default.

Two key players joined the Monarchs in 1922. One was former All Nations pitcher Bill "Plunk" Drake, who was secured in a trade with the St. Louis Giants. Drake had a good curve and excellent control. For the Giants in 1921, he pitched against the St. Louis Cardinals, losing 5–4 on an error in the 11th inning. According to Drake, during the winter after the 1921 season he had gone to Kansas City a couple of times and talked with J. L. Wilkinson about joining the Monarchs. Then, as Drake recounted the story, "unbeknownst to the people here in St. Louis—[Wilkinson] was way too sneaky for these people," the Monarchs traded Branch Russell and Dempsey Miller for him. Drake told John Holway that Rube Foster was perturbed, complaining "[t]hey got the best pitching staff in the league, now they've grabbed another good pitcher."

Drake said the Monarchs "used to advertise ball games at the picture show at 18th and Lydia. They'd put a ballplayer's picture on the screen. They'd say don't put Drake's up there he'll want a raise. I used to tell them, '[t]he hell with you, I'll go back and fish. I don't have to play no damn baseball.' I sometimes think I was a little too impetuous."[53]

The other major acquisition for the 1922 NNL season was Kansas City native Newton "Newt" Allen (1901–1988). A year earlier Wilkinson had noticed the 19-year-old Allen playing baseball on the lot at 17th and Paseo.[54] Allen was of slight build and didn't think he could make it as a professional ballplayer. However, astute judge of baseball talent that he was, the Monarchs' owner signed the youngster. Before he joined the Monarchs in 1922, Allen traveled with the reconstituted All Nations team. His starting salary with the Monarchs was $150 a month. Allen was so young his teammates called the rookie "Colt." At first he was unable to hit curve balls and laid down frequent bunts. However, over time he developed into a skilled hit-and-run batter, mastering the ability to hit the ball where it was pitched.

Defensively Allen was an excellent second baseman. When both Jackie Robinson and Allen were playing for the Monarchs in 1945, Dick Wilkinson said, Allen was a much better fielder than Robinson.[55] Ted "Double Duty" Radcliffe, whose nickname referred to the occasion in which he had pitched in one game of a doubleheader and caught in the other, and who played with Allen on the Monarchs for several years, rated him the best second baseman in the Negro Leagues. Fans selected him for the annual East-West All-Star Game five times.

Throughout Allen's long career with the Monarchs, the team's chief rivals, he noted decades later, were the Chicago American Giants. There were often fights. After one particularly vicious brawl in Chicago involving players and fans that had to be broken up by police, 18,000 came out in Kansas City when the teams next played, to see who would start the fracas. The American Giants' and Monarchs' owners were making good money!

The depth of the hostility between the players on the two clubs is illustrated in a story Newt Allen told to John Holway[56]:

> The American Giants first baseman Dave Malarcher once slid into me at second with his spikes high and put eighteen stitches on my shin. It took three years but I got sweet revenge. We were two runs up and Malarcher was on first. I took a throw at second for a double play, but instead of throwing to first I nailed Malarcher in the forehead. He was out for three days. The next time he was on first and rounding second for third I hit him in the back of the head. It was just one of those "evil spirit" days, I guess. But he never slid into me with his spikes up again.

J. L. Wilkinson was, Allen let it be known, "one of the friendliest men I've ever seen. Could have had any ballplayers. Those who played against us wanted to play for him. He understood people. Your face could be as black as tar; he treated everyone the same.

3. Founding the Monarchs and the Negro National League (1920–1923) 37

Traveled most of the games. Sat in front with bus driver." When the Monarchs were playing in the South, Allen said, Wilkinson would sit with the black spectators in the grandstand.[57]

Wilkinson chose Sam Crawford, who had been with the team its first two years, as the Monarchs' manager for the 1922 season. Crawford followed the style of Rube Foster and was strict with his players. Newt Allen said, "Crawford made the ballplayers keep the hours and kept you out of the ballgame as punishment. He was strict on drinking and you could only stay up late if you were playing cards or dominos." More importantly, Crawford was also an excellent strategist. He used pinch runners and pinch hitters to great effect. On one occasion Crawford employed two pinch runners to bring a run home after a single—the first because he was faster and the second because he was smarter.[58]

During the 1922 pre-season, the Monarchs defeated a number of white teams, including the Topeka team of the Western Association, 11–8 and 4–1. On April 22 the Monarchs traveled to Leavenworth, Kansas, to play the Booker T. Washington team, composed of prisoners at the Federal Penitentiary. Seven men on the prison team were serving life sentences. The game was played on a diamond inside the penitentiary, and Monarch slugger "Tank" Carr was the first to hit a home run over the prison wall in a 10–4 Kansas City victory.[59]

The Monarchs-American Giants rivalry was white hot throughout the 1922 season. According to the *Call*, the season-opening series, played in Chicago, was "a disgrace to Rube Foster, as League president, and the Chicago fans." In the Sunday contest, with the score tied in the ninth inning and Dobie Moore coming to the plate, the Chicago fans swarmed the field to prevent a repeat of Dobie's home run the previous day. Foster, as league president and the local team owner, should have cleared the field or instructed the umpires to forfeit the game, the *Call* asserted. He did not, and the score was recorded as a 2–2 tie.[60]

While the Monarchs were playing in Chicago, a white mob in Kansas City bombed the home of H. M. Williams, a black veteran of the First World War, who had left part of his right leg on the battlefield in France. According to the coverage of the incident in the *Kansas City Call*, after Williams moved into the home he had purchased at 2216 E. 21st, a neighbor told him, "if you move in we will bomb you." A delegation of 14 white men ordered him to leave because it was a "restricted area." Williams told the group he intended to stay. Two weeks later a bomb destroyed the veteran's home. No arrests were made.[61]

The Monarchs' 1922 home opener was on Saturday, May 20. Elaborate festivities began at 12:30 p.m. with a large parade led by a squad of motor police, followed by bands, marching units, and a long stream of cars. The owner of the St. Louis Stars rode with Quincy Gilmore (but not Wilkinson or Baird) in a large touring car. The mayors of Kansas City, Missouri, and Kansas City, Kansas, joined in throwing out the ceremonial first pitch. It took 13 innings and four pitchers, but the Monarchs prevailed over the Stars before a crowd of 3,500, winning 3–2.

During the 1922 season, Monarchs games in Kansas City attracted both black and white fans. According to Quincy Gilmore's wife, Alberta, there were sometimes more whites than blacks in the stands during the early years. She often worked at the ball park and remembered an incident when the opposing team attacked some of the Monarchs players and both "blacks *and* whites ran on to the field…, yelling, 'You're not going to hurt our boys!'"[62]

In the early years, fan misbehavior at games was a recurring problem in the NNL. Kansas City was no exception. After a late May 1922 game against the Pittsburgh Keystones, the *Call* warned in a blaring headline: ROWDYISM MAY CAUSE MONARCHS TO LOSE [ASSOCIATION] PARK. Gilmore released a statement, saying "he was sorry to have to say that the conduct of a few Negroes present at the game might keep Negroes from playing ball at the park." He asked "every member of our Race to urge upon each other to see that nothing happens which will hurt the good relationship existing between the races at the ball games. There is nothing in Kansas City that brings the two races closer together than the Monarch ball games." Gilmore noted, "Mr. Wilkinson is doing everything in his power to give Kansas City a winning team." Attendance was down, Gilmore said, and unless it picked up, Mr. Wilkinson would not be able to bring in teams from the East.[63]

In a continuation of their bitter rivalry, the American Giants came to Kansas City on June 17 for the first time during the 1922 season. After the Monarchs won the series, 3–2, they were victorious in seven of their next ten games, including four of five from the league-leading Indianapolis A.B.C.'s. With attendance at home games continuing a downward trend, Wilkinson cut the Monarchs' roster, sending six players to his Omaha All Nations team to barnstorm against white teams. He had named John Donaldson as the All Nations' manager.[64]

As the 1922 season continued, issues with imbalanced scheduling remained a source of exasperation within the NNL. Through September 2, Chicago had played 46 league games, Kansas City 63, Indianapolis 73, Detroit 65, Pittsburgh 37, Cleveland 44, the Cubans 37, and St. Louis only 34.[65] As one commentator noted, the number of league games needed to be equalized to promote greater fan interest and bigger paydays for management.

Another major concern facing the NNL was expressed in an August 19, 1922, article in the *Chicago Defender*. Frank A. Young cited poor umpiring and repeated a call made two years earlier for "umpires of color." It wasn't right, he asserted, that thousands sat in the stands to watch talented black players and had only "pale faces" umpiring.[66]

At the end of the 1922 season, the Monarchs were in fourth place in the NNL standings, behind the Chicago American Giants, Indianapolis A.B.C.'s, and Detroit Stars, at 43–32 (see Appendix).

In the 1922 post-season the Monarchs, led by slugger Oscar "Heavy" Johnson, got their revenge against a talent-laden Kansas City Blues squad of the white American Association for the defeats of the year before.[67] The Monarchs-Blues series began on October 14 and was scheduled to continue until one team won five games. It would be over in six games. The *Call's* sports editor, Carl Beckwith, wrote a front page article in which he proclaimed: "Against a team of former big league stars, some of whom are good enough for the main show now," the Monarchs won five of six and have the right to the title "City Champions." A total of 12,000 witnessed the six games. The crowds were well-behaved. According to Beckwith, "[t]he series has done more to boost Negro-oriented ball in this town with the white fans than anything could have done…. [T]heir eyes are now open to the fact that it isn't lack of ability that keeps Negro ball players off the big time—it's color. These fans will be far more interested in the standing of the Monarchs next season than they were last." The writers of the daily [white] papers who followed the Blues all year were forced to admit, Beckwith pointed out, "the better playing was done by the colored lads."[68]

3. Founding the Monarchs and the Negro National League (1920–1923)

A comparison of statistics for the series shows that the Monarchs hit seven home runs to the Blues' two. Each team collected 59 hits, but the Monarchs scored 34 runs, the Blues only 24. Monarchs pitcher Bill "Plunk" Drake claimed, "when we played a team like the Blues, we were off salary. We played what you called 'cold' playing: You get a certain percentage of the gate receipts, which would run maybe a hundred or so dollars." The Monarchs' style of play was, as Drake called it, "smart baseball." Fifty years after the series, Drake told John Holway that the Blues and Monarchs players had mutual respect. He said, "we got a lot of recognition from the fellows. We talked with those boys, they'd come right over and chat with you and tell you what a good ball player [you were]. I've had a lot of white ball players say to me, 'It's a shame you're black,' meaning if I was white, I'd be playing up there, too."[69]

Monarchs pitcher Chet Brewer said after the bashing of the Blues, "[p]ublic sentiment was beginning to wonder why these boys couldn't play in organized ball." Pitcher Rube Currie was quoted in the *Call* as saying he felt black players were as mentally and physically fit as the white players. Not to be outdone, the white *Kansas City Star* repeated Beckwith's claim in the *Call*.[70]

In an Associated Negro Press (ANP) article entitled "Negro Baseball Breaking Down the Race Prejudice," Charles A. Starks pointed out that in the 1922 Blues-Monarchs series, "[m]ost of the quick thinking and action was displayed by the blacks." He quoted J. L. Wilkinson, who said that while "[t]here aren't as many Negro ball players as there are white, ... when a colored boy is a good athlete, a good baseball player, he's very apt to be mighty good."

While Wilkinson may not have seen himself as a racial reformer, his Monarchs were certainly playing an important role in the struggle against discrimination. In reflecting on the Monarchs-Blues series, Starks noted: "From a sociological point of view, the Monarchs have done more than any other single agent in Kansas City to break down the damnable outrage of color prejudice that exists in this city. White fans, the thinking class at least, can not have watched the orderly crowds at Association park during this past season and not concede that we are humans at least, and worthy of consideration as such."[71]

On Sunday, October 29, several players from the New York Yankees, who had played in the 1922 World Series, including pitcher Carl Mays and catcher Wally Schang, appeared in Kansas City on an All-Star team for a game with the Monarchs. The Kaysees won, 5–3.[72]

Babe Ruth also brought his Traveling All-Stars to Kansas City during the 1921 postseason. The Monarchs beat the Bambino's squad, 10–5. Ruth brought two other major leaguers with him, Bob Meusel and pitcher Jack Quinn. While the Babe recorded four singles against "Bullet Joe" Rogan and Rube Currie, "Heavy" Johnson doubled off Ruth and homered against Quinn.[73]

Upset by black teams winning so often in match-ups with white major league squads, Commissioner Kenesaw Mountain Landis banned the practice of white players appearing in their team uniforms in interracial exhibition games. Thereafter, while barnstorming against black teams, white ballplayers would have to wear "All Stars" on their uniforms. Ruth was fined $5,000 and suspended from the Yankees for 30 days for violating the rule.[74]

With the aura of the new league fading, NNL attendance dropped by 25 percent during the 1922 season. Only the Monarchs, American Giants, A.B.C.'s, and Detroit Stars turned a profit. The Monarchs flourished financially by booking more exhibition games to supplement the league contests.[75] As Buck O'Neil put it, "[w]hile other NNL teams were floundering, Wilkie was building a juggernaut."[76]

The Monarchs played in a series of Kansas City ballparks owned by whites. The first was Association Park, at 20th and Olive, built in 1903. It was the home of the Kansas City Blues, who had been founded as the "Cowboys" in the 1880s and renamed the Blues because of the color of their uniforms. African Americans were restricted to the top 14 rows of the single-level stadium, even when two black teams were playing.

In another move reflective of his commitment to racial equality, one of J. L. Wilkinson's first acts when his Monarchs began playing in Association Park in 1920 was to remove the "segregation signs" that had demarcated the "colored section." Wilkinson wanted patrons to sit wherever they liked regardless of race. The Monarchs were also allowed to use the home team's dressing room for their games.

Brewery owner George Muehlebach, who had acquired controlling interest in the Blues in 1917, built a new stadium for the team in 1923 at 22nd and Brooklyn. He named it after himself. The concrete-and-steel, 18,000-seat stadium had a state-of-the-art electric scoreboard. The Monarchs moved to Muehlebach Field on July 28, 1923. As in Association Park, Wilkinson's agreement with Muehlebach allowed black spectators to sit throughout the stands in the new stadium. The *Kansas City Call* noted, "[f]ans from both races will continue to be able to sit side by side, and, after a while, the same relation may be carried to the workshop."[77]

Wilkinson approached playing in the expensive new park cautiously. He reduced the number of home games scheduled, from 57 in 1923 to 30 the next year. That reduction enabled the Monarchs to schedule more non-league barnstorming dates, making the Monarchs the most successful team in black baseball in the late 1920s.[78]

In 1932 Muehlebach sold his interest in the Kansas City Blues and the stadium to a partnership that included comedian Joe E. Brown, future Hall of Famer Tris Speaker, and E. Lee Keyser of Des Moines—a boyhood friend of J. L. Wilkinson—who was the first to install permanent lighting in a minor league park (see Chapter 5).

During the Depression this group sold the Blues to former Chicago Cubs catcher and Kansas City, Kansas, resident Johnny Kling at a bargain price. In 1937 he sold the team and stadium to Col. Jacob Ruppert for $230,000, and the Blues became a New York Yankees farm team. Muehlebach Field was renamed Ruppert Stadium.[79]

Until the 1923 season, the only successful African American professional baseball league was the Negro National League. That would change when the Mutual Association of Eastern Colored Baseball Clubs formed on December 16, 1922, with five clubs: the Brooklyn Royal Giants; Lincoln Giants of New York; Bacharach Giants of Atlantic City, New Jersey; Baltimore Black Sox; and Hilldale Daisies of Darby, Pennsylvania. It became known as the Eastern Colored League (ECL). The principal architect was African American Hilldale owner Ed Bolden. In contrast to the flamboyant NNL President Rube Foster, Bolden, who worked in the Philadelphia post office, was "small, shy, quiet and modest." Like J. L. Wilkinson, he preferred to stay in the background.

As soon as the ECL started, Rube Foster let his complaints about the new league be known. In a letter published in the *Pittsburgh Courier*, he listed his grievances, which were very similar to the charges leveled by other owners against him.[80] Foster asserted that the ECL existed only as a booking agency for a white man, Nat Strong, who charged a higher booking fee than Foster (20 percent compared to 5 percent). Foster also claimed

3. Founding the Monarchs and the Negro National League (1920–1923)

Strong had manipulated Bolden into leaving the NNL. He further complained that the ECL was encouraging players to jump from NNL teams, claiming that as many as 30 players had left the NNL for the ECL.

Foster also was upset that one of the league's officers, James Keenan, and half of the ECL owners, were white. Calling the ECL a "colored league," Foster noted sarcastically, was like saying a street car was a steamship. He accused Bolden of "race betrayal" and contended white owners would impose the carnival attractions they were known for having players perform. Foster noted that the NNL had strictly avoided such gimmickry.

Of course, Foster conveniently ignored the fact, as Bolden pointed out in a response published in the *Amsterdam News*, that "J. L. Wilkerson [sic], one of the key NNL owners, and a league officer," was white. Bolden compared Foster to the Kaiser who "attempted to swallow the world with results, that are now history," and adamantly rejected proposals for a post-season playoff series between the NNL and ECL.[81]

For the 1923 season the Toledo Tigers and Milwaukee Bears joined the NNL, but the former lasted only one year. The Birmingham Black Barons were accepted as an associate member and later became a full member, staying with the NNL until its demise in 1932.

In early February 1923, several Monarchs traveled to Hot Springs, Arkansas, to train with white major leaguers. "O boy," Quincy Gilmore wrote to the *Call*, "what a time there will be in that burg when Babe Ruth, Frank Duncan, Carl Mays, Bob Mussel, Bullet Rogan, Waite Hoyt, Bill Gisentaner, Heinie Grohe, Tris Speaker, Dobie Moore, Grover Alexander, Hurley McNair and a few more of the country's great stars meet and talk over the great pastime."[82]

At a March 1923 meeting in Chicago, J. L. Wilkinson and other NNL owners voted to use African American umpires in all games, addressing a complaint that had plagued the league since it began. On April 26 Rube Foster hired seven African Americans to call league games during the season. The black umpires, who had to be moved from city to city, cost the NNL $4,000 more for the season than white umpires, who were paid only for games they worked. Some owners protested, but it was decided that the umpiring had improved markedly. The black umpires were retained for the 1924 season and the next year received a raise.[83]

The majority of the Monarchs left Kansas City's Union Station for spring training in Dallas on March 20, 1923. Gilmore wrote to the *Call* that "Boss Wilkinson provided the boys with their own private sleeping car so as not be bothered with the well-known Jim Crow laws of the South." Wilkinson was on the train with the team and told reporters that in his 20 years in baseball he had never had a stronger team than the current Monarchs. The Monarchs arrived at Dallas the next morning and were met by a delegation of black businessmen and hundreds of local fans. As they passed through the African American district, the streets were packed with enthusiastic spectators.[84]

After describing the likely 1923 Monarchs roster in another promotional article in the *Call*, Gilmore added, "last but not least, we have … one that will bring credit to the race. Yes, the owner, Mr. J. L. Wilkinson is the whitest of white men, and one that believes in giving his men a square deal." They had the greatest fans in the league and "more white patronage than any other city in the country. The Monarchs team, more than any other enterprise," Gilmore concluded, in a now familiar refrain, "brings the two races closer together in Kansas City."[85]

On Saturday, April 28, the 1923 home opener against Foster's Chicago American

Giants was preceded by the traditional parade and pre-game ceremonies. "Bullet Joe" Rogan led the Monarchs to a 5–0 win and the team won this series, 3–2. It was the first series in the history of the NNL officiated by African American umpires (Bert Gholston and Billy Donaldson).

After starting by winning eight of 11, the Monarchs dropped four in a row to the American Giants in Chicago. The losses put them in third place in the NNL standings. As the season continued through June, a 9–3 loss to the Cuban Stars led the *Call* on June 29 to chastise the Monarchs for their "indifferent play" and the fans for their declining support.

Sam Crawford's strict managerial style was rubbing the old-timers among the Monarchs the wrong way. They complained to Wilkinson, who replaced Crawford with José Méndez midway during the 1923 season. Méndez would continue as Monarchs manager through 1926. He was, according to Newt Allen, "one of the smartest managers we ever had" and won the respect of the players.[86]

On July 28, in their first game in the newly opened Muehlebach Field, the Monarchs lost to Rube Foster and his American Giants in a 6–0 shutout but were victorious in the other games in the series. The *Call*, on August 3, 1923, lambasted Foster for again allowing his role as on-field manager to take precedence over his position as NNL president. The wins placed the Monarchs atop the NNL standings, but Wilkinson expressed his disappointment that more fans had not turned out to see the games against the team's chief rivals in the new park. The next week the Monarchs piled up 52 runs in a five-game sweep of the Milwaukee Bears. Méndez and Drake combined for a no-hitter on August 5. However, attendance was still frustratingly low.

In Chicago the Monarchs-American Giants rivalry did bring out the fans. In one 1923 game, 17,000 crowded into Schorling Park in Chicago for a Monarchs win, and Wilkinson pocketed $2,222.90 as his team's share of the gate.[87] However, the competition between the two clubs had grown even fiercer and fights were frequent. After a particularly vicious assault by American Giants players and fans on the Monarchs, the players and their fans couldn't wait for the American Giants' next game in Kansas City. However, Wilkinson nipped the planned revenge in the bud. "I'm paying you to play ball," he told the Monarchs, "not to fight. Remember that. If you start any fights, you're gone, and I'll see you don't get on any team. I'll blackball you."[88]

The Monarchs clinched the 1923 NNL championship on Sunday, September 8, by beating the A.B.C.'s in both games of a home twin bill, 9–3 and 4–3, before a crowd of 6,000. However, reflecting the confusion in determining which games counted in the NNL pennant race, Rube Foster ruled the Monarchs would need to take at least two of five games in a series with the Detroit Stars to be declared league victors. They won two, and were, all had to recognize, the 1923 NNL champions. In awarding the 1923 pennant to the Monarchs at the NNL winter meeting, Foster heralded "the sterling quality and ability of the club from the west."[89]

On Sunday, September 29, the 1923 NNL champions finished the season with doubleheader wins against the St. Louis Stars on a field so drenched that "base runners were throwing mud like a fenderless Ford on a Missouri road."[90]

An ad announced that grandstand seats would be 75 cents and box seats only 35 cents more for a Sunday, October 21 game in which the Monarchs faced an All-Star team of major and minor league players. According to the *Call*, "[t]he local club's bit of the gate receipts will be divided among the Monarch players, the owner, Mr. Wilkinson, having decided on this means of showing his appreciation for the season's work."[91]

Despite ongoing problems, by the end of the 1923 season, the NNL had proven that African Americans could organize and successfully run their own professional baseball circuit. Without the firm and decisive leadership of Rube Foster and the support of key owners like J. L. Wilkinson, the NNL would not have lasted. Foster became known as the "Wizard of the Western Circuit" for leading the NNL teams to what would be a decade of relative prosperity. Other sobriquets for Foster were "the John McGraw of Colored Baseball," the "master mind of baseball," and the "great strategist and peer of baseball generals."[92]

Financial records for the NNL are murky at best, but data has surfaced for 1923, when total attendance at league games was said to be 402,436, with an average of 1,650 per matchup. Total receipts were $197,218. With total expenses of $162,425 (including $101,000 for players salaries) the league operated at a profit of $34,793. The earnings were split among the seven clubs operating at the end of the season. Monthly league salaries ranged from $125 for rookies to $375 for stars, with $175 being the average. Meal money was $1 to $1.50 a day. Players also received periodic bonuses. At the same time major league white players were making from $300 to $2,000 a month with $15 a day for meals. The average monthly wage per household nationwide was $105.50.

Only three teams were real moneymakers—the Monarchs, American Giants, and St. Louis Stars. The Monarchs would average $41,000 a year from league games during the first six years of the NNL. The American Giants averaged $85,000.[93]

In an article entitled, "Monarchs are a Mighty Team," *Kansas City Call* Sports Editor Charles A. Starks expressed the pride African Americans in Kansas City felt about their team and assessed the impact of the first four years of the NNL. Black baseball, Starks wrote, "is a source of interest, pride, and race glory." The sport would lead to "great strides in the development of national character.... Here in Kansas City," he wrote, "we see baseball as a wonderful contributor to the solution of an ancient race problem."

For Starks, the white psychology that "implies always the superiority of the whites and the inferiority of the blacks" was now dead. Black baseball was showing what was wrong with the sense of "moral depression" and "terrible inferiority" created by "white standards of valuation." "It has been recently proven too well," Starks noted, "that Negroes play the game with much more thought and snap than the average white player." He suggested the public would begin to question the results of a World Series championship between two white teams "when perhaps there are one of several colored teams in the country better than the contenders."[94]

CHAPTER 4

Negro National League and World Champions (1924–1929)

Between 1924 and 1929, the Kansas City Monarchs were the premier team in the Negro Leagues. They won Negro National League (NNL) pennants in 1924, 1925, and 1929, and finished second in 1927 and 1928. They appeared in two of the four World Series played against the Eastern Colored League (ECL), in 1924 and 1925, and were World Series champions in 1924. At the Monarchs' helm, as he had been since the founding of the club, was principal owner J. L. Wilkinson.

Though not as plentiful in the stands as in the white majors leagues, beginning during the 1924 season fans began to turn out in greater numbers for the Kansas City Monarchs and other NNL teams. By 1924 attendance in the white majors had reached ten million. That same year about 500,000 fans attended NNL games.[1]

Before the season, in a February 1, 1924, article, the *Kansas City Call* once again heralded the racial progress made in baseball in Kansas City and the key role played by J. L. Wilkinson. Previously restricted to the bleachers in Association Park, blacks now had access to much better seating, the *Call* noted. The first season the Monarchs played, Wilkinson "made arrangements for games between the Monarchs and several of the most respected [white] big league players in America," and that had continued each year. According to the *Call,* the Monarchs' owner had also forged a strong relationship with the Kansas City Blues of the American Association. Players on the Monarchs and Blues practiced together throughout the season. Although there had been rumors the Monarchs would not be able to play in Muehlebach Park when it began operation in 1923, the *Call* maintained that Wilkinson's close association with Blues owner George Muehlebach and Blues secretary John Savage had opened the door.

Before the start of the 1924 season, Milwaukee and Toledo left the NNL, and the Birmingham Black Barons and Memphis Red Sox replaced them. In order to cover the territory added by the two Southern teams, Wilkinson cut back on exhibition games, leaving his players more rested for league contests.[2] Quincy Gilmore was so enthusiastic about the Monarchs in 1924, he reported to the *Call* that he was "trying to get Boss Wilkinson to consent to send the team to Honolulu, the Philippine Islands and Japan right after the season ends." Several big league teams, Gilmore pointed out, had made the trip the previous year.[3]

Always on the lookout for good pitching, Wilkinson signed former American Giant

Jack Marshall and Centralia, Missouri, native Homer "Hop" Bartley for the 1924 Monarchs. With John Donaldson leaving the team to barnstorm in Northern states and Canada and Rube Currie reportedly jumping to the Hilldale club of the ECL, the Monarchs needed new arms. Wilkinson agreed to send the St. Louis Stars seven players in exchange for speedster "Cool Papa" Bell, but when St. Louis insisted the seven include "Dink" Mothell, Wilkinson withdrew the offer.

With José Méndez as manager, the Monarchs opened the 1924 season by sweeping four games from the American Giants in Chicago in early May. The fans in Chicago were adamant that the Monarchs' winning of the pennant in 1923 was accidental and their American Giants would take the 1924 championship. What are they saying, the *Call* asked, using stereotypical imagery typical of the era, now that "the Monarchs are on their way to Detroit with the scalps of the Foster tribe dangling from their belts?"[4]

The Monarchs continued their winning ways by accumulating ten more victories, scoring an average of nine runs per game before finally losing on May 26 to the St. Louis Stars. In June they won 14 games in a row. When the American Giants came to Kansas City for a series over the Fourth of July, Rube Foster's conduct again took center stage. Foster had exerted his presidential authority by ordering a replay of Sunday's game because of a disagreement over the starting time. This was not the first instance, the *Call* noted, of his abuse of power. Foster had caused one of the best umpires in the league to quit because of his constant haranguing, the paper claimed. In addition, he was using a white umpire at home despite the NNL's ruling that only Negro umpires would be employed. The *Call's* verdict: "Rube Foster must step down!"[5]

August brought eight more victories in a row for the charging Monarchs. In their 77 games in 1924, the Monarchs averaged more than seven runs per contest, scoring in double figures 20 times. The Monarchs secured the NNL pennant on September 13 with a victory over their archrivals, the American Giants.

"Bullet Joe" Rogan was the ace of the staff with 16 wins. He also was the top hitter with a .413 batting average and a slugging percentage of .652. The team average was .313, with eight hitters besting .350. Hurley McNair led in homers (eight). Rogan, Bell, and Drake all held opponents to fewer than five runs a game, but the Monarchs lacked a quality left-handed starter. Wilkinson added lefty Bill McCall late in the season in an effort to plug the gap. The Monarchs had a good-fielding, weaker-hitting catcher in Frank Duncan. They were strong at the corners with Newt Joseph at third and Lem Hawkins at first. Their middle infield was solid with Dobie Moore at short and Newt Allen at second.

Despite their success on the field, Wilkinson told *Call* Sports Editor Carl Beckwith in January 1925 that the Monarchs stood to lose $5,000 for the 1924 season.[6]

The bitter dispute between Rube Foster and Ed Bolden over contract jumping between the NNL and ECL, principally by players from the Western clubs of the NNL to Eastern teams, was blocking what fans and sportswriters had been loudly calling for— a World Series between the champions of the two leagues.[7]

In a January 5, 1924, article billed as "A Word to Baseball Fans," published in the *Chicago Defender*, Foster attempted to explain why the NNL could not financially support such a series. In the previous three seasons, Foster wrote, league teams had paid out $428,000 to players, $165,000 for use of parks, and $130,000 for transportation, room, and board. Beyond these amounts were the additional expenses each team had incurred— advertising, balls, bats, other equipment, park staff, umpires, etc. Teams made money on

In the 1924 Negro Leagues World Series the Kansas City Monarchs, champions of the Negro National League (NNL), met the Hilldale Daisies, winners of the Eastern Colored League (ECL). J. L. Wilkinson stands on the far right, next to his players. From the right the players are George Sweatt, Bill "Plunk" Drake, Bill McCall, Carroll "Dink" Mothell, Cliff Bell, Frank Duncan, Lemuel "Hawk" Hawkins, William Bell, Walter "Dobie" Moore, José Méndez, Newt Allen, Wilber "Bullet Joe" Rogan, Oscar "Heavy" Johnson, Harold "Yellowhorse" Morris, Newt Joseph, and Hurley McNair. On the far left may be the Monarchs' trainer, Frank "Jew Baby" Floyd. The Monarchs took the Series, winning five, losing four, with one tie (National Baseball Hall of Fame Library, Cooperstown, New York).

Sundays and holidays, Foster pointed out; weekday games lost money. Fans complained the NNL did not have as full a schedule as white major league teams. Foster countered that white owners were rich men. NNL owners simply did not have the resources to follow their example. A Negro Leagues World Series was beyond their means.[8]

Sportswriters and fans were not swayed by Foster's appeal. A steady stream of editorials appeared in African American newspapers during the 1924 season, demanding a playoff between the league champions. On August 14, Ollie Womack of the powerful syndicated Associated Negro Press (ANP) noted that the Monarchs, certain NNL champions, had "shown themselves to be the real Monarchs of Negro baseball in the West." If there was not a championship series between Kansas City and the ECL champions, Womack asserted, the players and fans would surely lose interest.[9]

J. L. Wilkinson and the Monarchs helped break the stalemate. In the September 4, 1924, issue of the *Chicago Defender*, an undated letter signed by Wilkinson's trusted secretary and business manager, Quincy J. Gilmore, was published. Presumably, if he was not the actual source of the letter, Wilkinson must have authorized Gilmore to write and send it. "On behalf of the Kansas City Monarchs, winner of the 1923 pennant, and the prospective winner of the 1924 National Negro League, I hereby issue a challenge," the missive announced, "to the winner of the Eastern League pennant for a series of games to determine the Negro world's championship." The letter called for a commission with representatives of both leagues to work out a plan for the series, following the example of the World Series between the white National and American League champions.

One rumor was that Wilkinson had told Foster the Monarchs would play the likely winners of the ECL pennant race, the Hilldale Daisies of Darby, Pennsylvania (near Philadelphia), in a post-season series whether Foster agreed or not. In any event, bowing to mounting pressure from the media and fans, Foster and Bolden asked white major leagues baseball commissioner Kenesaw Mountain Landis to arbitrate the dispute. Landis agreed, though he made clear he was acting independently, not in his official capacity. The ruling drafted by his office stipulated that Landis "would decide all questions related to future drafts, contracts, players, salaries, post-season games and any protest filed by teams" in the NNL and ECL.

In a telegram published in the *Pittsburgh Courier*, Foster pledged to endorse whatever agreement through compromise Commissioner Landis reached. He also said Western fans wanted to see the Monarchs meet Hilldale at the end of the current season and agreed not to insist NNL players who had already jumped to ECL clubs be forced to return.

Bolden responded by stating that if a 1924 Negro Leagues World Series did not materialize, he would not be to blame. He reiterated his position that the basic problem was not the "player question" but the NNL's refusal to refund his good faith deposit of $1,000 when his team resigned from the NNL in 1922. However, Bolden announced, "[t]he East will concede to the wishes of the fans."

The *Call* reported in mid–September that an agreement for a 1924 World Series had been reached. The only outstanding issue was "the assurance of the financial support of the fans [to] justify the enormous expense of the series."[10]

The first Negro Leagues World Series, matching the Monarchs, champions of the NNL, against the Hilldale Daisies, winners of the ECL, would last ten games, played between October 3–20.[11]

Ed Bolden's Hilldale Daisies finished with a record of 42–23 (.643). Kansas City had a record of 60–27 (.690). While the Monarchs were known for their power hitting, Hilldale featured pitching and speed. Hilldale had been consistent through the 1924 season, never losing more than two games consecutively. They had won 14 series, sweeping six.

With his wicked sinking curve ball, Hilldale ace Nip Winters won 20 games and had an ERA of 2.16. He had support from Phil Cockrell (a spitball specialist) and Red Ryan (master of the forkball). Scrip Lee (a submariner) and former Monarch Rube Currie were spot starters and relievers. The Daisies' staff held opponents to fewer than four runs per game. The Monarchs' pitchers included Bill "Plunk" Drake, William Bell, Clifford "Cherry" Bell, Harold "Yellowhorse" Morris, ace and dual threat "Bullet Joe" Rogan, as well as 40-year-old veteran player/manager José Méndez.

At catcher the Monarchs' Frank Duncan was being heralded as a "rising star" while at 35 years of age Hilldale's Louis Santop, renowned as a power hitter and premier catcher in his prime, was still performing well at bat, with a .343 average in 1924. Duncan was "a pitcher's dream" defensively, but at this point not as strong a hitter at .273.

The Monarchs' Lemuel "Hawk" Hawkins (.295) was an all-star first baseman, a dependable fielder and contact hitter. For Hilldale, first sacker Touissant "Tommy" Allen was also a top fielder, but not a threat at the plate, batting only .197 in 1924. At second base, Monarch Newt Allen (.275) was the best fielder in the NNL. His counterpart, Hilldale captain Frank Warfield (.313), was the best second baseman in the ECL and a threat to steal. Both were clutch hitters and team leaders by example. At third the Monarchs' Newt Joseph (.361) excelled, but no hitter was more feared than Hilldale's Biz Mackey (.332). Monarchs shortstop Dobie Moore (.356) was a tough out but his fielding was not as smooth as Hilldale's Judy Johnson (.342), who also hit well. With shortstop Jake "Country" Stephens out with a sprained ankle, Hilldale lost one of the top left sides of the infield in the Negro Leagues. Johnson moved over from third to short and Mackey, normally a catcher, stepped in at third.

In left field, the Monarchs' Oscar "Heavy" Johnson (.374) was a slugger who also hit for average. For Hilldale, Clint "The Beast of the East" Thomas (.282) covered more ground than any outfielder in baseball. Monarchs center fielder "Dink" Mothell (.278) was a dependable substitute at any position, and would likely share center with Rogan (.409) when "Bullet Joe" was pitching. George Sweatt could also fill in. Hilldale's center fielder, George Johnson (.250), had not had his best season but possessed power and outfield speed. Monarchs right fielder Hurley McNair (.346) had a great arm and was called the "toy cannon" because of his ability to launch a ball with his bat on any pitch. For Hilldale, Otto Briggs (.285) in right was a superb outfielder and one of the best leadoff hitters in either league.[12]

Noting that many of the Hilldale players had been "raided" from other teams (including pitcher Rube Currie, who jumped from the Monarchs), Buck O'Neil suggested the 1924 World Series "was Wilkie's boys, most of whom he had found himself, against Bolden's mercenaries."[13]

The first Negro Leagues World Series was announced as a best-of-nine match-up. In addition to the scheduled games in Philadelphia and Kansas City, Foster and Bolden had agreed to play games three, four, and eight and nine if necessary, in the cities that had finished second in the NNL and ECL during the season—Baltimore and Chicago.

The Series, witnessed by a total of 45,857 paying fans, was nothing short of spectacular. All games were cliffhangers, with each of the last eight decided in the winning team's final at-bat. In the view of some baseball experts, the 1924 Negro Leagues World

Series was not only a "seminal event in the history of the Negro leagues," but "ranks among the most dramatic postseason match ups in all of baseball history."[14]

A sizable contingent of Monarchs fans made the 1,200-mile trip by train from Kansas City to Philadelphia for the first game, played on Friday, October 3. It was a clear, warm day with some light fog. However, the turnout was not what the organizers hoped for. Only 5,366 fans paid to see the game in a stadium with a capacity of 18,000. Ticket prices throughout the series, set by the two leagues, ranged from $1.10 to $1.65 a seat.

Before the first pitch, Rube Foster and Ed Bolden met at home plate and shook hands, symbolically ending their long dispute. Foster then threw out the ceremonial first pitch as the game got under way a few minutes after 2 p.m.

An immediate controversy erupted when the white umpire hired to officiate disallowed Hilldale starter Phil Cockrell's patented spitball. The pitch had been ruled illegal in the International League, where the umpire worked. After a heated discussion among league officials, it was ruled that Cockrell could use the pitch.

The Monarchs' leadoff hitter, Lemuel Hawkins, doubled but was stranded. The Monarchs' ace, "Bullet Joe" Rogan, held the Hilldale nine off the base paths in the bottom of the inning. It remained a pitchers' duel until the sixth inning, when the Monarchs exploded with five unearned runs on three hits and four errors. Kansas City added one run in the top of the ninth, and Hilldale avoided a shutout by scoring twice in the bottom of the frame. The Monarchs were the first-game winners by a convincing 6–2 score. Rogan had allowed eight hits, struck out five, and was two-for-four at the plate. The sportswriters in attendance voted him the game's outstanding player.

On the day of the first game of the Series, the Monarchs ran the following ad in the *Kansas City Call:* World Series. Kansas City Monarchs (Negro National League Champions) Vs. Philadelphia Hilldales (Champion of Eastern League) Saturday, Sunday, Monday. Oct. 11, 12, 13. 2:00 p.m. Reserved, $1.10, Boxes $1.65.

The *Call* also published pictures and profiles of the Monarchs' players and Quincy Gilmore, as well as the following on J. L. Wilkinson:

> J. L. Wilkinson, the owner of the Monarchs, is the only white man connected with the National Negro Baseball League. Wilkinson is known to all of the local fans as "Wilkie," and has been connected with baseball for more than twenty-five years. He is the original owner of the Monarchs, and has been a pillar of strength to the league. He was the first owner ever to organize a baseball team of ladies; the original Bloomer girls were his. He has for years been owner of the famous All-Nations baseball team. Such stars as John Donaldson, the great pitcher; Joe Méndez, the Cuban pitcher and now manager of the team; Torrienti [sic], outfielder for the American Giants; "Plunk" Drake, the Monarchs pitcher; and several white major leaguers were developed under Wilkinson when he was the active head of the All-Nations. Wilkinson gives all of his time to baseball.

Better publicity and the arrival by train of more supporters from Kansas City helped increase paid attendance to 8,661 for the next day's game, also played in Philadelphia. It was another pleasant day. Hilldale gave the hometown crowd reason to cheer by recording 15 hits in an 11–0 rout. Nip Winters, known as the "Eastern Assassin" because of a blazing fastball that supplemented his wicked curve, allowed only four safeties. He had not lost since August 3, and six of his last seven starts had been complete games. Taking the loss was southpaw Bill McCall, whom Wilkinson had acquired from Birmingham in September. He started but did not record an out and was relieved by "Plunk" Drake, José Méndez, and "Yellowhorse" Morris.

The third game in the series was played at smaller Bugle Field in Baltimore on Sunday,

October 5, in part because Sunday baseball was banned in Philadelphia. Extra bleachers were placed in the outfield; any ball hit into the overflow seating was ruled a double. Knuckleballer Red Ryan was the Hilldale starter, and control pitcher William Bell was given the ball for the Monarchs. The 5,503 fans were treated to an exciting but frustrating 13-inning marathon called due to darkness with the score knotted at 6–6.

With the teams tied at a game apiece, the fourth contest was scheduled for Monday, October 6, again in Baltimore. There had been confusion in the papers about the start time, leading to an hour's delay. As light fog cleared, only 584 people were in attendance. Red Ryan, who had been pulled after four innings the day before, returned to pitch for Hilldale. Cliff Bell, who had not pitched since July 22 in a league game due to a sore arm, got the nod for the Monarchs.

The Monarchs drew first blood with two runs in the first inning on doubles by Allen and Rogan and a single by Moore. The visitors added one run in the third on another double by Allen and a single by Rogan. Hilldale tied the score at three apiece in the bottom of the third, on two hits and an error. A theft of home by Briggs, tying the game, proved to be the turning point. Neither team scored again until the bottom of the ninth, when Hilldale took advantage of two walks and two errors to score the winning runs without a hit. Though the Monarchs had eight hits to the Daisies' four, Rube Currie's 6⅔ innings of relief pitching earned him the 5–3 win as Hilldale took a two-games-to-one series edge.

After a five-day delay, the series resumed at Muehlebach Stadium in Kansas City on Saturday, October 11, for a three-game stand. Even though J. L. Wilkinson had arranged for soldiers from Fort Leavenworth to have complimentary tickets for the fifth game, the turnout was disappointing, with only 3,891 paid in the 17,500-capacity park.

The aces of the two teams, Rogan and Winters, took the mound. Both hurlers went the distance. The Monarchs jumped out to a two-run lead in the bottom of the first with a single by Joseph, a double by Allen, and a single by Moore. Hilldale got on the board in the fourth, with singles by Santop and Johnson. A sacrifice fly drove Santop home, and he successfully evaded Duncan's tag. In the ninth, Hilldale erupted for four runs on four hits, three singles and a home run by Judy Johnson. Rogan allowed ten hits in the game, Winters only four. The 5–2 Hilldale win gave the Philadelphians a 3–1 lead in the Series.

The weather was again warm for the sixth match-up on Sunday, October 12, at Muehlebach Stadium. J. L. Wilkinson may have been low-key, but he clearly knew how to use the press. The *Kansas City Call* had upbraided Rube Foster, and the NNL president had agreed to change the original booking so that one of the games in Kansas City would be on a Sunday. The sixth game drew the largest crowd of the series, with 8,845 in the stands.

The Monarchs' William Bell faced Phil Cockrell. Bell had pitched 12 innings in the 13-inning tie game. Cockrell had not pitched since the opener. Judy Johnson drove in Mackey and Santop with a two-out triple in the first inning. The Monarchs stormed back in their half of the opening frame, chasing Cockrell after two outs had been recorded. Scrip Lee relieved. Rogan, Joseph, Moore, McNair, and Sweatt all singled, and four runs crossed the plate. Hilldale scored two runs in the third, when Judy Johnson drove in Warfield and Mackey scored on Rogan's throwing error. The Monarchs added one run in the fourth when Bell doubled in Duncan. Hilldale notched a run in the sixth as Thomas doubled and Lee drove him in. With the game tied, 5–5, the Monarchs plated the winning run in the eighth inning when Sweatt tripled to score Moore, who had reached with a single. Drake relieved Bell in the ninth after "Tank" Carr singled to lead off. Sweatt's first- and eighth-inning hits proved to be the key blasts. Manager Warfield's decision to leave in a tiring Scrip Lee was also decisive as Moore notched three hits and scored two important runs in the 6–5 win. Kansas City had closed to within one game of Hilldale, who maintained a 3–2 series edge.

After an off day, the teams endured a 12-inning marathon in the next 1924 World Series game, played on Tuesday, October 14, in Kansas City. Originally scheduled for Monday the 13th, the game had been bumped, with only a few days' advance notice to Wilkinson, by a benefit game at Muehlebach Field sponsored by the *Kansas City Journal-Post* for Children's Mercy Hospital. Babe Ruth was the main attraction in that contest, with tickets going at a reasonable $1 for choice seats. On Tuesday, only 2,539 attended the three-hour Monarchs-Hilldale game, but they got their money's worth.

The Monarchs' Cliff Bell faced Hilldale's ace, Nip Winters, who had been almost unhittable in the Series. Bell had lost Game Four. Hilldale scored first, recording two runs in the second inning on three hits. The Monarchs tied the game at two apiece in the fourth when Joseph reached on an error and scored after a double steal and theft of home. Drake singled, driving in Moore. The Monarchs went ahead in the eighth with Rogan walking, moving to second on a sacrifice, and scoring on a single by pinch hitter "Heavy" Johnson. Hilldale tied the game in the ninth when Judy Johnson singled and was driven in by Warfield.

José Méndez relieved Bell with men on first and third and only one out. He struck out Carr, and Rogan made a dazzling catch in center to end the threat. The game remained tied at three until the 12th. With two out, the Monarchs fans exploded in loud yelling and foot stomping as Sweatt tripled and was injured in a collision at third. Pinch runner William Bell scored the winning run when Judy Johnson's throw from short on a grounder by Rogan pulled Touissant Allen off the bag at first. Rogan had reached base four times in the game via three hits and a walk. Joseph was a slow runner, but was able to steal home when the Hilldale catcher, "Sleepy" Lewis, failed to hold the runners close. The mental error caused Winters to lose his composure, and he gave up a another run on a Duncan single. He pitched all the way in the 4–3 Hilldale loss. The series was now tied at three games apiece.

The final games were scheduled for Schorling Park in Chicago, after three days off. The eighth contest was played on Saturday, October 18, before a crowd of 2,608 that reportedly included an African prince. Rogan and Currie kept the score 0–0 until the sixth inning, when Hilldale took the lead after a single by Warfield. Mackey sacrificed him to second, and he scored on a single by Santop. Hilldale added a run in the seventh when George Johnson tripled and scored on a sacrifice by Carr.

Trailing 2–0 in the bottom of the ninth with two outs, the Monarchs rallied. "Dobie" Moore grounded toward Judy Johnson at short, but the ball took a big hop and bounced off the top of the fielder's glove. Two batters later, the bases were loaded when Frank Duncan hit a foul pop up. If catcher Louis Santop had caught the ball, the game would have been over, but he muffed it in a play reminiscent of the 1912 major leagues World Series between the New York Giants and Boston Red Sox, when Giants catcher John Tortes "Chief" Meyers failed to make a critical catch.[15] Duncan then lined a grounder right at third baseman Biz Mackey, but the ball went through Mackey's legs into the outfield, and the winning run scored for a 3–2 Monarchs victory.

It was the Monarchs' third straight one-run win. The crowd rushed on to the field and carried Duncan on their shoulders in a victory parade. In the Hilldale club house, the veteran Santop was reduced to tears after a tongue-lashing from manager Frank Warfield. In the loss Currie had pitched brilliantly, scattering eight hits and allowing no runs for 8⅔ innings.

The Monarchs had regained the lead in the Series, four games to three. One more win and they would be the first Negro Leagues World Series champions.

In warm, 81-degree weather a larger crowd (6,271) gathered for the ninth game at Schorling Park, played on Sunday, October 19. Winters, who had allowed only four runs in 29⅔ innings for a 1.21 ERA in the Series, returned to the mound. With their ace pitching, Hilldale was favored to win the Series despite being down by a game with two to play.

Monarchs manager José Méndez gave the ball to William Bell, and Kansas City took an early lead in the second inning. Moore reached on an error by Carr, moved to second on a sacrifice by McNair, and scored on Carr's second error of the inning. Hawkins made it to second on the miscue and throw to the plate. He scored when William Bell singled. Hilldale tied the game in the fifth inning when Warfield doubled and scored on Mackey's single. Santop singled and Mackey crossed home plate when Rogan misplayed the ball. Méndez called on Drake to relieve Bell.

Hilldale went ahead in the eighth. Winters walked, then scored when Briggs singled and Rogan committed a second error. With the bases loaded, Santop popped out. Kansas City drew even in the bottom of the eighth when "Heavy" Johnson and Moore singled, allowing Joseph, who had reached on a force out, to score.

Judy Johnson doubled and moved to third on a fielder's choice in the top of the ninth. Thomas reached first when Drake's throw failed to nab Johnson. Méndez relieved Drake with no one out and runners at the corners. Johnson scored on an error by Hawkins. The Monarchs went 1–2–3 in the bottom of the ninth and, after the 5–3 Hilldale win, the Series was now knotted at four games each. Nip Winters had his third World Series win, giving up only one earned run. The Monarchs had committed five errors on the chewed-up infield.

With the Monarchs and the Daisies tied at four games each, with one tie, it would take a tenth game to decide the first Negro Leagues World Series. The temperature had plummeted about 30 degrees by game time. Because of the cold and the game being on a Monday (October 20) only 1,549 fans turned out.

In an unexpected move, Monarchs player-manager José Méndez took the mound. He had not started a game since July 26 and was suffering from a viral infection. Doctors had instructed the gaunt Cuban not to play, but he ignored them. Junk ball artist Scrip Lee, a World War I purple-heart recipient, made his first Series start for Hilldale.

Both hurlers would go the distance in one of the best pitchers' duels in baseball history. Méndez used guile rather than speed to hold Hilldale to three hits and recorded a 5–0 shutout. He never allowed a runner past first. Lee matched Méndez until the bottom of the eighth, when the Monarchs broke loose for all five of their runs. For the inning, Lee had changed from throwing submarine style to an overhand delivery. It didn't work. Moore singled, was sacrificed by McNair to second, and scored on "Heavy" Johnson's double. Duncan walked, and Méndez singled to load the bases before Allen singled. Johnson and Duncan scored, with Méndez and Allen moving up a base on the throw to the plate. Mothell doubled to bring in Méndez and Allen. Hilldale could not mount a rally in the top of the ninth, and the game and first Negro Leagues World Series were over.

4. Negro National League and World Champions (1924–1929)   53

After 18 days and 2,614 miles, the Kansas City Monarchs were the 1924 Negro Leagues Champions. The two umpires who called the Series said the level of play was equal to that of the white leagues where they worked, and the players on both teams were "perfect gentlemen and sportsmen."

The Monarchs celebrated their World Series win with a party at Chicago's Sunset Inn. The *Kansas City Call* exuded: "Let no hint of how long the party continued, nor the condition of the guests on leaving. Just remember that it happened in Chicago—and guess the rest." It went on, "Negro sport has done what Negro churches, Negro lodges, Negro businesses could not do. The series has shown that a Negro can get attention for a good deed well done, and that publicity is no longer the exclusive mark of our criminals."[16]

After their Series triumph, the Monarchs returned to Kansas City and displayed the victors' trophy at Stark's Shoeshine Parlor. Two months later, someone broke into the back room where the Monarchs stored their uniforms and other equipment. The stolen goods showed up at a pawnshop and were traced to Oscar "Heavy" Johnson. Rather than publicly humiliate Johnson, Wilkinson traded him to the Baltimore Black Sox of the ECL.

Total gate receipts for the 1924 Negro World Series were a disappointing $52,113.90 and expenses $28,650.46, including $9,384.63 for park rental, $5,094.80 for team transportation, a $4,941 War Tax, and $208.60 for baseballs. Of the $23,463.44 profit 35 percent went to the players, 35 percent to club owners, 10 percent to the two league commissions, 12 percent to the second-place teams (American Giants and Baltimore Black Sox), and 8 percent to the third-place teams (Detroit Stars and Lincoln Giants). The winning share for each of the 16 Monarchs was $307.96. As the losers, 17 Hilldale players received $193.23 each.

By comparison, gate receipts for the 1924 Major Leagues World Series between the Washington Senators and New York Giants totaled $1,093,104. The players' share was $331,093, with each member of the winning Senators team earning $5,959.64 and the losing Giants players $3,820.29 each.[17]

How important was the 1924 World Series in NNL and Monarchs history? Seventy years later, when the American League Kansas City Royals had a special Negro Leagues Night at Kauffman Stadium, Buck O'Neil was asked what uniforms the Royals players should wear to honor the Monarchs. It could have been the best team he said he played on, the 1942 Monarchs, or the last Monarchs team he managed (1955), but he chose the white pinstripes of the 1924 season.

In 1924, as a 12-year-old, O'Neil had been sitting in his Florida home reading the *Chicago Defender* when he saw a picture of the participants in the first-ever Negro Leagues World Series. In the line, he saw one white gentleman in a business suit, wearing a fedora. What was a white man doing in the picture, O'Neil later remembered thinking. It was, of course, J. L. Wilkinson, whom O'Neil would later come to know well and deeply respect.

Although the NNL had begun play in 1920, it was not until November 8, 1924, that the Articles of Incorporation were officially signed, notarized and registered with the state of Illinois. The Articles stated that the NNL was chartered with $2,500 in common stock at $25 a share. The shares belonged to the five directors: Willie Foster, Russell Thompson, Rube Foster, Walter M. Farmer, and J. L. Wilkinson. Wilkinson was the only white owner and stockholder. The role of Thompson and Farmer, both of whom were from Chicago, is not known. Willie Foster, the majority shareholder and later a pitcher for the American Giants and the Monarchs, was Rube's younger half-brother. The official name was specified as The Negro National League of Professional Baseball Clubs.

Wilkinson's address in the Articles was listed as 4118 Agnes St., Kansas City, Missouri. He paid $500 for 20 shares of stock. Willie Foster owned 40, Rube Foster 20, Thompson 15, and Farmer five.

The league owners accepted the change at the December 5, 1924, meeting. The NNL Charter was revised again on September 21, 1925, to increase the number of directors from five to nine. Of the original directors, only Rube Foster and J. L. Wilkinson were retained.[18]

By the 1925 season, Rube Foster's various roles were beginning to take a toll on his health. He was manager, owner, and general manager of the Chicago American Giants. As president of the NNL, Foster carried the responsibility for resolving players' contract disputes and saving financially troubled teams. He also found venues for teams to play at and scheduled league games.

In a November 1924 article published in the *Chicago Defender*, Foster reflected on his baseball career. He had remained committed to the game his whole life, he wrote, though he had had to endure critics who thought those who play black baseball are "low and ungentlemanly." When the NNL was founded in 1920, Foster had wrecked his own American Giants, he pointed out, to equalize the league's teams. Despite his best efforts, he noted, NNL teams were losing money for wont of businessmen who could place baseball on a solid economic base. "Men can own ball clubs and be successful if they would only hire some brains to run their clubs," Foster lamented.[19]

Despite his criticism of their leadership skills, J. L. Wilkinson and his fellow owners re-elected Foster as President of the NNL at the winter meeting after the 1924 season. On February 2, 1925, they released a statement saying they had examined the books under Foster's supervision and found "everything in good order."

On May 26, 1925, Rube Foster was almost asphyxiated by a gas leak in an Indianapolis rooming house where he was staying. He was briefly hospitalized but insisted on traveling with the American Giants to Kansas City. His mental faculties continued to deteriorate in the year ahead. Some speculated that the gassing was not accidental but a suicide attempt.

By the 1926 season, there were troubling episodes that could not be ignored. "Wee Willie" Powell, an American Giants pitcher, saw Foster running up and down in front of his house on Chicago's Michigan Avenue, chasing imaginary fly balls. Foster took to locking himself in his bathroom at his office and refusing to exit unit someone came in through the window and led him out.

The last straw was Foster's hearing voices in his home, destroying furniture, and threatening a friend with an ice pick. He was brought before a "Psychopathic Court," deemed insane, and placed in an asylum in Kankakee, Illinois, in September 1926, a month before the American Giants won the 1926 Negro Leagues World Series from the Bacharach Giants. Because Foster had no contract with then American Giants owner John M. Schorling, all compensation to him from the team he had painstakingly built ended when he was hospitalized.[20]

Though the 1924 season was disappointing financially, Wilkinson and other NNL owners were confident that with the NNL and ECL now at peace, the coming season would be more successful. Many good, young players were emerging. The season would have 100 games, divided into a first half (May 2–July 8) and a second half (July 9–September 17).[21]

The first Monarchs exhibition game of the 1925 season, on April 4, was a 13–1 shellacking of Wilkinson's All Nations team in Kansas City, Kansas. The next week 3,000 fans made the trek from Kansas City to Topeka, Kansas, to see the Monarchs throttle the white Topeka club, 9–0.

The Monarchs opened the 1925 season on the road (May 1–3), winning one of three games against the Detroit Stars. They moved into a second place tie two weeks later by sweeping three games from the St. Louis Stars. Challenging fans to attend the regular season home opener against Detroit on May 23, Quincy Gilmore asked in a promotional article: "Do you remember what the white people of the city did on the day the Blues opened the season? Well, the Negroes are going to do the same thing for the Monarchs, and the 23rd is going to be one of the greatest days for our people they have ever had."[22]

The Monarchs took 12 of their next 14 games and won the first half of the 1925 pennant race with a convincing 31–12 record. By early September, the St. Louis Stars held the second-half lead, but the race tightened when Kansas City defeated St. Louis in four of five games. The Stars hung on and were the second-half winners with a 38–12 record.

The Monarchs again went on the road in 1925, winning almost every exhibition game they played. People would drive up to a hundred miles to see a game between the Monarchs and a local team, or another touring club. J. L. Wilkinson commented, "[t]he colored ball players play the game with all the spirit of the college athletic teams. I believe that's the main reason the Monarchs are so popular."[23]

A seven-game NNL playoff series between the Monarchs and St. Louis Stars determined who would meet the ECL champions in the second Negro Leagues World Series. Divisional playoffs in major league baseball would not occur until 1969, 44 years later. With Muehlebach Field unavailable, the Series was played in St. Louis and Chicago.

"Bullet Joe" Rogan was the star of the inaugural NNL playoffs, winning four games. The Monarchs took the first game, on September 19 at the Stars' park in St. Louis. Rogan was the 8–6 winner with the help of homers off the bats of Allen, Duncan, and Moore.

The second game, also in St. Louis on September 20, showed off the base running of the Stars' speedster "Cool Papa" Bell. In the third inning, the center fielder beat out an infield roller, stole second and third, and scored on a single. St. Louis won, 6–3. St. Louis took the lead in the playoffs, winning the third game, also played in St. Louis on September 23, by a score of 3–2.

The playoffs moved to Chicago for Games 4–7. Excursion trains brought fans from both Kansas City and St. Louis to cheer on their favorites. Rogan was again the pitching and hitting star in the fourth game on September 26, recording four safeties, and the Monarchs prevailed 5–4, tying the playoffs at 2–2.

The next day the Stars were the victors, 2–1, to go in front in the Series. Kansas City took a 1–0 lead into the ninth inning, but St. Louis scored twice to win. However, the Monarchs won Games 6 and 7, which were played as a doubleheader, to take the playoffs.[24]

The 1925 Negro League World Series was essentially over before it started due to a freak injury suffered by Monarchs pitching ace "Bullet Joe" Rogan. His infant son had run a needle into his father's knee, leaving the Monarchs' star unable to play. Hilldale won five of the six games to become the only ECL team ever to win a Negro Leagues World Series.[25]

Hilldale's Rube Currie won the 12-inning opener, 5–2, at Kansas City on Thursday, October 1. The Monarchs came back to take the second contest the next day, 5–3, beating spitballer Phil Cockrell behind rookie Nelson Dean. José Méndez, who had relieved William Bell, lost Game Three on Saturday, October 3 (3–1). "Plunk" Drake was the loser in the fourth game on Sunday, October 4, 7–3. The series shifted to Philadelphia, and Hilldale won the fifth game, 2–1. The sixth and final game was played in weather just above freezing, and Hilldale emerged victorious, 5–2.

The 1925 Negro League World Series was a financial failure, with a total attendance of only 20,000. The gross receipts were $21,000, leaving only about $6,000 to distribute after expenses. Each of the 14 Monarchs received only $57.64 for 12 days' work.

On January 7, 1926, the *Pittsburgh Courier* printed a mock obituary for the Monarchs as Negro Leagues world champions, beginning, "[i]n loving memory of the Kansas City Monarchs, infant prodigy of the United National League and only child of J. L. Wilkinson.... Kansas City departed this life at the tender age of one year."

At the seventh annual NNL winter meetings, held in Philadelphia, Quincy Gilmore was appointed league secretary. Owners learned that the Memphis Red Sox would no longer be in the league and that the Birmingham team would be run by the league office if a new set of owners could not be found. At a joint session, NNL and ECL owners decided to maintain financial viability by holding down player salaries. With the cap of $3,000 per month, assuming 15 men per team, the average salary would be only $200 a month or $1,000 for the 1926 season.[26]

By 1926 radio stations were beginning to carry major league games, and attendance at both NNL and white minor league games suffered. Additionally, few of Kansas City's 30,000 African American residents could afford the price of Monarchs tickets. Wilkinson found he needed Sunday draws of 4,000 or 5,000 fans to break even. As a means of remedying the situation, he authorized a cut in the price of box seats for Monarchs games in Muehlebach Field from $1.10 to 75¢. That brought their price lower than box seats in any other city in the NNL. Wilkinson also scheduled more non-league exhibition games away from Kansas City.

To stimulate attendance, Wilkinson directed Gilmore to work with leaders in the black community to form one of the first and most successful fan organizations in the Negro Leagues—the Monarchs Boosters. One of its main projects was planning the popular festivities at the first home game of the season.

Robert Sweeney was active in the Boosters from the late 1920s until the team folded. In a 1981 interview with Janet Bruce Vaughn, he described how on the night before the opening game there would be big dinner that Wilkinson and all the players attended. According to Sweeney, "Wilkie was quite a promoter and knew how to make money.... He was a fine man and did a lot of good."[27]

The Boosters also sponsored events so fans could meet the players. With encouragement from the Monarchs, local black ministers promoted the games at church services, making sure they let parishioners out by 1 p.m. on Sundays to allow them time to get to the afternoon games. Free admission was sometimes given to ministers. The Monarchs also played benefit games for churches and organizations like the NAACP. On the road, Wilkinson would arrange for players to be invited into local churches to give inspirational talks.

In addition, pictures of Monarchs players were projected onto the screens at movie theaters. The players were portrayed as "local heroes and ... role models." Articles about the Monarchs were sent to 36 black and white newspapers across the country.[28] At "ladies days" admission was either free or half-price for women. In a 1926 advertisement, the Monarchs offered box seats to women for little more than general admissions prices, announcing, "[i]f you fannettes want to display new hats and dresses this summer, you can do so at an added expense of only $.15." Wilkinson also used women as ushers, both as an attraction for men and to "elevate the tone of the crowd."[29]

In preparation for the 1926 season, Wilkinson continued to focus on improving travel conditions for the Monarchs ... and saving money. He gave up the aging Pullman railroad car the team had been using and bought a new, 18-passenger Derris bus for $8,000. It was "a parlor bus of the latest type, with specially constructed cushions and semi-reclining backs and plenty of leg room."[30] The Monarchs saved thousands of dollars in transportation costs by using the bus. The Pullman cars were more comfortable, but with the buses the Monarchs could get to towns that did not have train depots. Wilkinson could make more money at the smaller venues than bigger ones because an appearance by the Monarchs was a bigger event and the Monarchs received a higher percentage of the gate.[31]

Sportswriter Paul Fisher described how Wilkinson orchestrated the arrival of the Monarchs' bus for a game in Pittsburg, Kansas, during this period[32]:

> Abruptly at Fourth Street, the traffic breaks. A moment passes. Into the vacuum an army of boys and girls come sweeping and planing on their bikes, the vanguard for the Monarchs' bus carrying the team. At the fairgrounds, scores of little boys and girls stand dryly on the plot of grass where the bus unloads. Each of the 16 Monarchs picked his thralls. Each one goes marching with this little girl carrying his sunglasses ... this little Negro boy with his baseball shoes ... ["Bullet Joe"] Rogan, the old soldier of the 25th Infantry, who usually marches with quick steps, comes last, accommodating his steps slowly to two tough little Irish kids who are choked with their good fortune, each holding one of Rogan's hands just like little old sissies.

Before the 1926 season began, Wilkinson announced that Rogan would "fill the position as manager left vacant by the resignation of José Méndez, who has handled the reins for two seasons."[33] "Bullet Joe" was not new to the manager's role, as he had filled in on occasion during the past two seasons. The acquisition of Cristóbal Torriente from the American Giants to play center field allowed Rogan to move to first base when he wasn't on the mound.

In addition to Torriente, two other new players were added to the 1926 roster. One was Thomas Jefferson (T. J.) Young, who reportedly was "three-fourths Choctaw." A big, fast, young catcher who had been farmed out to the Chicago Union Giants the past two years, Young was described by one sportswriter as "the Lusitania docked among a lot of small tugboats."[34] Young would remain with the team in various capacities until 1931. The other acquisition was Bob Saunders, a right-handed pitcher from Los Angeles.

Méndez cited health concerns as the reason for his resignation. After the 1926 season, he left the team and retired to Cuba. In early November 1928, the sad news reached J. L. Wilkinson and the Monarchs that Méndez had died at the age of 41 in Havana during a tuberculosis epidemic. As a pitcher, the *Call* eulogized, Méndez was "skillful, wily, possessing a classic collection of deliveries which proved baffling to opponents and left them wondering how it was accomplished. He was acclaimed by many sportswriters as the wizard of the diamond. At short he played a great game; sensational, easy and efficient."[35]

With the help of the new Boosters Club, the Monarchs staged an elaborate Opening Day extravaganza on May 1, 1926, with "festivities and ceremonies befitting a club which has won three league pennants and a world championship."[36] The parade was led by Marmons, Hupmobile 8s, Rickenbackers, Chryslers, Hudsons and new Fords. As 2,500 fans waited in Muehlebach Field, the 1,000 participants in the parade arrived, swelling the attendance.

The Monarchs swept all five games in their opening home series against the St. Louis Stars. They then won eight of their next ten games at home, though bad weather held down attendance.

After a 15-inning victory on another Ladies Day, May 17, a post-game celebration turned tragic. Walter "Dobie" Moore, who had been a Monarch since the team was organized, was shot by Elsie Brown, in whose Kansas City house the party was taking place. In trying to escape, Moore jumped from a second-story window, shattering the bones in his right leg into six pieces. According to a statement given by Miss Brown to the police, "she and Moore had quarreled and … he … struck her three times, [once] in the ear, the eye and the back of the head." When Moore threw something at her, she said she grabbed her pistol and shot him. Had his career not been cut short, "the Black Cat" may have become the finest African American shortstop of all time. Some thought he already was. J. L. Wilkinson's son Dick said Moore was "just as good as Jackie Robinson" and added, "Dad always said he would have been one of the great ones."[37]

The Monarchs came out on top in the first half of the 1926 NNL pennant race with a record of 24–6. After opening the second half with five straight victories at home, they departed on their Derris parlor bus for a ten-game exhibition series, appearing before enthusiastic crowds in Horton, Frankfort, Smith Center, and Oberlin, Kansas; and Wymore, Nebraska. On the trip Newt Allen amused himself by "shooting jackrabbits from the window of the bus going 45 miles per hour."[38]

The Kaysees returned home for nine games, then went on a two-week, 13-game barnstorming tour ending in Great Bend, Kansas, on August 24. Along the way they played in Abilene, Pratt, Eldorado, and Garden City, Kansas; and Tonkawa, Oklahoma, among other towns.

With Dave Malarcher having replaced Rube Foster as manager of the American Giants, the Chicagoans won three of five games in a decisive late-August series against the Monarchs at Schorling Park. In early September the Monarchs Boosters Club sponsored a round trip "Xcursion" to Chicago for $10.

A playoff series to determine the 1926 NNL pennant winner was scheduled, but the *Call* reported that "[a]s far as Mr. Wilkinson … is concerned, … [h]e can take the bus out for a few exhibition games in Kansas and make more money, with far less expense, than he can in the playoff series."[39]

Despite the Monarchs owner's reservations, Wilkinson agreed to participate in the 1926 NNL Playoffs series.[40] Beginning on Saturday, September 18, the first four games between the Monarchs and American Giants were held in Kansas City. The Monarchs won the first three, 4–3, 6–5, and 5–0. The American Giants were victors in the fourth contest, 4–3.

The remaining games were scheduled for Chicago's Schorling Park. The fifth game, played on Saturday, September 25, was the first time "Bullet Joe" Rogan and Rube Foster's half-brother and the American Giants' ace, Willie Foster, had faced each other. Foster did not make it out of the fourth inning, and the Monarchs prevailed, 11–5.

The Monarchs needed only one more win the next day to secure the league championship. However, that game went to the American Giants, 2–0, with Rube Currie recording a two-hit shutout. On September 27, the American Giants squeaked by, 4–3, with a walk-off run in the bottom of the ninth to close within a game of tying the series.

A doubleheader on September 28 would determine who would meet the ECL champion Bacharach Giants in the 1926 Negro Leagues World Series. Snow was falling as the eighth game began. With Foster again facing Rogan, it would be one of the most memorable pitching duels in baseball history. The Monarchs threatened to break a scoreless tie in the eighth inning when Cristóbal Torriente came to bat with a man on third and one out. The Cuban, a veteran of Wilkinson's All Nations team, had been traded to the Monarchs after eight years with the American Giants. However, he had left the team in mid–August after accusing Monarchs trainer Frank "Jew Baby" Floyd of stealing his $250 ring. Now back with the team after reconciling with Wilkinson, Torriente had his chance for redemption. Though he batted .407 in the playoff series, on this occasion he was no match for his former teammate; Willie Foster fanned him. The American Giants' ace ended the threat by enticing Newt Joseph to pop up. With two men on base in the bottom of the ninth, Rogan gave up the winning hit to Sandy Thompson.

Like José Méndez, outfielder Cristóbal Torriente (1893–1938) was already a star in Cuban baseball when J. L. Wilkinson signed him to play for All Nations in 1913. Torriente was a stalwart for Rube Foster's Chicago American Giants (1919–1925) before Wilkinson enticed him to join the Monarchs during the 1926 season. With Méndez and Wilkinson, Torriente was inducted into the National Baseball Hall of Fame in 2006 (National Baseball Hall of Fame Library, Cooperstown, New York).

Now tied at four games each, the playoff would be decided by the second game of the doubleheader, the ninth contest in the series. It was shortened to five innings by mutual agreement to allow the winner time to make the opening contest in the 1926 World Series. The teams' aces would perform the Herculean task of pitching both games of a doubleheader. When Rogan saw Foster warming up to pitch, he decided he had no choice but to take the mound also. Foster emerged victorious, shutting out the Monarchs, 5–0, in the five-inning game. On the train ride back to Kanas City, Monarchs pitcher Clifford "Cherry" Bell angrily shot his pistol through the roof of the Pullman car, because he claimed he needed the World Series money to support his daughter after the girl's mother had abandoned her.

The American Giants went on to win the best-of-nine 1926 Negro World Series, defeating the Atlantic City Bacharachs five games to three (with two ties). Each Monarch received $443 as his share of the World Series profits that totaled $23,457.65. The injured "Dobie" Moore, trainer Frank "Jew Baby" Floyd, and Quincy Gilmore were voted full shares by the players.[41]

After the 1926 season, Wilkinson decided to trade Cristóbal Torriente, mostly because he had missed a number of exhibition games and also because it was obvious to the Monarchs' owner he "was on the back side of a celebrated career, his power having diminished to an alarmingly low level." Torriente was sent to Detroit, and the Monarchs received pitcher Harry Kenyon, a graduate of Arkansas Baptist College.

Monarchs Newt Allen and Frank Duncan joined a post-season NNL all-star team that toured Japan. They won 14 straight games but were two weeks late for the 1927 spring training, "much to the anger of the league owners back home."[42]

In a retrospective on the 1926 season, the *Call* commented: "As there are no oil millionaires with bloated bankrolls holding franchises in the league, it can readily be seen that it took courage and faith in the future of the organization to complete the season."[43]

By 1927 white politicians recognized the social and economic value of black baseball. For example, Detroit Mayor John Smith welcomed NNL and ECL owners to his city for their annual joint meeting, January 11–13, 1927, telling them he "was pleased to note the representatives of both leagues were white and colored, interested in the game and working harmoniously together for the advancement of colored baseball." In a cost-saving move, the owners agreed to reduce the salary cap from $3,000 to $2,700 a month for each team, including the manager.[44]

At a meeting in St. Louis on January 27, the NNL owners voted to replace Indianapolis with a Cleveland franchise and accept the applications of the Birmingham and Memphis teams which had been released from the Southern League. Wilkinson "presented a plan providing for equalization of transportation costs." He was asked to detail the proposal and present it later for consideration. Judge William C. Hueston of Gary, Indiana, was selected unanimously as NNL president. The owners retained Quincy Gilmore as league secretary/treasurer and required him to post a $10,000 bond.

In an oft-repeated complaint by journalists who covered the Negro Leagues, the *Call's* A. D. Williams charged that NNL and ECL "owners are slow to recognize the importance of getting news which fans are anxious to read to the press in a timely manner, while it is news. Most owners are good business men in other respects, but they fail to understand that the fan, who is almost entirely responsible for the future success of the game, deserves to be informed of what is going on."[45]

Just six weeks before the 1927 season was set to begin, Gilmore was still working to complete the NNL schedule. His efforts were complicated by the owners' agreement to play exhibition games in the South and the decision to return to Negro umpires. Written contracts had been sent to prospective Monarchs players, but none had yet been returned—signed or unsigned.[46]

For the 1927 season Wilkinson embarked on a campaign to rebuild the Monarchs' pitching staff, signing Maurice "Dolittle" Young, Owen "Buzz" Smaulding, Admiral "Deacon" Walker, George Mitchell, Carl "Lefty" Glass, and William "Steel Arm" Tyler. Wilkinson's recruitment of Maurice Young (1904–1984) was typical. Young pitched for the Gilkerson Giants in 1926. After the season, Wilkinson wrote and invited him to the Monarchs' spring training in Kansas City. The Monarchs' owner watched Young pitch, then promptly offered him a written contract with a salary of $125 a month. As Young recalled a half-century later, the Monarchs were an educated group of players; some had college degrees. However, like ballplayers in any era, they liked to play practical jokes on teammates. Some on the team would lather up soap, he remembered, and come into your room while you were sleeping. They'd shout, waking you up, and then plaster you in the face with the soap. Young said they only did that once to him, because he carried a gun. According to Young, "Wilkinson was one of the best white fellows to colored fellows that I've ever known. He was the best. He'd give you money in the winter. Guys like [Newt] Allen and [Frank] Duncan and [Carroll "Dink"] Mothell, who had been playing for him a long time, he'd give them $100 or $1,000 because he knew they'd play it out next year."[47]

Young, who threw emery balls, and Duncan, who had to catch the dancing pitches, were soon at odds, and the 1927 season did not start well. However, the Monarchs rallied and finished the first half only a few percentage points behind the American Giants. The momentum did not last and the weak-hitting Monarchs finished the season in second place to the American Giants, who beat the Bacharachs in the nine-game 1927 Negro Leagues World Series.

In a series of commentaries in the *Kansas City Call* entitled "Behind the Curtain of Negro Baseball," beginning on December 16, 1927, A. D. Williams laid out the issues he thought needed to be addressed in the NNL. There was something wrong in the NNL (and, by extension, in the ECL), Williams wrote, known not only to owners but also to many thousands of fans. Patrons of black baseball "are demanding that something be done to elevate the game in the league to the standards which it had set as its goal at the time of the foundation of the league." He identified the problems the NNL needed to address as follows: (1) a lack of adequate financing; (2) poor scheduling of exhibition games by many teams that had their players working half or, at best, two-thirds time; (3) carrying too many players—as many as 18—on rosters; (4) a need for a six- rather then eight-club circuit; (5) better cooperation with the press in covering games objectively; (6) too many petty disputes among owners; (7) indecisiveness on which teams should be included in the league; (8) poor park management, with lack of respect for patrons by players, park attendants, even owners; (9) weak organization of the World Series, resulting in neither players nor owners receiving much compensation from them; (10) inadequate attention to the planning of league schedules; and (11) shoddy treatment of players by team owners.

The problems Williams identified were taking a toll. By mid–March 1928, the ECL was beginning to unravel. Hilldale, the Brooklyn Royal Giants, and Harrisburg left the league, citing the high player salaries they could no longer afford. In early June Alejandro Pompez's Cuban Stars also departed.

J. L. Wilkinson did his best to salvage the Negro Leagues World Series, proposing in February 1928 that "all games [in the World Series] should be played either in the East or the West, alternatively. The money saved on railroad fares would thus be available for the players."[48] However, the plan was not adopted. With the ECL in shambles, there would be no 1928 World Series.[49] It would not resume until 1942.

Before the 1928 season, Wilkinson released outfielder Wade Johnston, first baseman Lem Hawkins, and pitchers Clifford Bell and Nelson Dean. To replace Hawkins at first, the Monarchs' owner had already signed George Giles, a teenage infielder, who batted left-handed. Giles had been enamored with the Monarchs since watching them defeat his hometown Manhattan, Kansas, team in 1923. Added to the club were even more youngsters for the Monarchs' outfield: Larry "Goo Goo" Livingston, Leroy "Ben" Taylor, Eddie "Pee Wee" Dwight, and Reginald Hopwood. Livingston and Taylor were both students at Wiley College, a black college in Marshall, Texas, with which Wilkinson and the Monarchs would have close relations over the years. Taylor had a reputation as a hothead and had not done well with Birmingham or Indianapolis. However, Wilkinson saw his

Eddie "Pee Wee" Dwight (1905–1975) was a speedy outfielder for the Monarchs (1928–1929, 1933–1937). He also drove the Monarchs' bus and assisted J. L. Wilkinson with publicity during barnstorming tours. Dwight's son, Eddie, Jr., was the first African American to be selected as an astronaut by the National Aeronautics and Space Administration (Kenneth Spencer Research Library, University of Kansas Libraries).

potential as a hitter and signed him.⁵⁰ The Monarchs experimented at shortstop with "Hallie" Harding, another college man.

Eddie "Pee Wee" Dwight (1905–1975) was playing sandlot ball in Kansas City as a teenager in 1924 when Wilkinson first saw him and recognized his potential. That same year he entered professional baseball, signing with the Tennessee Rats. The next season he played for the Indianapolis A.B.C.'s. Wilkinson obtained his contract and sent him to the Gilkerson Union Giants to gain more experience. According to his wife Georgia, "If you got an offer to be a Monarch, you took it and dropped everything. Didn't worry about the future. If Mr. Wilkerson [sic] contacted you and asked you to play, you said yes, because you knew he wouldn't have asked you if you weren't good enough."⁵¹

In a trade announced on March 30, 1928, Hurley McNair, Grady Orange, and George Mitchell of the Monarchs were sent to Detroit in exchange for veteran pitcher and future Hall of Famer Andy "Lefty" Cooper. According to the *Call*, "Owner Wilkinson decided that he could use a player of the type to a good advantage as he would be in the lineup at the beginning of the season." Alfred "Army" Cooper, also a lefty, who had come to the Monarchs owners' attention years earlier, had just been discharged from the 25th Infantry. He was another of Wilkinson's signees during the 1928 season.

In an example of his support for disadvantaged youngsters in the community, Wilkinson provided baseball uniforms for a team at the Jackson County Boys Industrial Home. The Jackson County Court, which included Harry Truman, announced, "if the Monarchs officials could be such fine sports they would do their bit by sending the boys out bats, gloves, breast protectors and balls."⁵²

After spring training in Hot Springs, Arkansas, the Monarchs played exhibition games against Wiley College and white teams in Clarksville, Arkansas, and Joplin and Springfield, Missouri, among other towns.⁵³

The 1928 NNL season opened for the Monarchs on April 28. Replete with the now traditional Opening Day festivities, the first home game was on May 15 against the Cleveland Tigers. Two weeks into the season, the Monarchs had a record of 8–8. In mid–June their record was 17–15. They would win the first-half NNL pennant race.

During the season the Monarchs continued to play frequent road games against local white teams to keep the club afloat financially. For example, a crowd of 3,000, including several hundred African Americans, was on hand to watch the Monarchs topple the Wichita Henry Clothiers in a doubleheader on Sunday, June 17, 5–0 and 10–4.⁵⁴

The Monarchs were fighting for the second-half pennant in early August, when NNL president W. C. Hueston joined J. L. Wilkinson in the owner's box at Muehlebach Field for a series with the St. Louis Stars. However, a doubleheader loss, plagued by errors, set back the Monarchs' hopes.

To attract fans, Wilkinson tried another promotion by hiring long-distance runner Eddie Garner, who had attempted to complete a 168-mile marathon from Kansas City to Joplin. Garner was stopped short after running for 104 miles and 23 hours through rain and mud. However, Wilkinson took advantage of the publicity the stunt generated and had Garner run an exhibition race against the fastest Monarchs players between the games of the Sunday, August 11 doubleheader.⁵⁵

A sweep of the Cuban Stars in mid–August put the Monarchs back in first place, but by early September the Monarchs were out of the 1928 pennant race. Only a series of exhibition games in Missouri and Kansas remained in their season. St. Louis and Chicago played for the NNL championship.

While the *Kansas City Call* was thoroughly covering the Monarchs in particular and black baseball in general, the weekly was also making sure its readers were aware of the discrimination and violence African Americans faced. As it did each year, the *Call* reported in early 1929 on the ongoing crisis of lynchings in America. Nationally, in 1928, there had been 11 lynchings. One was in Missouri. Near the end of the year, in Hattiesburg, Mississippi, Emanuel McCallum, 40, had been pulled from his bed and hanged from a tree because of an argument with a white man over money. Two weeks into the New Year, the *Call* reported that 2,000 cars had been in a parade in Jackson, Mississippi, after the lynching of Charles Shepherd was announced several hours in advance. A crowd of 6,000 was present. Shepherd was burned alive and his arms, legs, ears, nose were cut off as souvenirs.[56]

In another cost-cutting move at the outset of the 1929 season, the NNL decided at its winter meeting to reduce rosters to 14 players in order to save an estimated $20,000 in annual salaries. At the same gathering, Quincy Gilmore announced his resignation as Monarchs and NNL secretary to launch a new black circuit—the Texas-Oklahoma-Louisiana (TOL) League. He was soon appointed to a five-year term as the TOL's organizing president and began to recruit teams for a 100-game, split-season schedule.[57]

Throughout his career, J. L. Wilkinson encouraged those who worked for him to take advantage of opportunities for advancement. He enthusiastically supported Gilmore and the new league. In a speech at one of the TOL's first meetings, Wilkinson told the gathered owners that with Gilmore as the league's leader, "its success [was] assured." He also said if the owners focused on good publicity, proper player discipline, and fair treatment of umpires, they would do well. He agreed to schedule exhibition games between the Monarchs and TOL teams.[58]

Before the 1929 season began, the *Call* warned of the resumption of an East-West baseball war. The Homestead Grays had announced they would play Sunday games in Cleveland during the 1929 season, breaking an agreement that specified teams in the East would not play home games further west than Pittsburgh.[59]

The Monarchs held their 1929 spring training in Shreveport, Louisiana, where, as Wilkinson had promised, they played exhibition games against the Shreveport entry in the new TOL. The only Monarchs holdout was George Giles. The Monarchs' owner had refused Giles' request for a $25 a month raise, money the first baseman said he needed to get married. Wilkinson responded, "I could go down to Louisiana and get three players for what you are asking." Giles jumped his contract with the Monarchs to sign with the Gilkerson Union Giants. Although Wilkinson told Chet Brewer he would never take Giles back after he jumped, one of the first players the Monarchs' owner contacted when he reorganized the Monarchs in 1931 was Giles.

During the 1929 season, *Call* Sports Editor A. D. Williams continued to critique how the NNL was functioning. In May he reported that while the *Call* was able to publish TOL standings, "[t]he careless manner in which the publicity of the NNL is handled makes it almost impossible to furnish a standing of the clubs. No official standing has been received from headquarters of the league this season." In June Williams complained that NNL umpires were allowing players to stand around and argue a point for five or ten minutes until fans became disgusted and left the park.[60]

By August 1929, the Monarchs were reporting a $4,000 deficit. Although they continued to field excellent teams, Wilkinson's Monarchs were suffering from sagging home attendance. Games with white semi-pro teams in Missouri and surrounding states were now "crucial to the club's financial stability."[61]

On August 26, the Monarchs were in Wichita to play the Henry Clothiers once again. To spark fan interest, Wilkinson arranged for the first game of the doubleheader to be played like a golf match, with the team scoring the most runs in any inning given the advantage of that frame. The team with the most innings won was declared the victor.[62]

Their excellent home record, coupled with remarkable success on the road, had led the Monarchs to victories in both halves of the 1929 NNL pennant race, enabling them to avoid a playoff. It was the Monarchs' fourth pennant in the ten years the NNL had been in existence. NNL President Hueston called the 1929 Kansas Citians "a ball club full of fight, augmented with exceptional ability."[63]

As the end of the 1929 season neared, A. D. Williams chastised Kansas City African Americans for their lack of support of the Monarchs. "If there ever was a club deserving the support of a city—it is them," he wrote. "Their brand of baseball is second to none in the country. The Monarchs owner ... [has] always placed a real ball club on the field, and this year the club was even better than some of the clubs bearing the Monarchs label in the past. I wonder where that old Monarch loyalty is."[64]

In keeping with Wilkinson's pledge to support Quincy Gilmore and the Texas-Oklahoma-Louisiana League, the Monarchs played the Houston Black Buffaloes, champions of the TOL, in a best-of-seven, post-season series. All the games were played in Houston, with the Monarchs' owner on hand for the raising of the flag before the first contest on September 21, 1929. Large crowds turned out to see the Monarchs sweep what was billed as a World Series in four games: 12–10, 3–2, 6–2, and 10–1. Kansas City fans were able to see highlights of the first two games in a motion picture shown at the Lincoln Theater. Wilkinson told a *Call* reporter the Houston team had played "a great series and made the Kansas City club play up to standard to beat them."

After the series, L. D. Livingston left the Monarchs to visit his home in Fort Worth, planning to rejoin the team in Dallas. However, he discovered that being a Monarchs player did not give him the respect in Texas that he and his teammates enjoyed in Kansas City. When a Dallas policeman who stopped Livingston learned he played for the Monarchs, the officer promptly arrested him. At the police station, the Monarchs outfielder had to pay a $20 bribe in order to be released.

The Monarchs completed the 1929 post-season by playing a three-game series with the champions of Mexico, the San Louis Cubans. They won the first game on October 5, 11–2, with a fired-up Livingston slamming two homers, in front of 2,000 fans. The Monarchs also took both ends of the Sunday doubleheader.[65]

Over the years, many Kansas City Monarchs players participated in winter ball in California, playing in interracial games well before the color ban in "organized baseball" was lifted. In the 1920s, Joe Pironne organized a four-team Southern California Winter League. Three of the teams, with such stars as future Hall of Famers Babe Ruth, Lou Gehrig and Mickey Cochrane, were white; one was black.

The black squad was variously known as the Los Angeles Stars or White Sox or the Philadelphia Royal Giants. "Bullet Joe" Rogan brought a number of the Monarchs with him to play on the team. By 1926 virtually the entire squad was made up of Monarchs. Rogan's club played a team of white All Stars, including future Hall of Famer Tony Lazzeri, in a five-game series in Los Angeles in October and November 1926. Pironne, who played for a different white team each season, avoided having a league championship between black and white teams by regularly canceling the title game. Pirrone and the other white players likely feared they would lose the championship to the black team and did not want to face the potential embarrassment.

In one game during the 1929 winter season, Chet Brewer got into a fight with a white player. It started when the player yelled at Brewer after being hit by a pitch: "You black, blankety blank! You hit me purposely." Brewer dropped the ball and the two got into a fistfight, with the Monarchs pitcher raising a big lump over his opponent's left eye. Other players and fans joined in, and only the quick response of a half-dozen black police officers averted a full-scale riot.[66]

In a "Progress Edition" on July 27, 1928, celebrating its tenth anniversary of publication, the *Kansas City Call* paid tribute to a number of black institutions, among them the Kansas City Monarchs. The article featured a portrait of a young J. L. Wilkinson taken in Des Moines in 1913, where he "started his baseball connections." He was, the *Call* asserted, "the man who is responsible for Kansas City being on the baseball map of the nation, so far as the Negro is concerned." Then the *Call* offered a summary of Wilkinson's career to date, ending with the note that "all the Monarchs clubs have displayed a deportment on and off the field which would do honor to the most exacting conventional English family.... Both races are true supporters of the club which bears the colors of the diamond throughout the circuit of the NNL."

As the end of the Monarchs' first decade approached, J. L. Wilkinson was recognized by black sportswriters as the NNL's best promoter. A. D. Williams of the *Call* said "the stocky, pleasant-voiced" Wilkinson was a "baseball genius."[67] Others were trying to exploit his success. Wilkinson told the *Wichita Eagle* many barnstorming teams had begun to try to cash in on the Monarchs' popularity by taking similar names—Monarchials, Monarivons, etc."[68]

Toward the end of the 1928 season, Monarchs players paid for a spread in the *Call* as a tribute to their owner. It read in part[69]:

> We have a man—the best club owner in the world to work for—who is familiar with the game as it is today, who knows how to plan for the future, who believes in us at all times, who stands for a fair and square deal to all, who gives the best and expects the best in return, who loves and is loved by his players, who believes that charity begins at home, who knows and appreciates real ability, who instills the fighting spirit in his club, who practices what he preaches, who never turned on a friend.
> Because of the Man, we have the best Ball Club—the best ball park in the loop, the best training quarters, the best traveling conditions, the best baseball town in the loop, the best playing conditions, the best fans to play to, the best paid ball club in the loop, the best baseball atmosphere, the best baseball trainer in the loop, the best publicity of any ball club, the best team spirit in the loop, and last but not least—the best, the best of everything that matters to a great ball club.

It ended by listing the Monarchs players and with the statement: "This advertisement paid for by the players of the Kansas City Monarchs baseball club, who appreciate the sterling worth of J. L. Wilkinson, owner of the Monarchs."

Despite the overall decline in black baseball, the 1920s had been an excellent decade for the Kansas City Monarchs, thanks in large measure to the leadership of J. L Wilkinson. Although there are slight differences among sources in reported league standings, during the 1920s the Monarchs had played approximately 507 league games and won 381, for a remarkable winning percentage of .751. In their first ten years the Kansas City Monarchs had the NNL's best overall won-lost record five times, finished second four times, and third once.[70]

The question now facing J. L. Wilkinson, the Kansas City Monarchs, and all of black baseball was how to survive the most serious economic crisis in the history of the country—the Great Depression. It was just beginning as the 1929 season came to an end.

CHAPTER 5

The Innovator— Night Baseball and Barnstorming (1930–1936)

The Great Depression was a disaster for African Americans. With the collapse of the cotton economy in the South in the 1920s, 700,000 blacks had migrated to Northern industrial cities in hopes of finding jobs. However, black unemployment soared, even before the stock market crash in 1929. By 1932 the jobless rate among African Americans in major cities had reached 75 percent. Although largely free of the lynchings and strict Jim Crow legislation that plagued the South, blacks in the North experienced the indignities of extra legal discrimination that could arise at any time.[1]

In 1930 Kansas City ranked far behind other cities with Negro Leagues teams in African American population. Chicago's black population was 233,903; New York's was 327,706; Philadelphia had 219,599; Detroit's 120,066; Indianapolis had 43,967; and Kansas City's was only 38,574.[2] With such a small fan base, J. L. Wilkinson realized the Monarchs would have to expand their schedule in order to draw enough spectators to pay the bills.

To meet the economic and demographic challenges the Depression posed, Wilkinson adopted two strategies reflecting his vision, entrepreneurial spirit, and willingness to take risks that could have resulted in financial ruin for his family. One was night baseball; the other was for the Monarchs to become an exclusively barnstorming team without league affiliation.

As he prepared for the 1930 season, Wilkinson realized he would need to expand the hours during which games could be played in order to attract more fans. Those who had enough disposable income to attend games worked on weekdays and often Saturdays. Giving them an opportunity to attend games that began when their workday was over was the key.

As we have noted, Wilkinson had experimented with night games earlier in his career. In 1930 he was ready to stake not only his reputation as a successful baseball executive, but everything he and his family owned, on the gamble of baseball after dark. Since most of the Monarchs' games would be played on the road, the challenge was even more difficult. The lighting system would have to be portable, able to be set up, illuminate a playing field, and be quickly dismantled in order to be transported to another venue.

Wilkinson's second strategy was to build on the success of the Monarchs' barnstorming tours and devote the entire season to games mostly in small towns, as far away as Canada and Mexico. He saw the handwriting on the wall and pulled the Monarchs out of the failing NNL at the end of the 1930 season. Wilkinson's team would remain unaffiliated for the next six years (1931–1936), depending for revenue solely on a few exhibition games at home and extended barnstorming tours. They would play as many as 200 contests a year against league and independent black teams; the dwindling number of white pro, semi-pro and amateur teams; and, frequently, the renowned House of David bearded baseball team.

In January 1930, J. L. Wilkinson described the innovative, portable lighting system he was developing that would allow night baseball to be played in small towns around the Midwest and beyond beginning in the upcoming season, and his rationale for it[3]:

> According to the present plans the lights will flood the playing field to the extent that the entire playing will be clearly visible to the players and fans. The greatest difficulty will be experienced with high fly balls which cannot be seen well after reaching a given point, but ... the game will be played under slightly changed rules which will take care of this feature by limiting bases on such batted balls, thus giving each team an even break on such plays. The lighting system will be transported on two special built trucks and will be set up at angles from two sections of the playing field, well out of range of the activities of the field.
>
> In traveling with baseball clubs throughout the country for a number of years, I found that hundreds of people who wanted to see baseball games could not on account of working conditions which did not allow them to get off until after dark. I have often thought of some remedy in this and in working out the night baseball problem I figured it would allow these ardent baseball fans, who have heretofore been denied the privilege of witnessing their favorite sport, a chance to do so at a time that their work would permit. I am well aware of the fact that night baseball will not permit the exact brand of ball as played ordinarily, but with the rules under which [it is played] it will not be far from the regular day time game.

Wilkinson announced, "Iowa and Nebraska cities where the Monarchs are well known have indicated that they would like to contract for games at night." Night baseball would also allow two league clubs to play a day game, then move a short distance for a "night tilt, thus keeping the clubs always busy and making money, catching up some of the slack experienced by rain, etc. while playing their regular league schedule." At present only exhibition night games were planned, the Monarchs owner concluded.

Some baseball writers were quite dubious about Wilkinson's proposed portable lighting system. *The Sporting News* predicted night games would not catch on, because, "[t]he night air is not like the day air; the man who goes to baseball after he has eaten a hearty meal is apt to have indigestion if he is nervous and excited."[4] *Kansas City Call* sports editor A. D. Williams acknowledged the idea was controversial but noted, "sufficient tests have been made to encourage the originator to go ahead with the new invention." Rules would be adjusted to protect the safety of players and spectators. For example, the ball would be softer than a regulation baseball. "Believe it or not," Williams emphasized, "there's method in the supposed madness of friend Wilkinson. There's one thing about him—he knows his baseball ... and the highway to the dollars."[5]

J. L. Wilkinson was not the only baseball executive ready to try night baseball in 1930. At the white Western League's winter meeting, E. Lee Keyser, owner of the Des Moines Demons, had stunned fellow owners by announcing his intention to install a permanent lighting system in the Demons' stadium in Des Moines and play night baseball in 1930.[6] He had been inspired, he said, by the great success in 1929 of the Drake University Bulldogs football team in installing permanent lighting.

Lee Keyser and Wilkinson were good friends. Their association went back to Wilkinson's days in Des Moines, before he moved to Kansas City, and the two had stayed in contact over the years. Now the two associates would enter into a competition to see

In 1930 J. L. Wilkinson risked everything his family owned to develop an innovative portable lighting system the Monarchs could use while barnstorming and at Muehlebach Field in Kansas City. The lights were carried on these trucks and assembled by the crew shown. The gamble of night baseball paid off, attracting the curious and fans who could not get away from their jobs for day games (Kenneth Spencer Research Library, University of Kansas Libraries).

whose team could play the first successful night game. Keyser is often credited with winning the race when the Demons played under the lights at their season opener on May 2, 1930. However, by that time Wilkinson's Monarchs had already played a game using their new portable lighting system.

Confirming his now well-established commitment to innovation in baseball, Wilkinson said[7]:

> I am sure there is a bright future for dark time baseball. As little as one may think about it right now, there will be many of the smaller leagues taking up the idea as the months roll past—and who knows but that the big leagues as well will adopt the new plan. It will mean much to the game and will allow many who have no daytime to devote to attending the national pastime to witness baseball games without inconvenience. From all indication at this time the novel game will go well in this section—and after all that is the section in which I am most interested right now.

Wilkinson knew if a successful lighting system were developed, baseball would be revolutionized. As he put it, "[w]hat talkies are to movies, lights will be to baseball." He also knew implementing his vision would require hard work and a huge financial investment. He would have to hire the best electrical engineers to design and build the big plant and accessories, and cars and trucks would have to be purchased to move equipment that could be set up and dismantled in an hour or less. Workers to set up, run, and dismantle the system would also have be employed.[8]

Wilkinson's initial estimate of the cost of the portable lighting system was a staggering

$50,000, which would be roughly one million dollars today. Other sources indicate Wilkinson sank as much as $100,000 of his family's money into the portable lighting system.[9] Dick Wilkinson claimed his father and mother "mortgaged everything they had that he could and probably went a little beyond that to get the lighting started."[10]

The Monarchs owner's daughter, Gladys Wilkinson Catron, agreed with her brother, and said her father had discussed his plan for the lighting system with her mother, Bessie, before mortgaging everything. "The man was the head of the house [then, but] Dad was never a domineering man. They always did talk things over. She always knew what he was planning," Gladys said in a 1980 interview.[11]

According to Janet Bruce Vaughn, "[t]he need for funds [for the lighting system] caused Wilkinson to take on Thomas Y. Baird, a Kansas City billiard parlor owner, as a partner."[12] We now know, of course, that Tom Baird had been involved with the Monarchs financially since the team began in 1920, though he had largely kept out of the public eye.

J. L. Wilkinson was not the first to come up with the concept of night baseball. Attempts at lighting games after dark apparently date from 1890, the year after Thomas Edison invented electric lights. Other trials occurred between 1890 and 1910. "Plunk" Drake told an interviewer he had seen a team called the Nebraska Indians play under a primitive lighting system using kerosene lamps as early as 1913 or 1914. Dick Wilkinson also pointed out the Monarchs had experimented with lighting for night games played in Altoona, Iowa, and around Des Moines in first two decades of the twentieth century, using arc lamps and burning kerosene, but "the engineers couldn't seem to get the poles high enough." In 1927 a Lynn, Massachusetts, team of the New England League played Salem under the lights.[13]

Acknowledging he had seen lights used in night football games, J. L. Wilkinson said the system the Monarchs were building "will furnish three times more light than was produced with a system used at a game between Haskell Institute and the University of Kansas, played before 6,000 in 1929." He concluded with the claim the Monarchs had already scheduled many night games beginning in April and many more were being negotiated.[14]

Both Wilkinson and Keyser approached the Giant Manufacturing Company of Omaha to engineer the lights, a portable system for the Monarchs and a permanent arrangement for the Demons. Although Wilkinson was not the first baseball man to experiment with lighting games so they could be played at night, he was certainly the one who made the innovation practical. As Wilkinson's son, Dick, said of the plan, it was "really quite ingenious."[15]

According to Dick, "[t]he lights were on cables and telescoped steel poles, and they had a Ford truck under each light, one behind first, one behind third, and one in the outfield." Each pole, which extended 40 feet in the air, had six 1,000-watt, non-glare bulbs. The power was supplied by a 100-kilowatt Sterling Marine generator with a 250-horsepower, six-cylinder engine, carried in a 28-passenger bus with very little room left. The motor itself was almost as large as a Ford car, having a triple ignition, triple carburetor system and many other features that insured "constant and efficient service." It sucked about 15 gallons of gasoline per hour.[16]

The *Kansas City Call* reported that by early April 1930, "the massive plant for the night game [was] nearly [completed] at the headquarters of the Monarchs." It would soon be ready to display to club owners and newspapermen from around the country. Colleges

This photograph shows one of J. L. Wilkinson's portable lighting system trucks with its 40-foot pole, holding six 1,000-watt bulbs. Power for the lights was supplied by a specially built 250-horsepower generator carried on another truck (Kenneth Spencer Research Library, University of Kansas Libraries).

were also interested. The Haskell Indians had already found night football a success and with the "improvement offered by the new Wilkinson type of glare-free lighting the game will be at its peak and will eventually be used by most of the big colleges."[17]

In one of its infrequent stories on the Monarchs, the *Kansas City Star* reported that the lighting system produced an estimated illumination power of 198,000 watts. It would take less than an hour after the trucks carrying the system into a ballpark arrived "for a crew of twelve uniformed men to set it up and about the same time to dismantle it after the game."[18]

Another account at the time noted that "[t]he organization is handled in circus style, and it will take about thirty men including the players to handle.... The consumption of electricity used for games will be more than that consumed by the average city, just bottled up and focused on one spot, lighting the sky so that it can be seen for miles and miles."[19]

Floyd Ogle, who worked the lights for Wilkinson, recalled: "My truck covered the third base area ... five big reflectors were assembled at front—7,500 watts of light on this one truck. Poles were winched straight up and tied off with ropes. Power was from a bus chassis with a big motor and generator in it and a cable strung to each truck." He added, "I was 18 years old at the time and had two exciting seasons with the team."[20]

According to J. L.'s son Dick, his Uncle Lee, who was 20 years younger than his father and had traveled with the Monarchs earlier, took on more responsibilities when the team was traveling with lights.[21]

J. L. Wilkinson was present on April 17, 1930, when a smaller version of the new portable lighting system was tested at a park in Independence, Kansas. After seeing the lights, he said, "Now, imagine our plant throwing out just three times that much light and you have an idea of what the plant we have will mean to night baseball."[22]

By April 23 the Monarchs had completed spring training in Houston, Texas, and were ready to test their new lighting systems as they traveled north. However, inclement weather postponed the planned first use of the innovative system in several small towns in Kansas and Oklahoma.

Finally, on Monday night, April 28, 1930, Wilkinson led a "strange-looking caravan"—a bus, trucks, and four taxicabs rented from Monarchs player Newt Joseph's Kansas City cab company—into Enid, Oklahoma, where the Monarchs were scheduled to play the Phillips University Haymakers at Alton Stadium under the portable lights. A standing room only crowd of 3,000 ecstatic fans packed in to see baseball history being made. A big piece of canvas was stretched in center field to provide a lighted background against the blackness of the night sky. Balls hit over the temporary fence would be ruled doubles. Wilkinson nodded, the generator coughed, and the lights blazed on to the amazement of the people and the crowing of some confused roosters. Curveball artist William Bell and T. J. Young were the Monarchs' battery in the historic game, a 12–4 victory. A sudden downpour caused the contest to be called after eight innings.[23]

"It was beautiful," pitcher Chet Brewer later remembered. "It was light as day." Monarchs first baseman "Dink" Mothell told the *Call*: "This night ball playing is the real stuff.... Night ball seems to give this club a lot of ambition to whale the ball out of the lot and if we keep it up we will sharpen our hitting power to such an extent that we should be able to lead the league from the standpoint of hitting percentage at least."[24]

"The only hard part was when a fly ball was hit," second baseman Newt Allen recalled. "You'd have to wait for it to come out of the dark to catch it. But we got used to it and developed a pretty good judgment of where the ball was."[25] Allen was being generous. In fact, batters were horrified to stand before pitchers who threw what looked to them like "dark gray blobs." The pitcher had trouble picking up the catcher's signs so special signals based on the position of the catcher's hand on the mitt were developed.[26]

Fielders could only hope they weren't hit in the face by line drives they couldn't see. A new ground rule had to be implemented—two bases for any batted ball hit so high into the darkness it could not be seen by fielders. As one player said, when a ball went so high you couldn't see it, "you just looked up and prayed, dear Lord, bring it here."[27] Opposing pitcher Scrip Lee refused to take the mound for one of the Monarchs' early night games, because he said he'd thrown a ball into the air and although it dropped a foot in front of him, he couldn't see it.

The racket of the gas engines that powered the lighting system was also an issue, and not just for the players and fans. At one game the engines were so loud that animals at a nearby zoo were awakened.[28] The glare also bothered some spectators. However, none of these problems stopped fans from flocking to see what many had considered impossible—baseball games played under the lights.

A day after the first night game in Enid, on Tuesday, April 29, 1930, the Monarchs played the Empire Oilers, with the lights on, at Conoco Park in Ponca City, Oklahoma. The caravan then headed south, where the Monarchs carried their lights to Oklahoma City, Dallas, and Houston, averaging 15,000 fans for each of six games.

The portable lighting system did not guarantee that the Monarchs would win. On May 3, 1930, they were shut out, 1–0, under lights by a team called the Black Indians in San Antonio.[29]

On May 6, in Waco, Texas, Monarchs lefty John Markham, a rookie, pitched the first night no-hitter against a white team, the Waco Texas League Cardinals, before a throng of 10,000. He faced only 28 batters. The Monarchs had eight runs and 14 hits. The *Call* noted, "the field was as light and clear as in the day time and not a single error was committed by either club."[30]

Twelve thousand fans came out in Memphis on May 11 to see the Monarchs and Red Sox under the lights in the 1930 NNL opener. By the time the Monarchs reached St. Louis on May 17, Wilkinson had paid for his lights. More than 4,000 turned out to see the St. Louis Stars play the Monarchs in an illuminated night game, an incredible 800 per cent increase over typical attendance. By this time Wilkinson's innovation was beginning to draw the attention of big league executives. After seeing the lights at the game in St. Louis, Sam Breadon, owner of the Cardinals, said he intended to order a permanent set for Sportsman's Park.[31]

The Monarchs returned to Kansas City for their NNL home opener on May 23, but their first night games in Kansas City were not played until June 13–14. The reason for the delay was that Muehlebach Field was much larger than the parks in which the portable lighting system had been used. Wilkinson said, "the entire plant [had to be] rebuilt for the games [at Muehlebach Field]." He added that "[f]orty flood lights [would] be used to flood the field with light, each with a capacity of 4,300 watts, the largest lighting plant of its kind in the world." Some of the additional lights would be placed on the roof of the stadium.[32]

In an article before the games titled "Father of Night Baseball Brings His Hobby Here," the *Kansas City Star* noted that the Monarchs players called their owner, "Mistah Wilkie." "For almost a quarter of a century," the *Star* commented, J. Leslie Wilkinson had "been engaged in his peculiar racket, or, better, business, as it is on that standard that it has been conducted since the beginning. Wilkinson is strictly a business man with a highly developed sense of values. His work has been a profession to him, and he has reaped the rewards, as his bank balance will show." Wilkinson had not been affected, the *Star* observed, by "years of association with varied types and characters.... He is no different from the shrewd, tactical business man of the industrial or manufacturing world." Wilkinson had, the *Star* continued, turned the Monarchs into "the most celebrated Negro team the sport has ever known." When large lighting companies told him portable lights for night baseball games were impractical, Wilkinson proceeded with his own plans. This kind of persistence was typical, Wilkinson told the *Star*, of the spirit found among Negro baseball teams, who, unlike white clubs, must "battle with all their strength in every game." According to the *Star*, in addition to being skilled ballplayers the Monarchs were known as "talented showmen and clever entertainers" who did not waste "any opportunities for comedy." Newt Allen, for example, "usually carries a flower in his teeth while playing."[33] The *Star*, it seems, was perceiving the Monarchs through the filter created by the expectations whites had for black baseball.

Twelve thousand spectators were in attendance at Muehlebach Field to see the Monarchs beat the Nashville Elite Giants, 15–8, in the first game under the newly installed lights. Thomas Hickey, president of the American Association, who had earlier banned exhibition games between the Monarchs and Kansas City Blues, said, after seeing his first night game, he was "more impressed than ever by its possibilities. I regard baseball under the lights as [a] success."[34] There was no indication in game reports that the Monarchs had employed the comedic routines the *Star* had claimed were typical.

After a month of league games, Wilkinson took his popular portable lights to the East for two weeks. On the way, at about 11 a.m. on Monday, July 14, 1930, several members of the Monarchs were hurt in an automobile wreck on Highway 40 near Warrenton, Missouri. Most seriously injured were L. D. Livingston, who suffered a lacerated scalp; Andy ("Lefty") Cooper with cuts; and business manager Quincy Gilmore with a badly wrenched shoulder and cuts. Gilmore had rejoined the Monarchs after the collapse of the Texas-Oklahoma-Louisiana League he had organized.[35]

The 16-day eastern tour drew 30,000 fans to the night games played. The first was on July 16, 1930, when the Monarchs took on the Homestead Grays in Cleveland, where the Grays played their home games. Apparently, J. L. Wilkinson did not share the concern of other NNL owners about the Grays playing home games outside the East in violation of an inter-league agreement. Six thousand fans were in the stands at Hooper Stadium for the contest. That weekend the Monarchs and Detroit Stars met under the lights in Detroit. Seven thousand fans filled the stadium, and another seven thousand had to be turned away.

A number of the night games on the Eastern swing were played in smaller towns. Dick Wilkinson recalled that 10,000 people knocked down the fences in a tiny stadium in Hershey, Pennsylvania. "There were 2,000 in the park and 8,000 outside. They had no money to get in, so they just stood around and looked." On some occasions, Dick said, "we had to call the police department to keep the curious out of the way so we could erect the lights and save them from injury."[36]

On August 3, 1930, the Monarchs were back at Muehlebach Field to face the Grays again. Wilkinson assured fans, "[t]he lights will be perfectly arranged when the game is called tonight and one of the prettiest sights ever witnessed in a ball park will be offered."[37]

Although J. L. Wilkinson's portable lighting system did not illuminate a baseball diamond like sunlight, as its supporters claimed, it did make possible, better than any previous effort, the playing of night games. It is not an exaggeration to say the system saved the Kansas City Monarchs and other professional baseball teams during the Great Depression (Kenneth Spencer Research Library, University of Kansas Libraries).

Grandstand seats were only 60c, and box seats 75c for what turned out to be an epic pitchers' duel between 45-year-old "Smoky Joe" Williams of the Grays and 23-year-old Chet Brewer of the Monarchs. In 1930 the spitball was still legal in the Negro Leagues. In addition, both hurlers cut the ball, using, a reporter observed, "everything but a blacksmith's file." One sportswriter labeled the game the "Battle of the Butchered Balls." Brewer's emery ball proved almost impossible to hit. Williams retaliated by spitting tobacco juice on the ball and throwing sidearm, causing Monarchs batters to jump back. "Smoky Joe" struck out 27 and Brewer 19 in a contest that saw Oscar Charleston walk in the 12th inning for the Grays and race home all the way from first to score the game's only run.[38]

    Baseball historian Henry Metcalfe summed up well what J. L. Wilkinson accomplished by envisioning and then implementing night baseball with a portable lighting system: "With a tip of his characteristic wide-brimmed hat to the myth of American ingenuity, the cult of the inventor, and innovator, and the language of the traveling medicine show, Wilkinson bet the house on developing night baseball." With his portable lighting system "Wilkinson and his barnstorming Monarchs became the bright shining stars of the vast baseball-crazed heartland."[39]

Larry Lester described the importance of the innovation in these insightful words: "Wilkie presented a new science to the game, long before televised baseball games, radar guns, lap-top computers, pronto replays, plastic grass, faxed scouting reports, caged stadiums and carnival scoreboards, maybe even before aluminum bats and Teflon baseballs."[40] As Buck O'Neil wrote in his autobiography, "I do believe that if it wasn't for [Wilkinson's] lights, Negro baseball wouldn't have survived the Depression."[41]

Although Wilkinson's partner Tom Baird was supportive of the development of the portable lighting system, he acknowledged that "Wilky," as he called him, should be known as the "Father of Night Baseball."[42]

Within a few years most Negro Leagues games during the week were played at night, with Sunday afternoon reserved for doubleheaders. The president of the Mississippi League, which launched night baseball on June 16, 1930, claimed it saved the circuit, increasing attendance 32,409 over 1929, with three fewer games. By 1931 all eight Pacific Coast League teams were committed to playing night games.[43]

However, most white major league owners and officials were not initially impressed. Ban Johnson, former president of the American League, claimed, "[n]ight baseball has created a curiosity interest for the time, especially among women; but, in my opinion, it is not an interest that is of an educational or permanent nature. Night baseball is not natural. It cannot be permanent. It will never take hold of the major leagues." Other opponents called the idea "outdoor vaudeville" and claimed the lights "profaned a great game God meant to go with sunlight." It would be another five years before a major league game was played at night.[44]

When NNL founder Rube Foster died on December 9, 1930, Joe Green, former owner of the Chicago Giants, said, "the league died with him."[45] At the winter meeting of the NNL on January 23–24, 1931, Foster's friend and colleague J. L. Wilkinson was among those offering eulogies during a memorial service.

In *Only the Ball Was White*, Robert Peterson paid Foster the following tribute: "If the talents of Christy Mathewson, John McGraw, Ban Johnson, and Judge Kenesaw Mountain Landis were combined in a single body, and that body were enveloped in a black skin, the result would have to be named Andrew (Rube) Foster."[46]

Foster's biographer, Robert Cottrell, summed up Rube Foster's contributions not only to baseball but to American sports and American life in these words: "Without Foster's vision and organizational acumen, [Satchel] Paige, [Josh] Gibson, [Buck] Leonard, and even [Jackie] Robinson would likely have remained mere footnotes in American sports history. The country and its often tortured race relations would, as a consequence, have been more troubled still." Perhaps the greatest tribute to the master mind of black baseball was what a bleacher fan said of Rube Foster: "After him, they ain't no more."[47]

In a *Kansas City Call* editorial, A. D. Williams offered his analysis of what it would take to save the NNL in the post–Foster era. What was needed, he asserted, was "an efficient man of baseball to head the 1931 season of the Negro National League. A man who knows baseball, a man who has spent most of his life in the game and knows what it is all about. A man who can devote his time—all of it—to the grand old game. Look where you may—say what you will—but you have only one man, right now who fits the shoe. Believe it or not, he who hesitates is lost." Leaving no doubt as to the one person he thought could be the savior for the NNL, Williams placed his editorial under a picture of J. L. Wilkinson.[48]

J. L. Wilkinson was not the first owner of a black team to see the financial advantages of barnstorming. By 1930 it had been a staple for African American teams for decades. However, Wilkinson was the innovator who embraced barnstorming as his main strategy, alongside night baseball, for surviving the economic challenges of the Great Depression.

Barnstorming comprised over half the yearly schedules of teams like the Monarchs, even while they were affiliated with a league. Historian Leslie Heaphy has determined that more than 650 towns in the United States served as venues for touring black clubs.[49] Most of these games were played either with other black teams, or local amateur or semi-pro white town teams, but by 1931 barnstorming contests between white major leaguers and Negro Leaguers were especially popular moneymakers. It has been estimated that Negro Leaguers won the majority of the games played against white major league teams (89–67–1).[50]

However, barnstorming was not a racial utopia. Those who cheered the Kansas City Monarchs at the games often refused to serve them food or pump their gas. The Monarchs often did not stay in hotels but instead "relied on a loose network of black boardinghouses and private homes." If none were available, they slept in their bus or in tents they carried with them.[51]

In pinning the hopes of the Monarchs and black baseball on barnstorming, Wilkinson clearly understood the tenor of the times. During the Depression most people in small towns still had enough money to splurge on a once-a-summer opportunity to see some of the world's best baseball players. The Monarchs focused their barnstorming between North Dakota and Texas, with some trips north into Canada and the Western states as well as south into Mexico. Wilkinson always received at least half the gate, and often left with 80 or 90 percent.

Several years into the Monarchs' commitment to rely exclusively on barnstorming, Frank Young, who served as the *Kansas City Call's* managing editor from 1934–1937, commented that the Monarchs "see no reason why they should be in any Negro League. Barnstorming pays better than any so-called league."[52]

In a 1971 interview, Bill "Plunk" Drake recalled barnstorming in the early days. "We'd go out in the small towns in Iowa," he said, "and we would take our tents and we would put them up and we would sleep in those tents, … and in the evening we'd go fish, and we had just a dandy good time…. I played for an awful good man, J.R. Wilkerson [sic] … [F]rankly speaking, the Monarchs lived awfully good."[53]

During the 1930s, J. L. Wilkinson developed a close relationship with another sports entrepreneur, Abe Saperstein. Although the two were different in temperament and background, they shared an ability to sense what would attract the interest of fans. Saperstein (1902–1966) was born in London, but grew up in Chicago. Standing just five-foot-three on his tiptoes, the diminutive Saperstein took a job at the Welles Park Recreation Center in the Windy City. There he met Walter Ball, a former Negro Leagues player who wanted to take a baseball team he had organized on tour around Illinois. Saperstein convinced Ball to let him be the booking agent for the team.

Within a few years Saperstein had established a black basketball team with appeal to white audiences: the Harlem Globetrotters. He scheduled exhibition games wherever and whenever he could and seasoned basketball "with slapstick comedy and trick shots." Saperstein was soon being called "The Great White Father of Negro Basketball." He continued to be heavily involved in black baseball as well.[54]

Although Abe Saperstein was Wilkinson's junior by 24 years and had a much different demeanor, the two men developed a close working relationship and friendship.

When the Monarchs' owner decided to begin using Saperstein as a booking agent, his son Dick asked why he was using the Chicagoan when they could book games themselves. His father responded, "Saperstein needs a little help right now. Son, I believe that man is going places. You've got to understand, one day he'll be a great sports promoter."[55]

It turned out J. L. Wilkinson was right. By the late 1930s Saperstein was booking for the Ethiopian Clowns baseball team and most of the independent Negro American League (NAL) games. By 1939 he had also worked his way into the promotion of the annual Negro Leagues East-West Game, receiving five percent of gate receipts. Like Wilkinson, Saperstein won the respect of his players. For example, Ted "Double Duty" Radcliffe called him one of the greatest figures in black baseball. Another player, Sug Cornelius, heralded his publicity and administrative skills.[56]

As Tom Fredrick has noted, Wilkinson's visionary experience with the All Nations team and the Kansas City Monarchs gave Abe Saperstein a professional blueprint. Wilkinson's personal and early financial support of Saperstein garnered enduring affection and respect in return. "I don't think Abe ever forgot it,'" Dick Wilkinson commented. In the years to follow, Sapersetin would send postcards and call the Monarchs' owner when he was on tour with the Harlem Globetrotters. If he came through Kansas City, he'd visit the Monarchs' owner for several hours. "They had a big time going over old times," Dick added.[57]

Sapersetin's Harlem Globetrotters may have adopted the "race identification" originated by Wilkinson's All Nations team, but, according to historian Mark Ribowsky, Saperstein went "far beyond Wilkinson's tasteful showbiz inclinations with the All Nations" and "molded magnificent black athletes into the worst white assumptions of how Negroes behaved." To this, Ribowskey maintains, Wilkinson's Monarchs were "a counterbalance of dignity and class."[58]

A widely held belief in white baseball circles was that black baseball was a shady enterprise controlled by unscrupulous booking agents and racketeers. White booking agents like Abe Saperstein, Nat Strong, and Eddie Gottlieb were often maligned, but they put together games with white semi-pro teams and non-league black games through which black clubs like the Monarchs made the most money. They also promoted special events in venues like Yankee Stadium, the Polo Grounds, and other big league parks.

White major league owners like the Yankees' Jacob Ruppert may have viewed black baseball with contempt, but by 1930 they could no longer pass up the money to be made renting out their major and minor league parks. Ruppert's Yankee Stadium, "The House that Ruth Built," held its first black baseball game on July 6, 1930, drawing 15,000 mostly African American fans. By the end of the 1930s every big league park—except Sportsman's Park in St. Louis, Wrigley Field in Chicago, and the two parks in Boston—were being rented out to Negro Leagues teams. Rentals at minor league parks, like Muehlebach Field in Kansas City, were also essential to the balance sheets of Ruppert and other owners.[59]

In early April 1931, the *Kansas City Call* ran a banner headline proclaiming: MONARCHS OUT OF NATIONAL NEGRO LEAGUE. J. L. Wilkinson had announced that the Monarchs were withdrawing from the NNL and would play independent baseball. The Monarchs owner explained, "membership in the league has been a losing proposition for some years." The current Monarchs players, Wilkinson noted, were free to pursue other contracts. However, a number had said they would go with the Monarchs if Wilkinson reorganized them as an independent team.[60]

The refashioning of the Monarchs as an independent, barnstorming team did not happen quickly. In May 1931 the *Call* noted former players had "scattered to all four corners of the country."⁶¹ A month later, after meeting with former Monarchs players in Chicago, Wilkinson decided to proceed with a plan to reorganize the team and named "Bullet Joe" Rogan as manager. Among those who signed with the independent Monarchs were "Dink" Mothell, Newt Allen, Frank Duncan, T. J. Young, Grady Orange, Charley Beverly, and the timeless veteran, John Donaldson.⁶²

After barnstorming in Wisconsin and Illinois, the new Monarchs returned to Muehlebach Field on July 26, 1931, and defeated the Chicago Giants in a doubleheader, 9–4 and 4–0. Three more players, former Monarchs Chet Brewer, Henry McHenry, and Alto Lane, had joined the team. The next day they were back on the road for games in Kansas and Nebraska. By August 9 they had returned to Kansas City to play at Muehlebach Field on weekends and pick up other games in small towns during the week. Nearly 9,000 fans of both races were present on August 16 for a doubleheader with the Cuban House of David.⁶³

The barnstorming Monarchs played anyone and anywhere if there was a dollar to be made. In just one stretch they played teams in Oxford, Nebraska; Norton, Kansas; Wymore, Nebraska; Formosa, Kansas; Nicodemus, Kansas; Guide Rock, Nebraska; McCook, Nebraska; and Harrington, Kansas. Then it was back on the road east for games against the Mills club in Chicago and the Homestead Grays in Akron, Ohio, with stops in small towns and cities along the way.

The Homestead Grays and Monarchs played nine games billed by promoters as a championship series in late August and early September 1931. Beginning with a game in Akron on August 28 before a crowd of 10,000, the teams traveled to Pittsburgh, Cleveland, and Canton before playing the final three match-ups in Kansas City.⁶⁴

Reprising the type of promotion first used with his Bloomer Girls and All Nations teams, Wilkinson scheduled games with the Cuban House of David during the Arlington Fair in Omaha on September 19, 1931. Back at Muehlebach Field, 10,000 chilled Monarchs fans saw their team beat the Original House of David, 11–2. Another House of David–Monarchs game in Trenton, Missouri, drew 5,000 fans, more than had turned out to see Babe Ruth in the small town two years earlier. On October 4, the Monarchs faced Pittsburgh Pirates infielder Colt Tierney's team, which included Bill Terry, Paul and Lloyd Waner, and Babe Herman, before a crowd of 10,000. There were five games in the series, with some played in St. Louis.⁶⁵

To extend the lucrative barnstorming season, Wilkinson took the Monarchs south through the rest of October and November for games in Texas and Mexico. On this trip the Monarchs beat the Mexican Nationals and an all-star team composed of the best players from the white Southern League.⁶⁶

Buck O'Neil recalled that the Depression had made Wilkinson even more willing to travel for games in distant locations. According to O'Neil, the Monarchs' owner always insisted on exemplary behavior and dress, giving good impressions of African Americans in towns that had not seen one before. The Depression, O'Neil claimed, "brought black and white a little closer together, if only because people were too poor to be picky about the company they were keeping."⁶⁷

Newt Allen remembered the barnstorming Monarchs sharing roadside camps and meals with white people heading westward to escape the Dust Bowl. It was so hot, he recalled, the team sometimes cut its games to seven innings. "Even golf balls were melting," he claimed. Willie Foster, who was with the Monarchs in 1931, said he would have written home for money but couldn't afford a three-cent stamp.⁶⁸

5. The Innovator (1930–1936)

Wilkinson, who earned the respect of his players by sharing the hardships of travel when they barnstormed, said he found life interesting when traveling with the team. "They [the Monarchs] never permit things to become dull, keeping the party lively with their spontaneous humor and wise cracks." "Many occasions," Wilkinson recalled, "we ... had to get out and push [the bus] over miles of muddy roads in order to keep engagements."[69]

"Lefty" Bryant, who joined the Monarchs in 1937, recalled, "[s]ometimes there were places on the road where a black man could not get off the bus and go in and eat. [Wilkinson] would go in and get the food and bring it to us. He always saw that we had plenty of food. That J. L. was one of the finest persons I ever knew."[70]

Since major league salaries were drastically reduced during the Depression, big league ballplayers scrambled to book post-season games against the Monarchs, knowing that all would go off well and they would make good money. "Funny thing what depression will do," wrote Bob Boyd in the *Kansas City Call*. "Make an All-Star big league team come 'south' and play a professional colored team."[71] The *Chicago Defender*'s Fay Young opined in a syndicated article early in the Depression, "Wilkie gets credit for being the outstanding baseball promoter in the country and a believer in winning teams."[72]

In the 1930s the Monarchs found a money-making machine called the House of David baseball team. In 1903 Benjamin Franklin Purnell had established a religious community in Benton Harbor, Michigan. He named it the Israelite House of David. Purnell's stated purpose was to gather the 12 lost tribes of Israel for the "Ingathering" to await the return of Jesus Christ and be among those who would inherit the earth. To show their piety male members did not shave their beards or cut their hair. The commune followed a strict vegetarian diet and a healthy lifestyle with rigorous exercise.

Nine years later the House of David baseball team began play when a group of boys in Purnell's community took to the diamond and defeated some local Benton Harbor teams. After beating factory teams around western Michigan, the House of David nine began touring more widely. House of David players performed sleight-of-hand tricks with baseballs and may have been among the first teams to use the "pepper" pre-game warm-up drill. Early on they traveled mostly in the East and played Negro Leagues teams such as the Pittsburgh Crawfords. Their fame spread when Hall of Fame pitcher Grover Cleveland Alexander (1887–1950) signed on as player/manager of the House of David team in 1931 after retiring from the major leagues.

Taking advantage of the growing popularity of the House of David team, the Monarchs began scheduling games with the bearded nine in the early 1930s. On occasion, Olympic champion Mildred "Babe" Didrikson was signed to play second base or pitch with the House of Davids to boost fan interest. Often the Monarchs and House of David team traveled together. The Monarchs toured an area, defeating local teams, followed by the House of David team, who bested the same clubs. Then the Monarchs and House of David staged "championship" games in the same little towns, guaranteeing large crowds. A Winnipeg, Manitoba, sportswriter reported, "[t]he exhibition of baseball the House of David and the Kansas City Monarchs dished up may never be equaled again. You don't see many games that go eleven innings with errorless ball, and a pitcher [referring to Grover Cleveland Alexander] knocking at baseball's Hall of Fame."[73]

By 1934 the popularity of the original Hall of David team had spawned a number of variations. Those loyal to Purnell remained the Original or Israelite House of David. Those who followed Purnell's wife, Mary, who had left the community, called themselves

T. Y. (Tom) Baird was co-founder of the Kansas City Monarchs with J. L. Wilkinson in 1920. He remained with the team in a largely behind-the-scenes role until buying out Wilkinson and assuming full ownership in 1948. One of the most successful schemes with the Monarchs in which Baird was directly involved was, beginning in 1931, booking games with the popular House of David team, a bearded club started by a Michigan religious commune. Here Baird (standing, fifth from the left) is shown with the Davidites and members of the crew that assembled the portable lights for night games. Standing (seventh from the left) is Iowan Ray Doan, who collaborated with Baird and Wilkinson in booking games (Kenneth Spencer Research Library, University of Kansas Libraries).

the Israelite House of David as Re-organized by Mary Purnell, or simply the City of David.

Impostor teams who had no connection with the House of David community also co-opted the brand. One of the first, the Cuban House of David, had already begun touring in 1931. It replaced the Havana Red Sox and was owned and operated by white promoter Syd Pollock. The Cubans featured an "assortment of sideburns, mutton-chops, and flowing beards."[74] The Spring Valley House of David and Colored House of David also copied the bearded look.[75]

The Original House of David parlayed its success into East, West, and Central traveling squads. In addition to Alexander, another future Hall of Fame pitcher, Mordecai "Three Finger" Brown, was recruited to add luster to the teams. In the first-ever night game in Sportsman's Park in St. Louis, on September 22, 1931, Alexander led the House of David against the St. Louis Cardinals. The game drew over 9,000 fans in comparison to 450 for an afternoon Cardinals game against the Reds the same day. Alexander was

In 1931 Grover Cleveland Alexander (1887–1950) signed on to manage the House of David team that frequently played against the Monarchs. Alexander had already achieved fame as a future Hall of Fame major league pitcher (1911–1930). He and Christy Mathewson are tied for the most National League wins (373). "Donkey ball" was a fan favorite and was staged as part of bills that featured the Davidites. Alexander allowed himself to be photographed on a donkey but refused to take part in the sideshow himself (Kenneth Spencer Research Library, University of Kansas Libraries).

not required to grow a beard, but he could not thwart gimmicks such as donkey ball, in which players competing riding donkeys. After he left the team, Alexander is reputed to have said, "I was advertised like the elephant in the circus and had to pitch an inning or so every game."[76]

As late as 1953, the House of David was still renting the Monarchs' portable lighting system. It was used on August 21, 1953, for "Goose Tatum Night" in the Chicago Cubs' Wrigley Field, the first night game in the historic park's history.[77]

In 1932, as the Depression deepened, the Monarchs' future was again uncertain. Monarch George Giles remembered, "Wilkie said he wasn't going to start up in '32.... So we all went to the Homestead Grays or the Detroit Wolves [of the new East-West League]."[78] The now-defunct NNL's last president, William Hueston, was trying to rally support to revive the league for the 1933 season, but J. L. Wilkinson offered him no hope, saying, "[I] just can't see the league at present." He also laid to rest rumors the Monarchs were planning to join the East-West League or move the team to Chicago, Cleveland, or Detroit, citing the loyalty of Kansas City fans to the Monarchs.[79]

Wilkinson persevered, and the reorganized Monarchs opened the 1932 season on Saturday, July 9, in Chicago against the American Giants after a one-day "spring training."

Among the successful promotions during the Monarchs-House of David games of the 1930s were those featuring Mildred "Babe" Didrikson (1911–1956), a gold-medal winner in track and field events at the 1932 Olympics. She also excelled in a variety of other sports. To the delight of fans, Didrikson took the field as a pitcher or at second base for the House of David (Kenneth Spencer Research Library, University of Kansas Libraries).

Their lineup for the game included "Cool Papa" Bell in center, George Giles at first, Newt Allen at second, Willie Wells at short, T. J. Young behind the plate, "Dink" Mothell at third, Leroy "Popsickle" Taylor in right, Curtis Harris in left, and Quincy Trouppe in a rare appearance on the mound. Wilkinson had acquired Bell, Wells, Young, Harris, and Trouppe from the Homestead Grays, who had been unable to pay their high salaries. He

5. The Innovator (1930–1936)   85

Taken at a Monarchs practice about 1932, this is one of the few shots showing co-owners T. Y. Baird (fourth from left) and J. L. Wilkinson (fifth from left) together on the field. Longtime Monarchs business manager/secretary Quincy (Q. J.) Gilmore (1882–1954), who worked with Wilkinson from 1920–1935, is third from the left. Next to Wilkinson is Carroll "Dink" Mothell (1897–1980), who was a valued utility player for the Monarchs (1920, 1923–1934). He also played for All Nations (1921–1923) (Kansas State Historical Society).

also claimed he was negotiating with Babe Ruth and other big leaguers to play games during the fall in Kansas City.[80]

After series against the A.B.C.'s in Indianapolis and the Mills in Chicago, the revamped Monarchs went on a terror across the Midwest and into Canada, reeling off an impressive 20 straight victories. When Wilkinson's team reached Jamestown, North Dakota, for a game, it would be the first time in his professional career that "Bullet Joe" Rogan, who was on the Jamestown roster, was playing for a team other than the Monarchs. It would also be the last. Wilkinson convinced Rogan to rejoin the Monarchs to play out the rest of the 1932 barnstorming season, and he remained with the team until he retired in 1938.[81]

The Monarchs finally played their first 1932 home game on Sunday, August 7, against the American Giants, winning 8–1. The Tuesday game of the series was played under the lights. The Monarchs then went back on the road, playing in Iowa, Kansas, Oklahoma, Nebraska, Wisconsin, Illinois and Michigan. They returned to Muehlebach Field on September 23 and beat Grover Cleveland Alexander and the Original House of David squad, 5–4. On October 2, 1932, John Donaldson brought his Fairmont, Minnesota, All-Stars to Kansas City.[82]

The Monarchs then traveled to Wichita to face a major league all-star team. Before the game, Washington Senators first baseman Joe Kuhel claimed, "[t]he Monarchs ...

haven't got the hitting power. The only way they could ever beat a club like ours is to have enough pitching to hold us scoreless."[83] The game featured future Hall of Fame brothers Paul and Lloyd Waner, who recorded hits, but the Monarchs won the game, 6–2, not only with good pitching but solid hitting, including a home run by Willie Wells.

On October 20, 1932, the Monarchs arrived in Mexico City for an historic set of games. Quincy Gilmore chronicled the trip in a series of dispatches to the *Kansas City Call*.[84] He wanted it understood that "[j]ust as soon as we crossed the border, we were treated as real men." Gilmore wrote that one day in Mexico City he saw "a young colored lady [as dark as he was] walking down the street on the arm of a Mexican student as white as any white student in the States."

In the Monarchs' traveling party were Frank Duncan, Tom Young, George Giles, Newt Allen, Willie Wells and his wife, Carroll "Dink" Mothell, "Cool Papa" Bell, "Turkey" Stearnes (who told the *Call* when he began play in 1920 he was "all chest, no hips or legs," so his teammates came up with "Turkey" as a moniker[85]), Leroy Harris, Chet Brewer, Charley Beverly, Bertram Hunter, "Bullet Joe" Rogan, J. L. Wilkinson, Tom Baird and Quincy Gilmore.

Playing in uniforms with American flags on the sleeves, the Monarchs won 14 games and lost only two. Gilmore proudly wrote, "we have been told that the Monarchs are the best behaved baseball club that has ever visited the Republic of Mexico."[86]

Despite the Monarchs' record of 74–6, 1932 was the nadir for organized black baseball. It was the first time since 1920 there was no major Negro League in operation. However, it was also the harbinger of a new era when strong personalities in the mold of Rube Foster would emerge. They were led by Cumberland Willis "Cum" Posey of the Homestead Grays and W. A. "Gus" or " Big Red" Greenlee of the Pittsburgh Crawfords.[87]

Most significantly, Greenlee organized the second Negro National League in 1933. The Grays, American Giants, Indianapolis A.B.C.'s, Detroit Stars, and Columbus Blue Birds joined the Crawfords in the new league. This version of the NNL would survive, with changes, until 1948. Eager to have the Monarchs in the new NNL, Greenlee invited Wilkinson to all league meetings and granted the Monarchs associate membership, allowing them to schedule games in league cities, but the Monarchs' owner declined the offer.[88]

It is important to note that Wilkinson was not fundamentally opposed to a new black league. He had himself tried unsuccessfully to organize a few owners in 1932. Two years later he convened a meeting in Kansas City to discuss a possible new, Western league, perhaps in association with Southern clubs, but the attempt failed.[89]

The 1933 campaign would be the last great season of the first generation of Monarchs players. After opening with a barnstorming tour of Kansas, Oklahoma, Arkansas, and rural Missouri, the Kaysees returned to face former Olympic champion Jim Thorpe's touring Oklahoma Indians on June 4 in Kansas City, Kansas.[90]

Since the white American Association team, the Kansas City Blues, was in town, limiting access to Muehlebach Field for the Monarchs, Wilkinson's team soon went back on the road, with games as far north as Winnipeg, Canada. Touring in North Dakota, Minnesota, and Wisconsin, the Monarchs were almost unbeatable, surging to a record of 42–4 by July 4. From the road, Wilkinson told the *Call* that "he had no intention of joining the [new NNL] at present and the possibility that he would join next year was so far distant that he didn't care to discuss it."[91]

By late July, Wilkinson and the Monarchs had returned to Kansas City for two games against Syd Pollock's Cuban Stars. The Monarchs and Cubans split the twin bill, with the

Kansas City loss ending a long winning streak.[92] After another barnstorming swing through Kansas and Nebraska, the Monarchs returned briefly to Kansas City to face the Memphis Red Sox of the Southern League for a doubleheader on August 6, winning both games. In a game arranged by the two pioneers of night baseball, J. L. Wilkinson and Lee Keyser, the Monarchs thrashed the Des Moines Demons of the white Western League in Des Moines on the evening of August 7, 14–3.[93]

For Wilkinson the most lucrative contests during the 1933 season were against white Western League teams like the Demons and Grover Cleveland Alexander's Original House of David.[94] One four-game series against the House of David squad in Winnipeg attracted 20,000 paying fans, in addition to many who looked on from beyond the field for free. Enthusiastic crowds also came out in large numbers in Wichita, Topeka, and Dodge City, Kansas; Bartlesville, Oklahoma; and Carthage, Missouri, to see Alexander and his "bewhiskered" crew take on the famous Monarchs.

Back in Kansas City for Labor Day doubleheaders on September 3–4, the Monarchs won three of four from the Nashville Elite Giants.[95] On September 19, 1933, they beat the Eastern House of David, 6–1. More important than the score was the appearance of a "great girl pitcher in the lineup"—Jackie Mitchell, who had already gained national recognition by striking out Babe Ruth twice in a single game.[96] After the game, the Monarchs returned to barnstorming against Alexander's Original House of David.

On Monday night, October 2, 1933, a major league all-star contingent, including Cardinals "Gashouse Gang" favorites Dizzy Dean and Pepper Martin, faced off against the Monarchs at Muehlebach Field. Dean was effective on the mound, striking out five and allowing only one hit in three innings against Wilkinson's team. However, led by Rogan the Monarchs rallied in the eighth and ninth innings and won the game 5–4.[97]

The two teams met again the next day under the lights in Oxford, Nebraska. The Monarchs' hard-throwing hurler Chet Brewer beaned Dean, who dropped as though he had been shot. The dazed Dizzy was carried to the bench, and Wilkinson and the Oxford manager rushed off to get medical help. Within ten minutes an ambulance arrived, but the medics couldn't find the injured Cardinal. They were amazed to see Dizzy trotting in from the outfield. He had recovered and insisted on continuing in the game. Wilkinson told a reporter, "[i]f that blow didn't wreck him I guess nothing could."[98]

On Sunday, October 8, the Monarchs defeated another major league all-star team made up mostly of Pittsburgh and Brooklyn players by a score of 6–4 before a crowd of 3,500 at Muehlebach Field. According to Wilkinson, these two groups of major leaguers presented "the strongest lineup ever to have appeared in recent years in Kansas City against the Monarchs." The Monarchs and All-Stars next played a game in Joplin, Missouri. After games in Oklahoma City and Wichita, the series and the Monarchs' season came to an end with a 3–2 Kansas City win.[99]

The Monarchs finished their 1933 campaign with a remarkable record of 134 wins and just 14 losses. More importantly, Wilkinson's barnstorming strategy had been a financial success. The *Chicago Defender* noted, "[the] Monarchs are playing through Nebraska and other western points at a very high rate of profit and laughing merrily as the associated clubs [of the NNL] wallow in [debt]."[100]

While the Monarchs were playing white teams before integrated audiences, acts of horrific violence were an ongoing reality for African Americans. In 1933 in St. Joseph, Missouri, just 30 miles north of Kansas City, Lloyd Warner, a black teenager who had been released to a mob by the sheriff, was lynched. After hanging him, the mob burned his corpse and gouged his eyes out while a crowd including women and children cheered them. Eight men were arrested but, after a jury failed to convict any of the assailants, all charges were dropped.[101]

Following on the success of the initial white major league All-Star Game on July 6, 1933, owners of black teams scheduled the first African American All-Star East-West (E-W) Game on September 10, 1933, at Comiskey Park, home of the Chicago White Sox. A dark, dreary day limited attendance, but up to 20,000 people braved the drizzle to attend.

The concept of a Negro Leagues All-Star game had originated with two Pittsburgh sportswriters, Roy Sparrow and Bill Nunn, but, as we have noted, the driving force was Pittsburgh Crawfords owner Gus Greenlee, who enlisted the aid of Tom Wilson, owner of the Nashville Elite Giants, and Robert Cole, owner of the American Giants. The three were the E-W game's first promoters and pocketed most of the gate receipts for the first few years.

In 1936 J. L. Wilkinson and Horace Hall of the American Giants joined Wilson and Greenlee in promoting the E-W game. That year the contest, with players only from the teams of the four promoters, "lacked the all-star quality of previous years."[102] With the formation of the Negro American League (NAL) in 1937, an agreement to divide the proceeds of the E-W games equally among NNL and NAL clubs was reached.

Held every year from 1933–1962 the E-W games were one of black baseball's most successful ventures. The games attracted crowds of over 50,000, even during the depth of the Depression. In some years, two games were played, one at Comiskey Park in Chicago and another in New York, Cleveland or Washington, D.C., Buck O'Neil, who participated in three E-W games as a Monarch, said the E-W games were a matter of racial pride. In most years black papers, including the *Call,* ran lists of players eligible for the E-W game and included ballots fans could clip and send in to select the two teams. A million votes were cast the first year.

Despite the large turnouts of fans at the E-W games, players were not fairly compensated. During the early years of the E-W contests, the players received virtually nothing. As one owner suggested, "they are on salary anyhow, and we don't need to give them anything." By 1939 each player was paid $25 for participating in the game, $20 more than the meager amount grudgingly given them four years earlier. With the game consistently drawing over 40,000, the players' call for a larger share of the proceeds grew louder. In 1943 NAL officials yielded to pitching phenomenon Leroy "Satchel" Paige's demand for $800, annoying his fellow players. The next year Paige boycotted the game when his insistence on an even higher fee was rejected. When Satchel responded that he would donate his entire fee to the Army/Navy relief fund if the leagues did likewise, the owners refused, with NAL President J. B. Martin noting, "Paige is not running Negro baseball." Other players joined in by demanding that their fee be hiked. NNL players asked for $200; NAL players demanded $100.[103]

By March 1934, Wilkinson had given up on the effort to find a new league home for the Monarchs. With that frustration and the financial challenges of maintaining a team during the depths of the Depression, it was clear, according to the *Kansas City Call,* that "[o]wner Wilkinson of the Monarchs has stayed in baseball during these stressing times for the sake of his men who have played for him, during the more prosperous years."[104] In January 1934, the Monarchs' owner had optimistically announced that, regardless of whether they associated with a league again, the Kaysees would train in Texas and barnstorm as far north as Seattle, Portland, Tacoma, Walla Walla, and Vancouver, where clubs had already been contacted.

Members of the 1934 Kansas City Monarchs included (standing, from left)—Quincy Gilmore, T. J. Young, George Giles, "Turkey" Stearnes, Frank Duncan, Moocha Harris, Carroll "Dink" Mothell, "Cool Papa" Bell, Newt Allen, Willie Wells, J. L. Wilkinson; and (kneeling, from left)—Chet Brewer, Newt Joseph, "Bullet Joe" Rogan, Charles Beverly. The team barnstormed all the way to the Pacific Northwest and rushed back to Denver to be the first all-black team to be allowed to participate in the prestigious *Denver Post* Tournament (Kansas State Historical Society).

In mid–April Wilkinson filled in his ambitious plans for the 1934 season. He told the *Call* that within the next ten days he intended to sign "some of the best known players in the country to play for the Monarchs." The schedule would begin on April 29, with barnstorming games in the south, a home opener on May 10, then a tour through western Canada to Vancouver and a return through the Pacific Northwest.

Wilkinson also said that for the first time, the Monarchs had been invited to play in the annual *Denver Post* tournament, where the first prize was $7,500. According to the Monarchs' owner, the team would also have a working agreement with both the Southern and Negro National Leagues. After the season the plan was for the Monarchs to journey to South America for games in Argentina and the Canal Zone, then return north, playing games in Old Mexico along the way.[105]

In an Associated Negro Press (ANP) release published in the *Call*, Dan Burley expressed regret that "J. L. Wilkerson [sic], owner of the Monarchs for years had his famous team in the old Negro National League, [but] can't be inveigled into the [new Negro National League]." However, Burley understood "[Wilkinson] sees ... the fans will pay for baseball if they see the right kind of opposition whether the bugaboo of league activity is stuck on it or not."[106]

In three Ford touring cars, the Monarchs embarked in July 1934 on a barnstorming tour taking them into the South, then up to the Dakotas, into Canada, and across the Pacific Northwest. They played more games in 1934 in Winnipeg, Canada (eight) than they did at home in Kansas City (four). The tour was clearly a success, with games against Grover Cleveland Alexander's Original House of David team drawing huge crowds. For example, "[i]n Spokane, Washington 4,500 packed in to see the crack Kansas City Monarchs traveling team beat [the House of David] 4–0," on July 19.[107] The Kaysees had shut out the bearded players the day before in Walla Walla. "Babe" Didrikson started the game on the mound for the House of David. She singled and stole second in her only at-bat. On the evening of July 28, 1934, the largest crowd for any event in ten years in Regina, Canada (3,100) watched an exciting 1–0 Monarchs victory over the House of David. That afternoon the Monarchs had beaten Moose Jaw before another banner group of spectators.[108]

Tragically, on August 10, 1934, Lem "Hawk" Hawkins, first baseman for the Monarchs from 1923–1927, was killed in a robbery attempt. He had turned to crime after his professional baseball career ended in 1930.[109]

In August 1934, the Monarchs became the first black team allowed to play in the popular *Denver Post* Tournament, at least in part as a result of a spirited campaign by the black press.[110] African American teams had been banned during the tournament's first 19 years. In the meantime it had become famous as "the biggest sporting event of the year in the Rocky Mountain area," and "the little world series of the west."

Baseball historians have pointed out that participation by black teams in the *Denver Post* Tournament was a significant step on the path toward the goal of integration of organized baseball. In addition to the Monarchs, another black team, the Denver White Elephants, was also allowed into the tournament in 1934. The Monarchs had to make a hurried, thousand-mile trip by car from Canada to reach Denver in time for the tournament, but they were there and ready on August 1.

In an effort to improve their chances in the *Denver Post* Tournament, after conferring with Monarchs manager Sam Crawford, J. L. Wilkinson leased some of the new NNL's top talent, including the American Giants' "Turkey" Stearnes and Willie Foster, as well as Sam Bankhead from the Nashville Elite Giants. The Monarchs' owner had already recruited his old stalwart, now 42-year-old John Donaldson, for the Western barnstorming tour.

In preparing to play in the tournament, the Monarchs collaborated with Ray Doan, the publicity manager of the House of David team, which had also been invited. Likely encouraged by Wilkinson, Doan rented for the House of David team (still managed by 47-year-old Grover Cleveland Alexander) "Satchel" Paige from Gus Greenlee's Pittsburgh Crawfords, along with Paige's personal catcher, William "Cy" Perkins. According to Timothy Gay, Doan, a fellow Iowan, had cultivated a close working relationship with Wilkinson, and, it should be added, Monarchs co-owner Tom Baird. Gay has written that the barnstorming arrangement was for Wilkinson to "serve as producer, providing resources and matériel; Ray, the director, would do the hard work. Ray did such an effective job promoting the House of David that the papers often called them 'Doan's Davidites.'"

In language typical of the times, the *Denver Post* described the Kansas City players and other Blacks in the tournament stereotypically. For example, Sam Crawford was "King Fish," referring to the white actor who portrayed a black in the popular *Amos 'n' Andy* radio show. Satchel Paige pitched "black magic" and was "The Chocolate Whizbang." Paige, in a fake red beard, blew away the House of David's opposition. His showmanship was on display as he warmed up pitching from a chair.

In first round play, on August 1, the Monarchs, showing no weariness from their long car ride from Canada, crushed the Greeley, Colorado, Advertisers, 12–1. Chet Brewer struck out 19, and John Donaldson was four-for-four at the plate. The Monarchs also won their second and third games.

In what turned out to be the decisive contest of the 1934 *Denver Post* Tournament on Friday, August 10, the Monarchs faced the Original House of David. Chet Brewer pitched well, but the day belonged to Satchel Paige. He scattered eight hits and struck out 12 in a narrow 2–1 House of David victory, witnessed by a crowd of over 11,000, the largest in the history of the tournament. Thousands more were turned away. The *Call* reported, "[t]he Bearded Beauties banked everything on Satchel, and the colored Whizbang did not disappoint." The House of David club tallied the winning run in the eighth inning when a collision at the plate resulted in Monarchs catcher Frank Duncan dropping the ball. After Paige retired the Monarchs in order in the ninth, "fans rushed helter skelter on the field to pound [Paige] on the back and subject him to more punishment than he received at any time from the Monarchs."

The Monarchs won their fifth game, a 5–4 squeaker over the Enid, Oklahoma, Eason Oilers, with Willie Foster making his first appearance. On August 13 the Monarchs lost again in their sixth and final game to the House of David, 2–0, before another huge crowd of 8,200. Alexander held Paige in reserve in the event a tiebreaker was needed. The lanky hurler had won three games, striking out 44 batters in 28 innings during the tournament. The House of David walked away with the $7,500 winners' share. The second-place Monarchs pocketed $4,800.

Before the 1934 *Denver Post* Tournament, there was speculation that white teams from Oklahoma would not play black teams, but given the choice between competing and defaulting, they opted to stay. However, the tournament committee ruled that henceforth only one black team would be allowed each year, and teams had to be all black or all white, not integrated. In 1936 an NNL All-Star team would win all of its seven games in the tournament, with Paige fanning 18 in the final game against another Enid, Oklahoma team. In 1939 the Ethiopian Clowns would take third. They won the tournament in 1941.

J. L. Wilkinson and Ray Doan also collaborated to promote an appearance of the Monarchs and the Original House of David in Wichita shortly after the 1934 *Denver Post* Tournament. Doan released a statement saying, "[w]e have the best ball club this season ... and feel certain of beating them again in Wichita." Wilkinson declared, "[m]y colored boys have been gunning for the Davids ever since we were beaten out of the *Denver Post* tournament championship. There was only one thing for me to do to please the boys, and that was to arrange another game with the Davids." He pointed out that the Monarchs had "won 30 games and lost but one in Wichita in the past eleven years." Quoted in the same article, Grover Cleveland Alexander contributed to the pre-game hype by claiming, "[t]he Monarchs used to have the best ball club but they don't now There's not a team in the country that can beat us in a series of games."[111] The promotional build-up paid off. The two teams took the field before a capacity crowd of over 8,000, and the Monarchs prevailed, 8–5. They returned to Wichita in late September and the Monarchs edged the bearded ballplayers once again, 7–6.

The Monarchs beat the white Western League Omaha Packers on Friday, August 31, 1934, 7–1, before a record-breaking crowd in Omaha.[112] The Kaysees continued barnstorming, including a series with the Homestead Grays, and then returned to Kansas City to play the Original House of David yet again, on September 26 and the Pittsburgh

Crawfords (and Satchel Paige) on September 30. "Babe" Didrikson was scheduled to pitch for the House of David, and the game was to be followed by two innings of donkey baseball. However, Didrikson did not show up, there was no mention of donkeys in the game write-up, and the game against the Crawfords was apparently cancelled.[113]

On Sunday, October 7, the Monarchs allowed only four hits and shut out a big league all-star team, 11–0, in Jamestown, ND, before 2,000 enthusiastic fans. Future Hall of Famer Jimmie Foxx of the Philadelphia Athletics was the best-known major leaguer among the all-stars. Chet Brewer held the major leaguers hitless through six innings. In the same edition, the *Call* endorsed Jackson County Judge Harry S Truman in the 1934 U.S. Senate race.[114] Lifelong Republican J. L. Wilkinson likely did not agree. His grandchildren remember their grandfather telling them he never had much use for Truman.

In the immediate aftermath of the St. Louis Cardinals' "Gashouse Gang" win over the Detroit Tigers in the 1934 World Series, the Monarchs met Cards pitchers Jay Hanna "Dizzy" Dean (1910–1974) and Paul "Daffy" Dean (1912–1981) and their all-star team in a post-season series (October 10–22). It would be called the Dizzy and Daffy Tour.[115] Besides the Dean brothers, most of the players on the white team were semi-pro pickups. Once again Ray Doan teamed up with J. L. Wilkinson to promote the series. Instead of the small-town circuit the Monarchs typically followed, the pair decided to focus on bigger markets, scheduling games in Oklahoma City, Wichita, Kansas City, Des Moines, Chicago, and Milwaukee.

The Dean All-Stars flew on chartered planes throughout the tournament, while the Monarchs traveled in Ford cars pulling trailers. Dizzy and Paul flew to Oklahoma City to begin the tour with a game against the Monarchs. Newt Allen told John Holway, "[w]e had so many people the grandstand wouldn't hold them. The ball game quit in the fifth inning—had to, people were all out in the outfield, and every inning they would press closer to try to see Dizzy." At least a half-dozen fights, including one in the press box, broke out as people elbowed for space. The huge crowd rendered Jim Crow segregation, common in Oklahoma at the time, impossible.

One of Wilkinson's skills was defusing the racial tensions that sometimes boiled over when the Monarchs played white teams. Quincy Trouppe, who played with the Monarchs in 1932 and 1934–1936, recalled a situation similar to the one that occurred in Oklahoma City: "I think having a white owner was the only thing that kept a real free-for-all from busting loose, involving everybody."

The Monarchs were victorious in the majority of the games played, but the real winner in the 1934 Dizzy and Daffy tour was the gate. 64,500 paid to see the contests. According to Dizzy, he and Paul received $14,000. This amount may reflect Dizzy's propensity to exaggerate. A suit filed against him by the Cardinals' treasurer, Bill DeWitt, who claimed to be Dean's manager, named $6,000 as Dean's profit. According to Dick Wilkinson, whatever he cleared, "Dean said he made more money playing exhibitions with Dad than he did playing the World Series." Hilton Smith told John Holway that, unlike some major leaguers, Dizzy Dean enjoyed playing exhibition games against Negro Leagues players. However, like the travel arrangements, the earnings were not equal. The Monarchs players received considerably less than the Dean All-Stars.

By 1934, in the depths of the Depression, black and white promoters were turning to any gimmicks they could dream up to boost attendance. In addition to the bearded House of David, sometimes featuring donkey ball and celebrities like "Babe" Didrikson, there were a number of traveling teams offering various forms of entertainment to

One of the most successful barnstorming tours J. L. Wilkinson and Tom Baird staged with white all-star teams was the so-called "Dizzy and Daffy" Tour, featuring Jerome "Dizzy" Dean and his brother Paul "Daffy" Dean. The two were members of the famed St. Louis Cardinals "Gashouse Gang," and the tour occurred in the aftermath of their winning the 1934 World Series. Shown here standing in front of the chartered plane on which the Dean All-Stars flew during the tour are, from the left, Wilkinson, Dizzy Dean and his wife Patricia, Paul Dean, and Baird (Kenneth Spencer Research Library, University of Kansas Libraries).

supplement the games: the Detroit Clowns, the Jewish Clowns, Jim Thorpe's Indians, the goateed Kentucky Colonels (replete in coveralls and straw hats), and the similarly dressed Hillbillies.

Comedic routines were common in the early years of black baseball, but had become relatively rare by the 1920s. However, inspired by the success of white novelty teams like the House of David, black promoter Charlie Henry fielded a team called the Zulu Cannibal Giants, with players in grass skirts, headdresses, and war paint. Playing to the worst white stereotypes, players staged "fights" with spears and shields and "crap games" with loaded dice. The most famous black novelty team, the Ethiopian Clowns (see Chapter 8), formed in 1935 or 1936 in Miami.[116]

According to Dick Wilkinson, in yet another promotional venture, his father sponsored the first National Football League game in Kansas City. It may have been a Washington Redskins exhibition game in 1934.[117] Whenever it was held, according to Dick, the football game was a financial flop. His father had to put up a $30,000 guarantee and made only $20,000.[118] Wilkinson's partner Tom Baird did not fare better in promoting professional football. In 1952 he reported losing $2,400 on a game between the Redskins and Chicago Bears at Blues Stadium in Kansas City.[119]

The Monarchs continued their winning ways in 1935, even though a number of their stars jumped to other teams. In addition, Carroll "Dink" Mothell retired due to a shoulder injury and Hurley McNair because of age.

In his final year as Monarchs manager, Sam Crawford did still have Chet Brewer, Charlie Beverly, and Andy Cooper, three of the best strikeout pitchers in the game. Wilkinson brought in several new players from the Monroe, Louisiana Monarchs: Willard Brown, Eldridge E. "Chili" Mayweather, and pitcher Floyd Kranson. Others added were Bob Madison and speedster Henry Milton, another Wiley College product. Milton joined Eddie "Pee Wee" Dwight in the outfield, giving the Monarchs two of the fastest runners in baseball. Wilkinson had traveled to Willard Brown's home in Shreveport, Louisiana, and offered him $250, a salary of $125 a month, and one-dollar-a-day meal money to sign with the Monarchs. Brown was making only $10 a week, "so you know I'm going to take that," he said.[120]

Another addition to the 1935 team was Quincy Trouppe, who briefly rejoined the Monarchs after a year in Bismarck, North Dakota. Wilkinson had given him an advance over the winter, which Trouppe had used to buy a new Ford.

Spring training in 1935 was held at Wiley College in Marshall, Texas. In a phone interview with the *Kansas City Call*, Wilkinson said he "was trying to give the KC fans a first class hustling ball club." The *Call* noted, "[t]hat has been his reputation. The Monarchs have been second to none. He expects to keep them as such."[121] After an exhibition tour through Oklahoma and Kansas, the Kaysees returned to Kansas City. They played a few games at home against their standbys, Grover Cleveland Alexander's Original House of David, and a team billed as the Chinese All-Stars from Honolulu. General admission was down to 40 cents.[122] The Monarchs played only nine home games in 1935, drawing a total attendance of just 18,000. On the road they played 153 more games and won 144 for the season.[123]

In 1935 Wilkinson purchased two new trailers, with bunks for eight, a shower, and a small kitchen to be pulled by the team's cars. Wilkinson told the *Springfield News Leader* they were "large rooms on wheels which include two lower and two upper berths, hot and cold running water, plenty of closet space for suits, shoes, and hats, wash basins, and even a shower." With a travel allowance of $1 a day, Monarchs players saved money by fixing their own meager meals. To pack in the most games, the team often traveled through the night, with the players sleeping in the trailers.[124]

Like other black teams, the Monarchs carried the minimum number of players possible. The three or four pitchers were expected to stay in for the entire game, and with seven to ten games a week, they got very little rest. Although outlawed in the white major leagues, pitchers in the Negro Leagues and on all black teams still threw an assortment of "doctored" balls—spitballs, emery balls, cut balls, mud balls and shine balls. Wilkinson instructed his players not to complain when umpires employed by the hometown teams made bad calls. He told them to hit whatever was close enough to reach. While white baseball in the 1930s emphasized home run hitting, black ball "featured tight pitching duels, bunts, sacrifices, hit-and-run plays, and daring base stealing."[125]

Some of the Monarchs' best games in 1935 were played against the mixed-race team in Bismarck, North Dakota, owned by a local car dealer, Neil Churchill. The main attraction for the Churchills was Satchel Paige, who was pitching masterfully. Paige was not the only outstanding player on the Bismarck team, which also featured Quincy Trouppe, Hilton Smith, Barney Morris, Ted "Double Duty" Radcliffe, and Red Haley. Wilkinson had let Trouppe return to Bismarck in June to catch Satchel Paige, saying he would rather give him his release than carry a dissatisfied ball player.[126]

According to Hilton Smith, when he played for Bismarck, there were seven whites and seven black players.[127] The Monarchs and Churchills first met on June 20, 1935, in Winnipeg with Paige and Brewer locked in a scoreless pitchers' duel. The game was called after nine innings due to darkness. Paige gave the fans a treat, striking out 17. Brewer fanned 13.[128]

The Monarchs also once again played a number of games during their 1935 schedule on the road against the ever-popular Original House of David. After nearly two months barnstorming all the way to Saskatoon and Calgary, Canada, and through the Pacific Northwest, the Monarchs returned to Kansas City on August 25, 1935, to face Alexander's House of David yet again.

In early September, after striking out 359 with Bismarck, Satchel Paige joined the Monarchs (for a $500 fee) and continued to dominate hitters.[129] For the year he notched at least 500 strikeouts. On September 27 Paige helped Wilkinson continue a streak of never having lost a game in Omaha in more than 20 years—five with All Nations and 15 with the Monarchs.[130]

In mid–September Wilkinson "loaned" Paige back to Neil Churchill and his Bismarck team for the National Semi-pro Tournament in Wichita.[131]

In August 1935, the *Kansas City Call* reported that the NAACP was trying to persuade Negro athletes not to participate in the 1936 Olympic games in Germany. The NAACP leaders called on the American Olympic committee to withdraw the entire U.S. team because the games were being hosted by a country "founded officially upon suppression of religious, political, and social liberty, and upon terror and brutality."[132]

In an effort to re-create their success of the previous year, in 1935 Dizzy and Paul Dean organized another all-star team and scheduled 20 games, beginning with three against the Monarchs. On Sunday, October 6, in Kansas City, Satchel Paige pitched a complete game, fanning 11 and allowing only three hits, but lost the contest, 1–0. Dizzy Dean pitched one inning and drove in the winning run with a sacrifice fly. Cold weather held paid attendance down to 2,000.[133]

The Monarchs got their revenge on October 13, beating an all-star major league team with three players from the world champion Detroit Tigers (Charlie Gehringer, Tommy Bridges, and "Schoolboy" Rowe) plus Joe Bowman of the Phillies. Paige and Beverly combined for a 6–0 win before a Muehlebach Field crowd of 3,000.

The "Paige effect" was already evident. When Rowe and his All-Stars and the Monarchs traveled to St. Joseph the next day, the 2,000 in the stands rebelled when Andy Cooper was announced as the Kansas City hurler instead of the anticipated Paige. Wilkinson had not yet fully grasped the significance of the fans' fixation on Paige. He told a reporter, "I didn't think they wanted to see Paige. I thought they came out to see the Deans."[134]

At a game in Omaha, many blacks were in the crowd of 5,500, chanting, "You can't beat the Monarchs in Omaha."[135] The next year the Ku Klux Klan burned down the stadium.[136]

Andy "Lefty" Cooper (1898–1941), who had graduated from Paul Quinn College in Waco, Texas, assumed the player-manager's role for the Monarchs in 1936. T. J. Young and Chet Brewer left for the New York Cubans, giving the Monarchs a rebuilding challenge once more. Wilkinson tried to sign Satchel Paige, but said he "couldn't afford to pay him $500 a month, which is what he'll get at Bismarck, North Dakota."[137] One of the new players the Monarchs' owner did ink was third baseman Andrew "Pat" Patterson, who had been a track and baseball star at Wiley College. Patterson joined Henry Milton and Leroy Taylor from Wiley. Woodrow "Lefty" Wilson and Floyd Kranson were Piney Woods College products. Two important, late-season additions were Hilton Smith and Quincy Trouppe from the Bismarck Churchills.

Hilton Smith (1907–1983) said J. L. Wilkinson called him during the 1936 season, while he was playing for the Bismarck semi-pro team, and asked him if he would be willing to finish the season with the Monarchs. Smith agreed and was paid $175 a month. He would become one of the best pitchers in Monarchs history. Monte Irvin said of Smith, "[h]e had one of the finest curveballs I ever had the displeasure to try and hit. His curveball fell of the table. Sometimes you knew where it would be coming from, but you still couldn't hit it because it was that sharp." Buck O'Neil claimed Smith actually had three or four curveballs, including a big one and a little one. Smith himself told Joe Posnanski "he could make a ball curve a dozen different ways—up and down, side to side, whatever he wanted."[138] In 1938 Smith pitched a perfect game against the Chicago American Giants.

After Satchel Paige joined Smith on the Monarchs in the early 1940s, the two often pitched in tandem, with Paige starting and Smith relieving and finishing the game. Smith went 129–28 over a six-year period. He was also an excellent hitter, often playing the outfield when he wasn't pitching.

Hilton Smith had this to say about the Monarchs owner: "Wilkinson demanded that Monarchs wear suits, ties, be clean, be of good moral character. Very shrewd, quite a baseball man. Everybody, *everybody* who played ball loved Wilkinson. He lost money and made money, finished with a lot of money. One year he made more than [the] government allowed; took us off salary and put us on percentage because the government was going to take it all."

Smith also said that Wilkinson never sent the team back to a town if the team had had any trouble there. Not only was he good at running the team as a business, the Monarchs owner, Smith said, "had played a little semi-pro ball himself and he really knew baseball." Smith credited Wilkinson with teaching him how to improve his curveball by throwing it harder, telling him, "Look, you've got everything, but use your wrist a little more, see if you can't get a little more hop on your ball." The Monarchs pitcher said he "took him at his word, and sure enough it worked."[139]

The son of a teacher and a graduate of Prairie View A&M University, Hilton Smith was, like J. L. Wilkinson, a quiet man. The two would remain good friends long beyond their days with the Monarchs. After his last year with the Monarchs in 1948, Smith became a schoolteacher, then a foreman at a steel plant. Like Buck O'Neil he also was a scout for the Chicago Cubs. He was posthumously inducted into the National Baseball Hall of Fame in 2001.

Once again the Monarchs were almost exclusively a road club in 1936, playing only nine games in Kansas City. The team clocked more miles in a month than many American and National League teams did in a season.

The Monarchs began the 1936 season on Easter Sunday, April 12, with a game at Muehlebach Field against Schneider Jewelers, an outstanding white semi-pro team from Kansas City, Kansas.[140]

On Friday, May 8, the Monarchs lost at home to another white team, the Omaha Robin Hoods of the Western League, 13–9. On May 17 they fell to the Israelite House of David, 3–1. The next Sunday at Muehlebach Field, in a sea of mud under threatening skies, the 2,000 fans, who paid only 40 cents for a grandstand seat or 25 cents more for a box seat, saw the Monarchs beat their archrivals, the American Giants, 10–8.[141]

On Monday night, May 25, 1936, the Monarchs departed Kansas City to barnstorm in Illinois, Wisconsin, North Dakota, Minnesota, and Nebraska. Some of the games were against semi-pro teams, others with white minor league clubs. Wilkinson said the Monarchs would not likely return home until July because of the difficulty convincing other teams to travel all the way to Kansas City.[142] By July 4 the Monarchs had played in Wyoming and Montana and were in Spokane, Washington, for a doubleheader. Instead of returning to Kansas City in July, they crossed the border into Canada to play games in Saskatchewan, then barnstormed through the northern Midwest as they wound their way south.[143]

After three months on the road during the summer of 1936, the Monarchs finally returned to Kansas City to play the Chicago American Giants on August 30. A crowd of 3,000 was on hand as the Monarchs took both ends of a doubleheader, 10–4 and 5–4. The next day they mauled the Chicagoans, 14–0, before a Ladies Night crowd. The American Giants remained in Kansas City to play a doubleheader on Labor Day, but only 500 showed up. It was the lowest attendance in years for a Monarchs-American Giants series.[144]

On September 20 the Monarchs faced off at Muehlebach Field against the NNL All-Stars, who had won the 1936 *Denver Post* tournament.[145] In the final game of the season, another major league all-star team, with players from the Senators, Indians, Dodgers and Phillies, stopped in Kansas City to play the Monarchs on Sunday, October 4. The Monarchs shut out the big leaguers, 4–0.[146]

On their barnstorming tours over the years, the Monarchs typically experienced little racial discrimination from other teams, in part because prejudiced players refused to take the field against them. However, they did receive constant racial taunts from white fans. Sometimes it was too much. In one game "Pat" Patterson went into the stands and punched a man who was hurling racial insults at him. J. L. Wilkinson fined him $50 and Patterson agreed, saying, "[Wilkie] was right for fining me. He explained to me ... you just don't bite the hand that feeds you."[147]

After Eddie Dwight retired as a player in 1936, he did publicity work for the Monarchs. Dwight also accompanied Wilkinson on barnstorming trips. Before the team had buses, Dwight would ride with Wilkinson in the front seat of one of the two big touring cars. According to Dwight's wife, Georgia, the team did encounter prejudice, even in Northern states. She told Janet Bruce Vaughn in 1978 that when Wilkinson learned how bad the discrimination was, he bought two buses so the Monarchs would not have to sleep in rooming houses or hotels any longer. She said the Monarchs' owner also minimized the racial hostility by developing a circuit of friendly communities to which the Monarchs returned year after year.[148]

Chapter 6

Joining the Negro American League (1937–1938)

After sustaining the Kansas City Monarchs through the six roughest years of the Great Depression as an independent barnstorming team, by late 1936 J. L. Wilkinson was ready to try league affiliation again. Showing his willingness to adapt to changing circumstances, the Monarchs' owner took the lead in the organization of the Negro American League (NAL), which began play in 1937. As they had in the first NNL, the Monarchs flourished in the new league, winning NAL pennants in 1937, 1939, 1940, 1941, 1942, 1946, 1953, and 1957, as well as their second Negro Leagues World Series championship in 1942.

The NAL originally featured an alignment of Midwestern and Southern franchises strikingly similar to the first NNL, including, in addition to the Monarchs, the Chicago American Giants, Detroit Stars, Cincinnati Tigers, St. Louis Stars, Indianapolis Athletics, Birmingham Black Barons, and Memphis Red Sox. The Indianapolis franchise changed its name back to the A.B.C.'s in 1938 and left the league the next year. Additions to the NAL during its tenure included the Jacksonville Red Caps and Atlanta Black Crackers for the 1938 season; the Cleveland Bears (later the Buckeyes) for the 1939 campaign; and the Cincinnati-Indianapolis Clowns, who entered the league in 1940 and remained until the franchise folded in 1962. When the second NNL ceased operation in 1948, the Baltimore Black Sox, Philadelphia Stars, Newark Eagles and New York Cubans joined the NAL for the 1949 season.

Chosen to head the NAL was Major Robert R. Jackson, a former postal employee active in Republican politics in Chicago. J. L. Wilkinson was elected to serve as NAL secretary. Abe Saperstein was the official NAL booking agent, but, according to some sources, was later replaced by Monarchs co-owner Tom Baird.[1] A nagging problem in the NAL would be, as it was at times in the original NNL, the superiority of two teams—the Monarchs and American Giants—over the other clubs.

With the NAL and the second NNL there were now two fully functioning black leagues for the first time since 1929. Because the NNL's teams were located in the East and the NAL clubs in the West and South, there was at first little friction over geographical boundaries between the two leagues. In addition, soon after the NAL formed, a crisis involving their own players diverted the attention of NNL owners from potential conflict with the NAL.

In April 1937, former New York Cuban player and future Hall of Famer Martin

Dihigo, who had been hired by the *Ciudad Trujillo* ("Trujillo City") team in the Dominican Republic, came north with instructions to recruit Satchel Paige. The owner of *Ciudad Trujillo*, Dominican dictator Rafael Trujillo, was intent on winning the Caribbean nation's league championship and believed the lanky hurler was the key to success. With Paige signed, other NNL stars, including "Cool Papa" Bell, Sammy Bankhead, and Josh Gibson, were enticed to join him. A total of 14 NNL players left their teams for a two-month season at salaries ranging from $1,500 to at least $3,000 for Paige. Paige said the opportunities extended to black players in the Dominican Republic were equal to those of white players in the major leagues.

Ciudad Trujillo won their league's championship after a tough seven-game series with San Pedro de Macoris. The fanciful story that Paige and his teammates were held in jail cells to keep them out of trouble and were told they must "win or die" has entered baseball folklore.[2] Whatever the truth of that tale, when the Dominican championship series ended, Paige and his compatriots flew back to the United States as soon as they could.[3]

Despite earlier failures to enforce penalties on players who jumped teams, NNL officials, led by league president Gus Greenlee, did make a concerted effort to impose a ban on Satchel Paige and six other players who had left their NNL teams for the Dominican Republic. The only exception was Josh Gibson, who had received permission from the Homestead Grays to play abroad.[4] In a sign of cooperation between the two black leagues, an agreement between NNL and NAL owners stipulated that the banned players would not be allowed to play for or against NAL teams. "When they return to the States they will have nowhere to play," Greenlee stated.[5]

However, to the owners' chagrin, promoter Ray Doan booked a Western tour for the "Santo Domingo All-Stars," composed of Paige and other players who had jumped to the Dominican teams. They also entered and won the annual *Denver Post* Tournament (and $5,179 in prize money) as the Negro All-Stars in August 1937.[6] When the All-Stars and Monarchs played in Kansas City on August 29, 1937, the game attracted the largest crowd of the season.[7] In the end, the NNL fined Paige and the other offenders only a week's pay. Defections to the Caribbean and Latin America, especially to Mexico, would continue to plague black teams and leagues for years to come.

The 1937 NAL pre-season began for the Kansas City Monarchs with several weeks of spring training in Shreveport, Louisiana, and a series of games in Mexico.[8] Andy Cooper was the 1937 Monarchs manager. Pitcher Chet Brewer was among those who defected to the Dominican Republic, but his shoes were more than filled with the addition of Hilton Smith. Remarkably, 44-year-old "Bullet Joe" Rogan remained on the team. Other rising Monarchs stars were first baseman Eldridge "Ed" Mayweather, leadoff speedster Henry Milton, and shortstop turned outfielder Willard Brown.

In many contests both at home and on the road, Brown (1915–1996), who would replace Josh Gibson as the premier home run hitter in black ball, was the major draw. For example, at Muehlebach Field in 1937 he hit a home run immediately after the public address announcer said that a jeweler on 18th Street would give a diamond ring to the first player to hit a four-bagger. Brown would be known as Home Run, Willie, and, most often, *Ese Hombre* ("That Man" in Spanish). He so often hit monster home runs when playing in Latin America that fans would say when he came to the plate, "Here comes *Ese Hombre*." Other Monarchs called him Sunny, because they knew Brown loved sunny days.[9] He would be inducted into the National Baseball Hall of Fame in 2006, in the same class as J. L. Wilkinson.

The Monarchs Boosters went all-out for Opening Day of the 1937 NAL season in Kansas City on May 15. Before the game against the American Giants, more than 12,000 fans were treated to a gala with "two fifty-piece bands, a contingent of high school cadets, the VFW, and a parade of 50 decorated cars."[10] The Monarchs lost to the American Giants and their ace, Willie Foster, in the opener, 2–0, but on the 16th Hilton Smith pitched a no-hit, no-run game with 5,000 fans cheering him on.[11] The next week the Monarchs took three of four from the Cincinnati Tigers. Games during the week were typically played under the Monarchs' lighting system. On the Monday night of the series with the Tigers, the game had to be shortened when rain affected the lights.[12] The Monarchs closed their first home stand May 29–31, winning three of four against the Birmingham Black Barons.[13]

After a two-week road trip, the Monarchs returned home on the weekend of June 18, to face the St. Louis Stars. To spark fan interest, Wilkinson arranged for fan giveaways—including a premium 14-pound turkey at the Ladies' Day game. Despite the promotion and free admission for women, the crowd was sparse.[14]

There were glitches in the operation of the new league, at least one involving J. L. Wilkinson in his role as the first NAL secretary. The *Kansas City Call* complained that while the new NNL was sending in regular updates on the league's standings, Wilkinson was not able to get the information from team owners to forward to the *Call* and other papers. "Many have been slinking away to see major league games in preference to their own men in action," the *Call* noted. "Those who pay to go through the turnstiles have a right to know about where their team stands in the percentage column." Unless the club owners woke up, the league would soon find itself in financial difficulties, the paper warned.[15]

By winning three of five from the American Giants in the Windy City over the Fourth of July holiday, the Monarchs edged out the Chicagoans in the first half 1937 NNL pennant race.[16] A few weeks later, before the largest crowd of the season at Muehlebach Field, the Monarchs won two of three from the Chicago team. Newt Allen, Willard Brown, Frank Duncan, Andy Cooper and Hilton Smith made the lineup for the West's entry in the East-West Game, played in Chicago on August 8.[17]

In the middle of the 1937 season, infielder Byron "Mex" Johnson, who had a degree in education from Wiley College, was teaching high school in Little Rock when Wilkinson sent him a round-trip train ticket. When Johnson arrived in Kansas City during a game, Wilkinson came down to the field to say, "I know you've been riding most of the night, Johnson, but do you feel like going out and trying out? This is a good time." "Mex" went in and turned a double play to the roar of the fans.[18]

Despite his auspicious start, Johnson almost didn't make it with the Monarchs because he couldn't hit curveballs. Fortunately for "Mex," "Bullet Joe" Rogan, who was always ready to help a rookie, worked with him until he was comfortable with the pitch. The next year Johnson was the starting shortstop in the East-West game.

The American Giants were the second-half NAL pennant winners. The Monarchs met their rivals in a best-of-seven playoff series to determine the league championship. On Sunday, September 12, in Chicago, they played a thrilling 17-inning game marked by five double plays. It ended in a 2–2 tie when the game was called due to darkness. The next night, in Milwaukee, American Giants manager Jim Taylor protested the game because of a call at home and pulled his team. Reached by phone, NAL President Jackson ordered the game resumed the next night, and the Monarchs scored three runs in the

6. Joining the Negro American League (1937–1938)

eighth inning for the win. In the end the Monarchs took the series, 4–1, with the one tie, to become the first Negro American League champions.[19]

After winning the playoffs, the Monarchs resumed barnstorming in Kansas against a team made up of white players from the Kansas City Blues and other American Association teams.[20] Wilkinson arranged a 60–40 winners/losers split of the gate for each game. In a matchup under the Monarchs' portable lights in Larned, Kansas, Willard Brown rocketed a shot that would have been a homer except for hitting one of the lighting wires and bouncing back onto the field.

After the series with the American Association team, the Monarchs participated in another exhibition tour with an all-star white professional team. The promoters for both tours were J. L. Wilkinson, Tom Baird, and Ray Doan. The second club headlined 18-year-old Cleveland Indians pitching sensation Bob Feller, who was joined by a talented group of major leaguers, including Lon Warneke, Lou Fette, Johnny Mize, and Vince DiMaggio. Wilkinson and Baird made sure most of their best Monarchs players would be available for the games with the major leaguers in Iowa, Kansas, and Oklahoma. They included Andy Cooper, Frank Duncan, Slug Cornelius, Hilton Smith, Newt Allen, Ted Strong, "Pee Wee" Dwight, Henry Milton, Willard Brown, and "Bullet Joe" Rogan.

The third game, played in Des Moines on October 8, was the first in which Bob Feller pitched. He struck out five Monarchs in two innings, and the major leaguers won, 1–0. At Manhattan, Kansas, on the chilly evening of October 9, about 1,800 people showed up to watch the Monarchs fall, 6–3. As he did in other games in the series, Lon Warneke, when not pitching, kidded the players, crowd, and umpires, often making quips over the public address system.

In the wake of the Monarchs' success over the years against all-star major league squads, an uncharacteristically boastful Wilkinson told the *Wichita Eagle* his team could compete with the New York Giants or Yankees, the two teams in the 1937 white major leagues' World Series.[21] The Monarchs' owner pointed out, "[w]e've been very fortunate in Wichita, having won 39 victories in 42 games here in 13 years. Right now we have a great team to cope with the major leaguers. The Monarchs are desirous to see just what they can do against such pitchers as Feller and Fette." That night 2,000 spectators paid to watch the Monarchs win, 5–4, despite a home run by Feller in the ninth.

Feller pitched only one inning of the last game in the series at Oklahoma City, because he had to catch a flight to the West Coast, where another lucrative tour and a screen test for a possible motion picture role awaited him. The Monarchs humiliated the major leaguers, 10–0, pounding out 16 hits, and as the game ended, the handful of fans still in the stands booed lustily. Hilton Smith went the distance and held the major leaguers to only three hits. The *Daily Oklahoman* headlined its coverage of the game the next day, "Negroes Win Farce."[22]

By the end of the 1937 season, black professional baseball desperately needed reform. The signs were declining attendance and waning support of teams, a lack of organization, increasing vulnerability to player raids by foreign teams, and competition for the support of African American sporting fans from athletes like boxer Joe Louis.[23] These problems would continue to plague the Negro Leagues in years to come.

Veteran columnist Fay Young, writing in the *Chicago Defender* after the 1937 season, commented on the decline in black attendance. He wrote that many fans now had automobiles and drove into the country rather than going to ball games. Others had acquired radios and stayed home. However, Young pointed out, "it is a sad state of affairs [in

Chicago] when such a club as the Monarchs can draw but 5,000 on a Sunday—and at a double header at that." Attempts to stimulate attendance—Ladies' Day, free Saturday admission to boys under 16, season passes, even an automobile giveaway—had produced only modest results, Young noted.[24]

Reliance on appeals to race pride for support of teams had been crucial during the establishment of black leagues but was beginning to wear thin. Respected black poet and former NAACP secretary James Weldon Johnson warned that the concept was "a mighty shaky business foundation." All black businesses, including baseball clubs, Johnson said, must provide excellent quality and prompt service if they expect to succeed. In the highly regarded 1936 Carnegie-Myrdal study of black American life, black poet and scholar Sterling Brown had concluded: "Negro professional baseball is in need of much more capital, much more centralized organization instead of individualistic entrepreneurs."[25]

As sportswriter Russ Cowan noted, J. L. Wilkinson and other NAL owners could not just sit and watch money gush like oil from a newly opened well. An NAL owner had taken on, Cowan warned, "one of the toughest assignments in the field of sports. He must not only be a good business man, but he must also be an excellent promoter, a top publicity man, and one capable of spending long hours helping his manager select players for the team."[26]

When attempts at reform were made, they too often missed the mark. For example, Quincy Gilmore, who was still serving as the Monarchs' business manager and traveling secretary, proposed in early 1938 the formation of a national organization of Negro semi-pro, amateur, and traveling teams as a way of bringing more unity to black baseball. It was to be called the National Negro Semi-Pro and Amateur Baseball Association, and Gilmore would be its president. Q. J. was able to convince 176 representatives from teams in Missouri, Kansas, Nebraska, Iowa and Colorado to attend a planning meeting in Kansas City on March 6. More meetings were held, and several states put together schedules, but the scheme proved too elaborate and costly to implement fully.[27]

In 1937 Winfield Welch, player-manager of the black Shreveport, Louisiana, Acme Giants, signed a line-drive-hitting first baseman from Sarasota, Florida, named John "Buck" O'Neil.[28] Welch recognized that although O'Neil was not a power hitter, he "had instincts, intellect, and a savvy for hustle."

The young player was tearing the cover off the ball for the Acme Giants when first seen by J. L. Wilkinson and manager Andy Cooper during the Monarchs' 1937 spring training in Shreveport. Wilkinson approached O'Neil and, according to Buck, told him the Monarchs would like to sign him to play first base. There was only one problem. The Monarchs' current first baseman, Ed Mayweather, had broken his leg and Wilkinson felt he had to give the injured player a chance when he recovered. "But I'm going to send you over to Memphis to play with the Memphis Red Sox," O'Neil remembered the Monarchs' owner telling him. Welch agreed to the transfer, and O'Neil joined the Memphis team.

The situation with O'Neil was a classic example, Welch would later complain, of how "the mighty Kansas City Monarchs kept poaching his prime players." Welch said only later did he realize he had been duped when asked by Wilkinson to send O'Neil to the Red Sox. As soon as the Monarchs had first base open, Wilkinson "pulled O'Neil from Memphis and started him on his legendary career with the Monarchs." Welch always said he "never got a dime for filling Buck's pockets with quarters."[29]

In his autobiography, O'Neil marveled that Wilkinson "had the power to get other teams to do him favors like that."³⁰ Wilkinson traded Mayweather to St. Louis and O'Neil joined the Monarchs in 1938, signing for $100 a month, from which $1-a-day meal money was deducted. Even so, he said, "I was able to kick some money home." Ironically, the practice of signing a player, without compensating his team, would famously come back to haunt the Monarchs' owner in 1945 (see Chapter 9).

According to O'Neil, when he joined the Monarchs in 1938 the lineup was loaded. Ted Strong (1914–1978) was a lanky, switch-hitting shortstop with tremendous power. He would later switch to the outfield and went on to play for Abe Saperstein's Harlem Globetrotters basketball team. Also on the 1938 Monarchs were infielders "Packinghouse" Adams and Roosevelt "Indian Joe" Cox, who, because he could pass for white, often bought food for the team from restaurants that would not serve blacks. The veteran catcher, Frank Duncan, was, according to O'Neil, mean on the field and sweet off it. During the 1938 season Wilkinson traded Duncan to the American Giants, receiving Junius "Rainey" Bibbs in return. In the outfield were two of the fastest ballplayers O'Neil had ever seen, Bill Simms and Henry "Streak" Milton, and two of the strongest, "Turkey" Stearnes and Willard Brown.

The real strength of the Monarchs in 1938 was pitching. One sportswriter said the Monarchs' infield should be arrested for vagrancy because they mostly stood around doing nothing. The ace was O'Neil's good friend Hilton Smith, who had outstanding control, a fastball that moved, and an unrivalled curveball. He also had, according to O'Neil, "the guts of the devil." The other pitchers were Frank Bradley, Floyd Kranson, Johnny Markham (a knuckleballer), Randolph Bowe, and Andy Cooper, who was managing the team when O'Neil arrived. O'Neil said Cooper was the best manager he ever played for. He was stern when he needed to be, but also a father figure and teacher who earned the trust of his players. "Bullet Joe" Rogan had finally retired as an active player when O'Neil arrived and split his time between umpiring and working in the post office, though he also continued to help young Monarchs players.

O'Neil called the team on which he played "the Monarch family." The Booster Club "took good care of us," O'Neil emphasized. When the Monarchs won a championship, the club gave the players a gold charm for their watch chains. The players took care of one another as well. O'Neil remembered a young player who couldn't read and was trying to hide it. When he and Hilton Smith discovered their teammate was unable to read, they offered to help him learn. O'Neil and Smith obtained a primer and worked with the young player at night. Eventually he got his high school diploma.

"We slept together, ate together, and after the game, we'd drink and dance together," O'Neil remembered. "We were always aware of our image. There was a tailor on 18th Street named Meyers, whom Wilkinson kept on call to make sure everyone had a nice set of clothes. The Monarchs weren't allowed to wear their baseball jackets outside the park. A Monarch never got into a fight on the street. A Monarch never shot craps on the bus or in the hotel."

Owners loved it when Monarchs patronized their nightclubs in Kansas City's jazz district, because they always attracted a crowd. Had Wilkinson not worked out an agreement with many of the bartenders to limit drinks to Monarchs players who were showing they couldn't handle it, "we all might have become drunks," O'Neil recalled. As it was, some Monarchs did succumb, but most kept themselves in check, enjoying the music of Count Basie, Charlie Parker, Cab Calloway, Lionel Hampton, Fats Waller and other musical greats.

During the Monarchs' 1937 spring training in Shreveport, Louisiana, J. L. Wilkinson spotted a player who, alongside Satchel Paige and Jackie Robinson, was to become the most famous Kansas City Monarch. John "Buck" O'Neil (1911–2006) joined the Monarchs in 1938 and remained with the team, except for his service in the U.S. Navy (1944), until 1955, serving as the team's manager from 1948 to 1955. After gaining national recognition in Ken Burns' 1994 documentary *Baseball*, O'Neil spent his remaining years as an ambassador for the Negro Leagues Baseball Museum, which he helped found, and baseball in general. O'Neil and Wilkinson were close friends (National Baseball Hall of Fame Library, Cooperstown, New York).

"By the time I got to the Monarchs, blacks were in a new world," O'Neil recalled in his autobiography. "I know that overall, of course, we weren't yet where we should be. There was still a ways to go, and still is today. But to be a Monarch was a taste of something special, the good life."[31]

Forty-five years later, O'Neil amplified his description of how the Monarchs were viewed in the community, telling the *Kansas City Times* that we were "educated and refined" and "mothers wanted to introduce us to their daughters."[32]

After training in Texas, the Monarchs opened the 1938 NAL season at home on May 13 against the American Giants. The park where they played was now called Ruppert Stadium to honor Colonel Jacob Ruppert, who had purchased the Kansas City Blues and made them a farm team of his New York Yankees. Following the traditional Opening Day parade and ceremonies, the two old rivals split a doubleheader, with 6,000 in attendance.[33] While maintaining their league schedule, the Monarchs continued barnstorming, working in a ten-day tour of Canada in late July. They would finish the 1938 NAL season with a 32–15 record in league games.

Times were changing. By 1938 the open racism common among major league baseball players of the time was no longer accepted without protest. In a July 29, 1938, interview,

New York Yankees outfielder Jake Powell told a Chicago radio announcer who asked him how he kept in shape during the off season, "I'm a policeman and I beat niggers over the head with my blackjack." Though Powell tried to back-track, telling audiences in Harlem he felt "colored players" were good enough to be big leaguers and that he was not prejudiced, his remarks produced a furor in the black press. Commissioner Landis suspended Powell for ten days, but that did not satisfy the critics. Fay Young called for Powell's banishment from baseball and a boycott of the Yankees. "Nothing in recent years," Young wrote, "has stirred the Race population ... as did Powell's insult to our race.... My race is not pacified by the 10-day fine and Judge Landis and Powell's boss don't need to think we are."[34]

At the same time, some white sportswriters were stressing that Negro Leagues players were performing at a high level. Lloyd Lewis of the *Chicago Daily News* attended the 1938 East-West Game on August 21, won by the NAL All-Stars, 5–4. He judged the caliber of play a little above that of the American Association, the top white minor league, and a little below that of the white majors. However, he was impressed by a speed of play not seen in white ball for 20 years. It reminded him, he wrote, of the "golden age, the days of McGraw and Tinker and Cobb and Chance." American League president Will Harridge took a look at the 40,000 fans at the East-West Game and predicted the bars of segregation keeping black players out of the big leagues would be down in five years or less. A month later, in September 1938, Jimmy Powers of the *New York Daily News* asked former major leaguers to name black players they considered good enough for the major leagues. Seventeen were listed.[35]

CHAPTER 7

J. L. Wilkinson and the Rebirth of Satchel Paige (1938–1939)

Though he was only one-third of the way through a career in baseball that lasted from 1924 until 1967, by the fall of 1938 Leroy "Satchel" Paige had already achieved acclaim not only as one of the best pitchers in the Negro Leagues but all of baseball. By his own account Paige would pitch for more than 100 teams during his more than three decades as a professional baseball player.

Ever the self-promoter, Satchel Paige claimed he was born with control and had trouble walking hitters. He warned batters they would have to hit by sound, because his pitches would be so fast the hitters wouldn't be able to see them. His windups included the Model T, windmill, and hesitation. He said he threw "bloopers, loopers, and droppers … [a] jump ball, bee ball, screw ball, wobbly ball, whipsy-dispsy-do, a hurry-up ball, a nothin' ball and a bat dodger." However, it was his fastball, by whatever name, that confounded hitters the most. Sportswriter Dan Burley said Paige's fastball created so much friction as it went over the plate bats caught on fire when "by some unforeseen accident the wood became connected with the horsehide."[1]

Paige's showboating was unique. Advertising himself as "The World's Greatest Pitcher," he guaranteed he would strike out the first nine men he faced, and, more often than not, he did. In non-league contests, Paige sometimes brought in his outfielders, saying he was going to strike out the next batter, and he usually did. Jimmie Crutchfield, a college-educated outfielder who played with Paige on the Pittsburgh Crawfords, said, "When Satchel got to the ballpark it was like the sun just came out…. He was terminally unpredictable, the prize inside the Cracker Jack box of baseball."[2]

By 1938 J. L. Wilkinson was well aware of the marketing potential Satchel Paige represented. Wilkinson's Monarchs had seen Paige on opposing teams over the years, and the Monarchs' owner had taken advantage of Paige's practice of assuring he could be "rented out" to clubs other than the one for which he was playing. The Monarchs had "borrowed" Paige for exhibition games, including series against the Dean Brothers All-Star Team in 1934 and 1935 (see Chapter 5). Now Wilkinson was about to take full advantage of Paige's star power, and the Monarchs' owner and his legendary pitcher would become close and lasting friends.

Leroy Robert Paige was born in Mobile, Alabama, on July 7, 1906. "Satchel" was the nickname he acquired as a boy of about six. To make money, Leroy carried suitcases at the railroad depot in Mobile and figured out he could handle more by hanging several from a pole. "Looks like a satchel tree," another young porter offered, and the moniker stuck.³

When Paige was caught shoplifting at the age of 12, he was sent to the Industrial School for Negro Children in Mount Meigs, Alabama. He claimed reform school was good for him. He had a clean bed, warm meals, a little schooling, sang in the choir and learned to play drums. Most importantly, he was taught how to pitch a baseball. While at the school Paige grew to 6'3", but weighed only about 130 pounds. Other boys called him "the crane" for his high kick that caused batters to swing at his foot as it came down. "Blacking out the sky" is what Satchel called his motion.

Paige began pitching for a black semi-pro team, the Mobile Tigers, at the age of 18. He was already supremely confident. When the owner of the Chattanooga Lookouts of the white Southern League offered Paige $500 to put on white face and take the mound against their rivals, the Atlanta Crackers, Paige refused, saying, "I would look good in white-face, but nobody would have been fooled…. Only one person can pitch like me."

Paige's reputation for not honoring contracts also appeared early. His first pro deal, which he signed in 1926, was with Chattanooga of the Negro Southern League for $200 a month, but he soon jumped to the New Orleans Pelicans because they offered him an old car in addition to the salary. He moved on to the Birmingham Black Barons (1927–1930), Baltimore Black Sox (1930), Nashville Elite Giants (1931), and Cleveland Cubs (1931). He was, he said, "the travelin' man," always ready to take a better offer.

By 1930 his fastball was overpowering, and his control, on which he worked tirelessly, was rapidly improving. In a July 1, 1928, game against the Kansas City Monarchs, Paige threw 15 consecutive strikes with a fastball described as "so infernally fast that two were needed to see it." Always on the lookout for new talent, J. L. Wilkinson took note of the 22-year-old phenomenon.

The consummate entertainer, Paige would almost always be late to the ballpark, sometimes arriving with a police escort. With all the players in place, he would walk so slowly to the mound, the crowd started laughing. Paige said he joked between pitches but never while pitching. What he threw, he said, was always "thoughtful stuff."

Paige pitched thousands of innings from 1930 to 1938, for whatever team would pay him the most. For three seasons beginning in 1932, he was the ace of the Pittsburgh Crawfords, pitching in relief when he wasn't starting. His teammates included some of the game's real stars—Josh Gibson, "Cool Papa" Bell, and Oscar Charleston. The Crawfords' owner, Gus Greenlee, capitalized on Paige's appeal, renting him to traveling and semi-pro teams for $500. When Greenlee turned down Paige's request for a raise, Paige left the Crawfords for one of the House of David teams and pitched the bearded nine to victory over the Monarchs at the 1934 *Denver Post* tournament (see Chapter 5).

In 1934 Paige pitched for the Monarchs in a game against an All-Star team put together around the popular pitching duo, Dizzy and Paul Dean of the St. Louis Cardinals' "Gashouse Gang." The Monarchs hired Paige again the next year for another series against the Dean All-Stars (see Chapter 5) and for other exhibition games. Dizzy Dean told Paige, as they were saying good-bye after one of the tours, "You're a better pitcher'n I ever hope to be, Satch." On another occasion, Dizzy said, "If Satch and I was pitching on the same team, we'd cinch the pennant by July fourth and go fishin' until World Series time."

During the mid–1930s, Paige also pitched for car dealer Neil Churchill's integrated team in Bismarck, North Dakota, for $400 a month, a car, and the right to hire himself out to other teams between games. Paige said he did not know the team had white players until he arrived in North Dakota. The ethnically diverse team, reminiscent of Wilkinson's All Nations team (see Chapter 2), also had a Cuban, Jew, Lithuanian, Italian, Irishman, Swede, and German. "I'd cracked another little chink in Jim Crow," Paige observed in his autobiography.

While playing for Bismarck in the summer of 1935, Paige said Sioux Indians had given him some snake oil. They told him it was "hot stuff" and not to put it on anything but snake bites. Figuring it might be good for him in the cold North Dakota air, Paige put some on his arm after pitching and it loosened him up. He began using the concoction after every game. With the help of stars like Quincy Trouppe, Hilton Smith, Chet Brewer, and "Double Duty" Radcliffe, the Bismarck team won the 1935 National Baseball Congress Tournament in Wichita. After the tournament, the Churchills barnstormed their way to Kansas City, where on September 15 Paige took the mound with Radcliffe as his battery mate. Paige struck out 15 Monarchs, and the Churchills won the game, 8–4.

By this time Satchel Paige's antics were wearing thin on his teammates. They tolerated him because they realized fans were paying to see him, and they benefited financially. In an April 11, 1935, column in the *Philadelphia Tribune,* Ed Harris wrote: "Guys like Paige may be interesting as the devil to the fans sitting in the grandstand. But to his teammates, he's usually a pain where you don't want to be kicked. The pet of the club owners is always giving somebody else a lot of trouble and getting away with it."

In the spring of 1936, Paige made up with Gus Greenlee and rejoined the Pittsburgh Crawfords. That August he led a powerhouse group of NNL stars to compete in the *Denver Post* tournament. They won easily. He also pitched the last two innings of the 1936 East-West Game for the East. Paige's schedule was hectic. September found him pitching for a semi-pro team in Texas and taking time to fly to New York for a game against the Black Yankees before 20,000 at the Polo Grounds.

In 1937 Satchel left the Crawfords again, this time to play for a month in the Dominican Republic for *Ciudad Trujillo,* a team sponsored by dictator Rafael Trujillo. He went 8–2 and won the championship game (see Chapter 6). When Paige and the other players who had jumped to the Dominican Republic returned to the States, they formed an all-star team that outdrew Negro Leagues clubs. Greenlee offered him $450 a week, but Satchel told him, "I wouldn't throw ice cubes for that kind of money." The Crawfords' owner sold Paige's contract to the Newark Eagles, owned by Abe and Effa Manley, for $5,000, but the "travelin' man" went to Mexico instead of reporting to the Eagles. Enraged, Greenlee demanded that Negro Leagues owners ban Paige for life.

In Mexico, Satchel Paige's arm hurt so much he could barely throw. Virtually every batter he faced hit him hard. At times he said the spicy Mexican food was to blame for his arm trouble; on other occasions he said he had run out of the special oil the Sioux Indians had given him. In fact, the years of pitching in so many games had caught up with Paige. Some have speculated that he suffered a debilitating rotator cuff injury, perhaps while trying to master throwing a curveball. Looking back, ten years later, the *Kansas City Call* suggested alliteratively, "[t]he great one owned a wing that was as dead as a new bride's biscuit.... It was at that time that J. L. Wilkerson [sic], owner of the Monarchs, toyed with the idea of employing Satch, who was nursing the once-poisonous paw in pathetic pity."[4] Indeed, almost everyone in the baseball world except Wilkinson thought Paige was washed up.

7. J. L. Wilkinson and the Rebirth of Satchel Paige (1938–1939)

When no other baseball executive was interested, J. L. Wilkinson called Paige, who remembered the conversation well.

"Satch, this is J. L. Wilkinson. I own the Kansas City Monarchs. Remember me?"

Paige recounted, "I remembered good. I'd put in some time for Mr. Wilkinson.... 'Yes, sir, Mr. Wilkinson,' I said."

"Satchel, Tom Baird, my partner, and I just got your contract from Newark. When can you report to Kansas City?"

"I can be there tomorrow."

"Make it next week and meet me there."

Paige said he felt, "I'd been dead. Now I was alive again. I didn't have an arm, but I didn't even think of that. I had me a piece of work."

Wilkinson's signing of Paige turned out to be transformative for the Monarchs as well. As John Holway described the moment, the Monarchs' owner's decision "represented the second great achievement that would help bring the Monarchs a new dynasty [the first being night baseball]. It was an achievement born of baseball acumen, of wisdom about muscle and bone, skill and sporting spirit. Wilkinson decided to give Satchel Paige a second chance." As it turned out, "Wilkinson saved Satchel Paige's career. And Paige rejuvenated the Monarchs."

When Paige met J. L. Wilkinson in Kansas City, he explained that he couldn't throw. The Monarchs' owner responded that the plan was not for him to pitch but to play first base. Then Paige asked when he could join the Monarchs. Wilkinson was quiet for a moment and said, "You're not going to play with the Monarchs. We've got a Monarchs traveling team, a barnstorming team. We planned to send you up North on a tour with them. You couldn't pitch with that arm of yours, and you haven't played first enough to hold it down in the Negro Leagues."

Paige said, "that good feeling I'd had just sort of floated away." However, he said to Wilkinson, "I guess that's how it will be."

When Paige asked why he was being given a job if he wasn't good enough to play for the Monarchs, Wilkinson told him he thought Paige could still attract fans. A despondent Paige responded that he didn't see how his name was going to lure many fans any more.

Wilkinson was quiet again for a moment, then said, "It'll lure enough. Anyway, I thought you needed a hand."

According to Paige, "That's how Mr. Wilkinson was. I found that out later. If you were down and needed a hand, he'd give you one."[5]

As Wilkinson's son Dick commented, "Satchel had a 'whalebone arm,' all bone, not much muscle. Dad could tell by looking at a ball player whether he could play ball or had potential. They talked, and Dad gave him another chance."[6]

J. L. Wilkinson and Paige may have been pleased that Satchel would be playing again, but Effa and Abe Manley were furious. Effa was particularly incensed. She believed the Monarchs' owner, whom she referred to as the "Nordic Wilkinson," should have sided with her when Paige jumped his contract with the Manleys' Newark Eagles to play in Mexico. Manley accused Wilkinson of being no different from other white booking agents or ballpark owners, interested only in making money, and she threatened to sign players from the Monarchs in retaliation. Wilkinson responded to Mrs. Manley's outrage calmly, telling her "no one had offered Paige a contract, so I picked him up." Technically, he was right. The deal in which the Crawfords had sold Paige's contract to the Eagles was contingent on Paige showing up, and he hadn't.

Stubbornly refusing to back down, Effa Manley wrote to the presidents of both the NNL and NAL, demanding that Wilkinson be ordered to send Paige to Newark immediately. She claimed, "[i]f organized baseball is not strong enough to do this, it is not strong enough to call itself organized and anything may happen. Whatever decision you reach remember there is a big race issue involved, 'Negro Baseball.' It is probably at the crossroads, and its future may depend on your handling of this present situation. I pray you will have devine [sic] guidance at this time."

In the end, Paige was allowed to remain with the Monarchs, and the Eagles were permitted to keep two NAL players they had signed in violation of inter-league rules. However, Effa Manley's antagonism toward Wilkinson did not abate. A year later she included Wilkinson in an anti–Semitic slur, accusing him of being in collusion with Ed Gottlieb, Abe Saperstein and "all the other Jews who want to join them where Negro baseball is concerned." In her mind, Paige "was basically the creation of a powerful Jewish coalition that was making money off him."[7]

According to Monarchs pitcher Chet Brewer, the first thing the Monarchs' owner did after signing Paige in 1938 was to take him to a dentist and get him a new set of teeth. Wilkinson just had a way, Brewer said, of knowing what a player needed.[8] In a 1971 interview, Bill "Plunk" Drake said, "Wilkerson" [sic]," whom Drake called an "awful good man," even took Paige to Chicago for treatment of his stomach trouble.[9]

Buck O'Neil remembered that Wilkinson sent Paige to play in the West, all the way to Canada, on a team called at various times the "Second Monarchs," "Junior Monarchs," or "Kansas City Travelers." The players on the main Monarchs squad often laughingly called them the "Baby Monarchs."

With the Monarchs traveling squad, Paige would often perform a "pepper show," doing tricks with the ball like rolling it across his arm and chest to the other arm and hand, and some shadow ball playing, slow-motion

Without the support of J. L. Wilkinson, the career of the pitcher many regard as the best in baseball history, Leroy "Satchel" Paige (1906–1982), would likely have ended in 1938. Instead, with Wilkinson guiding each step, Paige's baseball journey continued into the 1960s. Paige first pitched for the Monarchs' traveling squad (1939–1940) then (as shown here) for the Monarchs A-team (1940–1947), before signing with the Cleveland Indians (1948–1949). He ended his major league career with the St. Louis Browns (1951–1953) and a symbolic appearance with the Kansas City Athletics (1965). In addition, Paige made hundreds of special appearances for other teams with Wilkinson as his mentor and manager (National Baseball Hall of Fame Library, Cooperstown, New York).

throws, and gags. Taking the pitcher's mound, he would soft-toss his way through a few innings with what he called his "Alley Oops and bloopers." Then he would play first or occupy the first base coaching box to the delight of the crowds in the small towns where the team played.

As Paige remembered the traveling team, the other players at first treated him like he "was dead and buried." About the only one not like that was Newt Joseph, an old-timer who played on the team and served as the traveling club's secretary. It was Joseph who told Paige, "maybe we can work that arm of yours out." At least, Paige said, he was making spending money.[10]

Before long the Monarchs "B" squad was outdrawing and outearning the main team. Wilkinson wisely began advertising the Travelers as "Satchel Paige's All-Stars." They played games against "community teams, post office teams, industrial league teams, church squads, Sunday-school teams, railroad-sponsored teams, pharmacy-sponsored teams, and any local nine that came together with enough cash to sponsor the contest, cover travel expenses, and guarantee a reasonable gate."[11] For many semi-pro teams, the entire year's budget was dependent on booking Paige. He kept many teams solvent just by appearing.

The Monarchs' traveling team included young talent as well as older players such as Newt Joseph, George Giles, and "Cool Papa" Bell. Paige respected Wilkinson for giving jobs to older players like him who were ridiculed as past their prime. Of course, J. L. Wilkinson the savvy businessman also realized that the well-known names of the oldsters, especially Satchel Paige, would still be draws at the box office. Before sell-out crowds the Paige All-Stars toured the Northwest and played in the California Winter League as well as barnstorming in the Midwest. Backed by Wilkinson, Paige refused to play in towns where they could not eat or sleep. Wilkinson also made Frank "Jew Baby" Floyd the star pitcher's personal trainer.[12]

During Paige's second year with the Monarchs' traveling team, while barnstorming in Canada, his arm and overpowering fastball miraculously returned. O'Neil said he was told Paige's arm came back as a result of treatments administered by Floyd. In any event, batters no longer had to hold back when Paige pitched as they had been instructed to do by Wilkinson when the games were booked. Newt Joseph immediately phoned the Monarchs' owner and told him Paige was ready to join the main team. As it had been before, Paige's control was excellent. "He could throw the ball right by your knees all day," said "Cool Papa" Bell. However, Wilkinson told Paige there was no rush, and that he should just stay with the traveling squad on the road. In fact, the Monarchs' owner had not received league approval to reinstate Paige, though he was sure it would eventually come because of the hurler's box office appeal. Patience, he knew, would in this case be a virtue.[13]

Satchel Paige remained with the traveling team during the 1939 season, and the Monarchs, who had trained in Memphis, maintained their NAL schedule while also playing barnstorming games as far north as Canada. Always open to new promotional ideas, Wilkinson agreed to a Monarchs bathing beauty contest during a game with the American Giants on July 2. Thirty-six women, sponsored by area beauty parlors, entered and paraded around Muehlebach Field in bathing suits. Wilkinson and the Monarchs won at the gate, as the promotion drew more than 10,000 spectators.[14]

On August 6, between games of a doubleheader against the Toledo Crawfords, 1936 Olympics champion Jesse Owens, billed as the "world's fastest human," appeared in a series of sprints against Monarchs and Crawfords players and local track stars. The promotion drew 4,200 fans.[15] It was not the first time the Monarchs' owner had exploited Owens's popularity. Soon after the 1936 Olympics, Wilkinson and other team owners began hiring Owens for races against cars, motorcycles, horses, and college students.[16]

After the Monarchs won the first-half NAL pennant race in 1939, they met the winners of the second half, the St. Louis Stars, in a three-game playoff series in early September for the league championship. Satchel Paige's All-Stars were guests of the Monarchs management at the Sunday doubleheader on September 3. After splitting the twin bill, the Monarchs won the third game on Monday, shutting out the Stars, 7–0, to become NAL champions.

The Monarchs ended the 1939 season with what were advertised as two "dream games" against Satchel Paige's All-Stars the last week in September at Ward Field in Kansas City, Kansas.[17]

The dispute over who held rights to Satchel Paige festered until June 27, 1940, when the NNL and NAL owners finally came to an agreement that both leagues had a justified claim on him. However, Paige indicated he wanted to stay with the Monarchs. Almost 30 years before Curt Flood challenged the reserve clause in major league baseball, Paige contended that slavery was over and he could play for whomever he pleased. The leagues' owners tried to strong-arm Paige into leaving the Monarchs for the Eagles and told him that unless he did "there will be a war between the two leagues." However, as historian Donald Spivey has noted, "Paige and Wilkinson ignored the threats. Paige was declared ineligible for the 1940 East-West All Star Game in Chicago, but he just continued barnstorming."[18]

In late September 1940, after Paige had completed two years on the Monarchs' traveling team, Wilkinson decided the time was right for the pitcher to rejoin the main squad. He signed Paige to a new contract for the 1941 season and sweetened the deal with something he knew Paige would love—a new car. To test Paige out, he put Paige to work before the 1940 season ended. Paige's first start in Chicago against the American Giants drew 10,000 fan; the next game in Detroit brought out 12,000. Having showcased Paige's box office appeal, Wilkinson next sent him to the Puerto Rican Winter League, where he was named the Most Valuable Player.[19]

Wilkinson took full promotional advantage of Paige's return to the Monarchs by "loaning" him to pitch the 1941 season opener for the New York Black Yankees on May 15.[20] Mayor Fiorello La Guardia threw out the first pitch before 20,000 fans, setting an attendance record for an Opening Day Negro Leagues game. Paige pitched all nine innings, struck out eight, and won the game over Philadelphia, 5–3. The game was covered not only by the black press but also the *New York Times*.

A week later Paige pitched the Monarchs' home opener. He let it be known that, because of the good relationship he had forged with J. L. Wilkinson, his habit of jumping teams was over. With his fastball reduced, as Paige put it, from "blinding' speed" to "just blazin' speed," he relied more on a curve, a knuckleball "Cool Papa" Bell had taught him, and a slow sinker.[21]

Midway through the 1941 season, Paige's reconciliation with Negro Leagues owners was largely complete. It helped that Wilkinson was willing to "lend " Paige to any NNL team for exhibition games. According to his Monarchs teammate Chet Brewer, Wilkinson would "rent" Paige and pocket 15 percent off the top of the gate receipts.[22]

Wilkinson now also booked more games for the Monarchs in the East. The stipulation was that Wilkinson and his partner, Tom Baird, would receive a higher percentage of the gate for giving their opponents the privilege of having Paige on the field.[23] Eddie Gottlieb promptly booked another doubleheader in Yankee Stadium for July 20, 1941, featuring Paige's Monarchs and three NNL teams. Philadelphia and other NNL clubs also booked the Monarchs on the Kansas City team's Eastern swing. A large crowd showed up at Parkside Field in Philadelphia on July 17 in response to advance publicity that promised Paige "will definitely hurl part of the game."[24]

Satchel Paige received 276,418 fan votes for the 1941 East-West All-Star Game, 100,000 more than the next pitcher, the Monarchs' Hilton Smith. After he was cleared to play by owners of the two leagues, Satchel pitched two innings during the July 27 game in Chicago.[25]

Because Paige was perpetually late, Wilkinson sometimes had Chet Brewer ride with him. After one harrowing trip, Brewer told the Monarchs owner, "I don't want to ride with Satchel any more. He's going to get us both killed." Paige would pitch a game at Yankees Stadium on a Sunday, then take off in his big Cadillac and not show up until the next Sunday. "The Monarchs put up with it," Brewer said, "because they were making money off him."[26]

Monarchs catcher Joe Greene remembered: "Sometimes it would be fifteen or twenty minutes before game time, and [Wilkinson] would say, 'Where's Satchel?' And you'd hear some sirens, and Satchel would be in a cab surrounded by police cars and motorcycles. Satchel loved excitement, and he loved to create it."[27]

At the same time Wilkinson was treating Satchel Paige with dignity and respect, the white media, now well aware of the public's interest in the lanky Monarchs hurler, continued to portray him stereotypically. In a June 1940 edition, *Time* magazine featured Paige in a condescending article, calling him "Satchelfoots." A month later the *Saturday Evening Post's* Ted Shane wrote an article in which he said Paige had "apelike arms" and a "Stepinfetchit accent in his speech."[28]

Frazier "Slow" Robinson, who played with and became close to Satchel Paige, said he believed "J. L. Wilkinson knew what made Satchel tick." He "knew that as long as Satchel lived out of a suitcase" he was liable to vanish at any time. So Wilkinson took Paige under his wing, as he did his own children. When he helped Paige buy a house in Kansas City, it was the first time Paige had any home to go back to. Paige paid for the house, but he would have never done it on his own, Robinson pointed out.[29] In *Maybe I'll Pitch Forever*, Paige credited his second wife, Lahoma, with convincing him to buy the house and working out with Wilkinson a way to hold back money from his paycheck to put into savings.[30]

According to Paige biographer Larry Tye, "[h]ome ownership had precisely the effect on Satchel that Wilkinson had hoped: it settled him down. He would remain a devoted Monarch for as long as he remained in the Negro Leagues and a devotee of J. L. Wilkinson as long as he lived." As Paige told the *Pittsburgh Courier* in 1943, his contract jumping days were definitely over. "I am going to play with the Kansas City Monarchs as long as the owner and manager will have me."[31] According to "Slow" Robinson, "Wilkinson let him know the value of making money while you were able to make it. Especially playing baseball." Wilkinson was showing him "if he wanted to make something of himself, he'd have to change his way of living."[32]

Paige filled his Kansas City house with Chippendale chairs and roomfuls of trophies and guns. Not surprisingly, it was J. L. Wilkinson, whose wife Bessie had owned and operated an antiques store in Kansas City since 1931, who led Paige into the world of collecting, and Paige took to it with the same gusto he had for hunting and fishing. He bought Chinese vases, a complete set of Wedgwood, Sévres French China, Royal Vienna dishes, some 18th Century Chippendale and Queen Anne pieces for his dining room, and a big Chinese cabinet for Fischer Hungarian dishes.[33]

"Working for Mr. Wilkinson was something no man'd forget," Paige himself recalled. "He was as good a boss as you could ask for. And he was a real promoter." With the Monarchs' owner's portable lights, Paige remembered pitching in as many as three games in one day. In one three-game stretch in the East, Paige said he drew 105,000 fans, pitching between three and six innings each game.[34]

By 1945 others were noting the positive effect J. L. Wilkinson was having on Satchel Paige. In a May 16, 1945, *Philadelphia Tribune* column, Dr. W. Rollo Wilson noted that Paige had changed his *prima donna* lifestyle since recovering from his arm problems and playing with Wilkinson's Kansas City Monarchs. "He retained the on-duty color and slugged off the off-duty trimmings," Wilson wrote. "Now, he travels with his fellows, in uniform every day, and is on the field for all pre-game activities. The snob is now a regular fellow."[35]

Intent on getting his moneymaker to as many appearances as possible, J. L. Wilkinson leased a small plane in July 1946, a two-seat, single-engined Cessna. The pilot was his son, Dick, who had been captain of a B-24 American Liberator bomber on multiple missions during World War II. "Satchel Paige" was stenciled on the side of the Cessna. The day after the plane was delivered, Dick flew Paige from Kansas City to Madison, Wisconsin, without any problems. On the return flight, however, they encountered a storm system and bounced up and down all the way to Kansas City. "You trying to kill me! Get me out of here!" Paige yelled at Dick. Although he said he would never get in the plane again, Paige relented after Dick told him that he would lose $500 if he did not fly to Oklahoma. Again, the first leg of the flight was fine, but mechanical trouble made for a hectic return to Kansas City. After only two flights, the Cessna was returned to its owner when Paige let it be known in no uncertain terms that he would not fly in it again. Dick's father didn't force the issue.[36]

According to Paige, after J. L. Wilkinson "decided to kind of retire" and Tom Baird was his boss, he took a sizable pay cut from the Monarchs for the 1948 season. Even though he was almost 42 years old, he still thought he was "too young to take any cut in pay."

During the summer of 1948, Paige was on a barnstorming tour in Iowa with his All-Stars when Dick Wilkinson, who was traveling with the team, got a phone call from his father in Kansas City. Dick recalled years later: "Dad called me on the phone and said, 'The Majors want Satch to report to Cleveland.' I walked over to Satchel and said, 'you're going to the Majors. Dad says get home.' He looked at me with a big grin and said, 'Oh boy!' He jumped into his Cadillac and took off. That's the last time I saw Satchel."[37]

According to Paige, the first indication the Indians were interested in him had come in a letter from Abe Saperstein, who told him Bill Veeck was looking for pitching help. Saperstein recommended Paige and Veeck brought him to Cleveland for a tryout on July 7, 1948, Paige's 42nd birthday. Manager Lou Boudreau caught as Satchel hit the strike zone on 46 of 50 throws. Veeck told him, "Satch, I'm just sorry you didn't come up in your prime. You'd have been one of the greatest right-handers baseball has ever known if you had." Veeck signed Paige the same day, offering him a $10,000 signing bonus and $5,000 a month—a total of $25,000 for the season. After Satchel told Veeck he thought

7. J. L. Wilkinson and the Rebirth of Satchel Paige (1938–1939) 115

In an effort to book Satchel Paige at more of the lucrative special games that teams all over the country were clamoring for, in July 1946 J. L. Wilkinson leased a single-engine Cessna plane (shown here). The plan was for Wilkinson's son Dick, who had flown B-24 bombers in World War II, to serve as Paige's personal pilot. However, being in a small plane buffeted in bad weather convinced Paige to refuse to ride in the Cessna and, after only two flights, the scheme was scuttled (courtesy NoirTech Research, Inc.).

"Mr. Wilkinson and Mr. Baird" should get something for taking him on when his arm went dead, the Indians owner agreed to give them $5,000 (according to Paige, or $15,000 in other sources) for his contract. Veeck also gave Abe Saperstein a finder's fee.[38]

Most importantly for the Indians and Paige, the turnstiles kept twirling whenever the lanky hurler pitched. More than 200,000 showed up to see Paige's first three major league starts, and the huge crowds continued.[39]

Paige's plaque in the National Baseball Hall of Fame at Cooperstown describes his start in the Majors: "Paige made his debut for a Cleveland club involved in one of the tightest pennant races in American League history. That summer and fall, Paige went 6–1 with three complete games and a save and a 2.47 earned run average. Cleveland won the AL pennant in a one-game playoff against Boston, and then captured the World Series title in six games against the Braves. Paige became the first African American pitcher to pitch in the World Series when he worked two-thirds of an inning in Game 5."[40]

The veteran Bill "Plunk" Drake, who had pitched with Wilkinson's All Nations team and the Monarchs and always claimed he taught Paige the hesitation pitch, said after observing Paige's performance in 1948: "I haven't seen no big league pitcher that could do any more than Page could do.... What do you think would happen if he went there at 25?"[41] Bob Feller said of his Indians teammate, "he could throw the ball through a keyhole and did.... The color of a ballplayer meant nothing to me. Can you hit, run, throw, pitch? If you can do that, you belong here."[42]

However, the aging Paige could not sustain the high level of performance that had made him famous. After a weak 4–7 performance for the Indians in 1949, which he attributed to a return of his stomach trouble, and the sale of the team by Bill Veeck, Hank Greenberg, the new controlling owner of the Cleveland club, offered Paige a contract of $19,000 for the 1950 season. Satchel asked his wife Lahoma what he should do, and she said, "Maybe we'd better see Mr. Wilkinson. He'll know. Maybe he can tell us what to do." When Paige went to see him, Wilkinson advised him to accept the offer because he would be better off with a steady job than trying to make a living from barnstorming. Wilkinson also told Paige to contact the Indians right away because it had been a couple of weeks since the offer was made. Paige called Hank Greenberg, and the deal seemed settled, but Greenberg called back and told Satchel that Lou Boudreau, who was still the Cleveland manager, said he couldn't use the aging pitcher. On January 29, 1950, Greenberg announced the release of Paige, saying, "[o]lder players will have to make way for rookies."[43]

A distraught Paige once again turned to his mentor J. L. Wilkinson and asked if he could find some work for him. Paige said he did not want to hook up with a black team, because "I want to stay loose so those big boys can call me if they want me." Wilkinson contacted Eddie Gottlieb and Abe Saperstein, and pitching offers soon started arriving.

When Bill Veeck purchased the St. Louis Browns in 1951, he made good on his promise to give Paige a job if he was able to acquire a new team. Paige's record for the 1951 season was 3–4. When it was rumored that Paige was being offered a salary of $22,000 for the 1952 season, he retorted he had "made lots more in 1950 barnstorming for J. L. Wilkinson, my manager." However, Paige would continue to pitch with the Browns through 1953 and was selected to play in three major league All-Star Games.[44]

Paige then went back on the road and, according to his own estimate, by 1961 he had pitched in more than 2,500 games, winning about 2,000. He claimed he had pitched as many as 153 games a year.

In 1965, at the age of 58, Paige appeared one last time in a major league game, appropriately for the Kansas City Athletics, pitching three innings of shutout ball. Athletics owner Charlie Finley would have signed him as a coach, but Paige wouldn't break the barnstorming contract he had entered into with Abe Saperstein after the 1961 season. So the lanky hurler resumed barnstorming until illness kept him home. Paige worked briefly as a sheriff's deputy in Kansas City and ran unsuccessfully for the Missouri legislature, before the Atlanta Braves took him on in 1968 as a coach so he could qualify for a major league pension.

Satchel Paige was elected to the National Baseball Hall of Fame in 1971 as the first selection of the Committee on Negro Baseball Leagues. When Paige's induction was announced, he said of J. L. Wilkinson and Tom Baird, "If you needed help they helped you. Mister Wilkinson was the only man I know whose check you could cash anywhere and I mean anywhere in the world."[45] He told reporters that he would "go into the Hall in a Monarchs uniform. I want it that way. Kansas City is my home."[46] After being inducted, reminiscing about his baseball career, Paige said, "I played some good cities and some good ball clubs—but they didn't treat me like Kansas City did."[47]

7. J. L. Wilkinson and the Rebirth of Satchel Paige (1938–1939)

Leroy "Satchel" Paige died in Kansas City on June 8, 1982, one month before his 76th birthday.

According to two of the greatest major league hitters of all time, Joe DiMaggio and Ted Williams, Satchel Paige was the best pitcher they ever saw. Paige was also in a class all by himself in terms of what he was paid. During the best years of black ball, he regularly made $30,000–40,000 a year. Far behind was the next highest-salaried player—Josh Gibson—who made about $1,000 a month during his peak in the early 1940s.[48]

Though he was schooled in a reformatory, Paige bought a typewriter and wrote drafts of his autobiography, a 96-page version in 1948 (*Pitchin' Man*) and a 300-page 1962 version (*Maybe I'll Pitch Forever*). "Unlettered yes, but not unlearned," Larry Tye, has suggested.[49]

Another Paige biographer, Donald Spivey, linked J. L. Wilkinson, Abe Saperstein, Bill Veeck, and Satchel Paige as "the four [who] together wrote in bold and bright ink for future generations the how-to book of promoting professional team sports and marquee athletes." They also showed that "black and whites could work together for mutual self-interests in professional athletics."[50]

His friend Buck O'Neil had more stories to tell about Satchel Paige than any of the countless other ballplayers, black and white, he had known. One is particularly moving. When the Monarchs were on the road in Charleston, South Carolina, Paige said to O'Neil, "We're gonna take a little trip." At Drum Island, where slaves had once been auctioned off, there was a big tree with a plaque on it, marking the site of the slave market. Buck and Satchel stood there in silence for about ten minutes. Finally, Satchel said, "Seems like I been here before." And Buck said, "Me too, Satchel." According to O'Neil, Robert Leroy Paige was "a little bit deeper than most people thought."[51]

Satchel Paige was, as a *Collier's magazine* writer put it, "one of the last surviving totally unregimented souls." To paraphrase Paige himself, he did as he did.[52]

No discussion of the great Satchel Paige would be complete without a listing of his six tongue-in-cheek rules for "How to Stay Young," which he had printed on his business card.[53] According to Paige, an East Coast sportswriter penned the list after Paige told him how he stayed in shape. The "rules" speak for themselves.

1. Avoid fried meats, which angry up the blood;
2. If your stomach disputes you, lie down and pacify it with cool thoughts;
3. Keep the juices flowing by jangling around gently as you move;
4. Go very light on the vices, such as carrying on in society. The social ramble ain't restful;
5. Avoid running at all times;
6. Don't look back. Something might be gaining on you.

CHAPTER 8

The "Black Yankees"— The Monarchs Reach Their Peak (1940–1945)

African American baseball enjoyed its best times during the war years of the 1940s. Between 1940 and 1946, when black employment in manufacturing rose by thirteen percent, fans flooded to the ballparks. According to Rachel Robinson, when her husband Jackie entered the Negro Leagues in 1945, "black baseball had never been better. ... While major league attendance declined during the war years, the Negro League teams played to packed stadiums. ... There was something in the play and players of the Negro Leagues that captured the essence of black life in America—the ... playing of the game with skill and grace and enjoyment, despite the obstacles."[1]

As a number of Monarchs would say when they looked back on those glory days, it was a time when every young white boy wanted to be a New York Yankee, and every African American boy wanted to be a Kansas City Monarch because they were the "Black Yankees."[2]

As black baseball reached its zenith during World War II, increased prosperity at home and the fight against fascism abroad were feeding the growing demand for greater integration in American society. Ironically, in the years ahead desegregation would threaten the viability of the Negro Leagues and other black-owned and supported "shadow" institutions.[3]

The reality for too many young African Americans in 1940 was still the scourge of racism. In a classic example of the miscarriage of justice based on racial bias, five of the nine "Scottsboro Boys," African American teenagers falsely accused of raping two white women in 1931, were still in prison. Early in 1940 the *Kansas City Call* printed a petition with spaces for signatures. When returned to the *Call's* office, the signed petitions were sent to Alabama Governor Frank Dixon, demanding that the remaining "Scottsboro Boys" be set free.[4] It would take until 2013 for all nine convictions to be overturned.

The Monarchs again held their spring training at all-black Wiley College in Marshall, Texas, in late March 1940. After two weeks in camp, the Monarchs played exhibition games in Jacksonville, Dallas and New Orleans,

In the spring of 1940, long-time Monarchs trainer Frank "Jew Baby" Floyd fell ill and was in need of hospitalization. In one of many examples of his genuine concern for Monarchs employees, J. L. Wilkinson sent out an appeal for assistance for Floyd. "He has a wife and children to support," the release stated. "He was one of the crucial 'behind the scenes' people for the Monarchs; like a 'hen presiding over a brood' he has watched over the Monarchs players, keeping them in good physical condition as well as in mind and spirit." By the next week pledges of support arrived from fans, and several teams had offered to hold benefit games. The campaign raised enough money for Floyd to have surgery at the University of Missouri hospital in Columbia in July. By October 1940 Floyd had fully recovered and returned to his position as Monarchs trainer.[5]

Just before the 1940 season began, Kansas City sportswriter Parke Carroll paid tribute to Tom Baird for his contributions to baseball since his days running semi-pro teams, and J. L. Wilkinson, whom he named as the "principal owner of the Monarchs." Carroll noted that the Monarchs had been traveling up to "40,000 miles a year by automobile and bus playing 180 games." He quoted Baird as saying that the "most enthusiastic players are in Mexico where soldiers surround the diamond and visiting players welcome the protection."[6]

At the Monarchs' home opener on May 26, 1940, prominent African American citizens, including C. H. Calloway, president of the Kansas City branch of the NAACP and respected "crusader for Negro rights," were on hand at Ruppert Stadium. A crowd of 7,000 cheered from the 40-cent grandstands and 65-cent box seats as the Monarchs doubled up on the Memphis Red Sox, 2–1 and 5–2.[7] By mid-June the Monarchs were in the NAL lead with an 11–5 record. For the first time, Tom Baird was named in the *Kansas City Call* alongside J. L. Wilkinson and Quincy Gilmore as representatives of the Monarchs at an NAL owners meeting.[8]

In July 1940, the Monarchs barnstormed in Kansas and Oklahoma. In August they faced off against the popular Ethiopians Clowns (see below), playing in towns as far north as Winnipeg, Canada, as well as small towns in Minnesota, South Dakota, and North Dakota.[9]

In late September, Satchel Paige finally made his debut with the Monarchs A-team, beating the Palmer House All-Stars in Chicago, 2–1. The *Call* reported that while in Chicago with the team, J. L. Wilkinson was injured in a car accident. The automobile was destroyed, but Wilkinson rejoined the Monarchs after only a few days' recuperation.[10]

As the 1940 season drew to a close, the *Call* celebrated the Monarchs as eight-time pennant winners who had made Kansas City "the leading baseball city in the middle and southwest." The Monarchs were victorious in both halves of the 1940 NAL pennant race. Once again they were league champions. The Monarchs had built a "name nationally—known as tops in organized baseball." The architect of the Monarchs' success was, the paper wanted readers to understand, "John [sic] L. Wilkinson, white, ... [who] has been in the baseball game twenty years and is considered as one of the smartest owners in baseball."[11]

However, Wilkinson and Baird rejected an offer from Cum Posey to play his Homestead Grays in what would have been the first Negro World Series since 1927. The Monarchs' owners apparently thought the series would be a financial failure.

By 1940 Negro Leagues baseball had become a two-million-dollars-a-year business, the second or third largest black-owned industry in the United States, employing hundreds and offering players salaries from $250 to $1,000 a month. Despite the improved economic climate, the owners of African American teams were not enriching themselves. As one commentator observed, black baseball was not "a highly profitable business, but an enormous struggle to keep your head above the water." Survival depended almost entirely on ticket sales.[12]

To bolster attendance at Monarchs games, Wilkinson tried a variety of new promotions during the 1940 season. He sponsored a Ministerial Alliance night in recognition of the support of the Monarchs by Kansas City's black clergy and a "popularity contest" with a cash prize given to the most popular girl attending the game that day.[13] On Labor Day the Monarchs hosted another beauty contest. The winner was 19-year-old Mary Jo Weaver, who won $50 and a loving cup. A planned two-inning Labor Day game featuring Monarchs old-timers was canceled when one of them, Sylvester "Hooks" Foreman, suddenly answered the "call of the Great Umpire," as the *Call* described his passing. Instead of an old-timers game, a short memorial service was held for the deceased catcher instead, with the announcer calling solemnly for the "battery of Rogan and Foreman."[14]

In an *Associated Negro Press* (ANP) article published during the 1940 season, Al Moses responded to criticisms of Negro Leagues players. He pointed out that many black players made less than half what white players in the minor leagues were paid, and were not supposed to fly into tantrums like Leo Durocher. Perhaps while "loafing" they were thinking how, Moses suggested, to stretch their salaries to feed and clothe their families.[15]

Jesse Williams (1913–1990) was barnstorming with the American Giants and facing the Monarchs during the summer of 1940 when J. L. Wilkinson approached the shortstop and signed him. He remained with the Monarchs, off and on, from 1940 until 1956. According to Williams, he was treated well by Wilkinson and Baird although his pay was not the best. In the 1940s the top Monarchs, except for Satchel Paige, were getting only $500 a month, Williams said, while minor league players for teams like the Kansas City Blues were making $750 minimum. However, it wasn't the money that was important; it was being a Monarch, he said.[16]

As pitcher "Lefty" Bryant, who played for the Monarchs in 1940, 1941 and 1946, put it, "I don't think Wilkinson exploited us; he didn't do us that way. He was liberal with his money, but he wasn't gracious with it…. He paid you what he felt you were worth, not what you thought you were worth."[17]

Wilkinson was also consistent through the years in insisting that his players be well-behaved. Although manager Andy Cooper wanted to bring Frazier "Slow" Robinson over from the traveling team in 1940 to catch for the Monarchs, Wilkinson refused, believing Robinson had been involved in a fight in Reno a year earlier with the House of David team. In his autobiography, Robinson commented, if the Monarchs owner "thought you was gonna be a little troublemaker, they wouldn't bring you in."[18]

Election ads in the *Kansas City Call* urged voters to mark their ballots in the 1940 election for Democratic Senate candidate Harry S Truman, "for 30 years a proven friend, justly deserving the vote of every Negro … a stalwart supporter of the anti-lynching bill and vigorous champion of Negro rights."[19]

As a result of the U.S. rearmament program begun in 1941, more African American workers were employed, but they were not being fairly compensated. A. Philip Randolph, head of the Brotherhood of Sleeping Car Porters and a civil rights leader, had to threaten a massive march on Washington to pressure President Franklin Roosevelt into creating the Fair Employment Practices Commission (FEPC). It was charged with minimizing racial discrimination in hiring and pay. On June 25, 1941, FDR issued Executive Order 8802 banning discrimination in defense industries.

Seven years later President Harry Truman issued Executive Order 9981 ending segregation in the armed services.

At a February 1941 meeting in Chicago, NAL and NNL owners considered ending their cooperative agreement that set rules governing players and contracts. The issue was the owners' failure to follow through in fining Satchel Paige and the other players who jumped their contracts to play in Latin America. Some owners wanted to repeal the ban, arguing that with the draft of younger players into the armed services, these players were needed. The NNL's Cum Posey said he could find no record of any of the players who had jumped paying a fine and claimed, "Paige is ruining Negro organized baseball." Since the clubs were deadlocked on the issue, NAL President Dr. J. B. Martin, who was chairing the meeting, called a recess so that the two leagues' representatives could meet separately. When they reconvened, Tom Baird proposed that teams take the players back with a $100 fine placed on each returnee. The motion passed on a 10–1 vote.[20]

An important addition to the Monarchs' roster in 1941 was Clifford "Connie" Johnson (1922–2004), who remained with the team through 1950. In a 1978 interview with Janet Bruce Vaughn, Johnson recalled that when he was 17, Monarchs catcher Joe Greene saw him throw and recommended him to J. L. Wilkinson, telling the Monarchs' owner the youngster had a superb fastball and curve. Johnson pitched for a semi-pro team before signing with the Indianapolis Crawfords, then the Monarchs for $95 a month. After pitching the 1941 season, he spent two years in the Army.

When Johnson rejoined the Monarchs in 1943, he was paid $300 a month. Like virtually all of Wilkinson's players, Johnson remembered how well the Monarchs were treated in the black community. Johnson said that in the Negro Leagues you were expected to be something of a showman, in addition to being a good baseball player, because the fans expected it. He remarked that since he was from the South, he expected discrimination while traveling with the Monarchs and never thought much about having to go to the back of a restaurant to be served. One of the Monarchs who made it to the major leagues, Johnson was signed by the Chicago White Sox in 1952, traded to the Baltimore Orioles in 1956, and retired in 1958.[21]

The Monarchs opened the 1941 season on the road on May 18 in Chicago against the American Giants. The Chicago White Sox management offered the use of Comiskey Park since the American Giants' stadium had burned down earlier in the year. The big question before the game was whether Satchel Paige, who was negotiating contract terms with Wilkinson, would join the team in time to pitch. He did, and the Monarchs won, 2–1. At their May 25 home opener, the Kaysees faced the Memphis Red Sox. The cost of a grandstand ticket had risen to 55 cents, with box seats 25 cents more. Wilkinson ran two full-page ads in the May 23 *Call*, and 18,000 fans turned out to see Satchel Paige pitch. He did not have a good game, as the Red Sox batters pummeled the lanky hurler, driving him from the mound in the third inning. However, behind the solid relief pitching of Hilton Smith, the Monarchs rallied for a 7–6 win.[22]

In addition to having Paige pitch in the regular rotation with the Monarchs, during the 1941 season Wilkinson scheduled games for a team he called "Satchel Paige and his Negro All-Stars." On Sunday, June 8, 13,000 fans poured into Crosley Field, home of the Cincinnati Reds, to see Paige's All-Stars take on the Ethiopian Clowns.[23] A week later the Paige All-Stars beat the Cuban Giants in Portsmouth, Ohio, before 3,000 spectators. Paige was then "loaned" to the Giants for two games against the Clowns.[24]

By the summer of 1941, Satchel Paige was approaching the celebrity of Joe Louis and Jesse Owens. His notoriety allowed him to insist on integrated grandstand seating for a Fourth of July game in Sportsman's Park in St. Louis. A crowd of 19,000 showed up.

Despite a dominating performance by Hilton Smith, the next day's headline read "SATCHEL AND MONARCHS WIN AGAIN."[25]

While Paige and his crew were in Cincinnati, the Monarchs were barnstorming in Kansas and Oklahoma against the Jacksonville Red Caps before continuing league play with the American Giants in Chicago and Canton, Ohio. The *Call's* new sports editor, Sam McKibben, wondered if the 1941 Monarchs had contracted a case of "can't get going-itis." Their play was sometimes "dull, listless," he complained.[26] Back in Ruppert Stadium on June 29, the Monarchs upped their game and beat the New York Black Yankees twice, 3–2 and 10–2, with 8,000 attending.

Noting Kansas City was not one of the towns where a brawl drew a crowd, since fans were savvy and many were women, McKibben chastised Monarchs manager Newt Allen for shoving an umpire during a game at Ruppert Stadium on July 13, 1941. Ironically, right after the incident, an announcement came over the P.A. system that Newt Allen Day would be held on August 10, and "Owner Wilkinson" had given the first five dollars to the Boosters who were organizing the tribute.[27]

On July 27 four Monarchs played in the 1941 East-West Game for the West: Newt Allen, Ted Strong, Hilton Smith, and Satchel Paige. Paige had been the fan favorite, with over 300,000 votes. After the game, Newt Allen and Jim Ford of the St. Louis Stars got into a fistfight. Allen had committed two errors in the game, and Ford blamed him for the West's 8–3 loss. Other players separated them. NAL President Dr. J. B. Martin fined Allen and Ford $25 each and suspended them from league play for two weeks.[28]

With Wilkinson's support, the *Kansas City Call* mounted a spirited month-long campaign during the summer for a game at Ruppert Stadium between the Monarchs and Kansas City Blues, both of whom had been league champions the year before. The effort ended when the Blues management said their schedule was full and a game would not be possible.[29]

On Labor Day, Wilkinson once again held a Ministerial Alliance Night with free admission for clergy. Exploiting the popularity of the Ethiopian Clowns, who had just won the *Denver Post* tournament, Wilkinson scheduled a Monarchs-Clowns tour with doubleheaders in Louisville on September 7 and at Ruppert Stadium on September 21, with a couple of games in between.[30] The 1941 season ended with the Monarchs posting a 24–6 (.800) record in league games to win their fourth NAL pennant in five years.[31]

J. L. Wilkinson booked St. Louis's Sportsman's Park for a game on October 5, 1941, between the Monarchs and a white major league All-Star team fronted by Cleveland Indians ace Bob Feller, the major leagues' hardest-throwing pitcher. Despite lifting the segregation policy at the insistence of Satchel Paige for the Fourth of July contest, the park's management at first indicated that the policy would not be changed for this game. However, with ticket sales skyrocketing, blacks were allowed into the grandstands. A crowd of 20,000 black and white fans sat side by side without problem and witnessed a great game. Local hero Stan Musial won the contest with a home run off Paige.[32]

After the December 7, 1941, Japanese attack on Pearl Harbor, a rumor circulated that to conserve electricity night baseball would be banned. The Monarchs would have been hit particularly hard, since they played more than half their games after dark. As it turned out, only coastal cities like New York and Newark were affected.[33]

In a *Kansas City Call* editorial published a few days after the Pearl Harbor bombing, C. A. Franklin wrote: "A united America is the only answer that can and should be made to Japan's attack. Regardless of differences about domestic issues, we are now one about national policy. It is for us each to consider how best he can hasten victory over the foreign enemy." Franklin wrote that one thing the war would do for British and American whites—it would show where "master race" thinking leads.[34]

On April 12 and 13, 1941, the Kansas City Monarchs were in Florida to play the Ethiopian Clowns. The booking had drawn the ire of Cum Posey and other Negro Leagues owners who claimed the antics of the Clowns on the field were offensive and played to white stereotypes of black baseball. However, Syd Pollock, the Clowns' owner and business manager, pointed out that the Monarchs had contracted with his club several months earlier, and the games went ahead as scheduled.[35]

As the 1941 season progressed, NAL owners could not resist the prospect of making money from playing the Ethiopian Clowns despite their concern about the team. In June they agreed to allow NAL clubs to book the Clowns. In August the Clowns won the *Denver Post* tournament, beating a white team in the championship game, and by September even the *Pittsburgh Courier's* Wendell Smith, who had agreed with Posey in calling such teams offensive and often said so in his columns, acknowledged that the Clowns and Paige's Monarchs were the best drawing cards in black baseball.[36]

Many baseball historians in recent decades have ridiculed the Ethiopian Clowns and similar teams as unfortunate representations of the Jim Crow era, believing that black ballplayers on these clubs were fulfilling the racist roles expected of them by whites. Syd Pollock's son, Alan, has taken exception to that characterization, pointing out that "while black baseball was played seriously, with risk, improvisation, aggressiveness and daring seldom seen in white baseball, it was always fun. And that was exactly how the Clowns played baseball. Negro league owners no more stopped Clowns comedy than they did the windmill windups, showmanship and clowning of Satchel Paige with the Kansas City Monarchs." As Clowns catcher-manager Buster Haywood put it, "the Clowns outdrew every team in both leagues. We brought money and good baseball into the league, and that was our purpose, and the critics can say whatever they want about that!"[37]

J. L. Wilkinson, Tom Baird, and others associated with the Monarchs favored playing the Clowns not only because they drew crowds, but also because they played excellent ball. Looking back a half-century later, Buck O'Neil called the 1941 Miami Ethiopian Clowns "one of the greatest baseball teams ever assembled."[38]

The Clowns perfected comedy pepper ball and shadow ball, which had been part of baseball since before World War I. It was a staple for Satchel Paige and the traveling Monarchs during the late 1930s and early 1940s. In pepper ball, the players performed a juggling act with the ball. In one popular trick, a player would roll the ball down his arm bouncing it up and down, then pretend to hand the ball to a teammate, before rolling it back up his arm and flipping it to another player. It never happened the same way twice and required constant practice to maintain the crispness that allowed fans to follow the ball despite the speed.

Shadow ball was the Clowns' trademark. Typically, after the seventh inning, the Clowns would stage a second infield practice, but this time using an invisible ball. With silent-movie speed players would make spectacular plays, rifling the non-existent ball around the field. Then the players would switch to slow motion. Before it ended, a long imaginary fly would be hit deep to the outfield, and a Clowns player called Bebop would run from the bullpen in a grass skirt to catch the "ball" before firing it 400 feet to home plate. The routine ended with another Clowns favorite, known as King Tut, hitting a pretend pop-up and running around the infield under the direction of Bebop. Tut and Bebop followed this crowd pleaser with a raucous jitterbug dance.

Tut would often go into the stands for a laugh. As Buster Haywood remembered a game against the Monarchs in Dallas, a "Monarchs fan" pulled a "gun." After the cops disarmed him, Tut went up into the stands and lit a chain of firecrackers under the row of seats from which the cops had just hauled off the "fan." Everyone, including Tut, ran as he shouted, "What's that! What's that!" He ended up sitting in a woman's lap, shaking. Tut was also the principal in the famous water fight routine (picked up and used to this day by the Harlem Globetrotters). After throwing water from a bucket at the opposing team and umpire, Tut would throw a bucket of what turned out to be confetti into a row of well-dressed fans.

Pitcher Peanuts Davis (also called Peanuts Nyassas) was another star attraction for the Ethiopian Clowns. At a barnstorming game against the Monarchs in Winnipeg, Canada, in June 1941, Peanuts stole the show from Satchel Paige, with his "slow motion antics," giving the impression he couldn't get the ball to home plate. However, despite his clowning, Nyassas could "really fog 'em through" when he wanted. The fans loved it, as 10,000 turned out to watch the Clowns and Monarchs do battle at Fargo, North Dakota, and Winnipeg.[39]

Monarchs catcher Othello "Chico" Renfroe recounted the following story about an act involving another popular Clowns player. Goose Tatum, who also played with the Globetrotters, would pretend to be a dentist trying to pull Tut's tooth. Goose would try unsuccessfully to make the extraction. He then lit a firecracker, and Tut, who had a mouth full of corn kernels, would jump up hollering and spit out all the corn. "They did the same thing every game," Renfroe recalled, "but it always kept you in stitches. Any team that barnstormed with them made money. Small or large towns—they packed them in."[40]

In summing up the case for his father's team and their style of play, Alan Pollock put it this way: "Not just Tut, but all Clowns; not just all Clowns but all Negro leaguers, were symbols of joy ... within the national disgrace of segregated baseball. And their fans knew that."[41]

In a reversal of their earlier decision, at the annual meeting in Chicago in late December 1941, the NAL owners accepted an NNL resolution banning all clubs in both leagues from playing the Ethiopian Clowns and any Cuban team other than Alex Pompez's. Tom Wilson, president of the NNL, said in a statement at the meeting, "the Eastern owners had long been of the opinion that the painting of faces by the Clowns players, their antics on the diamond and their style of play was a detriment to Negro league baseball." J. L. Wilkinson, who now held the position of NAL treasurer, and Tom Baird were present at the meeting and either agreed or remained silent. Abe Saperstein, who was booking exhibition games for NAL clubs, was also in attendance. At the same meeting, Cincinnati was admitted as a NAL member.[42]

Baird, who was now, along with Wilkinson, consistently representing the Monarchs at league meetings, was among NAL owners at the NNL meeting in February 1942 when the two leagues decided to reinstate the World Series. They also agreed with a request from black sportswriters to improve press releases on games.[43]

The Monarchs' 1942 spring training was held in Monroe, Louisiana. In a prelude to the 1942 Negro Leagues World Series, on Sunday, April 26, the Monarchs played a doubleheader with the Homestead Grays in New Orleans' Pelican Stadium. An overflow crowd of 15,000 caused the gates to be closed and the sale of tickets stopped. On May 10 the Monarchs opened the 1942 NAL season in Chicago against the American Giants, followed seven days later by their home opener against the Memphis Red Sox.

According to Buck O'Neil, the 1942 Monarchs were the best team he ever played with, and he believed they could have given the New York Yankees a run for their money. The pitching staff, which many considered the best in all of baseball, included Satchel Paige, Hilton Smith, "Connie" Johnson, Booker "Cannonball" McDaniels, Jim "Lefty" LaMarque, and Jack Matchett. LaMarque was a Potosi, Missouri, native who had previously played for a white club. Wilkinson gave him a $500 bonus to sign with the Monarchs. The starting second baseman in 1942 was a rookie, William "Bonnie" Serrell, called the "Vacuum Cleaner" because of his range. At short was Jesse Williams. Newt Allen was still around, playing third, along with Herb "Baldy" Souell. In the outfield were Ted Strong, Bill Simms, and Willard Brown. Buck O'Neil was at first base, leading the league in at-bats; he would be chosen for the 1942 East-West Game.[44]

Andy Cooper died suddenly in 1941 and was replaced by William "Dizzy" Dismukes (1890–1961) then Frank Duncan (1901–1973) as Monarchs manager. Joe Greene took over for Duncan as regular catcher. Dismukes was also by 1941 the team's business manager, replacing Wilkinson's brother Lee, who had left the team.[45] According to Joe Greene, Frank Duncan was temperamental, but he was a good manager and all the players liked him. The Monarchs players policed themselves, Greene said. "We didn't allow anything to get between us and our baseball and winning. We liked to win. If a guy wasn't right for the team, we had a way of getting him off. He's got to weave himself into the team. Youngsters had to have good discipline. Can't stay out all night and play ball the next day."[46]

Quincy Gilmore agreed with O'Neil that the 1942 team was the best Monarchs club in a decade. The fan base for the team was expanding as the number of African Americans in Kansas City grew to 41,574, 17.3 percent of the total population.[47] However, as the season got under way, attendance at Monarchs games was declining. The *Call*'s Sam McKibben questioned why African Americans were supporting the white Kansas City Blues instead of their own Monarchs. At Blues games, blacks were still forced to sit in the bleachers, exposed to the sun and rain. "Apparently," McKibben wrote sarcastically, "rank discrimination doesn't spoil their enjoyment of the game." By contrast, at the Monarchs' home opener "whites and Negroes sat together, cheered together, slapped each other on the back." The *Call* suggested readers "encourage your white neighbors to subscribe to THE CALL and learn what the darker one-tenth of the American population is thinking and doing."[48]

Declining attendance at home did not mean the Monarchs were not popular on the road. On May 24, 1942, 30,000 fans jammed into Wrigley Field to see Satchel Paige and the Kaysees beat a team of former major leaguers, including Dizzy Dean, who were in the armed forces. Abe Saperstein was the game's promoter. It was the first time an African American team had played at Wrigley Field. Paige pitched seven innings and gave up only one run on two hits. Hilton Smith allowed only one hit in two frames of relief. The Monarchs won, 3–1; they recorded ten hits off Dean and two off other former big league pitchers. A white reporter who saw the contest heralded the "bang-up, hustling, showmanship kind of game" the Monarchs played. The reporter said Paige was as good as Christy Mathewson, Grover Cleveland Alexander or Bob Feller. Across town, only about 19,000 were on hand at Comiskey Field to see a doubleheader between the Chicago White Sox and St. Louis Browns.

On May 30 in Griffith Stadium in Washington, D.C., an estimated crowd of 25,000 saw Paige, whom Wilkinson had "loaned" to the Homestead Grays, beat the white all-stars 8–1. A third game, scheduled for June 7 in Indianapolis, was canceled when word got out that Bob Feller, who was in the Navy and had pledged to donate his $1,000 fee to the Navy Relief fund, had been forbidden by military officials to take part. Commissioner Landis joined military authorities in denouncing games ostensibly played for "relief," but which were in fact commercial enterprises. A number of black sportswriters observed that Landis's opposition probably had more to do with dismay over the drawing power of black baseball.[49]

Meanwhile, at Ruppert Stadium in Kansas City, the Monarchs were sweeping the Black Barons and American Giants to take an early lead in the 1942 NAL standings. On June 21, a "mild riot of bottle throwing" broke out when former Monarch, now umpire, Hurley McNair called Bonnie Serrell out on a long triple. The Monarchs "ganged McNair," but "officers averted a serious mishap." The *Call* editorialized: "POOR SPORTSMANSHIP and unwarranted attacks on officials must go." The paper also claimed that if Joe "Greene or John O'Neil were white or IF BASEBALL MOGULS were democratic," the Monarchs could sell Greene or O'Neil to a major league club for thousands of dollars."[50]

In mid–July 1942 at Ruppert Stadium, the Monarchs met the Jefferson Barracks All-Stars, who were 21–6 and featured some former major leaguers. The Army-Navy Relief Fund received 50 percent of the gate; the other 50 percent went to the Salvation Army Penny Ice Fund. The Ruppert management donated the park and all employees their services. In his "Sports Potpourri" column, Sam McKibben wrote about the game:

> Death claimed Segregation, Discrimination and Jim Crow, father, son and grandson, all pioneer residents of Ruppert Stadium. There were no mourners, just 6,000 enjoying a baseball drama. The ushers, who are usually rude to Negro patrons, were bubbling with friendliness. That's democracy at work. Whites seated next to Negroes without incident and asked, "Why don't they allow the Blues to play the Monarchs?" and "Why are Negroes kept out of the majors and minors?" There was no trouble-making, no vile language, no fights. The Ruppert management had contended that white patrons would object to sitting next to Negroes at ball games. Oh well, if it never happens again, it happened Friday night. There was no segregation, nor discrimination.

McKibben concluded by observing that whites benefited more than blacks as a result of the charity proceeds, but black fans came out in huge numbers in support of the game. A week later the segregated seating policy was back in place for a Blues game at Ruppert Stadium.[51]

In July 1942 an exhibition series featuring Paige's Monarchs and three NNL teams was witnessed by an estimated 36,000 fans in Yankee Stadium, one of the largest baseball crowds ever in New York City for a game between black teams.[52] Encouraged by J. L. Wilkinson, Chicago organizers staged "Satchel Paige Day" at Wrigley Field on July 26. More than 18,000 paying fans watched Paige get showered with gifts.[53]

Meanwhile, the Monarchs were barnstorming in the East. The highlight was a game against the Cubans at Yankee Stadium on August 2 that attracted 20,000 fans. During the Eastern tour, the Kansas Citians also played in Indianapolis, Toledo, Syracuse, Albany, Scranton, Philadelphia, Baltimore and Washington, D.C.

Impressively, two Monarchs were the top vote-getters in the fan balloting for the 1942 East-West All-Star Game. Satchel Paige received an astounding 235,672 votes, and Hilton Smith garnered almost 150,000. The game drew 44,897 to Comiskey Field in Chicago on August 16. The Monarchs had four other players on the West's team: Ted

Strong, Willard Brown, Joe Greene, and Buck O'Neil. Paige was not sharp, giving up three runs in the 5–2 win by the East. However, the score became inconsequential because it was one of the most profitable black sporting events in history, with each NAL and NNL team receiving $1,904.92.[54]

Several decades later, two members of the Monarchs of the early 1940s had vivid memories of their experience on the team. Newt Allen told John Holway that once "[w]e made so much money on a Sunday afternoon ball game against Birmingham with Satchel pitching three innings that after the ball game, why Mr. Wilkerson [sic] would give each man a $75.00 or $100.00 bonus. From St, Louis all the way into New York, he gave away to ball players $1,000 dollars each night that we played."[55]

Sammie Haynes (1920–1997), who played for the Monarchs from 1942–1945, when glaucoma forced him out of baseball, recalled,[56]

> [Y]ou were a part of the community. The baseball park was in close. You'd walk right by the stands and everybody knew your name and you'd talk to them before the game and after the game. And the fans looked at the guys in our league as heroes. But nobody had a big head. Everybody was always ready to go out to dinner with the fans, and sign autographs. Whatever they wanted we were part of it. We were happy to do it because we all really loved and respected each other.... I remember one time that we went about thirteen days without going to bed. We'd play one night, take a shower, get on the bus, sleep on the bus. When we finally got to St. Louis we went in the hotel. Couldn't sleep in the bed. Couldn't get accustomed to the bed. We'd slept in the bus so long we got accustomed to it. We didn't care. It was fun. We had a good time. The hardships were not hardships.

While the Monarchs were barnstorming with J. L. Wilkinson during the 1942 season, his partner Tom Baird was booking games for the House of David baseball team as far north as Ontario, Canada.[57]

The 1942 NNL-NAL World Series pitted the Kansas City Monarchs against the Grays.[58] Since the Monarchs won both halves of the pennant race, no playoff was necessary for them to be declared the NAL's 1942 champions. The Baltimore Elite Giants won the same number of games as the Homestead Grays but had one more loss, so the Grays represented the NNL in the first Negro Leagues World Series since 1927.

The 1942 Series would be remembered for the confrontation between two baseball immortals: Satchel Paige of the Monarchs and Josh Gibson of the Grays. Thanks to the second chance given to him by J. L. Wilkinson and the Monarchs, Paige was in his rejuvenated prime. However, he had lost three games to the Grays during the 1942 season, each by one run. Plagued by personal problems and prone to abusing alcohol and using illicit drugs, Gibson, who caught now while standing in a crouch with slightly bent knees, was in decline.

According to Buck O'Neil, Satchel Paige was playing his guitar and singing in the dugout before the first game of the 1942 World Series started while the Grays took batting practice. One of their players, Chester Williams, came over and said, "Man, you got nothin' to sing about. Don't you know we're gonna run you out of the ballpark?" Paige replied, "Chester, you see all these people in the ballpark? You know what Wilkie's gonna do?" What?" said Chester. "Wilkie's gonna give us all the money. He ain't gonna take no percentage out of it. That's right. We made a lot of money for Mr. Wilkinson this year. He's just gonna take out his expenses and give us the rest." Buck laughed as he recalled the moment and said, "[t]he first pitch hadn't been thrown, and already Satchel had us ahead."

In the first game of the 1942 World Series, played on September 8 at Griffith Stadium in Washington, D.C., before 5,000 fans, Satchel Paige started and won an 8–0 shutout. The Monarchs pitchers held Josh Gibson and Grays slugger Buck Leonard hitless.

According to Frazier Robinson, J. L. Wilkinson came into the locker room after the game, told the players he wanted them to divide the Monarchs' share of the gate, and gave a pile of money to them. "We couldn't believe how much money there was," Robinson recalled. "We knew we had played to crowds like this before, and we knew that our salaries were low. They just didn't pay that much…. Nobody complained though. We always said, 'Beats pickin' cotton.'" Buck O'Neil put a somewhat different spin on the windfall: "And Satchel was right. Wilkie did give us all the Series money, just like he'd said he would."

The next night Paige and Gibson traded taunts from opposite ends of Gus Greenlee's bar in Pittsburgh, where the second game was to be played. Paige said the two bet five dollars Paige would strike Gibson out in the game.

The second game, played in Pittsburgh on September 10, was one of the most memorable in World Series history. Paige entered the contest in the seventh inning with the Monarchs leading, 2–0. Two were out, and there was a Gray on first base. Paige called Buck O'Neil to the mound and told his first baseman he was going to walk the next two hitters to get to Josh Gibson.

O'Neil said he told Paige, "Aw, man you gotta be crazy!"

Then Monarchs manager Frank Duncan, joined by J. L. Wilkinson (in at least one improbable version of the story), came onto the field "waving their arms wildly." Unable to change Paige's mind, they shrugged, "It's your funeral."

While Gibson waited in the batter's box, Paige called for the Monarchs' trainer, Frank "Jew Baby" Floyd, to bring him a foaming glass of bicarbonate of soda, which he drank before letting out a big belch.

"The bases was drunk," Paige later recalled. To Gibson he said, "I heard all about how good you hit me. Now I fixed it for you. Let's see how good you can hit me now."

"I'm ready," Gibson replied testily. "Throw it."

Paige remembered saying to him, "'Now I'm gonna throw you a fastball, but I'm not going to trick you.' … I wound up and stuck my foot in the air. It hid the ball and almost hid me. Then I fired. Sidearm, knee-high. Gibson, thinking curve, took it for strike one. He didn't lift the bat from his shoulder."

"Now I'm gonna throw you another fastball, only it's gonna be a little faster than the other one," said Satchel. Strike two. Again Gibson's bat was motionless. One more to go. It was so tense you could feel "everything jingling," Paige later said.

The last pitch was a three-quarter sidearm curveball. Gibson got back on his heels; he was looking for a fastball. Knee high on the outside corner—strike three. Josh threw his bat "4,000 feet," Satchel recalled, and stomped back to the dugout.

Paige said he could not remember Gibson ever paying the five dollars he owed the Monarchs hurler. The Grays' Buck Leonard always said he had no recollection of Paige walking two batters to get Gibson to the plate.

The Monarchs had a 5–0 lead when the Grays scored four runs in the bottom of the eighth inning. However, the Monarchs held on, recording three insurance runs in the top of the ninth to win the game, 8–4.

The third game in the 1942 Negro Leagues World Series was played on September 13 at Yankee Stadium in New York before 30,000 fans. Paige started but left the game after only an inning, trailing 2–0. Matchett earned the win in relief as the Monarchs stormed back to win, 9–3. Strong and Brown homered for the Monarchs.

8. The "Black Yankees" (1940–1945)

The Series did not resume for the fourth game until September 24 at Ruppert Field in Kansas City. It was a contest made famous because the Grays owner Cum Posey signed four new players before the game. Three, including star pitcher Leon Day, were from the Newark Eagles and one, Buster Clarkson, was from the Philadelphia Stars. The Grays won, 4–1.

After the game J. L. Wilkinson lodged a protest with both the NAL and NNL, objecting to Posey's use of "ringers." Posey argued that Monarchs co-owner Tom Baird had agreed to the signings in exchange for certain "demands," but Baird denied he had. According to Frazier Robinson, although Wilkinson was not happy about Day being brought in from the Eagles to pitch, "he liked the idea of refunds even less. So we played." When the protest against the "Gray Eagles" was upheld, the game was replayed.

Jack Matchett started the replayed fourth game, held on September 29 at Shibe Park in Philadelphia. Satchel Paige was late arriving after being pulled over for speeding in Lancaster, Pennsylvania, where he reportedly had a liaison with a woman. The Monarchs trailed 5–2 in the third when Paige arrived. Monarchs manager Frank Duncan quickly put his star hurler on the mound. Gibson was due up but had pulled himself out of the game in the top of the inning. The Monarchs scored seven runs in the final six innings for a 9–5 win and claimed the 1942 Negro Leagues World Championship. Paige had pitched in all five games.

Al Moses claimed in an *Associated Negro Press* (ANP) commentary that the white writers who saw the Kansas City Monarchs during the 1942 season unanimously agreed they would be an "even bet to whip the St. Louis World's champions." Black writers rated them with the great teams of Rube Foster.

The 1943 season would also turn out to be eventful. Once again the NAL owners reversed course with regard to the Ethiopian Clowns, who were continuing to draw crowds wherever they played. At a February 1943 meeting, the owners not only agreed to allow NAL teams to play the Ethiopian (now Cincinnati) Clowns but also to let the Clowns join the league. With Syd Pollock as general manager, the Clowns would play their home games at Crosley Field in Cincinnati.[59]

More ominously, a federal ruling threatened the 1943 season before it began. The Office of Defense Transportation (ODT) issued an order effective March 15, 1943, banning the use of all privately owned buses by baseball teams. Both the NAL and NNL presidents pointed out to the ODT that since Negro Leagues teams appeared in several different parks each week, they would not be able to play enough games to have financial stability without bus travel. In addition, because black ballplayers were denied hotel accommodations in some cities, the buses were essential as sleeping quarters. The two league presidents also emphasized that Negro Leagues games provided much-needed entertainment for black war workers in 11 metropolitan areas as well as competition for military teams.

Unmoved, the ODT refused to grant black baseball an exemption to the ban. A Kansas City-based petition drive and the involvement of Senator Harry Truman of Missouri also failed to convince the ODT, which told the owners they would have to give up their private buses and use trains, public buses, and automobiles. Despite the ODT ruling, both the NAL and NNL decided to operate in 1943, relying more on train travel and hoping for a change in the policy.[60]

The *Kansas City Star* weighed in, pointing out that the previous summer the Monarchs had played a fundraising game that came to the aid of the Salvation Army's Penny Ice Fund and played in 18–20 army camps. The *Star* quoted "Wilkie" (as he was identified

Before the 1943 season, J. L. Wilkinson and the Monarchs received word that the Office of Defense Transportation (ODT) planned to issue a ban on the use of privately owned buses by baseball teams. The order would have crippled Negro Leagues teams financially. The *Kansas City Call* responded with articles condemning the ODT's ban and printing "Save Negro Baseball" petitions. Here Tom Baird (left), *Call* Editor C. A. Franklin (center), and Wilkinson (right) review the petition. The campaign to convince the ODT to reverse its order succeeded midway through the 1943 season, and the ban on private buses was lifted. In the meantime, the Monarchs had done their best to continue their schedule, traveling by train (Kenneth Spencer Research Library, University of Kansas Libraries).

in the article) saying, "with a long drawn sigh and wonder-what-we'll do look, '[w]e'll manage to carry on in whatever way we can.'" The *Star* also noted that Wilkinson and his partner (identified in the article as "Long Tom" Baird) had recently acquired a new bus and new tires.[61]

Before the 1943 season got under way, J. L. Wilkinson sat down with *Kansas City Call* editor C. A. Franklin to discuss the upcoming season and reminisce about the Monarchs' owner's baseball career. "When you've got a good combination and you know it, the only thing to do is to work it," Wilkinson said, noting the Monarchs would soon begin training in New Orleans. "We're going to make our schedules if we have to travel on train," Wilkinson stated. "We know that baseball is essential and we're going to play for war workers, both day and night games and on Sundays and week days." Wilkinson had made many contributions to the world of baseball, Franklin emphasized. The Monarchs' owner had introduced night baseball almost 15 years ago. The *Call* editor concluded that Wilkinson, who had become a grandfather the previous week, was "known as the 'godfather' of Negro baseball in Kansas City.... [H]e has not only lived baseball for the past 40 years but he has his whole family eating, sleeping and thinking baseball."

Wilkinson's son Dick, now a lieutenant in the U.S. Army Air Force, maintained his interest in baseball, the article noted. In his youth Dick had traveled with the Monarchs during the summers, carrying bats and acting as water boy and "general flunky." His father added, "[w]henever Dick writes home now, he wants to know what's happening to the Monarch combination. Well, if I were writing him a letter now, I'd say: 'We've got the combination. I hope they [the ODT] let us work it.'"[62]

The *Kansas City Star* reported that five months later, on August 1, 1943, Lieutenant Richard Wilkinson had completed the required 200 operational hours before pilots were typically taken out of combat service. The qualifying mission was the infamous Ploesti raid on Romanian oil installations that provided critical fuel for German tanks, trucks, and planes. The bombers flew out of bases in Libya, across the Mediterranean and Adriatic Seas, in what the *Star* described as a "suicide mission." Fifty-three out of an estimated 178 bombers, each with a crew of ten, were lost in the raid, which became known as "Black Sunday." Fortunately, the *Star* noted, Lieutenant Wilkinson survived, but his plane landed in the neutral country of Turkey, where he was interned along with about 70 other airmen, probably, the *Star* speculated, for the duration of the war.

By this time Dick had been in the Army Air Force for over two years, with many operations over France, Germany, and North Africa. He was a member of "Ted's Traveling Circus," a B-24 Liberator Bomber Squadron in the 8th Air Force. With a group of 8th Air Force bomber pilots, he was on the cover of the July 26, 1943, edition of *Life* magazine. According to the *Star*, Dick's wife and baby daughter Diane were living during the war with his parents, J. L. and Bessie Wilkinson, at their home at 7240 Wornall Road in Kansas City.[63]

Despite his assurance to Franklin, by early April Wilkinson and Baird had decided to suspend their plans for spring training, placing the 1943 Monarchs season in jeopardy. "It will be impossible for us to operate unless we use our bus," Wilkinson told the *Call*. "We would not be able to pay the exorbitant rates on the train and could not guarantee our players the promised salaries for the year. We might go down south and get stuck without a chance of meeting our obligations."

This prompted an editorial in the same issue by the new *Call* sports editor, W. Bea Harmon, suggesting that "[i]f [ODT] Director Eastman could be a Negro for a day and take a jim-crow trip through the south on either a bus or a train in normal times he would probably go out and shoot somebody. But if Director Eastman had to travel through the south with transportation conditions as they are in war-time America, he would probably go out and shoot himself." Harmon noted that if the 25 men who made up the Monarchs tried to take public buses they would get stranded in small towns when white passengers bumped them. To insist that black teams use public transportation was the same as telling them they would have to cease operations. "If Mr. Eastman is not willing to release 12 buses for use of Negro teams he should abolish jim-crow trains in the South," Harmon added. "Negro baseball is doomed unless fans take up the fight. Send your letters to the *Call*," she challenged fans.[64]

After Wilkinson and Baird canceled spring training, many of the Monarchs players returned to Kansas City, where they worked out at 18th and Paseo. Meanwhile, the Monarchs' owners continued to fight for a reversal of the ODT ruling. C. A. Franklin and the *Call* did their part by printing "Save Negro Baseball" petitions. Within a week, 84 petitions with 2,100 signatures had been turned in at the *Call* office. Syd Pollock, owner of the Cincinnati Clowns, sent the following telegram to the ODT: "One truck hauling beer from Kansas City will use more gas and tires than both leagues put together.... Unless immediate action is taken Negro baseball has been dealt a death blow. Won't you help save America's greatest sporting heritage for millions of Negro citizens?"[65]

Despite the ODT's bus ban and their initial misgivings, Wilkinson and Baird finally decided to go ahead with the 1943 season, and the Monarchs opened against the Black Barons in Birmingham on April 25. On their way north by train they played games in Memphis, Oklahoma City, and other towns. To replace Ted Strong, who had left the team to serve in the Army, Wilkinson signed a future major leaguer, 17-year-old Hank Thompson.

At the home opener at Ruppert Stadium on May 16, 1943, 8,500 saw the Monarchs take two from their longtime rivals, the American Giants, 2–0 and 1–0.[66] After winning three in a row from the American Giants at Comiskey Field in Chicago, the Monarchs traveled to the East by train. The Kaysees drew crowds of 20,000 or more at Shibe Park in Philadelphia, Griffith Stadium in Washington, D.C., and Yankee Stadium in New York.[67] A June 20 contest at Griffith Stadium was reportedly the first game played by black teams under major league lights. It was the largest crowd to see a game in the stadium since the 1925 World Series.[68] Wilkinson and Baird were clearly making the best of a bad situation.

Fortunately, the fervent campaign to reverse the ODT order proved successful and the ban was suspended during the second half of the 1943 season, allowing the Monarchs and other Negro Leagues teams to travel by private bus once again. The Monarchs' bus, purchased new in 1941 at a cost of $3,100, was still in excellent condition. Meanwhile, Mississippi passed new laws increasing the penalties for violating Jim Crow laws requiring separation of whites and blacks on buses, trains and other common carriers.[69]

In July 1943, sportswriter Fay Young described an encounter between J. L. Wilkinson and Washington Senators owner Clark Griffith at Griffith Stadium. Uncharacteristically, the Monarchs' owner bragged to Griffith, telling him that the Monarchs paid Satchel Paige more than the Senators' highest paid player. Griffith tried to laugh it off, but just then Paige walked into the office. Wilkinson asked the hurler to show Griffith the $1,500 check Paige had been given for the game against the Homestead Grays that had just been played.[70]

The 1943 East-West All-Star Game at Comiskey Park in Chicago on August 1 drew 51,723, the largest crowd to see a Negro sporting event to that time. The Monarchs had four players on the West's team: Jesse Williams, Willard Brown, Buck O'Neil, and Satchel Paige. Before the game, Paige and Josh Gibson held out for more money. They asked the

Opposite: **Two of the most proficient hitters on the Monarchs teams during the late 1930s and 1940s were outfielders Willard Brown (left) and Ted Strong (right). Brown (1915–1996) was a power hitter who was dubbed "Home Run" by fellow Negro Leaguers and "*Ese Hombre*" ("That Man") in Puerto Rico where he played winter ball. Brown was on the Monarchs from 1936–1944 and 1948–1950. He spent a month with the St. Louis Browns of the American League in 1947. Brown was inducted into the National Baseball Hall of Fame in 2006. Ted Strong (1914–1978) played for the Monarchs in 1937, 1938–1939, 1941–1942 and 46–47. Both served in the armed forces during World War II (Kenneth Spencer Research Library, University of Kansas Libraries).**

two league presidents for a $200 bonus each. The presidents reluctantly agreed, and Paige and Gibson kept the agreement to themselves. Actually, Paige took in $800. Each NAL club put in $50, and Wilkinson and Baird made up the difference.

For J. L. Wilkinson the record turnout at the 1943 East-West Game must have seemed a validation of his decades of hard work and sacrifice to promote black baseball. Just before the game he walked into the locker room. "You should see the crowd out there, Satchel," he told the pitcher whose career Wilkinson had resurrected and who had been instrumental in the growing popular support for the Monarchs and the Negro Leagues. In the game, Paige pitched three innings and earned the win. He was the first pitcher to win a game for both the East and West in the All-Star Game series.[71]

After another Eastern swing in August 1943, the Monarchs played a short series against the Cincinnati Clowns. With the turnstiles spinning, the two teams played multiple games before large crowds in Texas, Oklahoma, and Illinois. The season ended with a game called the North-South classic in New Orleans on September 26, won by the North, 5–2.[72]

After the 1943 season, NAL president J. B. Martin reported that all league teams had "made more money this last year than they ever made in the history of baseball." The Monarchs grossed more than $115,000, which probably included Wilkinson and Baird's booking income, and finished the year with a $53,000 profit. Wendell Smith noted, "Negro baseball has now attained the 'big business' classification. It has passed the stage of being merely a sport or a hobby."[73]

During the 1943 season, the Monarchs had lost Willard Brown, Buck O'Neil, Joe Greene, Hank Thompson, Jesse Williams, Ted Strong and Connie Johnson to the armed services. In total, at least 14 Monarchs served in the military during World War II.

In his autobiography, O'Neil described experiencing prejudice in the Navy. Many of the officers were from the South. He also felt cut off from his teammates. There was no coverage of the Negro Leagues in the armed services newspaper, the *Stars and Stripes*. What did help was receiving letters from J. L. Wilkinson and Tom Baird, who kept him apprised of how the Monarchs were doing and included clippings from black newspapers. "Those letters were so sweet," O'Neil remembered.[74]

Throughout World War II, Wilkinson adopted patriotically inspired promotions. He adjusted game times to accommodate swing-shift workers and gave free admission to soldiers in uniform. As a result, the Monarchs outdrew other teams (including the white Kansas City Blues, by then a farm team of the New York Yankees), attracting 6–7,000 black and white fans a game. The Monarchs joined with other African American organizations during the war in uniting behind what was called the "Double V" campaign, victory over "tyranny and injustice abroad and at home."[75]

Conditions for black ballplayers and others associated with Negro Leagues teams were still very difficult during World War II, especially while traveling in the South. The irony of African Americans putting their lives on the line in the fight for freedom abroad while suffering the indignities of racism at home was not lost on *Kansas City Call* sports editor Willie Bea Harmon. She addressed the issue directly, writing in her "Sportorial" column that U.S. Army General George Patton had slapped a soldier and was being disciplined because of the blow to troop morale. Strange the U.S. is

> not rocked when many of our great athletes now soldiers, sailors, Marines and Seabees ... are denied food on trains through the South.... What of the morale of the men—the colored men—... who get up each morning under a system which makes them serve for a "freedom" they never had? The nation is not rocked, but our enemies consider it a great sport for their headlines.[76]

Harmon also appreciated that J. L. Wilkinson was doing his best to support his players and those who accompanied them when they encountered racial discrimination. Harmon recounted the following story told to her by Monarchs trainer Frank "Jew Baby" Floyd, who had rejoined the team for the 1943 season. The Monarchs were warming up in Shreveport and Floyd was responsible for returning balls to the field. Wilkinson told him the balls were not being retrieved as they should. When Floyd asked those helping him what was happening, he was told, "You know how it is, you jest can't take those balls from the white boys." Floyd approached several white youngsters who were refusing to return the balls. One in particular, a boy about 12 or 13 years of age, ran away and when Floyd caught him, the boy began yelling that he'd "show [Floyd] where to get off." Soon the boy came back with his father and a riot squad. Floyd told Harmon he was taken to jail. When the case went to court, the judge said to Floyd, "[d]on't you know this is a white man's country?" The Monarchs' trainer was fined $550 for assaulting the boy and given six weeks on a prison farm, where he was beaten by the guards. The Monarchs had left town, but, according to Floyd, Wilkinson hired a lawyer, "and through a lot of hard work he got me released."[77]

At the annual winter meeting before the 1944 season, NAL owners re-elected J. L. Wilkinson as treasurer. Owners also decided that to be eligible for the NAL pennant teams must play at least 30 league games in each half, and each player must be a regular member of the team winning the pennant for 30 days prior to the end of the season.[78]

In a controversial move at the next league meeting, the NAL owners passed over Wendell Smith, who had been proposed as league statistician, choosing instead the J. Monro Elias Agency for the 1944 season. The agency was paid $25 a week to send out releases to 30 African American weekly papers and 50 white daily papers. The price was low because the firm hoped to sell the service directly to newspapers.[79]

The Negro Leagues continued to benefit from the wartime economy. In 1944 the Monarchs topped $100,000 in gate receipts and earned a profit of $56,281.37. Other NAL executives recognized that J. L. Wilkinson and the small group of other white owners "had put their money into Negro Baseball when it was at its lowest ebb."[80] The Monarchs had become one of the strongest and best-financed franchises, and Wilkinson continued to earn high regard for his treatment of players.[81]

As the 1944 season approached, Abe Saperstein's work as a promoter and booking agent of black baseball continued to draw mixed reviews from Negro Leagues officials and sportswriters. Some accused him of profiteering, but J. L. Wilkinson, NAL President J. B. Martin, and writer Wendell Smith, among others, remained steadfast in their support of Saperstein.[82]

The Clowns moved from Cincinnati to Indianapolis for the 1944 season. As Wilkinson had said earlier, "when you have a combination, you play it." The Monarchs had made good money playing against the Clowns in 1943, so the Monarchs' owner readily scheduled exhibition games with the Clowns in New Orleans, Houston, and other cities during April 1944.

The Monarchs opened the 1944 NAL season on May 7 against the Red Sox in Memphis. Wilkinson withheld Satchel Paige in league games from the beginning of the season until late May, when the weather was more favorable and there was less chance of the lanky right-hander injuring his pitching arm.[83] The Kaysees' home opener was with Memphis on May 21 and featured the Booster Club's gala opening ceremonies.[84]

Wilkinson continued his now well-established routine of a heavy dose of exhibition games, occasionally mixing in special promotions. For these games he was willing to have Paige pitch. Exploiting the draw at the gate of two of the most colorful pitchers in baseball history, Satchel Paige and Dizzy Dean, Wilkinson scheduled them to hurl for the Atchison Merchants and Sherman Field Soldiers at an exhibition contest in St. Joseph on May 9, 1944.

On June 4, before a crowd of 15,000 spectators, the Monarchs played an exhibition game against a team called the Chicago Firemen at Wrigley Field. Between games Jesse Owens raced against a fellow Olympian, sprinter Helen Stephens from Fulton, Missouri.[85]

On July 2, 1944, Satchel Paige threw 15 strikeouts in an 11-inning confrontation with the New York Cubans at Ebbets Field, home of the Brooklyn Dodgers. Paige had a one-hitter going into the ninth, but his defense deserted him and he lost, 3–2. It was Satchel's first Flatbush appearance. A paying crowd of 14,000 was on hand.[86]

Paige was again in the lineup for a league game when the Monarchs met their historic rivals, the American Giants, in Chicago on July 9. He took the mound for the second half of a doubleheader. However, the big news of the day was that J. L. Wilkinson had filed a protest objecting to Chicago's use of Alex Radcliffe on the grounds that the player had been "loaned" by the Indianapolis Clowns to the American Giants in violation of NAL rules.[87]

The 1944 East-West All-Star Game, played on August 14 at Comiskey Park in Chicago, was also controversial. The owners decided not to let fans elect the teams, in a move designed to neutralize Satchel Paige's bargaining leverage. After being spurned in his attempt to negotiate a higher participation fee, Paige proposed the game be deemed a benefit for wounded GIs. However, the owners would not go along, and Paige refused to play. With an anticipated attendance of 46,000, the players saw their own opportunity to bargain for a higher participation fee and voted to strike. They had been receiving only $50 plus a $15 *per diem*, but in 1944 they were demanding $200. The owners agreed to $150, and the game was played. Without Paige, the West won, 7–4. The only Monarch to participate was second baseman Bonnie Serrell. Despite the controversy, the game outdrew the white major leagues All-Star Game, which attracted only about 30,000.[88]

During the 1944 season, Wendell Smith and other black sportswriters began lobbying for a more organized World Series between the NAL and NNL. In August, Smith, Fay Young, and Sam Lacy were selected to serve on an "Arbitration Commission" which drafted a "World Series Agreement," requiring the two teams selected to submit lists of eligible players and post a $1,000 guarantee. Homestead and Birmingham represented the NNL and NAL in the 1944 Series, but the profits were negligible. Five Black Barons were seriously injured in a car wreck just days before the planned opening of the Series. With their lineup decimated, Birmingham lost.[89]

At the annual winter NAL meeting held in conjunction with the NNL meeting in New York on December 15–16, 1944, a committee to name a commissioner for the two Negro Leagues was selected. Tom Baird and "Dizzy" Dismukes represented the Monarchs at the meeting. For the first time in nearly a quarter of a century, J. L. Wilkinson did not attend a gathering of Negro Leagues owners.[90] Black sportswriter Dan Burley, writing under the pseudonym "Don [De] Leighbur," soon joined the call for the appointment of a NNL/NAL commissioner and described the difficulties whoever appointed would face. He would need "to have the experience of riding a bucking bronco, P. T. boat in the midst of a squall, sitting erect while riding the whip-the-whip at Coney Island ... and running through the revolving tunnel, all with perfect equilibrium," because it would be a tough job handling "the affairs of the rugged, tough, uncompromising bunch of brethren who own the various clubs in organized [black] baseball."[91]

Another issue facing NNL and NAL owners was the attempted formation of yet another Negro circuit, the Southern League, which planned to start the 1945 season with eight teams.[92] Under pressure from the NNL and NAL, the Southern League later clarified that it was a minor league with no intention of competing with the more established circuits.[93]

In the two years prior to the 1945 season, 11 regular Monarchs players had gone into the armed services. Wilkinson told the *Kansas City Star* that the Monarchs would play in 1945 "if at all possible." The Monarchs' owner told the paper that if the "white bigs" fielded teams, so would the Negro Leagues teams. He said, "[w]e believe we can scare up enough old-timers and kids to make up some pretty good ball clubs, although our losses to the armed forces have been heavy."[94]

The most famous player to join the Monarchs in 1945 was, of course, Jackie Robinson (see Chapter 9). However, there were other highly talented additions and returning players. One newcomer was Ted "Double Duty" Radcliffe (1902–2005) who joined the Monarchs in 1945. After only 12 games as a Monarch, Radcliffe was injured in a collision at home plate with a Birmingham Black Barons player and had to fly to Chicago for an operation. Radcliffe remembered the incident well: "I hadn't been with Kansas City but two weeks but Wilkinson paid the whole hospital bill. So you know what kind of man he was." Radcliffe grouped Wilkinson, Abe Saperstein, and Cum Posey as the three greatest men in black baseball.[95]

Othello "Chico" Renfroe (1923–1991) became the Monarchs' starting catcher in 1945 and remained with the team until 1947. He remembered how the Monarchs picked up players in little towns and bought them clothes, when they didn't even know what a suit was. "Mr. Wilkinson liked to make sure you dressed well. That was one of his musts," Renfroe remembered. "And I tell you, those guys could step out of those clubhouses Sunday sharp as a tack." The catcher acknowledged that despite Wilkinson's efforts to keep players in line, some had "bad attitudes," and he was one. He said he stood up one day in front of the team before a game in Wichita and urged his teammates to strike because of a dispute over meal money. As Renfroe told the story, "Mr. Wilkerson [sic] sent his son Dick down to ask what we were angry about…. [A]ll the old players kept their mouths shut, but I said we wanted more meal money…. Mr. Wilkerson said, 'Do the rest of you fellows feel the same way? If you do, raise your hand.' Nobody did and they left me standing there all by myself. So I learned a lesson about that."[96]

Another Monarch player who was with the team in 1945, Bonnie Serrell (1920–1996), learned that you didn't "jump a contract" with J. L. Wilkinson and get away with it. While still under contract with the Monarchs, Serrell left the team to play ball in Mexico. When Serrell returned, Wilkinson saw that he was blackballed. However, several years later Wilkinson did relent and convinced Tom Baird to let Serrell rejoin the Monarchs in 1949.[97]

Satchel Paige's box office appeal had certainly not waned in 1945, and Wilkinson was still eager to put him on the mound for exhibition games. On June 3 Paige pitched for an all-star team headed by Monarchs old-timer "Plunk" Drake against the Sherman Flying Field team, national semi-pro champs, in an exhibition game at Ruppert Stadium. The price of a general admission ticket was 95 cents; a box seat was 50 cents more.[98] On July 8 Wilkinson "loaned" Paige to the East Chicago Gainer's Giants for a game played in East Chicago, Indiana, against a team called Gary's Sportsmen's Club, featuring Dizzy Dean.[99]

By the summer of 1945, Wilkinson's trusted associate Quincy Gilmore, who had been with the Monarchs since the team's founding in 1920, was seriously ill. He had suffered two strokes and was confined to a hospital. On August 3 the Monarchs staged a benefit game for Gilmore. To honor Gilmore's reputation as a premier promoter, J. L. Wilkinson and Tom Baird arranged "gala entertainment." Satchel Paige offered to waive his usual fee and pitched.[100]

As the 1945 season drew to a close, the Monarchs had fallen to fourth place in the six-team NAL. Rumors spread that the Monarchs would not be allowed to play at Ruppert Stadium in 1946. Tom Baird took the lead in responding for the Monarchs. He noted that the Monarchs were outdrawing the white Kansas City Blues of the American Association at Ruppert Stadium. There was no chance, he said, that the Monarchs would be pushed out. Meanwhile, Blues management was again resisting appeals by both black and white fans for a Blues-Monarchs game. Apparently, Baird told Willie Bea Harmon, the Blues' officials figured the money they made would not be worth the embarrassment if they lost.[101]

CHAPTER 9

J. L. Wilkinson, Jackie Robinson and the Integration of Baseball (1945)

On April 15, 1947, Jackie Robinson stepped out of the Brooklyn Dodgers' dugout across an invisible color line onto Ebbets Field and into baseball immortality. He was the first African American baseball player in nearly three-quarters of a century to be a sanctioned member of a major league team.

Almost all who know the story of Jackie Robinson's breaking of the color barrier can name Robinson and Dodgers President and General Manager Branch Rickey as the two heroes of the drama. Rickey faced the near total opposition of other white baseball officials and owners when he let it be known he was about to bring a black player to the major leagues. Jackie Robinson had to confront a torrent of taunts and threats by racist fans, opposing clubs, and even members of his own team. Both men are justifiably acclaimed for their courageous actions in challenging racial discrimination in major league baseball. What they did changed America.

However, they were not alone. Before Robinson and Rickey's historical achievement, many had fought hard to end segregation in major league baseball. We will focus here on two leaders in the long campaign against apartheid in baseball—journalists Wendell Smith and Sam Lacy. Then we will relate the role played by J. L. Wilkinson and others in the Kansas City Monarchs organization in the integration of major league baseball, and, more specifically, in the Jackie Robinson story.

In his groundbreaking work on the history of blacks in baseball, *Only the Ball Was White*, Robert Peterson summed up well the reasons typically given before 1947 for maintaining the color barrier. First, one-third of all major-league players were Southerners who would refuse to play with or against blacks. Second, African Americans could not travel with a big league club because hotels would not accommodate them. Third, clubs trained in the South, where blacks and whites were not allowed to play together. Fourth, fans might riot in the stands if there was trouble between black and white players. Fifth, African Americans were not good enough to play in the majors. As Peterson pointed out, underlying all these reasons was a century of so-called "baseball tradition."[1]

Among the many who led the decades-long campaign to end apartheid in baseball, two black sportswriters, Wendell Smith and Sam Lacy, played central roles in the larger struggle and in particular Jackie Robinson's coming to the majors.

Wendell Smith (1914–1972) grew up in Detroit, where he pitched on an integrated

American Legion team. When he was on the mound for a 1–0 victory in a playoff game in 1933, a scout who saw the game signed Smith's white catcher as well as the losing pitcher to contracts, and told Smith he would have offered him a deal if it had been allowed. Smith did not let the rejection hold him back in his pursuit of a career in journalism. As a writer and editor, he would have a greater impact on baseball than as a player. Smith graduated from West Virginia State University in 1937 and joined the *Pittsburgh Courier*, where he remained for a decade.

As Jules Tygiel wrote in his highly regarded book on the breaking of the color barrier, *Baseball's Great Experiment*, Wendell Smith "could be bitterly sarcastic and vitriolic in his rage against Jim Crow, yet lyrical in his descriptive prose."[2] For example, in the *Pittsburgh Courier* on December 10, 1938, Smith compared major league owners to Adolph Hitler. "While Hitler cripples the Jews," Smith wrote, "the great leaders of our national pastime refuse to recognize our black ball players."

In a column earlier in 1938 (May 11), titled "A Strange Tribe," Smith challenged other African Americans. "Why," he wrote, "do we continue to flock to major league ballparks, spending our hard earned dough ... is a question that probably never will be answered satisfactorily.... The fact that major league baseball refuses to admit Negro players within its folds makes the question that much more perplexing.... We black folks are a strange tribe!"[3]

In 1939 Smith published the results of interviews asking eight major league managers and about 40 players their opinions on race relations. Five of the eight managers polled expressed willingness to sign blacks if their owners approved. For example, Pittsburgh Pirates manager Pie Traynor said, "it is a known fact that there are plenty of Negroes capable of playing in the big leagues." Of those opposed, St. Louis Cardinals manager Ray Blades said the "social prejudice that exists right now will have to be broken down." Casey Stengel felt the "unrest" in black baseball was a reason for continuing the color barrier but reflected his Kansas City background when he claimed he would gladly sign players of the caliber of José Méndez, John Donaldson, and "Bullet Joe" Rogan.

Among Smith's player interviews, the comments of "Dizzy" Dean stood out. Dean spoke glowingly of Josh Gibson, Oscar Charleston, and Satchel Paige, against whom he had played in his all-star tours (see Chapter 7), adding that when he played against black all-stars he knew if his team won they had accomplished something. Smith concluded his summary of the interview: "Open your door, Mr. Owner," Dean said, "the time has come."[4]

Sportswriter Sam Lacy (1903–2003) grew up in Washington, D.C. where he often joined his father in the Jim Crow section for Washington Senators games in Griffith Stadium. Later he shagged flies for Walter Johnson, worked as a Griffith Stadium vendor, and played semi-pro baseball around the D.C. area. Lacy competed against both black and white ball players and realized that skin color was not a determiner in a man's ability. After graduating from Howard University, he served as sports editor and managing editor of the *Washington Tribune* for five years.

In 1937 Lacy interviewed Senators owner Clark Griffith about the integration of baseball and was told to forget about it because "the climate wasn't right." Lacy said he told Griffith the climate would never be right if it weren't tested. He pointed out that when the Senators weren't playing at Griffith Stadium, black stars like "Cool Papa" Bell and Josh Gibson were, and they belonged in the majors.[5]

In his articles in the *Baltimore Afro American*, Lacy took a more nuanced approach than Smith. For example, in a piece entitled "Sepia Stars Only Lukewarm Toward Campaign to Break Down Baseball Barriers" (August 12, 1939), he noted that players like Vic Harris of the Homestead Grays worried what would happen to the rest of the players in the Negro Leagues if the stars got gobbled up by the big leagues. Jud Wilson of the Philadelphia Stars doubted integration would come because the big league "is overrun with Southern blood."[6]

In response to growing public clamor, on July 16, 1942, Commissioner Kenesaw Mountain Landis made the following, now-famous statement: "Negroes are not barred from organized baseball by the Commissioner and never have been during the 21 years I have served as Commissioner.... That is the business of the managers and the club owners."

Bowing to pressure from Wendell Smith and other sportswriters, Pittsburgh Pirates owner William Benswanger, who several years earlier had expressed interest in signing Josh Gibson, agreed to a tryout for three Negro Leagues players: Roy Campanella and Sammy Bankhead of the Newark Eagles and David Barnhill of the New York Cubans. The announced date of the tryout was August 4, 1942.

J. L. Wilkinson's response to Benswanger's announcement appeared in an *Associated Negro Press* (ANP) wire story titled "The Monarchs Owner is Elated," published in the *Call* on August 7, 1942. The article reported that, "J. L. Wilkinson, co-owner of the Kansas City Monarchs, champions of the Negro American League" has voiced his approval of the plan of William E. Benswanger, owner of the Pittsburgh Pirates, to give Negro baseball players a tryout with his team. "I think it would be a fine [day] for the game," the Monarchs' owner was quoted as saying, "although we would lose some of our stars."

According to the ANP, Wilkinson recounted that he had told Satchel Paige, who was then under a two-year contract with the Monarchs, he would not stand in his way if a major league club wanted to sign the talented hurler. The Monarchs' owner added that, next to Paige, Josh Gibson would likely attract the most attention from big league clubs, but "[t]here are at least a score of players who could make any major league team." As an example, he cited Monarchs pitcher Jack Matchett as "ready made material for the Brooklyn Dodgers."

A week later the ANP reported that the scheduled tryouts in Pittsburgh had not occurred and it would be "a long time" before a decision was made regarding the integration of the big leagues. With the exception of Wilkinson, the ANP observed, owners of Negro teams were "gloomy" about the prospect of losing their stars to the majors.[7]

On December 3, 1943, for the first time in baseball history, a black delegation was allowed to address a group of 44 major league officials. The representatives included publishers of African American newspapers; Wendell Smith, who mapped out the strategy for the meeting; a few other sportswriters; and the singer and former star athlete Paul Robeson. With Robeson speaking for the group, they demanded: (1) immediate steps be taken to accept blacks into organized baseball; (2) the elevation of players from Class C, B, A, and AAA teams to the majors without discrimination against blacks; (3) the same system to select players from semi-pro teams, sandlots, etc., be used in selecting black players; (4) a joint statement be issued by the Major Leagues that African Americans are available for trials. While the delegation was graciously received and the aging Commissioner Landis reiterated his point that each club was free to sign black players, there was no change. Owners remained either silent or evasive.[8]

A year later, on December 27, 1944, former Pittsburgh Crawfords owner Gus Greenlee, who had failed in his effort to rejoin the NNL, announced the formation of a new Negro League to be called the United States Baseball League (USL). Branch Rickey proclaimed his support of the USL in May 1945, saying no other Negro Leagues would be allowed to use Ebbets Field. Rickey's entry in the new league would be called the Brooklyn Brown Dodgers, with famed Negro Leaguer Oscar Charleston at the helm. In making the announcement, Rickey blasted the NAL and NNL because of their weak contracts and use of booking agents.

In 1945 Sam Lacy proposed the creation of a committee to include the big league owners, a baseball writer, and a Negro Leagues owner. The white major leagues endorsed the idea and named Branch Rickey and Larry MacPhail, but the Negro Leagues owners, including J. L. Wilkinson and Tom Baird, did not select a member. It may not have made a difference. The group accomplished little, mostly because of the resistance of MacPhail, who had purchased the Yankees with Dan Topping in 1945 and stood to suffer financially if segregation ended. In addition, Branch Rickey had no intention of sharing his plan, well under way in the spring of 1945, to sign one or more black players for the Dodgers organization.[9]

A year after Jackie Robinson was born in Georgia on January 31, 1919, his mother Mallie took Jackie and her four other children to Pasadena, California. Inspired by his older brother, Mack, a 1936 Olympic silver medalist, Jackie became a star athlete. After lettering in basketball, football, track, and baseball at Pasadena City Junior College, he enrolled at the University of California, Los Angeles in 1939, where he again excelled in all four sports. There Jackie met Rachel Isum, his future wife.

Robinson left U.C.L.A. just short of graduation in 1941 to play semi-pro football. A year later he was drafted by the U.S. Army, attended Officer Candidates School, and was commissioned a Second Lieutenant. On July 6, 1944, Robinson refused to move to the back of an Army bus. He was found not guilty during the resultant court martial and subsequently received an honorable discharge in November 1944.

Kansas City Monarchs pitcher Hilton Smith claimed he first met Jackie Robinson in 1942 when a team of black stars—including Robinson—played an exhibition game against a service team of white major leaguers. According to one account, Smith contacted J. L. Wilkinson after the encounter and urged him to sign Robinson right away. As Robinson recalled, playing with an all-black team was frustrating. Although they promised each player 20 dollars, the promoters never paid Robinson and his teammates. He said, "I decided then and there that Negro baseball was not for me."[10]

According to his wife, Rachel, Jackie's becoming a Negro Leaguer was the result of his grabbing at a lifeline. About to be discharged from the Army late in 1944, he did not have a college degree and, outside of sports, no marketable skills. He knew he had to help support his mother Mallie, and he wanted to marry Rachel. One day while waiting for his discharge papers to come through, as Rachel related the story, Jackie started throwing a ball around with another black GI who had played for the Kansas City Monarchs. Rachel said the two struck up a conversation, and the fellow soldier told him the Monarchs were looking for players. Jack wrote to the organization, Rachel claimed, and they invited him for a tryout. During spring training in 1945, he was signed at a salary of $400 a month, and when he got a spot on the team, he felt like he had hit pay dirt.[11]

Robinson himself said that during his final days in the Army, he was at Camp Breckinridge in Kentucky when he encountered a Monarchs pitcher he identified only as "a brother named Alexander" (probably Ted Alexander), who told Robinson the Monarchs were searching for players and there was good money to be made. "I was looking for a decent postwar job," Robinson said. "So I wrote the Monarchs. After checking me out, they responded rather quickly and accepted me on a tryout basis for spring training." Robinson said Wilkinson first offered him $300 a month, but Robinson countered with $400, and the Monarchs' owner agreed.[12]

In the spring of 1945, Jackie Robinson was not unknown to the readers of the *Kansas City Call*. The paper had covered his exploits as a UCLA football star and even his winning a ping-pong tournament while he was in the Army stationed at Fort Riley in Kansas.[13]

Robinson's joining the Monarchs was reported in an early March 1945 edition of the *Call*.

> Leading the list of well-known players added to the Monarch roster for the coming season is none other than Jackie Robinson, nationally known letterman at the University of California at Los Angeles and former lieutenant in the Army. Although Robinson is better known as an All-American football player out California way his prowess as a baseball player is known by several clubs in both leagues. Robinson has recently received a medical discharge from the Army and decided to cast his lot with the Monarchs.... He will play in the infield in the Monarch lineup."[14]

Fan interest in Jackie Robinson and the 1945 Monarchs was sidelined when President Franklin D. Roosevelt died on April 12. The *Kansas City Call* noted the passing of "a great friend of the little man" and the elevation of Missourian Harry S Truman to the Presidency. The article claimed that although Missouri was not a state in which public officials had had to take stands on "the Negro question," Truman had voluntarily taken the position the *Call* commended regarding the need for anti-lynching laws.[15]

Robinson's next appearance in game accounts in the *Call* was in a late-April 1945 description of a contest in New Orleans against the Indianapolis Clowns, a team about which the rookie undoubtedly had conflicted feelings. He recognized excellent athletes when he saw them, but the antics of the Clowns players must have offended him. According to the *Call*, Robinson hit an inside-the-park home run after the Clowns' center fielder misplayed a fly.[16]

Monarchs manager Frank Duncan was quoted as saying that Robinson was playing very well both defensively and offensively and that the Monarchs management considered him one of the best rookies in recent years. With Robinson in the lineup, according to the *Call*, the Monarchs' infield was a wall and their offense was strong.[17]

Robinson was indeed contributing on the field, and at the box office as well. On May 27, Robinson was perfect at the plate in both games of a doubleheader against the American Giants in Chicago. In the first game he walked three times and singled. In the second contest he doubled, singled, and tripled.[18] The next week he was two-for-five when the Monarchs took on the Black Barons in Birmingham.[19]

On Monday night, June 11, 8,100 fans saw Robinson hit a 350-foot-homer and go two-for-three against the Indianapolis Clowns.[20] On Sunday, June 17, 16,000 enthusiastic fans greeted the Monarchs rookie at Yankee Stadium, where he singled and scored in a 3–1 win over the Philadelphia Stars. After 27 games, he was batting .345.[21] The next Sunday a crowd of 20,000 was on hand at Griffith Stadium to see him tie the park record with seven consecutive hits in a doubleheader with the Homestead Grays. On July 4, Robinson moved to first base when the regular first sacker, Lee Moody, was injured.[22] On Sunday, July 8, he had two doubles in a game against Birmingham at Ruppert Stadium.[23] However, at times Robinson struggled defensively. Before 30,000 at Briggs

Stadium in Detroit, on July 22, with Satchel Paige pitching, the Monarchs rookie's error allowed the Memphis Red Sox to beat the Monarchs, 3–2.

On a tour of the East in late July, the *Call* reported, "Jackie Robinson is still the rage everywhere he plays. He is one of the best infielders in the league as well as in Negro baseball. Jackie has keen spirit and is one of the best competitors. He enjoys every minute of every game and performs in a scintillating manner."[24]

Despite his obvious enthusiasm on the field, Jackie Robinson was not excited about playing in the Negro Leagues. He had no intention of fitting into the "brotherhood-in-misery Negro League[s] mind set," having already won adulation as a multi-sport star on integrated teams at UCLA.[25] He came to the conclusion that black teams "were poorly financed, and their management and promotion left much to be desired. Travel schedules were unbelievably hectic." Moreover, the meals and accommodations were poor, Robinson complained. He began to wonder why he should "dedicate my life to a career where the boundaries for progress were set by racial discrimination."[26]

In a 1979 interview, J. L. Wilkinson's son Dick took issue with Robinson's description of travel conditions for Monarchs players during his time with the team. "The bus Robinson rode in 1945 was top of the line, newest you could buy, built in 1942, the last year they were built during the war," Dick said. "They didn't sleep in the aisles, as Robinson said—can't recall more than two days a year they slept in the bus. [His criticism] makes no sense at all."[27]

As the only Monarch who had been an athlete at a multi-racial university, and a loner who did not drink, smoke, or party, Robinson did not fit in well with his teammates. Hilton Smith called him "hard-headed," though he said Robinson was smart enough to know how far to go.[28] Robinson was soft-spoken, but he was tightly wound. He did not tolerate the practical jokes common among ballplayers. According to Rachel, "Jack quickly came to hate life in the Negro Leagues. Oh, the camaraderie among the players was wonderful. He always had fond memories of that." But as her husband wrote in *I Never Had it Made* (1972), she pointed out, he considered it "a pretty miserable way to make a buck."[29]

While most of his Monarchs teammates found Robinson overly priggish, J. L. Wilkinson respected his rookie's strong religious faith and strict morality. Despite the difficult situation in which he found himself, Robinson believed "that Providence was at work in his life, and that Providence deserved all thanks."[30]

Robinson also stood out in another way. He did not submit without objection, as other players often did, to prejudicial treatment when traveling. He responded not with anger as much as cunning. On a Clowns-Monarchs tour, the two teams stopped at a Mexican restaurant in the black section of a south Texas town. The restaurant refused to allow the players through the front door of the restaurant, and they were instructed to go around to the back for service. Robinson refused and the restaurant's manager was called. Robinson smiled, nodded toward the streets, and said, "surely you don't intend to send us back out hungry in our own neighborhood, do you?" The manager seated the two teams and they were quickly served.[31]

Hilton Smith recounted another story of how Robinson told a filling station operator in Oklahoma, where the Monarchs had been stopping for 20 years, to take the pump out of the bus's tank when the man told him not to use the "White men only" restroom. The bus had a 50-gallon tank and that man wasn't going to sell that much gas to one customer until the next time the Monarchs stopped. The operator backed down and said, "You

A smiling Jackie Robinson (kneeling, third from left) is shown here with his 1945 Kansas City Monarchs teammates: (front row) Frank Duncan (original photograph is cropped), John Scott, Robinson, Chico Renfroe, Chester Gray, Herb Souell, Walter Thomas, Sammie Haynes; (back row) Jesse Williams, Jack Matchett, Booker McDaniels, Jim LaMarque, Dozier Hood, Eddie Williams, Lee Moody, Hilton Smith, Ensloe Wylie (National Baseball Hall of Fame Library, Cooperstown, New York).

boys go to the restroom but don't stay long." Smith claimed from that day onward the Monarchs never got gas at a place where they couldn't use the restroom.[32]

Although not happy with his lot, Jackie Robinson almost always showed respect for his Monarchs teammates. Sammy Haynes, a center fielder who roomed with Robinson, remembered that Robinson once took a seat in a bus stairwell, saying, "I'm a rookie. This is my seat."[33] The ambitious rookie did at times alienate other Monarchs. He asked manager Frank Duncan to play him in place of Jesse Williams, an all-star shortstop who was well-liked on the team.[34] Duncan refused, but when an injury to Williams opened up the shortstop position, Robinson's performance on the field won his teammates over. In 41 games during the 1945 NAL season, he hit .345, with ten doubles, four triples, and five home runs. He was selected as the West's shortstop in the East-West Game played on July 29 in Chicago.

When J. L. Wilkinson asked Newt Allen for his evaluation of Robinson, the veteran told the Monarchs owner, "[h]e's a very smart ball player, but he can't play shortstop—he can't throw from the hole. Try him at second base."[35] Allen told John Holway in an interview, "Jackie didn't have the ability at first, but he had the brains. We had a ballplayer here that was a much better ballplayer than he was—Willard Brown. He could hit, run, throw. But Jackie had one-third ability and two-thirds brains, and that made him a great ballplayer."[36]

Though he agreed that Robinson deserved the recognition he received, J. L. Wilkinson's son Dick wanted it known that Robinson was not the first, nor necessarily the best, candidate among Monarchs players for the major leagues. He said there were "about ten of them who would have been outstanding major league players—[including] Méndez, Rogan, Donaldson, Moore, Paige, Duncan, Smith. They'd have made the major leagues easily."[37]

However, those who saw him play for the Monarchs said Robinson did the little things differently, with the aim of finding a way to win. For example, he was a great bunter. "Tell him something once and you never had to tell him again, he'd pick your brains and you'd never even know it," said Frank Duncan, Jr., an Elite Giant in 1945 and son of the Monarchs' manager. When he was on first and a teammate singled to left, Robinson would keep his eye on the left fielder and round second. He would fake returning to second, and when the fielder threw to the bag, Robinson would trot to third.[38]

Despite his brilliant play, the bitterness Robinson felt during his months with the Monarchs never left him. In an *Ebony* magazine article entitled "What's Wrong with Negro Baseball" published in June 1948, Robinson blistered the Negro Leagues, saying they needed a "housecleaning from top to bottom." He cited the Monarchs' failure to sign him to a contract "the first of many things I found to be wrong with the game." He also complained about the "low salaries, sloppy umpiring, and the miserable living conditions." Teams did not monitor players' behavior off the field, and some of his teammates did not go to bed at all, Robinson noted in the same article. The owners, he said, needed to take "more interest in their players rather than worrying so much about heavy schedules and getting in as many games as they can, regardless of the caliber of game that is played." He also challenged the "questionable business connections" of some of the owners and chastised rowdy fan behavior.

The outspoken Effa Manley responded to the article by calling Robinson "ungrateful and more likely stupid." She claimed she had received a letter from the Monarchs' owners thanking her for the way she had answered Robinson.[39]

Twice during the 1945 season, Robinson thought seriously about quitting the Monarchs. The first time J. L. Wilkinson talked him out of it by offering him an extra $100 a month. Hilton Smith claimed he also talked Robinson into staying, telling the rookie, "Jackie, you have a future."[40]

By the middle of August 1945, Robinson was, Smith later said, "pretty much fed up with life as a Monarch" and had determined he would leave the team after the season and a subsequent barnstorming tour. His plan was to marry Rachel Isum, find a job as a high school coach, and settle down in Los Angeles.[41] However, the course of his baseball career and his life was about to change dramatically.

Throughout most of his long tenure in baseball, Branch Rickey (1881–1965) had shown little outward interest in racial integration. Except for a positive response to a 1933 survey, Rickey had remained largely silent throughout the fight to end the color barrier. However, his administrative and organizational skills while with the St. Louis Cardinals (1919–1942) had earned him both admiration and fame. He was also well known for his pious living, rooted in the strong Methodist faith of his family.

As a businessman, Rickey had earned a reputation for his "ruthless attitude toward financial matters." Hall of Fame slugger Ralph Kiner claimed Rickey used "any means to sign a ball player for as little as he could get him." When he became the president and general manager of the Brooklyn Dodgers in 1942, Rickey was dubbed by sportswriter Jimmy Powers "El Cheapo." Roger Kahn, who knew Rickey well, wrote, "[h]e never went to a game on Sunday, but he banked the receipts of games played on the Sabbath."[42]

Rickey's most famous moniker was "The Mahatma" ("The Great One"). Sportswriter Tom Meany coined it after he heard the Dodgers' president quote the Indian independence leader Mohandas K. (Mahatma) Gandhi: "I object to violence because when it appears to do good, the good is only temporary, the evil it does is permanent."[43] Broadcaster Red Smith called the loquacious Rickey "a man of many facets, all turned on." Some reporters called his office the "Cave of Winds."[44]

Several practical factors account for Rickey's decision to take the lead in allowing African Americans into the major leagues: the player shortage during the war years, the more liberal social climate in Brooklyn in contrast to St.. Louis, and his willingness to embrace rather than resist what he saw as the inevitability of the integration of baseball. Black players were, Rickey recognized, a fertile ground for inexpensive talent and would give the Dodgers a competitive edge for years to come. As he put it himself in 1950, "I did not employ a Negro because he was a Negro, nor did I have in mind at all doing something for the Negro race, or even bringing up that issue. I simply wanted to win a pennant for the Brooklyn Dodgers, and I wanted the best human beings I could find to help me win it."[45]

To be fair, there was also a moral dimension to Branch Rickey's openness to the integration of baseball. He had been influenced, he told Jackie Robinson and many others, by an incident of racial discrimination he witnessed as a young man. In 1910, while coaching the Ohio Wesleyan College baseball team, Rickey was in South Bend, Indiana, for a game. The hotel where the team planned to stay refused to give a room to Charley Thomas, the team's one black player. Rickey balked, insisting Thomas be allowed to stay on a cot in his room. As Rickey told the story, Thomas sat on the cot for a long time, then began to cry and start tearing at one hand with the other, trying to scratch his skin off with his fingernails. When Rickey asked what he was doing, Thomas said, "It's my hands. They're black. If only they were white, I'd be as good as anybody then, wouldn't I, Mr. Rickey? If only they were white." Rickey recounted that he reassured the young player, "the day will come when they won't have to be white."[46]

Branch Rickey began scouting players of color in earnest after arriving in Brooklyn in 1942. The Dodgers' general manager knew Josh Gibson and Satchel Paige's talent but doubted that at their age (with a slowing Gibson 30 and Paige near 40) they could contribute at the major league level, especially with the intense mental and emotional pressure they would encounter. He knew he needed a talented younger player with self-confidence and moral courage.[47]

In March 1945, the Boston Red Sox and Boston Braves succumbed to political pressure and agreed to a tryout of black players. Wendell Smith was asked to choose the Negro Leaguers he considered the top candidates. He selected infielder Jackie Robinson of the Kansas City Monarchs, outfielder Sam Jethroe of the Cleveland Buckeyes, and pitcher-outfielder Dave Hoskins of the Homestead Grays. The promised tryout with the Braves did not occur, but on April 16 at Fenway Park several Red Sox coaches observed the three African Americans work out. As Robinson later remembered, "not for one minute did we believe the tryout was sincere." He told his wife Rachel it was a "humiliating charade."[48] When Wendell Smith asked why the players had not heard anything after the Boston tryouts, Red Sox General Manager Eddie Collins evasively responded his team was afraid to tamper with players under contract to Negro Leagues teams.

Kansas City Call sports editor Willie Bea Harmon sensed the potential financial implications. If the Red Sox or another white major league team signed Jackie Robinson, who was already a well-known athlete, Wilkinson and the Monarchs were in line to receive a sizable check for the sale of his contract, she contended. In her "Sportorial" column, Harmon commented that it was significant Smith had chosen Robinson as one of the players for the tryout. "If baseball is any one thing, that thing is big business. Robinson's name means big business if he can play ball.... Robinson's name is still magic in Sportdom."[49]

On April 17, 1945, Wendell Smith was returning to Pittsburgh after the Boston tryout when he stopped in New York to call on Branch Rickey. He told the Dodgers' president that Jackie Robinson was clearly the best candidate to break the color barrier. Rickey told Smith he had heard about Robinson as a football and track star but not as a baseball player. However, on Smith's recommendation, Rickey told the three scouts he had assigned to the Negro Leagues to pay particular attention to Robinson. After meeting Robinson, Dodgers scout Clyde Sukeforth told Rickey he saw in the Monarch rookie a "fire and an incredible will to succeed." That, in addition to Robinson's experience as an army officer, and the fact that he had already played with white athletes, made him, in the scout's view, a "can't miss."

The Mahatma took a trip himself during the summer of 1945 to Los Angeles to gather personal information about Jackie Robinson. One writer he consulted in California called Robinson "the Jim Thorpe of his race." However, Rickey was concerned about Robinson's fiery temper. He had heard that Robinson threatened to punch an umpire during a Monarchs game. Rickey called Wendell Smith, who told the Dodgers' general manager he knew Robinson could be "tough to get along with," and "when he was aroused, he had a sizable temper." However, Smith emphasized, the first black player in the white major leagues could not be "a Mickey Mouse." When Rickey told Smith he had decided to sign Robinson, Smith was tempted to break the story, but the Dodgers' president swore him to secrecy.[50] Interestingly, the Dodgers' president had not contacted J. L. Wilkinson, Tom Baird or anyone associated with the Monarchs to ask for permission to talk with Robinson.

On August 28, 1945, Brooklyn Dodgers president and general manager Branch Rickey signed Kansas City Monarchs rookie Jackie Robinson to a contract with the Dodgers organization. The historic signing marked the ending of the ban on African Americans ballplayers in major league baseball. J. L. Wilkinson strongly supported the breaking of the color barrier, but stated that Rickey should have been willing to purchase Robinson's contract from the Monarchs. Rickey refused to pay the Monarchs anything (National Baseball Hall of Fame Library, Cooperstown, New York).

On the morning of August 28, 1945, Clyde Sukeforth escorted Robinson into the Dodgers' offices in New York.

The Monarchs rookie assumed Rickey wanted to sign him to a contract with the Brooklyn Brown Dodgers, but the Mahatma told Robinson he wanted to offer him a contract to play with the major league Dodgers and their organization. When Rickey asked Robinson about his situation with the Monarchs, specifically whether he was under contract with the team, Jackie said, "No, sir, we don't have contracts." It was the answer Rickey already believed he knew, but he wanted to hear it from Robinson himself.

"Do you have any agreements—written or oral—about how long you will play for them?" Rickey then asked.

"No, none at all. Just pay day to pay day," Robinson answered.

During the meeting, Rickey unleashed a torrent of taunts to test Robinson's ability to withstand the racism the Dodgers' general manager knew would come. Struggling to keep his temper under control, Robinson asked, "Mr. Rickey, do you want a Negro who's afraid to fight back." "No!" Rickey famously yelled. "I want a ballplayer with guts enough *not* to fight back." During the meeting Rickey gave Robinson, a fellow Methodist, a copy of Giovanni Papini's *Life of Christ* and pointed to the passage that said the most revolutionary teaching of Jesus was his admonition not to resist evil but to turn the other cheek.

Two hours after entering Rickey's office, Robinson left having signed a contract that bound him to the Dodgers in exchange for a signing bonus of $1,500 and a salary of $600 a month.[51]

Rachel Robinson recalled that Jackie told her his first meeting with Rickey had aroused in him a "weird mixture of emotions" but that the Dodgers' president's "strength and apparent sincerity" impressed him enough to accept the offer. Years after both men were gone, Rachel said Rickey's support of Jackie in the next few years "cemented the lifelong trust and respect they felt for each other." Both were religious, she said, had unshakable integrity, and were determined competitors.[52]

Sworn to secrecy, Jackie Robinson told no one else about the contract he had signed with the Dodgers when he returned to the Monarchs. Without explanation, the rookie proposed that he play with the Monarchs until September 21, then be allowed to leave the team and return to California. According to Robinson, Dick Wilkinson chastised him for leaving the team without permission to go to New York and said he would have to play out the season or leave immediately. An offended Robinson left the Monarchs at once and returned to California.[53]

The *Kansas City Call* reported Robinson had been "suspended" and would not appear in the line-up during a series with the Indianapolis Clowns, September 18–19.[54] However, a week later, the paper published a statement from J. L. Wilkinson that announced, "Jackie Robinson, star shortstop for the Kansas City Monarchs," had not been suspended from the team. According to the Monarchs' owner, Robinson was still a member of the team until the end of the season. He did not play the last few games "because of an injury."

Wilkinson explained that Robinson, who, he said, had helped the team win top honors during the 1945 season, had returned to his home in California when it was determined his injury would keep him out the remaining games of the regular season. The Monarchs rookie's future plans were not known, Wilkinson explained. "But," he continued, "the Monarch fans would be glad to see him again next season out there forming that second-base-shortstop combination with Williams. Jackie left the team with clean hands."[55]

Someone in the Monarchs' organization may have misled Wilkinson, inventing the injury story as a palatable cover for Robinson's abrupt departure from the team. In fact, after returning to California, Robinson showed no evidence of a season-ending injury and played in the California League for the Kansas City Royals of Los Angeles.

The paradigm shift in baseball became official on October 23, 1945. In the offices of the Montreal Royals, with whom he would play during his first season in the Dodgers' organization, Jackie Robinson publicly signed the contract Rickey had negotiated with him. It stated that from then on Robinson would have no "written or moral obligation" to any other club.[56] A calm Robinson told the reporters present, "[o]f course, I can't begin to tell you how happy I am that I am the first member of my race in organized baseball.... I can only say I'll do my very best to come through in every manner."[57] The evening before, Branch Rickey, who did not attend the signing, told his friend, broadcaster Lowell Thomas, what was about to occur. Thomas said, "Branch, all hell will break loose." "No, Lowell," Rickey responded, "all heaven will rejoice."[58]

From the outset, the two Monarchs owners, J. L. Wilkinson and Tom Baird, were publicly supportive of the signing of Jackie Robinson by Branch Rickey, although they felt they had not been fairly treated. In the first *Kansas City Call* article after the signing, Baird was quoted as saying[59]:

> I am happy to know that Jackie Robinson has been signed to play in the big leagues. It is a well-deserved advancement for the Negro race. He has my best wishes for his success. The Monarchs management stands behind the idea of any man's advancement. We have no [intent] to hold any player down. I do think, however, that we should have been consulted in the matter. That would have been the proper way, but we shall do nothing to impede Jackie's progress. He played great ball for our team this season, fielding consistently and hitting .345. Of course, we would be happy to know that he would be with us again next season.

Two days earlier, on the basis of an *Associated Press* report that went nationwide, the *New York Times* had claimed Baird was actually more defiant, saying he planned to lodge a formal complaint with Commissioner Happy Chandler, telling him, "[w]e won't take this lying down. Robinson signed a contract with us last year and I feel that he is our property."[60]

It is possible that the more circumspect Wilkinson convinced his co-owner to change his tone after this initial comment. Wilkinson's first public statement on Robinson's signing clearly backed away from his partner's contention that an appeal to Commissioner Chandler was in order. "Although I feel the Brooklyn club or the Montreal club owes us some kind of consideration for Robinson," Wilkinson said, "we will not protest to Commissioner Chandler. I am very glad to see Jackie get this chance, and I'm sure he'll make good. He's a wonderful ballplayer. If and when he gets into the major leagues he will have a wonderful career."[61]

In the October 26 *Call* article, Baird himself backed away from the statement cited on the 24th. He claimed,

> I was misquoted by the Associated Press story, if there was an implication that we are going to start a fight to keep Robinson out of the league, or were going to cause him any trouble. We are glad of his advancement and hope more Negro players get the same opportunity. We are not in Negro baseball just to make money; we want to see the Negro race advance to full participation in American activities.

That was Tom Baird's official public position. However, in private conversations, he was and remained bitter. He told some reporters, ostensibly off the record, "I have been informed that Mr. Rickey is a very religious man. If such is true, it appears that his religion runs toward the almighty dollar."[62] Three years after the signing of Robinson by the Dodgers, Baird was still insisting Rickey "owes us a moral obligation. Whatever he might have offered would have been okay with us—but he has ignored our efforts to obtain something for our great shortstop which is preposterous."[63] Baird also later complained that Rickey "was not even gentleman enough to answer or acknowledge [the] many letters I wrote him."[64]

J. L. Wilkinson's reaction to Rickey's signing was also undoubtedly more complex than his restrained first public statement suggested. Although he always went along with the sentiment that Rickey's signing of Robinson was to be heralded, the Monarchs' owner also said, "we have been out some expense in training players such as Robinson" and "something should be done to prevent white organized baseball from just stepping in and taking our players."[65] Wilkinson was perhaps most honest about his feelings when he told Hilton Smith the only thing "that ever hurt him in baseball was for them to take Jackie Robinson from him without him getting compensated anything."[66]

J. L.'s son Dick was more direct in his criticism of Branch Rickey and defensive of his father. When Jackie Robinson was signed by Rickey, "few thought to remember the man who had made it possible—J. L. Wilkinson," Dick said. "Dad never got paid for Jackie. Rickey never paid anybody for anything. Nothing could be done about it in those days. If you'd raised a voice about the money, they'd said, 'Oh, you're trying to hold a man back.' Dad wasn't like that anyway."[67]

From the outset, and for the rest of his life, Branch Rickey replied testily when anyone suggested he should have paid the Monarchs' owners when he signed Robinson. He always claimed, "the Negro organizations in baseball are not leagues, nor, in my opinion, do they have any organization. As at present administered they are in the nature of a racket."[68]

Rickey also claimed since there were no reserve clauses restricting other teams from signing players, he was just doing what any team in the Negro Leagues had been doing for years. Rickey had spent $25,000 scouting black players, and "El Cheapo" wasn't inclined to add to that total by paying the Monarchs. However, when Rickey signed more Negro Leagues players, including Roy Campanella and Don Newcombe, he "made certain the black players put into writing the lack of contractual agreements with their Negro League teams."[69]

It was true the Monarchs did not have a formal, signed contract with Robinson, but as Tom Baird later explained, "[o]ur league constitution stipulates that a player agreeing to play by signed letter or telegram is the property of the club concerned.... We had Robinson on our payroll in 1945 and we paid Social Security and withholding taxes in his behalf. He was our property all right, and Rickey knew it."[70] Baird said at a NAL meeting in Chicago in March 1948, "[t]elegrams and letters exchanged with Robinson were, as far as we were concerned, a binding contract. We paid what we promised."[71]

Others in the Monarchs' management expressed their support for Robinson. "Dizzy" Dismukes, Monarchs business manager and traveling secretary, said he had faith in Robinson and believed he would make good on any ball team. Manager Frank Duncan said he was happy at the selection made by the Dodgers.[72]

Jackie Robinson's reaction to the complaints that Rickey had "stolen" him from the Monarchs was always to come vigorously to his mentor's defense. In a February 11, 1946, *Atlanta Daily World* article, Robinson said: "I wasn't signed to a contract because [Wilkinson and Baird] didn't know whether or not I would make good, so they didn't want to have trouble getting rid of me."[73]

Seven years later Robinson was still defending Rickey passionately, saying in a 1953 article, "Vicious men may insult him, foolish men may make fun of him and petty men may not understand him. But when the vicious, the foolish, and the petty men are forgotten, Mr. Rickey will be remembered. And all decent men will respect the memory and the blow Branch Rickey struck in the cause of human progress."[74]

In response to Robinson's explanation, which he repeated over the years, Baird and Wilkinson released a statement published in *The Sporting News*: "Any ball player knows that he can be given his release at any time. Robinson was signed by the Monarchs by letter and telegram. According to the rules and regulations of the Negro Leagues, any player accepting terms by letter or telegram or playing with a club becomes the property of that club." To clarify that they were not attacking Robinson, the Monarchs' owners added, "We have always held Jackie in highest regard, both as a player and a gentleman." It was regrettable that Branch Rickey chose to "spirit Robinson away, instead of dealing honorably with us."[75]

Reaction to the signing of Jackie Robinson in the black press as well as among NNL and NAL players and officials was mostly positive. The *Pittsburgh Courier* responded, "it would not have approved of the raiding of black players by the Brooklyn organization if these had not been extraordinary circumstances." The newspaper told Baird he may have had a legal and moral justification for challenging Rickey but advised him to drop the matter. The signing of Robinson, the newspaper said in a November 3, 1945, editorial, "transcended everything else at this time." Sam Lacy wrote in the *Baltimore Afro-American*: "Alone, Robinson represents a weapon far more potent than the combined forces of all our liberal legislation." The *Chicago Defender* was more confrontational, calling Baird "as unselfish as any plantation owner."[76]

Satchel Paige was upset that he was not the first black player chosen for the major leagues. Privately, he said, "[t]he signing of Jackie hurt me deep down.... I'd been the one who'd opened up the major league parks to the colored teams. I'd been the one who everybody said should be in the majors." However, he was gracious in public. "They didn't make a mistake by signing Robinson," he said. "They couldn't have picked a better man." Paige also said he felt for Wilkinson and Baird. They "wanted to see the colored ballplayers get ahead. They were too fine gentlemen not to be happy. But they were burned up at the way it'd happened. The Dodgers'd just signed Jackie without giving them anything for him."[77]

When asked what he thought about Jackie Robinson going to the majors, Buck O'Neil said, like other players, he was happy about it. He recalled that he "couldn't stop smiling for days."[78] Buck Leonard said that although there were a number of better players in the Negro Leagues, Robinson was the "ideal man"[79] However, Leonard also knew the signing of Robinson was the death knell for the Negro Leagues. After Robinson joined the Dodgers, "we couldn't even draw flies," he said.[80] Hilton Smith echoed the sentiments of many Negro Leagues veterans: "it all came down to this, he had played with white boys."[81]

Henry Aaron was a teenager when Jackie Robinson broke the color barrier. Aaron recalled seeing Robinson for the first time when the Dodgers came to Aaron's hometown of Mobile, Alabama, for an exhibition game in 1948. The future Home Run King wrote in his 1991 autobiography, "That same day, I told my father I would be in the big leagues before Jackie retired. Jackie had that effect on all of us—he gave us our dreams. He breathed baseball into the black community, kids and grown-ups alike."[82]

In a press release responding to the signing, NAL President J. B. Martin praised

9. J. L. Wilkinson, Jackie Robinson and the Integration of Baseball (1945)

The legendary Satchel Paige with his teammate Jackie Robinson, Kansas City Monarchs, 1945.

Fort Riley, Kansas in 1943 with Roscoe Devore.

In 1945 J. L. Wilkinson's Kansas City Monarchs featured the now veteran, but still wildly popular, Satchel Paige and the rookie phenomenon Jackie Robinson. Publicly, Paige applauded Robinson's breaking of the color barrier in major league baseball two years later. Privately, he was incensed that his record had not earned him the right to be first. The inset shows U.S. Army Lieutenant Jackie Robinson (right), with a friend from Pasadena and fellow soldier, Roscoe Devore (National Baseball Hall of Fame Library, Cooperstown, New York).

Branch Rickey for his "moral courage in making the initial step that will give Negro ball players a chance to participate in the major leagues, in this our great democracy." When asked what he would say to Rickey, Martin intoned, "I feel that I speak the sentiments of 15 million Negroes in America who are with you one hundred per cent, and will always remember the day and date of this great event." However, Martin also said, "we feel Mr. Rickey is too big not to compensate the Kansas City Monarchs."[83]

Behind the scenes Martin was working with NNL and NAL officials to see that there would be no recurrence of the "theft" of a Negro Leagues player by the white leagues without just compensation. Not surprisingly, most Negro Leagues owners were supportive of the signing of Robinson by Rickey in their public statements, but privately they were outraged. On his deathbed, Homestead Grays owner Cum Posey complained, "it's like coming into a man's store and stealing the goods right off his shelves."[84]

Before the 1946 season, the Negro Leagues owners approached Commissioner Chandler and National League President Ford Frick, asking for their help in meeting the challenges of losing additional players to the majors. In 1947, when Jackie Robinson joined the Dodgers, Frick would famously tell St. Louis Cardinals players threatening to not take the field against Robinson, "If you [strike] you will be suspended from the league. You will find that the friends you think you have in the press box will not support you, that you will be outcasts.... This is the United States of America and one citizen has as much right to play as another. The National League will go down the line with Robinson whatever the consequences."[85] However, Frick never displayed the same concern for the Negro Leagues owners' right to field teams. And when the owners of black teams asked Chandler if he would become their commissioner, as well as the white major leagues commissioner, he told them to go back and clean up their own organizations, then come back and ask for recognition. In particular, he told them they would have to purge themselves of the "numbers men" in their leagues. It was just a delaying tactic. He had no intention of acting.[86]

White baseball officials were more critical in public of Rickey's signing of Robinson than their black counterparts. True to form, Clark Griffith and Larry MacPhail, who stood to lose the most money if the Negro Leagues failed, were critical of Rickey's signing of Robinson. Griffith said, "In no walk of life can one person take another's property without paying for it." Larry MacPhail's son Lee, also a major league executive, testily said of Rickey, "There but for the grace of God goes God."[87]

George Weiss, who in 1947 was the general manager of the New York Yankees, said signing black players would attract black fans, and white patrons "don't want to sit with Negroes and they'll stop coming to our games at the Stadium. To bring in Negroes is to court financial ruin."[88]

On February 16, 1948, speaking before the annual football banquet at Wilberforce University, Branch Rickey told the audience his fellow owners had unanimously adopted a report finding that "black players would jeopardize the profitability of major league baseball." According to Rickey's grandson, not a single owner stood up for him. His grandfather, he said, never got over the bigoted attacks of men he had considered colleagues and friends.[89]

Present and former major league players were mixed in their reactions to the signing of Robinson. Most were positive, but there were exceptions, foreshadowing the prejudice Jackie Robinson would encounter when he joined the Dodgers in 1947. Rogers Hornsby said, "[t]he way things are, it will be tough for a Negro player to become a part of a closely knit group such as an organized ball club. I think Branch Rickey was wrong in signing Jackie Robinson to play with Montreal and it just won't work out."[90] Upon hearing of Robinson's signing, the most popular Brooklyn player at the time, high school dropout Fred "Dixie" Walker, said, "As long as he ain't with the Dodgers, I ain't worried."[91]

In the *Kansas City Call*, the editorial response was thoughtful. In his commentary on the Robinson signing, C. A. Franklin's wrote[92]:

> Negroes like Robinson who are products of the better colleges in the U.S. know how to get along with their mates.... They have no inferiority complex and therefore no chip-on-the-shoulder attitude. Negro players have already proven themselves capable in competition with white major leaguers.... The Negro player's success will depend on the Negro public. How will they deport themselves under the excitement of the game? Negro fans will have to maintain a brand of public conduct, not merely as good, but far better than the average.

Otherwise, white fans would stay away and, forced to choose between old patrons and new, management would get rid of Negro players.

In the same edition of the *Call*, new sports editor John L. Johnson commended J. L. Wilkinson and Tom Baird for their support of the signing of Robinson by Rickey, but had a caution.

> There should be, however, a lesson in Robinson's going for owners of Negro clubs. It is estimated that Negro baseball drew better than $2,000,000 through the turnstiles this year. This is not peanut money. There is considerable cost in training players until they become capable of playing jam-up baseball. If the owners of Negro baseball clubs are not organized sufficiently to prevent any Tom, Dick or Harry from plucking out of their team any desirable player they want, they should so organize, and the sooner the better. If a baseball magnate wants a player, let him pay the price. This is the American way.

When Robinson signed with the Brooklyn Dodgers, Wendell Smith wrote eloquently that Robinson carried "the hopes, aspirations and ambitions of thirteen million black Americans heaped on his broad, sturdy shoulders." While others continued to bask in the glow of Rickey's signing of Robinson, or lamented it, Smith was thinking ahead.

In a December 19, 1945, letter he asked Branch Rickey what provisions had been made for Robinson's accommodations at the Montreal Royals' 1946 spring training camp in Florida. Rickey responded that there would be "two colored boys" at the Daytona Beach training camp. The other turned out to be pitcher Johnny Wright. The Dodgers' president asked Smith to come early to make arrangements for "these boys," adding that he hoped Smith would assure that they not say or do anything out of turn.

Wendell Smith and his friend, Sam Lacy, were at the Dodgers' spring training, providing the support Jackie and Rachel Robinson so desperately needed to make it through the rough period ahead.

When Robinson debuted for the Montreal Royals on April 18, 1946, and slammed a three-run homer in his second at-bat, Wendell Smith wrote, "[o]ur hearts beat just a little faster and the thrill ran through us like champagne bubbles." What Wendell Smith foresaw, perhaps better than anyone else besides Branch Rickey, was that bringing Jackie Robinson to the major leagues would be profitable. And it was. In Robinson's first year with the Dodgers in 1947, black attendance at Ebbets Field, home of the Dodgers, rose 400 percent over 1946. Black and white fans turned out *en masse* when the team was on the road. The first season of integrated baseball in the twentieth century set a new attendance record of 19,994,832. As Smith put it in a bit of doggerel: "Jackie's nimble, Jackie's quick, Jackie's making the turnstiles click."[93]

Over the years, many civil rights leaders have spoken about the impact Jackie Robinson's becoming a major leaguer had on them and the movement to overcome segregation in American society. Immediately after the signing, Walter White, secretary of the NAACP, said, "I am delighted that big league baseball has grown up to its name."[94]

Nearly two decades later, Dr. Martin Luther King, Jr., told his closest aide, Wyatt Tee Walker, that Robinson's example in breaking the color barrier in baseball inspired him to pursue racial integration on a national level. "Without him I would never have been able to do what I did," King said. "Back in the days when integration wasn't fashionable, Jackie understood the trauma and the humiliation and the loneliness which come with a pilgrim walking in the lonesome byways toward the high road of freedom. He was a sit-inner before sit-ins and a freedom rider before freedom rides."[95]

Of all the reactions to the signing of Jackie Robinson by Branch Rickey, the comment of one anonymous African American fan perhaps says it best: "Yes, sir, democracy means much more to me today than it did yesterday."[96]

Finally, all things considered, distinguished Negro Leagues historian John Holway summed up succinctly and well the crucial contribution of J. L. Wilkinson to Jackie Robinson's acceptance into the major leagues, when he wrote, "the signing of Robinson ... produce[d] many saints, and if one can be beatified to represent them all, that man is James [sic] L. Wilkinson, the Monarchs white owner."[97]

CHAPTER 10

Final Years for Wilkinson and the Monarchs (1946–1964)

The year 1946 was the last in which the Negro Leagues came first in the hearts of African American fans. Soon they would be devoting their attention more to those in their race who had made it into the previously all-white major and minor leagues. The shift began during the 1946 season as the *Kansas City Call* and other African American newspapers covered Jackie Robinson's exploits with the Montreal Royals of the International League, alongside their articles on Negro Leagues teams. Sportswriters like the *Call's* John L. Johnson continued to emphasize the skill and stamina of players on NAL and NNL teams, but added admiration for what Robinson was doing "for the race and for democracy."[1]

The Monarchs' receipts totaled $155,921.20 in 1946. With expenses of $95,915.84, the team's profit was $60,005.56.[2] Attendance was 100,000. By comparison, in 1946 the Chicago Cubs of the National League had an attendance of 1,342,970, spent $1,192,284.25, and had receipts of $1,930,823.03. One reason for the disparity in income was that major and minor league parks typically charged black teams 20–25 percent of gross receipts for rent. The Monarchs and other Negro Leagues teams also had to pay park workers and cover the expense of lights for night games, and white promoters like Abe Saperstein received up to 30 percent of the gate to book the parks.[3]

In 1946 the Monarchs did what they could to encourage fan support, spending $7,040.40 on publicity.[4] One way the Monarchs got out the word about their frequent barnstorming tours during the late 1940s and early 1950s was through cards placed in the windows of businesses. The cards could also be tacked to trees or telephone poles and handed out. Once a date had been booked, the Monarchs would send a form to whoever had set up the game in the town, with a space for the number of cards wanted. For example, for a game with the Pierre, South Dakota, Cowboys, 100 cards were requested by the business manager of the team, Pete Adams of Adams Clothes Shop.[5]

Tom Baird, who was taking over responsibility for promotion of the team from J. L. Wilkinson, kept a list of all the local papers where the Monarchs traveled so he could send them information.[6] For example, when the Monarchs barnstormed in Louisiana, he sent news of the games to the *Louisiana Weekly* and *The Item*, both New Orleans papers. A few radio stations were on his list, including KPRS in Kansas City and WEDR in Birmingham.[7]

When the NAL owners met in Chicago to plan the 1946 season, J. L. Wilkinson was not present. He had clearly begun to withdraw from the central role he had played in running the Monarchs for over a quarter of a century. In his place, Tom Baird represented the team. When the Kansas Citians gathered for spring training in Houston in late March, "Dizzy" Dismukes was in charge. There was no mention of Wilkinson accompanying the team, as he so often had in past years.[8]

The Monarchs opened the 1946 season in Chicago against the American Giants on May 10 before 12,000 fans and at home on May 12 with a record-breaking, standing-room-only crowd of 16,000 at Ruppert Stadium. Ticket prices were 60 cents for the bleachers, $1.00 for the grandstand, and $1.50 for box seats. John Johnson commended the fans for their good behavior—not one fight and no whiskey in evidence.[9] The Monarchs had a strong starting line-up, even though they had lost Jesse Williams and Booker McDaniels to the Mexican League.

By the end of the first week of June 1946, the Monarchs had won 12 straight games. Although their hitting was not as proficient as expected, strong pitching carried the team as the pattern of Paige-relieved-by-Smith continued. Particularly impressive on the pitching staff was "Connie" Johnson.

Alongside its story on the Monarchs' successes, the *Call* relayed the word that in Montreal Jackie Robinson was batting .347 and playing such fine ball it was predicted he would be in a Brooklyn Dodgers uniform before the season ended.[10]

On June 30, 1946, a crowd of 5,156 at Ruppert Stadium watched the Monarchs take both games in a twin bill against the Birmingham Black Barons. In the second contest, former Monarch Hurley McNair, who was now an umpire, pulled a knife on the Barons' manager, Tommy Sampson, who had shoved him during an argument. McNair chased Sampson around the diamond until one of the Barons players threw his skipper a bat, causing the chase to be reversed. The fight ended only when police rushed onto the field with drawn pistols. The fans joined the fracas by throwing pop bottles, apparently at the umpire.[11]

On July 14, 1946, the largest crowd ever to watch an African American baseball game at the Polo Grounds saw Satchel Paige and the Monarchs blank the New York Cubans, 11–0. Paige was on the mound for five innings, allowing only four singles. Hilton Smith relieved him and gave up two hits in the final three frames.[12]

Throughout the 1946 season, racial tensions in the country continued to affect baseball. On August 11, at a game in Ruppert Stadium, almost 8,000 spectators, one-fourth of them white, stood for a moment of silence in protest against the "Nazi-like disregard for … human life" shown in the murder of four blacks, two of them women, in Monroe, Georgia, a few days previously. The protest was made at the request of the Kansas City branch of the NAACP. Meanwhile, traveling in the South with the Montreal Royals, Jackie Robinson "kept his head" while being subjected to racist taunts by fans and opposing players.[13]

On Friday, August 16, 1946, "Q. J. Gilmore Appreciation Night" was held to recognize the Monarchs' business manager's long and faithful efforts in behalf of the Kansas City ball club. A gift of $967.43 was presented to Gilmore. Another "Gilmore Appreciation" game was held in 1947 as J. L. Wilkinson and Tom Baird announced their intention to hold such a night annually to raise funds for their now incapacitated colleague.[14]

The Monarchs needed to win one game in a doubleheader with the Indianapolis Clowns on Sunday, September 1, to clinch the second-half 1946 NAL pennant. A crowd of 12,491 gathered to see the Monarchs lose the opener, 4–3. Satchel Paige was dozing in the locker room when he heard that the Monarchs had fallen short in the first game and it would be up to him to win the second. He held the Clowns to six hits, and the Monarchs won, 6–1.[15]

Despite his negative feelings about the months he spent with the Monarchs in 1945, in a letter to the Paseo Y.M.C.A. of Kansas City written during the 1946 season, Jackie Robinson readily gave his permission to use his name in the formation of the integrated Jackie Robinson Junior Baseball League for youngsters 17 and under. Wilkinson and the Monarchs served as the league's sponsor.

Meanwhile, across the state in St. Louis, youth leagues were still segregated. Umpires forfeited a game because one of the players for the Visitation Parish team was an African American, in violation of municipal rules that did not permit blacks to play in league games.[16]

The 1946 Negro Leagues World Series pitted the Kansas City Monarchs against the Newark Eagles.[17] Abe and Effa Manley's Eagles featured pitching sensation Leon Day, who had started the season with an Opening Day no-hitter. Mike Manning and Rufus Lewis were also outstanding Eagles moundsmen. Future major leaguers and Hall of Famers Larry Doby at second base and Monte Irvin at shortstop anchored the infield. Biz Mackey was the manager of the Eagles, who cruised through the season, winning nearly 75 percent of their league games. They had also drawn well at the gate.

The Monarchs also had several soon-to-be major leaguers. Two would be Hall of Famers: Satchel Paige and Willard Brown, who played briefly for the St. Louis Browns. The third was Hank Thompson, who also spent time with the Browns before going on to a nine-year career with the New York Giants. He was the first African American to play in both the American and National Leagues.

According to Frazier Robinson, while a Monarch, Hank Thompson shot and killed a man in self-defense in a bar in Dallas. Asserting that J. L. Wilkinson was "the best friend a ballplayer in trouble could have," Robinson recalled that the Monarchs' owner worked things out and Thompson wasn't charged, though Thompson always said "that guy [he shot] was always with him."

The first game of the 1946 Series was played at the Polo Grounds in New York City on September 17, with a number of major league scouts in the stands. Smith started and Paige relieved for a change, and the two combined to beat Leon Day, 2–1, before a crowd of 19,423. Hank Thompson homered.

Two days later, 10,000 fans cheered on the Eagles in Newark. Boxing legend Joe Louis tossed out the first pitch, and Newark won, 7–4. Brown homered in the sixth to give the Monarchs a 4–1 lead, but Doby's two-run homer off Paige led to the comeback Eagles victory.

The Monarchs' bats were on fire in a 15–5 win in the third game, played at Ruppert Stadium in Kansas City on Sunday, September 22. A total of 8,492 fans paid $1–$2 each to see the contest.

The fourth game, played the next day, Monday, September 23, was also in Kansas City. Lewis threw a four-hitter in an 8–1 Eagles win before a much smaller crowd of 3,836.

The fifth match-up was in Chicago at Comiskey Park under the lights on September 25 before 4,000 spectators. Smith led the Monarchs to a 5–1 win.

The Series returned to Newark with the Eagles needing to win two straight to take the title. The Monarchs surged ahead in the first inning of the sixth game, played on

At times, as shown here, the front page of the *Kansas City Call* included an article on the exploits of the Kansas City Monarchs next to an entry in the paper's ongoing coverage of the struggle of African Americans for justice (*The Kansas City Call*, September 27, 1946).

September 26, with Brown again showing off his power with a four-bagger. However, the Eagles were not intimidated and evened the score in the bottom of the first. They hung on for a 9–7 win, forcing a seventh and deciding game.

A crowd of 7,500 fans was justifiably angered when three of the best Monarchs players were no-shows for the finale on September 28: Willard Brown, Ted Strong, and Satchel Paige. Nonetheless, the seventh game was exciting. Rufus Lewis started for the Eagles and was given an early lead when Irvin drove in a run in the first. O'Neil tied the score in the sixth with a home run. Johnny Davis gave the Eagles a two-run lead with two RBI in the bottom of the sixth, but the Monarchs pulled within one the next inning. O'Neil was robbed in the eighth when Day ran down a long drive in center to keep the Eagles in the lead, 3–2. The Monarchs nearly tied the game in the ninth, but a pop-up ended the game and the Series with the tying run on second. The Monarchs had outscored the Eagles, 36–34, in the Series and may have won the championship had three of their stars not bolted before the deciding contest.

The early departure of Paige and Brown was probably to join the Feller/Paige All-Star tour described below. The two future major leaguers anticipated a bigger payday on the tour than in the World Series and wanted to make sure they would not be left behind.

Strong's leaving the Monarchs during the 1946 World Series is a more intriguing story. In an interview published after the Series J. L. Wilkinson told the *Call* that Strong had "deserted the Monarchs." According to the Monarchs' owner, Strong simply walked out on the team when it was fighting to win the World Series. "He left without notice or explanation," Wilkinson said. "And because he left us without a regular right fielder to replace him, I am of the opinion we lost the championship to the Newark Eagles." According to Wilkinson, Strong did not go to Chicago for the fifth game. He started to board the bus but after putting his luggage on board, he abruptly removed it and left by taxi. Monarchs manager Frank Duncan was forced to use pitchers in right field for the final three games and had to recall Jim Greene, who had been out with a broken thumb.

In an interview with the *Call's* sports editor, John Johnson, Strong claimed his action in leaving the team was the result of his having been approached by "three unknown Negroes who tried to 'proposition' him on the Chicago game." Strong said the men offered him $750 cash if he would "confirm" whether the Monarchs were going to win or lose the fifth game in Chicago. They were strangers to him and looked like gamblers. "I told them I would have nothing to do with their scheme.... I don't know whether they had talked to other team members or not."

Strong told Johnson another factor in his deciding to leave the Monarchs was general dissatisfaction "as a result of long rides in an overcrowded bus and sometimes no rooms after a two-day ride because the man who was supposed to get them failed to do so." The Monarchs players had scheduled a team meeting in the summer to discuss their concerns, Strong claimed, but it was never held. He said that after the last series with the Clowns he had a charley horse and asked for two days off, but was given only one. Everything added up to provoke him, he said, and the effort by the men to "buy" him blew his top. He acknowledged he wished he had talked it over with someone and was sorry if his absence caused the Monarchs to lose the Series.

Strong wanted *Call* readers to understand that neither J. L. Wilkinson nor Tom Baird knew of the unfavorable conditions that troubled the team. "If they knew of these things, I'm sure something would be done about them," Strong emphasized. He praised the two owners, saying, "both were swell men to work for, that Wilkinson had done him favors which he appreciated."

In the midst of its 1946 World Series coverage, the *Call* reported Jackie Robinson had won the International League batting crown with a .349 average. It was doubtful, the *Call* observed, any other player could have done so well, with the crushing odds that faced him.

In the late 1930s, when Bob "Rapid Robert" Feller was an inexperienced teenager in his first years with the Cleveland Indians, J. L. Wilkinson introduced him to barnstorming with Negro Leagues players. Feller, who became a savvy entrepreneur himself, respected Wilkinson's baseball knowledge and business acumen. Feller said that it was during his service with the U.S. Navy in World War II that the idea of organizing his own barnstorming tour with Negro Leaguers came to him. In an interview with Fay Vincent, an elderly Feller said as soon as he was discharged from the Navy, he contacted Wilkinson, asked his advice, and the two made a deal. Feller would put together a major league All-Star squad, and Wilkinson would organize a team with the best players of the Negro Leagues, to barnstorm after the 1946 season.[18]

Two of the best pitchers in baseball history, both Hall of Famers, the Monarchs' Satchel Paige and Bob "Rapid Robert" Feller (1918–2010) of the Cleveland Indians, fielded all-star teams for a barnstorming tour after the 1946 season. The 30-day tour was the brainchild of Feller, who had been inspired by J. L. Wilkinson's earlier barnstorming successes. The series was a huge windfall, drawing 400,000 fans whose ticket purchases lined the pockets of the black and white players (*Kansas City Call* [October 4, 1946]).

Feller recruited for his All-Stars some top major leaguers, including Mickey Vernon, Charlie Keller, Vince DiMaggio, Bob Lemon, Johnny Sain, Ralph Kiner, Phil Rizzuto, Spud Chandler, Dutch Leonard, and Stan Musial. Musial joined the tour after the 1946 World Series ended. Afraid his star would suffer an injury, Red Sox owner Tom Yawkey paid Ted Williams $10,000 *not* to sign with the tour.

In addition to the obvious choice, Satchel Paige, who was an eager participant, Wilkinson tapped five other Monarchs for the team: Hilton Smith, Hank Thompson, Willard Brown, Othello Renfroe, and Buck O'Neil. Three members of the NNL champion Newark Eagles were also signed: Monte Irvin, Leonard Pearson, and Max Manning. Paige's preferred battery mate, with whom he had played on the Bismarck Churchills, Quincy Trouppe, by then manager of the Cleveland Buckeyes, was the first-string catcher.

Jackie Robinson, Roy Campanella, and Buck Leonard turned down offers. Eight future Hall of Fame players were on the two teams: Feller, Paige, Musial, Lemon, Rizzuto, Smith, Irvin, and Brown.

Somehow Feller secured Commissioner Chandler's permission not only for a 30-day barnstorming tour but also for a start date during the Red Sox-Cardinals World Series. The schedule called for games in 31 towns in 17 states, with 13,000 miles of travel. The teams crisscrossed the country in state-of-the-art DC-3 airplanes leased from Flying Tigers Airlines. "Bob Feller All-Stars" was painted on one plane and "Satchel Paige All-Stars" on the other. Flying allowed the teams to play one game in the afternoon and another in the evening, hundreds of miles away.

The first game of the tour was in Pittsburgh, Pennsylvania on September 30. Paige's All-Stars were the victors, but, as in all barnstorming tours, the take at the gate, not the win, was what mattered.

The first doubleheader in different cities was on October 1, with an afternoon game in Youngstown and a contest under the lights in frigid Cleveland, Ohio. The two teams played in Yankee Stadium in early October on a Friday night and Sunday afternoon. On the Saturday in between they were in Newark. Then it was on to the Midwest, and finally up and down the West Coast, from Vancouver to San Diego. More than 10,000 fans were turned away from the first game in Los Angeles, which was attended mostly by African Americans.

One of the best games was played in Kansas City on October 13. Feller's team was leading, 2–1, going into the bottom of the ninth. The Yankees' Spud Chandler was on the mound with two outs. Willard Brown reached on an error, bringing John Davis to the plate. He took a ball, then unleashed a terrific cut at a waist-high fastball. In the Paige All-Stars' dugout, "Dizzy" Dismukes said, "Lord, if he throws Davis another one like that they'll never find the ball." He did, giving Paige's team a 3–2 victory.

The series was successful, drawing an estimated 400,000 fans. Both black and white players were paid well—at least $100 a game, with generous meal money. For the black stars, except for Paige, it was the biggest payday they had ever seen for an exhibition series. Feller, who fronted the entire cost, an estimated $50,000, told Fay Vincent, "we were interested in one thing, making money. I mean what else is there; yes we put on a good show; there was racial rivalry, not amongst the players, but amongst the fans. And we got a few laughs; they're great friends of mine. They love me dearly. I love them dearly. I know all the guys. We made more money in that month of October than we made all year round."

However, in the immediate aftermath of the barnstorming series, Feller was not so fulsome in his comments about the Negro Leaguers. In the October 30, 1946, edition of *The Sporting News,* he told Steve George that he hadn't "seen one Negro ball player good enough to make the grade in the big leagues—Well, maybe Satchel Paige—when he was young—but when you name him, you're done. Not even Jackie Robinson is big league timber."

After the 1946 Feller-Paige All-Stars extravaganza, Commissioner Chandler banned future barnstorming until after World Series games were completed.

Would Branch Rickey call up Jackie Robinson to the Brooklyn Dodgers? That was the question throughout baseball after the 1946 season. Robinson told the Associated Negro Press: "The good Lord was on my side last year, I hope he's with me this year." He said he was hopeful he would move up to the Dodgers not so much for the personal benefits as for the path that would be opened for other Negro ball players in future years.[19] The speculation continued into late March 1947 with Rickey coy as to whether Robinson would join the Dodgers. However, on April 10, he announced that Brooklyn had purchased Jackie Robinson's contract from the Montreal Royals. Robinson played his first game at Ebbets Field five days later.

It was not smooth sailing for the Brooklyn rookie. Robinson faced a near-revolt among his Dodgers teammates. It did not end until manager Leo Durocher and Branch Rickey took decisive action. Robinson also faced viciously racist taunting from opponents. In a famous column entitled "Lynch Mobs Don't Always Wear Hoods," *New York Post* columnist Jimmy Cannon responded[20]:

> You don't always lynch a man by hanging him from a tree. There is a great lynch mob among us and they go unhooded and work without the rope.... Their weapon is as painful as the lash, the hot tar, the goose feathers, or the shotgun. They string up a man with the whisper of a lie and they persecute him with ridicule. They require no burning cross as a signal of assembly and need no sheet to identify themselves to each other. They are the night riders who operate 24 hours a day.
>
> They lynch a man with a calculated contempt which no court of law can consider a crime. Such a venomous conspiracy is the one now trying to run Jackie Robinson out of organized baseball.... We should all be ashamed of it, not only those connected with the sport, but any one who considers this his country. It is an indication, I believe, that as a people we are a failure and not as good as the laws by which we live.
>
> We have been involved in a war to guarantee all people the right to a life without fear.... In such a world it seems a small thing that a man be able to play a game unmolested. In our time such a plea should be unnecessary. But when it happens we must again remember that all this country's enemies are not beyond the frontiers of our home land.

Despite the bigotry he endured, Jackie Robinson went on to have an excellent season in 1947, winning Rookie of the Year honors on a unanimous ballot and helping the Dodgers reach the World Series. The *Call* had almost as many stories about Robinson's performance with the

When Jackie Robinson began his major league career in April 1947, Branch Rickey's prediction that black fans would flock to see him proved accurate. For an appearance of the Brooklyn Dodgers' rookie in St. Louis for games against the Cardinals on June 14–15, 1947, Missouri Pacific Railroad organized a "Jackie Robinson Special" to take fans across the state from Kansas City. Needless to say, many who made the trip were Monarchs supporters, whose enthusiasm was now focused more on the former Monarchs player than the team from which Branch Rickey had raided him (*Kansas City Call* [May 16, 1947]).

JOIN THE CROWD ON THE

JACKIE ROBINSON SPECIAL

VIA

MISSOURI PACIFIC LINES

SEE TWO GAMES

BROOKLYN DODGERS

VS.

ST. LOUIS CARDINALS

SPECIAL TRAIN

Lv. K. C., 8:30 a.m., June 14
Ar. St. Louis 2:30 p.m. June 14
Lv. St. Louis 6:30 p.m. June 15
Ar. K. C., 12:30 a.m., June 16

ROUND TRIP FARE
INCLUDING TAX

$12.99

FOR FURTHER
INFORMATION
CALL OR WRITE

MISSOURI-PACIFIC TICKET OFFICE
1029 GRAND   K. C., MO.
TEL. VI 6100

ALSO

CONSOLIDATED TICKET OFFICE
906 N. 6th   AT. 1550
KANSAS CITY, KAS.

Dodgers in 1947 as accounts of Monarchs players. When the Dodgers played the St. Louis Cardinals in June, before a huge crowd of nearly 30,000, a special round trip excursion by train from Kansas City to St. Louis for $12 was advertised in the *Call*. Hilton Smith noted, "everybody wanted to go over [from Kansas City] to St. Louis to see Jackie. So our league began to go down, down, down."[21]

As the years went on, Jackie Robinson became an outspoken participant in the civil rights movement. In 1962 he called on the NAACP, of which he was a national board member, to become more militant, saying the organization was "not meeting the needs of the masses."[22] Although the stress would show, and contribute, his wife Rachel believes, to his early death at only 53, Robinson had a ten-year, Hall-of-Fame career with the Dodgers. Today Major League Baseball celebrates "Jackie Robinson Day" every April 15, and his number 42 has been retired throughout both the National and American Leagues.

As the 1947 NAL season approached, J. L. Wilkinson remained active in the Monarchs' management, telling the *Call* he predicted the team would be as strong as, if not stronger than, last year's club. Once again he emphasized that nothing would be spared to field a winning team.[23] However, he continued to step aside from league activities. At the NAL winter meeting in January, Wilkinson was not a league officeholder for the first time in many years.[24]

The next month, Abe Saperstein's application for his Cincinnati Crescents to join the league was denied. Plans to add teams from Detroit and St. Louis fell through when funding did not materialize, so the NAL continued as a six-team league. At a June meeting, NAL President J. B. Martin reaffirmed the league's support for integration. However, Branch Rickey turned down an invitation to attend the meeting at which he would have been given an award for his role in the breaking through baseball's color barrier.

Despite the "Robinson effect," fans continued to support most NNL and NAL teams in 1947. The Monarchs' home opener in May at Blues Stadium drew 16,846. Two East-West Games, one in Chicago on July 29, which drew 48,112, and another two days later at the Polo Grounds in New York, with 38.402 in attendance, demonstrated the continued popularity of black professional baseball.[25]

During the 1947 season, J. L. Wilkinson and Tom Baird continued to rely on games with the still-popular Indianapolis Clowns to boost gate receipts at home. On June 8, 12,262 turned out for a Clowns-Monarchs doubleheader.[26] They met again on June 29 and August 17 in Kansas City. The two Monarchs owners also depended for revenue on barnstorming in surrounding states as well as "loaning" Satchel Paige to other teams.

There was also a dramatic change in J. L. Wilkinson's health during the 1947 season. In July he and several Monarchs players were involved in a serious car accident in Chicago. Wilkinson ruptured the retina in his right eye. As a result of complications during cataract surgery at the Kansas University Medical Center, he lost all vision in his left eye, leaving him with 25 percent vision, according to his son Dick. He was no longer able to read or drive.[27]

The inevitable decline of professional black baseball began as the 1947 season progressed. The impact of the integration of the major leagues was greater, and occurred sooner, on the NNL teams in the East. For example, the Newark Eagles lost half of their fan base between 1946 and 1947. The 1947 Negro World Series drew limited interest, both from fans and the press.

According to critics, after years of taking the support of black fans for granted, the Negro Leagues owners had failed to make necessary changes in administration and publicity. With attendance declining, owners, including Wilkinson and, especially, Baird, turned to a strategy of black player development, offering to sell their best players to white major and minor league teams.[28] Larry Doby of the Newark Eagles signed with Bill Veeck's Cleveland Indians in July 1947 to become the first black player in the American League. In contrast to Rickey, Veeck negotiated directly with the Eagles' owners, Abe and Effa Manley, and paid them $15,000.[29]

Besides the Dodgers and Indians, most major league teams in 1947 remained reluctant to add black players. An exception was the St. Louis Browns, who signed two Kansas City Monarchs, infielder Hank Thompson and outfielder Willard Brown, on July 17. J. L. Wilkinson and Tom Baird negotiated an acceptable sale price of $5,000, with the assurance of more if the two players lasted longer than a month with the team. Baird praised Browns Vice President Bill DeWitt, who "made it very plain from the start of our negotiations that he wanted to do business with Mr. Wilkerson [sic] and me, and not the players. Everything was up and above-board."[30] Some sportswriters were starting to call the Monarchs the "foremost Negro preparatory school for the major leagues."[31]

In his "Sport-Light" column, John L. Johnson addressed why the Monarchs sold Thompson and Brown to the Browns, knowing the deal would deprive them of a chance to win 1947 Negro Leagues World Series[32]:

> Well, first, there is J. L. He's a square shooter, if there ever was one. J. L. Wilkinson and T. Y. Baird, owners of the club, believe in giving a man a chance. That is the reason they sold Thompson and Brown. It was not the money, for the Monarchs are and have been for years a money-making club. They sold these players because they wanted the men to have an opportunity to enter the majors....
>
> J. L. ... has built the Monarchs, made their name a conjuring word throughout the country; this man who has been a tower of strength to the league, a friend to every player of the team, and well liked by each in turn, is just that kind of guy.
>
> He never sees his team play anymore. He sits at home in his room—his eyesight almost gone. He has suffered much in the past few months. He has undergone one eye operation and has still another to undergo. And there is not too much hope.
>
> But eyesight or no, he still guides the destiny of the team.... [T]he players ... know that he's a square shooter all the way, that they can always go to him man to man. He's still one of the men who has done much for Negro baseball.
>
> Because he shoots square and always has, he has no regrets about selling Thompson and Brown. He believes in giving a guy a chance. That's the kind of management that is behind the Kansas City Monarchs. J. L. is on the level.

When the expectation that blacks would flood to Sportsman's Park in St. Louis to see Thompson and Brown and boost the shaky finances of the Browns did not come to pass, the two players were released on August 23, 1947, and returned to the Monarchs.[33]

The admission of a few black players to the major leagues in 1947 did not mean, from the perspective of most journalists, that the Negro Leagues should disband. As one New York writer put it, "[t]here are Negroes who join white churches, but is that a sign that there is no need for the countless Negro churches we have?"[34]

However, NNL and NAL owners knew changes needed to be made. They voted at their December 1947 meeting to submit an application for admission to the National Association of Professional Baseball Leagues, but it was rejected because of the overlapping of regions with the white majors and minors. With joining organized baseball not an option, owners turned to other strategies. In January 1948, NNL and NAL owners agreed to a 25 percent reduction in total payroll limits per team to $6,000 a month. Needless to say, it was not a popular move with players.[35]

As the 1948 season approached, J. L. Wilkinson was nearly 70 years old and ailing. As Dick Wilkinson recalled, "my dad saw the handwriting on the wall. With Jackie [Robinson] going to the Majors, he knew the great days of the Monarchs were over. He knew he had to sell the team."[36]

Consequently, after nearly 30 years as Principal Owner and President of the Kansas City Monarchs, J. L. Wilkinson agreed to sell his interest in the team to his long-time partner, Tom Baird. The contract, dated February 5, 1948, called for Wilkinson to be paid $27,000 by Baird. He also would receive one-half above $500 of the sale price for any member of the Kansas City Monarchs on the 1947 roster, "and half of money received for assignment and transfer of the player Jackie Robinson." The contract also stipulated that J. L. Wilkinson or his son Dick could use the name "Kansas City Traveling Club except in Denver and the states of Kansas, Iowa, and Nebraska and all cities where the Kansas City Monarchs Baseball Club played in 1947." As long as either J. L. or Dick continued to operate the Monarchs' traveling club, Baird could not give the rights to anyone else. The contract further stated that if the Monarchs Baseball Club ceased operations after 1948, rights to the team would revert to Wilkinson or his son.[37]

After buying his partner's share in the Monarchs, Tom Baird announced that Wilkinson "plans to take a rest." He said he expected a strong team for the 1948 season. Players, Baird revealed, would report to San Antonio for spring training about April 1.[38]

By June 30, 1948, Baird's Monarchs showed a net profit of $9,173.78 for the first two months of the season, with gate receipts of $39,775.15 and expenses of $30,601.37 (including $16,518.43 for player salaries, $2,345.56 for hotels, $2,227.28 for publicity, and $1,019.09 for transportation).[39]

James "Cool Papa" Bell (1903–1991) was the manager of the traveling Monarchs. According to Dick Wilkinson, Bell "was a lot like my father, never drank or smoked. I near even heard him swear. A fine man. A fine ball player too."

In the estimation of many who saw him on the diamond, "Cool Papa" was the fastest man ever to play baseball. He once stole two bases on one pitch, and he often scored from first on a sacrifice. Perhaps Bell's most famous feat was scoring from second on a ground ball to win the 1934 East-West Game. In 35 games against big leaguers, Bell hit .391 and stole 15 bases. Paul Waner called him "the smoothest center fielder I've seen." Bill Veeck placed him alongside Tris Speaker, Joe DiMaggio, and Willie Mays as the best outfielders he had ever witnessed. Jackie Robinson put Bell with Hank Aaron and Mays in his all-time, all-star outfield.[40]

In a 1971 interview, Bell said of his experience managing the traveling team, "[w]hen we played in the Monarchs territory we were the Kansas City Stars. Outside the territory we were the Kansas City Monarchs with Satchel Paige. A lot of scouts thought we was the league team and we sold about thirty-eight ball players that I had scouted, started and developed to the major leagues. They didn't all make the majors, but they were in the farm system." Elston Howard and Ernie Banks were among the players Bell groomed. Bell said Paige stayed with him just over a month into the 1948 season, before he was sold to the Cleveland Indians.[41]

In another interview, with John Holway, Bell said Paige wanted him to manage the traveling team. Bell remembered Satchel telling him: "[y]ou never made money in baseball. This may be your chance to make some money." Bell said, "I was supposed to get one-third of every ballplayer that they sold to the majors that I found and developed."[42]

Dick Wilkinson went on the road with the traveling team, but eventually left, disgusted, he said, because no one seemed to be able to control Satchel Paige. He did not return to baseball, pursuing a successful business career outside the game, with a beer distributorship and two car dealerships.[43]

Until J. L. Wilkinson's health began to fail and he purchased full rights to the Monarchs name, Tom Baird, as we have seen, had played a largely behind-the-scenes role in team operations. However, he had made important contributions to the success of the Monarchs. For example, during the 1930s Baird had played a key role in promoting both the original House of David baseball team and the Monarchs, arranging for the two teams to barnstorm separately and together. He also collaborated with Indianapolis Clowns owner Syd Pollock in promoting the popular and profitable Monarchs/Clowns tours.

Looking back on those barnstorming days three decades later, Baird and Pollock reminisced about having to be on the lookout for ticket sellers skimming money. At one Clowns-Monarchs game in the late 1930s, the two posed as ticket-buying fans to catch one cheating seller.

When J. L. Wilkinson sold his interest in the Monarchs to his longtime partner Tom Baird in 1948, the contract allowed him to own a Monarchs traveling team. The team was managed by James "Cool Papa" Bell (1903–1991). Bell, considered by many the fastest man ever to play professional baseball, already had a distinguished career in the Negro Leagues (1922–1946), including playing for the Monarchs (1932–1934). A switch-hitter, Bell compiled a career average of .337 and had incredible range as a center fielder. As manager of the Monarchs' traveling team, he earned the respect of all who played for him, including Satchel Paige. Inducted in 1974, Bell was the fifth Negro Leaguer selected for the National Baseball Hall of Fame (National Baseball Hall of Fame Library, Cooperstown, New York).

More than a quarter-century later, laughing and thanking Pollock for grabbing his raised hand to prevent him from committing assault and battery, Baird said, "But somehow, Syd, I still wish you'd have let me hit the son of a bitch."[44]

After buying out Wilkinson's interest in the Monarchs in 1948, Baird would become, by the time he sold the Monarchs in 1955, "the longest-serving owner in black baseball history." Baird continued to have numerous other business interests in addition to the Monarchs. He owned rental properties and operated two successful bowling alleys, one in Kansas and the other in Missouri. He collected rent from a local flower shop, a tavern, a hotel, and long-time Monarchs secretary Quincy Gilmore and his family. Baird also owned property in Kansas, where he paid for a search to find oil that proved unsuccessful. In addition, he belonged to many local organizations such as the Kiwanis Club.

Like J. L. Wilkinson, Tom Baird rarely commented on the state of race relations. They both let their actions in treating their black players and employees fairly and with compassion speak for them. However, Baird did have this to say in 1950[45]:

> You know, I was born in Arkansas—in the free Ozark hill country. But I early learned to look on men, white and black, for what they individually are. I've lived over on the Kansas side where I started out in semipro baseball, and the one thing that has grown upon me as the greatest need is for simple everyday contact between people. When people really know each other there is little room for suspicion and hatred.

Buck O'Neil had been given a chance in 1947 to become the Monarchs' manager, but he believed the circumstances weren't right. After a Monarchs loss to the Indianapolis Clowns late in the season, Dick Wilkinson had become upset and took the bus keys from manager Frank Duncan. Dick tried to give the keys to O'Neil, who refused to accept them, saying they would have to wait until they got back to Kansas City so Duncan and Dick's father could talk it over. Hilton Smith also refused Dick's offer to become the Monarchs' manager.

O'Neil said he didn't blame Dick. Along with a lot of other people in black baseball, Dick and his dad knew that it was the beginning of the end for the Negro Leagues, O'Neil emphasized. In 1948, after he had taken control of the Monarchs, Tom Baird renewed the request for Buck O'Neil to become player/manager. This time he accepted. At 36 he knew he was at the end of his playing career. Baird called O'Neil "one of the best managers [the Monarchs] ever had. He was a leader, never raised his voice against a player and was quick to develop a potential star."[46] "Dizzy" Dismukes was the traveling secretary until 1951, when O'Neil took over that role as well.[47] O'Neil knew he had to field the best team he could to interest white teams in the Monarchs' players. The result was an intriguing mix of veterans and rookies.

Among the youngsters on the 1948 Monarchs was rookie Elston Howard (1929–1980). Buck O'Neil was unsure where Howard would play, but he knew the rookie could hit. Unlike Jackie Robinson, Elston Howard loved playing for the Monarchs despite the rigorous travel schedule. "Playing for the Monarchs," Howard would later say, "was a lot like playing for the Yankees." He remembered how well Monarchs players were treated. While in Kansas City, Howard and his teammates would eat at the Rose Room in the Streets Hotel, or at Arthur Bryant's barbecue place, at the corner of Eighteenth and Brooklyn, where they would often consume all they wanted—free of charge.

The Monarchs were strong when Howard arrived, still drawing up to 11,000 a game at Ruppert Field. O'Neil quickly realized that in Howard he had "a model citizen, a smart young player who would never stay out at night, wouldn't get drunk or chase after

In 1948 the Monarchs signed St. Louis native Elston Howard (1929–1980). Howard remained with the Monarchs for three years, until July 1950, when his contract was sold by Tom Baird to the New York Yankees organization. In 1955 he would become the first African American player to wear a Yankees uniform (Kenneth Spencer Research Library, University of Kansas Libraries).

women." His manager called him "a fine young man," who was liked by all his teammates."[48]

The rookie would make his mark on the field as well. In his first game with the Monarchs, Howard hit a 400-foot home run. However, O'Neil noticed that "Ellie," as his teammates called him, was lifting his left leg too high before making contact with the ball, leaving him slightly off-balance. Once that flaw was corrected, Howard was a much more consistent hitter.[49] Howard's highlight during the 1948 season was hitting three home runs one day and two the next. According to some records, he played catcher, left field, and first base while hitting .283 in 1948 and .270 in 1949.[50]

Tom Baird was ready to sell Howard's contract to a major league team after the 1948 season. In a letter to Lee MacPhail of the New York Yankees, dated February 23, 1949, Baird suggested that the Yankees send scouts to the Monarchs' spring training to take a look at Howard and Gene Baker. The Monarchs' owner called Howard "the best looking youngster I've seen in years." He said the Cubs were interested in Howard but that "the Yankees have first call on Monarch players."[51]

By 1950, when Howard roomed and forged a close friendship with teammate Ernie Banks, major league scouts frequented the team's games. After the season, the Braves expressed interest in Howard, and Baird offered to sell his contract for $7,500. However, Boston backed away because of the likelihood, they contended, that Howard would be drafted into the armed services.[52] He was indeed called up and sat out the 1951–1952 seasons.

In a letter to Lee MacPhail on September 3, 1950, Baird acknowledged receiving $5,000 from the Yankees as initial payment for Howard and another Monarch, right-handed pitcher Frank Barnes. In the same letter, Baird said Jack Sheehan of the Cubs "was sore as a wet hen account [sic] I didn't give him a chance to deal for Howard."[53]

According to Howard's wife, Arlene, Tom Greenwade, the Yankees' scout who had signed Mickey Mantle, handled negotiations. In the end, the Yankees paid Tom Baird $25,000 for Howard and Frank Barnes.[54] Barnes never made it to the Yankees, but did play briefly for the St. Louis Cardinals during the 1957, 1958, and 1960 seasons. After a five-year stint in the minor leagues, in 1955 Elston Howard became the first black New York Yankee and remained with the club until he was traded to the Boston Red Sox in 1967. During his major league career he was a 12-time All-Star, six-time World Series champion, and American League Most Valuable Player (1963). His final game was in 1968. Elston Howard died of a rare heart condition in 1980, and four years later the Yankees officially retired his #32.

Arlene Howard said her husband was forced to endure the same type of racial discrimination Jackie Robinson had faced as the first black Dodger nearly a decade earlier. During spring training for most of his career, Howard was unable to stay in the hotel where his white teammates and coaches were billeted. He was placed instead in rooming houses in the black section of St. Petersburg, Florida. Yet he kept his positive attitude and was welcomed and respected by his Yankees teammates. Howard became especially good friends with fellow St. Louisian and catcher Yogi Berra and shortstop Phil Rizzuto.[55]

In a last hurrah for the Monarchs, about 19,000 supporters turned out on Opening Day of the 1948 season.[56] At a Sunday, August 1 doubleheader in Kansas City, the Monarchs met the Birmingham Black Barons. Tom Baird already knew about the Barons' outstanding young center fielder, Willie Mays. "Cool Papa" Bell had spotted Mays when the

Monarchs' traveling squad was playing the Barons in July. Bell had tried to convince Baird to sign Mays for the barnstorming squad and then bring him up to the Monarchs in 1949, but to no avail. After Mays rose to stardom, "Cool Papa" shrugged and said, "Look what a ballplayer Mays made."[57]

The Monarchs won the first half of the 1948 NAL pennant chase, and the Black Barons took the second half. Tom Baird sent his team to Birmingham for the opening of the NAL playoff series with instructions to uphold what he called "the million dollar name, Kansas City Monarchs." However, the Black Barons and Willie Mays were the series winners, three games to one.[58]

When the NNL folded in 1948, the three teams left (Baltimore Elite Giants, New York Cubans, Philadelphia Stars) joined the NAL, which split into an Eastern and Western Division, with five teams in each for the 1949 season. However, coverage of black teams was fading rapidly in the black press. When the Homestead Grays won the 1948 World Series, the *Pittsburgh Courier* buried the story amidst news of black players in the majors.[59]

Nine months after J. L. Wilkinson sold his interest in the Monarchs to Tom Baird, the *Kansas City Call* lamented the loss of the Monarchs' founder and principal owner, calling Wilkinson "one of [Negro baseball's] finest and smartest men."[60]

In the fourth year after Branch Rickey signed Jackie Robinson, Tom Baird was still angry and not ready to let the matter drop. For example, on January 20, 1949, he wrote a seething letter to Fresco Thompson, a Brooklyn Dodgers official who had told the *Associated Press* that the Dodgers were not stealing players, and "[i]t is my impression we also paid the Kansas City Monarchs for the release of Jackie Robinson."

Baird began his response to Thompson's assertion: "I feel that I should advise you that you were definitely under the wrong impression because Mr. Rickey never paid one cent for Jackie Robinson." He continued, "Rickey's acquisition of Negro baseball players reminds me of the fellow who found a rope and when he got home there was a horse on the end of it. I have been informed that Mr. Rickey is a very religious man. If such is trie [sic] it appears that his religion runs toward the almighty dollar." Baird pointed out that the Cleveland Indians and St. Louis Browns had asked his permission before signing Monarchs players, and that the practice of signing Negro players without compensating their teams should be called to "pull [a] Rickey." Baird concluded the missive by acknowledging, "[t]here is no doubt that Mr. Rickey should be given credit for removing the barriers and allowing Negro ball players into organized baseball. However, it appears that his unethical methods for obtaining Negro players does not meet with the approval of the public."[61]

Two weeks later, on February 11, 1949, Baird wrote to Lee MacPhail and complained that "[i]t seems as though the ethics are about the same with club owners when there are a few dollars involved whether they are white or black." He was apparently referring to a note he had received from booking agent William Leuschner saying that the New York "Giants were of the opinion that they had too many Negroes." Therefore, Baird told MacPhail, he assumed the Giants no longer wanted to sign Hank Thompson, and the Yankees could have him "when [he] is free of the trouble in Dallas," if they were interested. The next day Baird wrote MacPhail again to tell him the comment from Leuschner should be considered "confidential information."[62]

However, the Yankees did not follow through, and the New York Giants' interest in Thompson was revived. A memo dated March 2, 1949, in Baird's file indicates the sale of Thompson to the Giants for $5,000. The Giants assigned Thompson to their Jersey

City farm club. Included in the memo is the note saying that J. L. Wilkinson was to receive $2,250 (50 percent of the amount of the sale over $500), as stipulated in the 1948 contract in which Baird purchased Wilkinson's share of the Monarchs.

Two weeks later, Ford Smith was sold by the Monarchs to the Giants for $6,500 and also assigned to Jersey City, with Wilkinson pocketing $3,000. In June 1949, Baird sold Booker McDaniels' contract to the Chicago Cubs (who assigned him to their Los Angeles affiliate) for $7,500. Wilkinson received $3,500.[63]

Responding to pressure, the Pacific Coast League Oakland Oaks' owner offered Tom Baird $1,000 for Gene Robinson because, he said, the papers had been "on him to hire a Negro."[64]

In January 1950 the Monarchs also sold catcher Earl Taborn for $2,500 and Bob Thurman for $5,000, to the New York Yankees' affiliate in Newark. Wilkinson received $1,000 of the sale price for Taborn.[65]

On August 10, 1949, Harry Jenkins, Director of Minor League Operations for the Boston Braves, wrote Baird to inquire about the availability of Monarchs pitcher Gene Richardson. "It is our opinion," Jenkins commented, "the boy does have a chance to make it to the major leagues." He also wrote that he hoped the Braves could establish an affiliation with the Monarchs "to the advantage of each party."

Baird responded on August 24 that no price for Richardson's contract had yet been set, but that it would be more than $10,000. He pointed out that Richardson's record for the 1949 season was 14–4. Seven months later, Jenkins and Baird were still negotiating a price. In June 1950 they agreed on $2,000, with an additional $6,000 if Richardson made it to the majors within three years. Wilkinson received $750 as his share of the deal. However, on July 3, Jenkins wrote to Baird to say that the Braves were returning Richardson to the Monarchs because

Catcher Earl Taborn played for the Monarchs from 1946–1950. In January 1950, his contract was sold to the New York Yankees' affiliate in Newark, New Jersey, for $2,500. Because Taborn was on the Monarchs in 1948, J. L. Wilkinson received a portion of the purchase price ($1,000). Taborn finished his career in the Mexican League (author collection).

although "he has fine potential and is a good boy, ... his record forced us to return him."[66] He stayed with the Monarchs through the 1953 season.

With Buck O'Neil as their well-liked manager, as well as the Monarchs' reputation and ability to put a good team on the field, fans kept coming through the turnstiles during the 1949 season. The *Kansas City Star* quoted Baird as saying that he planned the biggest Opening Day in baseball, with five bands and 20 horseback riders in a large parade. He predicted that although the Monarchs might not draw as well they had on Opening Day in 1948, it would be a good turnout.[67]

The Kaysees were the only NAL team to draw well in 1949, attracting almost 30,000 fans to their first two Sunday games at Ruppert Stadium and nearly 100,000 for the season's home games.[68] The Monarchs won the first half of the Western Division NAL pennant in 1949, but Baird ceded the championship to the winners of the second half, the Chicago American Giants. With the Blues of the American Association having first dibs on Ruppert Stadium, he decided he would not make enough money in a playoff series without home games.

Attendance at the 1949 East-West Game slipped while support of the major league All-Star game increased when Jackie Robinson and other black players were selected to play.[69]

By 1949 only a handful of major league teams had realized that in order to scout Negro Leagues players effectively, they needed black scouts. Among the first African Americans who were recruited as scouts was "Dizzy" Dismukes, the Monarchs' traveling secretary, who picked up an annual stipend of $250 from the Yankees.

The White Sox hired another former storied Monarch, John Donaldson, as the first full-time black scout in the major leagues on June 29, 1949. Donaldson realized he would have to be selective, filing reports only on players he was certain could make the majors. As a premier pitcher himself, he naturally had an eye for hurlers. One of his favorites was the Monarchs' Connie Johnson. Donaldson had also been a gifted hitter, and he recommended Monarchs outfielders Elston Howard and Bobby Thurman and infielder Ernie Banks.

Above all, Donaldson had his eye on Willie Mays, "the player who could give him more credibility than all the strikeouts in the world." Donaldson failed to convince the White Sox to sign Willie Mays, though he did succeed in getting them to take Connie Johnson. When Donaldson lost Ernie Banks to the Cubs in 1953, he quit his White Sox job.[70]

By the end of the 1949 season, the NAL's survival was in serious doubt. Player sales had kept the league afloat, but declining attendance left several teams in dire financial straits. The Memphis Red Sox, for example, were struggling despite their recently built ballpark. While some, like sportswriter and former player Halley Harding, were calling the NAL "a joke," others came to the league's defense. In response to Harding's comment, Buck O'Neil pointed out that the NAL yearly gave jobs to 200 players, and even though salaries were modest "it beats hell out of loafing on.... Eighteenth and Vine."[71]

The Monarchs continued to draw well as the 1950 season began, attracting an Opening Day crowd of 16,490.[72] They benefited from the fact Kansas City did not yet have a major league team.

Thanks largely to the connections Tom Baird had developed, the Monarchs continued to make money from selling players. In addition to the sale of Frank Barnes and Elston Howard to the Yankees organization, Baird sold the contract of Gene Baker to the

Cubs.[73] Income for player sales in 1950 ($21,750) not only offset the Monarchs' nearly $25,000 drop in gate receipts from 1949, but also helped erase a $1,599.43 operating loss.[74]

In a May 1950 promotion J. L. Wilkinson would likely have endorsed had he still been with the team, two Monarchs games with the New York Cubans were televised in Kansas City in an effort to boost fan interest.[75]

However, the growing availability of radio broadcasts of major league games was undermining support of NAL teams. In a June 20, 1950, letter to Lee MacPhail, Baird claimed that a broadcast of the game between the Dodgers and Cardinals carried on KIMO in Independence, Missouri, had cost the Monarchs a drop of 1,000 to 2,000 in the number of fans at a competing NAL promotion at Blues Stadium.[76] Lacking any consistent radio coverage, NAL teams relied on articles in the black press, but weeklies continued to devote increased space to black players in the majors and minors at the expense of stories on the Negro Leagues teams.

An examination of the Monarchs' financial records illustrates the effect of various factors such as attendance, player sales, and competition from the major leagues. Gate receipts for the Monarchs totaled $74,245.95 in 1948, but two years later fall to $60,075.38. Barnstorming income dropped from $6,455.88 in 1948 to $977.38 in 1950. Income from the sale of players was $2,500 in 1948 and rose to $21,750 in 1950. Net profit was $15,353.82 in 1948 and $20,150.57 in 1950. The next year's net profit fell to $9,952.12.[77]

Although the Monarchs were still making money in the early 1950s, the departure of Negro Leagues pioneers like J. L. Wilkinson and Effa Manley, as well as the deaths of Cum Posey and Ed Bolden, left black baseball without the innovative leaders of earlier years. The one team besides the Monarchs able to hang on was the Indianapolis Clowns. Although criticism continued that they were pandering to stereotypical white expectations of black behavior, black writers like John I. Johnson of the *Kansas City Call* suggested "there is nothing wrong with making people laugh."[78]

The Monarchs won the NAL Western Division in 1950, but instead of staging a league playoff series with the Eastern winners, the Indianapolis Clowns, they went on a four-city barnstorming tour together.[79]

By 1951 the financial fragility of the NAL was increasingly evident. Player sales continued, but only at a modest profit. For example, the Monarchs received a total of just $1,000 for the sale of Bonnie Serrell to the San Francisco Seals of the Pacific Coast League. Baird entered into his files the note that "Wilkinson gets ½ of sale on players with the Monarchs when I bought the club. He gets ½ above $500." For the sale of Serrell and Connie Johnson to the St. Hyacinthe, Florida, minor league club, Wilkinson received $500.[80]

Baird's sale of players to white minor league clubs resulted in a warning from George M. Trautman, President of the National Association of Professional Baseball Leagues. Trautman told Baird in a latter dated April 5, 1951, that he had no right to assign players to clubs in the Association, because "you are not a member of the National Association and the National Association can recognize assignment of players only when two of its own clubs are involved."[81]

The Monarchs and Indianapolis Clowns, again division winners, did have a playoff series in 1951, with the Clowns coming out on top.[82]

By 1952 black baseball had declined from a peak of two leagues and 12 teams to a motley assemblage of six widely scattered NAL franchises willing to play exhibition games wherever there was a payday. A July 26 promotion at Yankee Stadium was typical. A doubleheader with the Stars, Clowns, American Giants and Monarchs attracted only 3,500 fans, and, as one writer noted, the comedic routine of the Clowns might have been a sell in rural areas but not in New York City.

However, despite competition from the recently integrated Kansas City Blues, the Monarchs were still able to turn a profit in 1952. Most of their money was made on the road. For example, on August 10 a Monarchs-Clowns game at Briggs Stadium in Detroit attracted 20,618.[83]

Baird (and Wilkinson) also continued to profit through selling players. In 1952 Baird sold the contracts of pitcher Eddie Locke, who played for the Monarchs in 1944 and 1945, for $3,000 (of which Wilkinson received $1,250) and shortstop Jesse Williams, a Monarch from 1943–1947, for $3,500 (of which Wilkinson pocketed $1,500) to Vancouver's Capilano Club of the class A Western International League.[84]

Also in 1952 the Boston Braves purchased the contract of Henry Aaron from the Indianapolis Clowns for $10,000. Tom Baird liked to say he had blocked the New York Giants from acquiring Aaron when a Giants representative tried to reach Clowns owner Syd Pollock during the NAL meetings on May 28, 1952, looking to make a deal. Baird claimed he intercepted the call and told the Giants official on the line that Pollock was not available. The Monarchs owner said he "detested the idea of Aaron and Willie Mays in the same lineup" and made sure the Clowns formalized their handshake agreement with the Boston Braves for Aaron's contract.[85]

Five years after Jackie Robinson had broken the color barrier, some major league teams still feared that having too many black players might alienate white fans. For example, the Braves passed on an opportunity to buy the contract of Jim LaMarque, a pitcher for the Monarchs. Tom Baird had written to Harry Jenkins, farm director of the Braves, on February 2, 1951, offering to sell LaMarque's contract for a mere $3,500, noting that "LaMarque ... is an intelligent looking Negro, in fact he might pass for an Indian." The Monarchs' owner said he had never met a finer fellow in his 31 years in baseball and that LaMarque "won't give you trouble about hotels or anything else."

On March 9, 1951, Jenkins responded, telling Baird, "[t]he truth is we now have three colored boys at Milwaukee and if we take another I am fearful the club would get top-heavy. I am certain you can recognize this is a factor to be considered."

A year later, the Braves again contacted Baird concerning the availability of LaMarque. When he learned of the team's interest, LaMarque, who had been playing in Mexico, wrote to the Braves, saying he considered himself a "free agent," and that if they were interested in signing him, they "will have to deal with me directly."

About the same time, the Braves wrote to Baird to say that their efforts to sign LaMarque had "gone by the boards," since they had been told he had unpaid bills in Mexico that were keeping him from being able to return to the United States. In fact, LaMarque was in the country, having rejected the offer of a free plane ticket from the Braves and paid his own fare. Despite a 15–5 record and 1.96 ERA in 1948, the 30-year-old LaMarque never played a single game in the majors.[86]

After over 30 years as a Negro Leagues owner, Tom Baird received special recognition "for his work in helping to improve relations between the races." The National Baseball Congress presented him with a plaque for supporting sandlot and town games that gave American youngsters the "opportunity to play America's National pastime with people from all walks of life." In late June 1952 he was honored between games of a Monarchs doubleheader with the Chicago American Giants.[87]

10. Final Years for Wilkinson and the Monarchs (1946–1964)

In a letter to the *Kansas City Star* dated January 6, 1953, Henry Rigney of Toledo commented on an article the *Star* had published on Baird and the Monarchs. "Tom, along with J. L. Wilkinson," he wrote, "has done more to perpetuate Negro baseball on a high scale than any man who has ever lived." Negro major league baseball, Rigney claimed, would not have survived "without the guiding influence of Tom and J. L."[88]

In February 1953, the Indianapolis Clowns signed the NAL's first female player—a 21-year old infielder named Marcenia "Toni" Stone, who had already played for several lower-level black teams. The $12,000 investment paid off, as the Clowns were soon attracting crowds not seen since the late 1940s.

At the Monarchs' opener with the Clowns, 17,205 curious fans turned out to see Stone. On June 21 a Clowns/Monarchs contest, with Stone in the lineup, drew 20,399 customers to Briggs Stadium in Detroit. At an Easter Sunday game in Omaha, Toni Stone came to bat against Satchel Paige. Ever the showman, Satchel asked Stone where she wanted the pitch. She said it didn't matter and stroked a base hit over second base. She scored her team's only run against Paige that day.[89]

Even though some games were drawing sizable crowds, Tom Baird's records show the Monarchs were now struggling financially. For example, on May 9 a game in Lafayette, Louisiana, had net gate receipts of $152.86.[90]

By 1953 the Kansas City Monarchs were barely hanging on financially. One of the misfortunes suffered during the season was a fire that destroyed the team bus during a barnstorming tour (Kenneth Spencer Research Library, University of Kansas Libraries).

J. L. Wilkinson may have retired from the game, but he still had opinions he was willing to make public. In 1953, when the Birmingham Black Barons started traveling with a harmonica player and pair of acrobats, he called it a "joke."[91] Apparently he had forgotten the wrestlers and bands he had on his All Nations teams four decades earlier (see Chapter 2).

Ernie Banks (1931–2015) joined the Kansas City Monarchs on June 4, 1950. "Cool Papa" Bell had first spotted Banks while serving as manager of the Monarchs' traveling team owned by Wilkinson. Bell enthusiastically recommended the youngster to Buck O'Neil, but, according to "Cool Papa," O'Neil told him the Monarchs did not need another shortstop. However, Bell persisted. In June O'Neil drove from Kansas City to Dallas and, with the authority of Tom Baird, signed the lanky shortstop without having seen him play.[92] It was a good decision. According to Baird, after observing him in a game, O'Neil told the Monarchs' owner, "he has everything a ball player should have."[93]

Baird shared his enthusiasm about the rookie with Lee MacPhail of the Yankees. On June 20, 1950, he wrote, "I signed Ernie Banks, 19-year-old shortstop and he looks like he will make a hell of a good ball player." Baird reassured MacPhail that if any of the Monarchs' young players looked good to the New York Yankees, "I will hang on to them for a while." Remarkably, the Yankees passed on Banks. After the 1950 season, Baird told MacPhail that the Brooklyn Dodgers had expressed interest in Banks but he had told them the rookie was too young and he would not sell his contract.[94]

Banks served in the Army during the 1951–1952 seasons and rejoined the Monarchs the next year. According to O'Neil, after Banks hit a home run with two men on to win the 1953 East-West Game, Tom Baird told the Monarchs' manager to take the shortstop to Wrigley Field the next day. At the meeting, which famed sportswriter Wendell Smith attended, the Cubs' Director of Scouting, Wid Matthews, signed Banks as the team's first black player, earning Baird $20,000.

Later, Matthews (who had been one of the Dodgers' scouts when Jackie Robinson was signed) told O'Neil that Baird was going to sell the Monarchs soon, and, when that happened, he wanted O'Neil to come work for him. His first assignment as a Cubs scout would be to sign Banks a second time, Matthews said, so O'Neil could get a fee.[95] Therefore, Banks, who became known simply as Mr. Cub, and who expressed his love for the baseball by joyfully proclaiming, "Let's play two!" actually signed twice with the Chicago team where he spent his entire major league career (1953–1971).

Ernie Banks was selected for the Major Leagues All-Star Game 14 times. He won the National League Most Valuable Player Award in 1958 and 1959, and was named to the Major League Baseball All-Century Team. He was inducted into the National Baseball Hall of Fame at Cooperstown in 1977, the first year he was eligible. The Cubs have retired his #14.

At the end of the 1953 season, the Monarchs and Indianapolis Clowns were the only viable franchises left in the NAL. Both teams considered withdrawing from the league but finally agreed to remain for the 1954 campaign. The NAL added two franchises, the Louisville Clippers and Detroit Stars, who were owned by Grand Rapids promoter Ted Rasberry, but things did not go well. After the 1954 season, the Clowns withdrew and became an independent touring team, emphasizing even more the comedic routines that drew white fans. Even the Monarchs had a deficit of over $10,000 in 1954.[96]

Hoping to draw on the novelty of a woman player, Tom Baird bought Toni Stones's contract before the 1954 season. In negotiations with Baird, Stone convinced him to pay her $400 a month, with the prospect of a $200 bonus at the end of the year. After a brief spring training camp in Norfolk, Virginia, the Monarchs played pre-season games against the Clowns across the "tobacco road circuit" before heading south to more lucrative contests in Florida. Stone resented the publicity photos the Monarchs staged that had her sitting in front of a make-up mirror in her uniform with a ball and glove on the vanity, pretending to apply powder to her face.

By the end of May 1954, the Monarchs were back in Kansas City and ready for their home opener. Only 7,000 fans, in comparison to 20,000 the year before, showed up. The game was broadcast on radio, and many fans stayed home to listen.[97]

A July 1954 match-up between the Monarchs and Clowns, booked by Baird and Pollock for Yankee Stadium, did not live up to expectations. Despite extensive promotion, only 7,500 were on hand, six times less than the combined crowds at Giants and Dodgers games the same afternoon—where Jackie Robinson, Don Newcombe, Monte Irvin and Willie Mays attracted many black fans.[98]

The integration of baseball clearly affected the attitude of young black players about signing with the Monarchs. During the 1954 season, at Buck O'Neil's recommendation, Tom Baird offered a contract to a teenage pitching phenomenon from Omaha named Bob Gibson, but the future Hall of Famer told the Monarchs' owner he had already agreed to play for the St. Louis Cardinals. As Gibson later said, "the Kansas City Monarchs were not the be-all and end-all for a Negro ball player."[99]

By mid-season Toni Stone was becoming disillusioned, realizing "[t]he Monarchs had come to conduct themselves less like a team than a collection of independent agents to get the best deals." She wrote to her husband that she was going to start looking out for herself and try barnstorming on her own terms. Stone became so irate after being called out on strikes she jumped on the back of the catcher, who had yelled "Pussy high" as the ball crossed the plate. What may have offended her more was the delight her teammates took in telling the story—over and over again.[100]

As late as September 1954, Tom Baird was complaining to NAL President J. B. Martin that the final standings submitted to the league by the Howe News Bureau were incorrect. The *Kansas City Call* listed the Monarchs in last place for both halves of the 1954 season. Baird told Martin that was never true and contended the misprint led fans to believe the Monarchs were not worth coming out to watch play. "I am not going to sit idle and take this kind of bad publicity for the Monarchs," he wanted Martin to know.[101]

By this point the continued viability of the Monarchs was in doubt. During the postseason they barnstormed until the weather got too cold, but the tension among players, including Stone, was getting worse. The tour over, she returned to California without the promised $200 bonus.[102]

By early 1955, Baird had come to the realization that barnstorming, which had kept the Monarchs financially viable for decades, was no longer effective. On January 20, he wrote to Oscar Rico of the Cuban Giants, who was seeking Baird's advice on a tour in the United States. He told Rico, "only a few years ago a traveling team could get by, but that has changed, and don't kid yourself." The Giants' only hope, Baird said, was for Rico to book games with the Indianapolis Clowns, who were looking for cheap clubs who were willing to put on "a fun show and comedy." The Clowns' owner, Syd Pollock, was, Baird commented, trying to make the team into the Globetrotters of black baseball.

In a letter the next day to a Cuban player who had asked his advice on playing in the United States, Baird lamented that the white minor leagues were quitting, only four teams remained in the NAL, and the Monarchs had lost over $5,000 during the 1954 season. Four months later, he confided in another letter to Rico that he would soon be 71 years old and should have retired several years earlier.[103]

By 1955 only Kansas City, Detroit, Memphis and Birmingham were left in the NAL. The Monarchs signed 49-year-old Satchel Paige for $250 a game and ten percent of the gate. Tom Baird also agreed to pay Paige ten cents per mile for any trip over 300 miles, since he liked to drive himself. The Monarchs' owner accepted these terms because he thought teams would pay extra "to have the honor of bringing [Satchel Paige] to their towns." He had already spent, he said in a letter to NAL President J. B. Martin dated June 3, $100 in long distance charges explaining to teams he had scheduled the Monarchs to play that Paige would indeed be on the roster.[104]

However, Paige's crowd appeal was finally fading. Even with Satchel Paige slated to pitch in the 1955 East-West Game, the once-popular attraction drew only 11,257 fans. Most damaging to the NAL "was the sudden shift in fortunes of the league's most successful valuable property, the Kansas City Monarchs."[105]

The Kansas City Blues relocated after the 1954 season to Denver, clearing the way for the American League's Philadelphia Athletics to come to Kansas City. The city purchased Ruppert Stadium, renaming it Municipal Stadium, and the new Kansas City Athletics attracted 1.4 million fans their first year.[106] African American spectators were more interested in the two black players—Vic Power and Bob Trice—on Kansas City's major league team than they were in the Monarchs.[107]

In a May 21, 1955, letter to Oscar Rico, Baird noted that the attendance at the Monarchs' home opener on May 15 had declined by over two-thirds and predicted, "it looks like the Athletics have killed all baseball in this territory."[108] The city required Baird to sign a contract that stipulated the Monarchs pay the Athletics 25 percent of the rental fee for each game played in the stadium. It was costing Baird about $3,000 a game (with charges such as $70 for cleaning restrooms and $90 for hauling trash), and he had to split what gate he did receive with the visiting team.[109] Although Baird had contracted for Monarchs games at Municipal Stadium through August 1955, after only a few contests at the venue, the Monarchs left the city for good to play only on the road, with Baird noting they were being charged "for everything but the flag pole."[110]

On June 17, 1955, Baird wrote Congressman Emanuel Celler of New York to complain that "Arnold Johnson's Kansas City Athletics trying to put me out of business was like the man that shot a dead horse, for I was going to retire at end of the 1955 season regardless of what happened." He also recounted the shoddy treatment he had received from Branch Rickey. After his experience with the Athletics and the Dodgers, Baird told the congressman he had learned that "all heels are not on shoes" and "[b]aseball was a sport until the millionaires bought most of the major league clubs for the publicity they get." Some, he said he had learned, were intent on making money "regardless of ethics."[111]

The Monarchs finished third, but Baird resisted league President J. B. Martin's appeal to field a team in 1956. In a June 9, 1955, letter to Martin, he said that he was not sure that he could keep going. "I am not an alarmist," he wrote, "but facts are facts and I know all owners are losing plenty.... I have been in baseball long enough to see what might happen to us."[112]

Although the Monarchs reportedly won the 1955 NAL championship, the league had become so disorganized that some sportswriters were not sure when the season ended and had less idea who won the pennant.[113]

10. Final Years for Wilkinson and the Monarchs (1946–1964)

In early 1956, after Baird had sent the bulk of his roster to various major and minor league teams, he sold the Monarchs franchise to Ted Rasberry for a mere $3,500.[114] Baird told the prospective owner he wanted to retire, liked the way Rasberry ran the NAL's Detroit Stars, and wouldn't sell the team to anyone else. Baird thought the new owner would maintain the Monarchs' prestige, Rasberry added in a 1981 interview. He retained the Kansas City Monarchs name but shifted the offices to Grand Rapids, Michigan.

Despite Rasberry's good intentions, his Monarchs were a rag-tag operation. He hired old Negro Leagues first baseman Olan "Jelly" Taylor as manager for the 1956 season, but soon replaced him with "Dizzy" Dismukes. The team maintained a barnstorming schedule as best it could. However, the Monarchs were now only a shadow of the team J. L. Wilkinson had established and nurtured. Rosters shifted, sometimes daily, and the Monarchs were occasionally no-shows for games because of bus breakdowns and player shortages due to missed paydays. Rasberry tried putting women on the team to draw crowds, but that didn't work.[115]

Although he rejoined the Monarchs in 1955 after his major league career ended, Satchel Paige retained J. L. Wilkinson as his agent, out of loyalty to the man who had given him a second chance in baseball. As he had for so long, Wilkinson helped Satchel book appearances in small midwestern towns. Occasionally, Paige would take the field in a game with Rasberry's Monarchs.[116]

On March 2, 1960, NAL President J. B. Martin wrote to Tom Baird, "[you] have done a lot of things for people. I know what you did for Satchel Paige, O'Neil and several other people, and you did a lot for [me] when you turned over the Chicago American Giants to me."[117]

On August 17, 1960, the Indianapolis Clowns and Monarchs played in Kansas City, Kansas. Tom Baird promoted the game, saying, "[i]t will be just like old times." He arranged for bands, drill teams, and majorettes. A respectable crowd of 9,503 attended. Monarchs greats "Bullet Joe" Rogan, Frank Duncan, Newt Allen, Buck O'Neil, Hilton Smith, "Army" Cooper, Jesse Williams, "Dink" Mothell and Eddie Dwight were honored.[118]

When they finally folded as a professional team after the 1960 season, the Kansas City Monarchs had won 17 pennants and two World Series despite having left league play from 1931–1936.[119] They limped along as a semi-pro team for a few more seasons.[120]

The final swan song for the NAL may have been the 1961 East-West Game, played in Yankee Stadium on August 20. Fifty-five-year-old Satchel Paige pitched the first three innings for the West, giving up only a scratch single. He was credited with the win, but only 7,245 were in attendance. Rebuffed in a last-ditch attempt to obtain a subsidy from major league baseball, the NAL finally collapsed officially in 1963.[121]

Near the end of his life, Tom Baird finally received some of the recognition he sought from the major leagues when he was signed to a scouting job for the Kansas City Athletics in 1961.[122]

On the day he died (July 2, 1962), Baird phoned *Call* sports editor Jay Cee Bee, who missed the call because he was at lunch. When Cee Bee returned the call an hour later, Baird's wife told him her husband was asleep and she would tell him to telephone the *Call* editor when he woke up. Baird never called back; he had died in his sleep.

In a short obituary, Cee Bee described Baird as the owner of the Kansas City Monarchs with J. L. Wilkinson from 1919–1947, when Baird bought out his partner. According to the *Call* sports editor, Baird's major achievements were in selling Monarchs players to the major and minor leagues. According to the *Call*, the former Monarchs owner had negotiated the sale of 29 players to the major leagues and nine to the minor leagues, including Satchel Paige, Hank Aaron, "Connie" Johnson, Gene Baker, Ernie Banks and Elston Howard.[123]

In its obituary, the *Kansas City Star* noted that in addition to his accomplishments with the Kansas City Monarchs, Baird had served as business manager of the Harlem All-Stars in 1957, and with his son-in-law, M. L. Wickstrom, in 1960 had built a $400,000, 16-lane bowling alley in Kansas City, Kansas. He was a member of the Masons and Kiwanis Club.[124]

When asked what he would say at the news conference on the day before his father's induction into the National Baseball Hall of Fame at Cooperstown, New York, on July 30, 2006, Dick Wilkinson responded,

> I'll just tell them what a great dad he was. I'll tell them how I traveled with him when I was a little kid. My dad was such a wonderful person. He never showed emotion. He never got mad. I never saw him curse. And he didn't drink or smoke. He just lived baseball. That's all he did.... He was the kind of guy who didn't care what color someone was. He just wanted to see how good they could play baseball.[125]

Dick told another interviewer, "He was the first one to share profits with the team, like they do now."[126]

In this undated picture, J. L. Wilkinson sat for one of his few photographic portraits (National Baseball Hall of Fame Library, Cooperstown, New York).

Years earlier, Dick had said his Dad would loan players money all the time—a couple of thousand a year. He said, "he didn't get back half of what he loaned. Didn't charge interest. If he'd got back all the money he loaned players he'd have been a wealthy man. Sometimes he'd loan money to a player from another team who came to town and was so broke he couldn't get out of town. His profit for a year might be only $5,000. Even so he'd pay players when they were injured, and cover doctors' bills ... long before health insurance."[127]

J. L. Wilkinson's three grandchildren—Diane Pond, Sharon Brescian, and Ed Catron—have their own vivid memories of their grandfather. Dick's daughter Diane remembers him as the grandfather "every granddaughter would love to have—a gentle man with no vices. There was nothing wrong with him." Since her father worked with her grandfather after World War II, Diane spent a lot of time in her grandfather's home in Kansas City and thought nothing unusual about meeting Jackie Robinson, Satchel Paige, and Buck O'Neil. When Wilkinson could no longer get out, a number of his former players would stop by to trade stories about their experiences. Diane remembers her grandfather always wore a suit and tie every day. She recalls his lovely handwriting and the drawings he would do as he taught her how to sketch birds.

Dick's younger daughter Sharon remembers sitting on her grandfather's lap listening to baseball games. She also remembers an old adding machine in her grandfather's home office and her grandmother's antiques stacked floor to ceiling in the house—in addition to the full inventory at her store. Both sisters remember their grandfather holding their hands as he walked them to the movie theater.

The Wilkinson grandchildren also recall that their grandparents had a chauffeur, Lee, who would come to the Wilkinson house each morning to make breakfast. They would always come down together when Lee had the meal ready. As Lee cleaned up, Bessie would get into a souped-up maroon hotrod she had purchased and squeal her tires as she turned on to Wornall Road on her way to the antique shop she owned for more than 40 years. At one point it was called the Welcome Antique Shop and was located at 216–18 West 75th Street.

They also remember that their grandparents had a Ford station wagon with wood paneling and a Ford Fairlane. Their grandfather was always so sweet and devoted to Bessie, always there for her, his grandchildren remember. He would always do anything she wanted. When he came back from a road trip with the Monarchs, Bessie would want to go out to eat and he would always take her. He never told her "no."

Bessie continued running her antiques store into her 80s, until she suffered a debilitating stroke. She was, her grandson Ed Catron recalls, a "flamboyant lady who loved fine, custom-made clothes and jewelry. She enjoyed trips to Chicago and New York to buy antiques." His grandfather did not keep alcohol in the house, but Ed's father had a flask in his car and Bessie would come out to the garage, ostensibly to look at an antique, and get a nip or two. She loved to entertain prospective antique buyers in their home and would often stay up late at night doing so. Ed remembers two complete sets of living and dining room furniture in their house—French and Chinese designs. One room had cases of cut glass from floor to ceiling.[128]

J. L. Wilkinson spent most of his final years at Bessie's antique store or at home, listening to baseball games on the radio. He was virtually blind as a result of the ruptured retina he had suffered in the July 1947 car accident and unsuccessful eye surgery.[129] Alberta Penn, the wife of his long-time traveling secretary Quincy Gilmore, came to Wilkinson's office to write checks for him and also helped out with inventory at the antique shop. She remembered Bessie as a "wonderful lady" who worked hard. As she recalled, Mr. Wilkinson sometimes took money from the antique store for the Monarchs, which Mrs. Wilkinson didn't like, but they worked it out.[130]

J. L. Wilkinson was living in the University Nursing Home in Kansas City, Kansas, when he died at the age of 86 on August 21, 1964. The headlines in the *Call* that day were about racial violence in Chicago and the fight between rival Mississippi delegations, one all-white and one integrated, to be seated at the upcoming Democratic Party's National Convention. Stories in the sports section were of the 33rd home run of Willie Mays during the 1964 season and Cassius Clay considering whether to become a Black Muslim minister.

Ed Catron remembers seeing box after box of records being carried to the trash from his grandfather's home office in the days after his death. Alberta Penn also recalled that all the Monarchs' records were discarded.

Over the years, Ed says, his mother, Wilkinson's daughter Gladys Wilkinson Catron, would share what material she had, including pictures, with researchers. Many of the objects and photographs were never returned.[131]

The obituary for J. L. Wilkinson in the *Kansas City Call* appeared two weeks after his death, in the "Sportlight" column of Jay Cee Bee. According to the *Call* sports editor, Wilkinson and Tom Baird were "very instrumental in helping to develop baseball talent in Negroes. The two were largely responsible in sending players to the major leagues." The columnist described Wilkinson as "Satchel Paige's best friend" and "personal manager." Along with Abe Saperstein, it was Wilkinson who "guided Paige into the major leagues with the Cleveland Indians," he noted. "Most of the players that wore Kansas City Monarchs' uniforms looked upon Wilky [sic] as a friend and benefactor. They could go to him with any of their problems and he would try to find answers for them."

Many of the old Monarchs, back to John Donaldson and the surviving members of the All Nations team, gathered for Wilkinson's funeral. The elderly Donaldson, who was born the same year as the Monarchs owner, drove from his home in Chicago to Kansas City for the service. Ed Catron remembers seeing the distinguished old pitcher paying his respects. According to the *Call* obituary, Donaldson and the other former players who had come to the funeral stood "with bowed heads and occasionally a whimper of a tear, [as they] said goodbye to their friend."[132]

"That guy was a doll," said Hilton Smith, who was also present at the funeral. "It was pretty bad, when I think about how they treated Wilkinson. They just took Jackie, made all that money off him, and Wilkinson was the man that was responsible for him playing and he didn't get a dime out of it. It was kind of shady, I thought. He really had kept it going and developed ball players."[133] "But," as historian John Holway noted in one of the few extended articles written on the Monarchs' owner, "they couldn't take the achievements, the memories, the legend of J. L. Wilkinson and his mighty Monarchs."[134]

As Larry Lester has written, "J. L. Wilkinson was an innovator, a promoter, a beneficiary and personal confidante to his players. He presented our national pastime with a formula for racial harmony and a quality product. Though not given the honor, Wilkinson—not Branch Rickey—was the forerunner of interracial baseball."[135]

A commentator offered this assessment of Wilkinson in the *Kansas City Star* when the Monarchs' owner was being considered for election to the National Baseball Hall of Fame[136]:

> Wilkinson deserves consideration for the Baseball Hall of Fame not just because he fielded great teams; not just because he put more players in the majors than any other black team; and not just because he embraced revenue sharing. In a time of great prejudice and inequality, Wilkinson possessed an impeccable reputation for treating African Americans humanely. Baseball owners today would be well served by studying the legacy of Wilkinson, a baseball owner who was light years ahead of his time.

J. L. Wilkinson's grandchildren remember seeing in the backyard of their grandparents' Kansas City home what may have been remnants of the innovative portable lighting system the Monarchs' owner had first developed in 1930, betting everything he and Bessie owned that it would work. Of course, it worked exceedingly well, as did so many of the ventures he undertook—from a multiracial team at a time when the Ku Klux Klan was in its resurgence to an important, but mostly forgotten, central role in the integration of professional baseball when racism was far from dead, and so many other achievements in between.

The Monarchs' founder and principal owner rarely talked about himself, and when he did it was with characteristic modesty. For example, when asked to comment about the Kansas City Monarchs and his long career in baseball after he had retired, Wilkinson had this to say: "They were a fine lot of men, and my memories are pleasant ones. Though we had a few trying moments in holding our standard up to an all-American concept, it was a well-spent fifty years.... Now I am happy that others are proud of our Monarchs' record on and off the baseball field."[137]

J. L. Wilkinson may have been a humble man of few words, but his bold actions speak volumes.

Epilogue:
The Long Road to Cooperstown

For its first 26 years, the National Baseball Hall of Fame at Cooperstown, New York, had no black honorees. That ended in 1962 when Jackie Robinson was inducted. Four years later, in his 1966 Hall of Fame induction speech, Ted Williams said, "I hope that someday Satchel Paige and Josh Gibson will be voted into the Hall of Fame as symbols of the great Negro players who are not here only because they weren't given the chance." Paige expressed his appreciation but wanted everyone to know that he and Gibson weren't the only Negro Leagues stars deserving of Hall of Fame recognition. "There were many Satchels. There were many Joshes," he said.[1]

A committee headed by Monte Irvin that included Judy Johnson and Roy Campanella was established in 1971 to recommend Negro Leagues players for induction into the Hall of Fame. That same year, Satchel Paige became the first selected. When word filtered out the Hall of Fame's plan was to place the plaques for Paige and other Negro Leagues inductees in a special exhibit at Cooperstown, Paige commented, "[t]he only change is that baseball has turned Paige from a second-class citizen into a second-class immortal."[2] Commissioner Bowie Kuhn responded by working to have the decision reversed, and Satchel's plaque was placed in the same room as those honoring Christy Mathewson, Babe Ruth, and Jackie Robinson.

The next Negro Leagues players inducted into the Hall of Fame were Josh Gibson (1972), Buck Leonard (1972), Monte Irvin (1973), "Cool Papa" Bell (1974), "Judy" Johnson (1975), Oscar Charleston (1976), John Henry "Pop" Lloyd (1977), and Martin Dihigo (1977). According to John Holway, the choices had a decidedly generational and Eastern bias. Left out were older, Western greats: Rube Foster, Bill Foster, Willie Wells, "Bullet Joe" Rogan, "Smoky Joe" Williams, "Turkey" Stearnes, and "Mule" Suttles, among others, Holway noted.

As pressure to recognize more deserving Negro Leaguers continued, the responsibility for further selection was given to the Hall of Fame's Veterans Committee. However, 16 of the 18 members of that committee were white and knew little of the Negro Leagues or black baseball. Not surprisingly, for the next decade only two black players from the pre–Jackie Robinson era were inducted: Rube Foster in 1981 and Ray Dandridge in 1987.[3]

By 1988 the 161 inductees selected for the Hall of Fame who were active before 1950 included 150 white and only 11 black players. As more writers and fans became aware of the disparity, demands intensified that more black players from the pre-integration era be inducted. There were still no blacks on the Hall of Fame Board of Directors, and the history of black baseball was confined in the Cooperstown museum to a small display case.

Filmmaker Ken Burns' acclaimed documentary, *Baseball* (1994), featuring Buck O'Neil as an articulate commentator, brought much-needed national attention to the stars of the Negro Leagues. An HBO film, *Soul of the Game* (1996), dramatized the breaking of the color barrier, focusing on Jackie Robinson, Satchel Paige, and Josh Gibson. The movie included several short segments with J. L. Wilkinson, played by R. Lee Ermey. However, the Monarchs' owner was not portrayed accurately. In the film, "Wilkie" angrily curses, something all those who knew him agree he never did.

In 1995 the Veterans Committee, with Buck O'Neil having replaced Roy Campanella, announced they would elect five more Negro Leagues players, one a year. The inductees selected were Leon Day (1995), Willie Foster (1996), Willie Wells (1997), "Bullet Joe" Rogan (1998), and "Smoky Joe" Williams (1999). Subsequently, in response to criticism that the Hall of Fame had unfairly established a quota, the Veterans Committee announced that two more Negro Leaguers would be selected. They were Norman "Turkey" Stearnes in 2000 and Hilton Smith in 2001.

A comprehensive study of African Americans in Baseball (1860–1960) funded by a $250,000 grant from Major League Baseball was authorized in 2000. Early the next year, the Hall of Fame's Board selected a research group led by Dr. Larry Hogan, Dick Clark, and Larry Lester to conduct a comprehensive study, in which more than 50 scholars participated. *National Geographic* published the book *Shades of Glory* (2006), edited by Dr. Hogan, using the research material generated.

Based on the study, a five-member screening committee identified 94 potential candidates in 2005. From that group, 39 were nominated. In order to be selected for induction, a nominee would need nine of the votes of a 12-member selection committee. Former Major League Baseball Commissioner Fay Vincent chaired the screening and selection committees but did not vote. Hall of Famer Frank Robinson served as advisor to the committee.

When Diane Pond learned that her grandfather was on the list of those being considered for Hall of Fame induction by the special committee, she and other family members put together a list of the reasons they thought J. L. Wilkinson should be selected: They summarized his impressive career as follows[4]:

- co-founder of the Negro National League (NNL) in 1920 and the Negro American League (NAL) in 1937;
- created the Kansas City Monarchs dynasty;
- only white owner when the NNL first organized;
- under his guidance the Monarchs won 17 Negro Leagues pennants and two of the four Negro Leagues World Series;
- the Monarchs sent 27 players to the major leagues, more than any other black team;
- signed the first black player, Jackie Robinson, and first black coach, Buck O'Neil, to integrate the major leagues;
- signed several other players who were first to integrate their teams from 1947 to 1959;
- innovator of night baseball in 1930, allowing the working man to see a professional team play during the week;
- innovator of team travel, media communications and player relations, including an open system of free player movement, i.e., free agency;
- pioneer for the first use of professional Japanese and Hispanic players in organized baseball with the All Nations team in 1912;
- established an all-women's team in 1909;

- supported other activities in Kansas City's black community, helping to intertwine the jazz and baseball communities in early years;
- helped Harlem Globetrotters owner Abe Saperstein get a start.

When the Hall of Fame released the profiles of the 39 candidates in the special election "James [sic] Leslie 'J. L.' Wilkinson" was among them. The selection committee met February 25–27, 2006, to conduct its final voting. The committee's choices included ten players with Negro Leagues experience—Ray Brown, Willard Brown, Andy Cooper, "Biz" Mackey, José Méndez, Louis Santop, "Mule" Suttles, Ben Taylor, Cristóbal Torriente and Jud Wilson; two pre–Negro Leagues players—Frank Grant and Pete Hill; one pre–Negro Leagues executive—Sol White; and four Negro Leagues executives—Cum Posey, Alex Pompez, J. L. Wilkinson, and Effa Manley.

Among the Monarchs players on the original list of 94 not elected were Newt Allen, Sammy Bankhead, William Bell, Chet Brewer, Ray Brown, John Donaldson, Frank Duncan, Oscar Johnson, Hurley McNair, Dobie Moore, Buck O'Neil, Ted "Double Duty" Radcliffe, and Bill Wright.

After the 2006 selection, a total of 41 Negro Leagues players and officials had been chosen for the National Baseball Hall of Fame. Fifteen were associated with the Monarchs: Ernie Banks, "Cool Papa" Bell, Willard Brown, Andy Cooper, Willie Foster, "Pop" Lloyd, José Méndez, Satchel Paige, Jackie Robinson, "Bullet Joe" Rogan, "Turkey" Stearnes, Hilton Smith, Cristóbal Torriente, Willie Wells, and J. L. Wilkinson. Among them, only

At the Hall of Fame induction ceremony in 2006, J. L. Wilkinson's son Dick (second from right) read from his father's plaque. Dick is shown here with Baseball Commissioner Bud Selig (right), then Hall of Fame President Dale Petroskey (left), and Hall of Fame Board Chairwoman Jane Forbes Clark (National Baseball Hall of Fame Library, Cooperstown, New York).

one was white.[5] At this writing no other Negro Leagues players or officials have been elected to the Hall.

Although they were ecstatic J. L. Wilkinson would finally receive Hall of Fame recognition, the Wilkinson family was deeply disappointed when they learned that Wilkinson's close friend Buck O'Neil had not been chosen. He had fallen one vote short of the nine votes required.

Dick Wilkinson spoke for his family when he told a reporter after the selection announcement that his father and Buck O'Neil should have gone in to the Hall of Fame together. They were, he said, friends and partners. When they met almost 68 years earlier, J. L. Wilkinson was already among the most famous and respected of the owners of the Negro Leagues. Dick remembered the day in 1938 when he and his Dad were watching the Monarchs show up for the first day of training camp on the Paseo in Kansas City. "This long, skinny guy came up carrying a bag," Dick recalled. "My dad didn't know. I didn't know. It was Buck." Over the next 18 years, as a player and the team's manager, O'Neil experienced "the essence of Wilkinson." When the Monarchs were traveling and hotels did not have enough rooms, Wilkinson shared his with O'Neil. "During that era, that was unheard of," said O'Neil.[6]

O'Neil's response to not being chosen for the Hall of Fame reflected the dignity he always displayed. He expressed his pride at the selection of some of his close friends for the Hall, including J. L. Wilkinson, who, he said, "didn't have a prejudiced bone in him." O'Neil pointed out, "[w]hile Wilkinson could have been lynched just for owning a black baseball team, he never allowed the ugly racial prejudice of his day to keep him from doing what he loved and believed—black baseball at its highest. J. L. Wilkinson, he looked down on no one and he brought out the best in everyone. That's J. L. Wilkinson. He brought out my best just by being himself, that's how he did it. Man, J. L. Wilkinson. I love that man." O'Neil had long kept a list in his wallet he pulled out whenever someone asked him who he thought deserved to be in the Hall of Fame. It had 11 names. First was J. L. Wilkinson.[7]

In answer to the question, "What has a lifetime in baseball taught you?" Buck O'Neil gave the following answer[8]:

> It is a religion. For me. You understand? If you go by the rules, it is right. The things that you *can* do. The things that you can't do, that you aren't supposed to do. And if these are carried out, it makes a beautiful picture overall. It's a very beautiful thing because it taught me and it teaches everyone else to live by the rules, to abide by the rules. It also teaches you humility. Hit a grand slam home run to win the game one day and the next day miss the ball and lose the game. It also teaches you that there's always a tomorrow. You got me today, but I'm coming back.

Although he was a man of fewer words, whose "loyalty and dependability" as well as "calm and stoic way is his legacy," J. L. Wilkinson would have agreed. On the heavenly diamond, the two friends are surely still enjoying one another's company and the game they both loved so much.[9]

Appendix: Kansas City Monarchs Rosters and Records During the J. L. Wilkinson Era (1920–1948)

Note: No official rosters for the Kansas City Monarchs or other Negro Leagues teams or records for league play were kept. The following reconstructions are based on the research of respected scholars of the Monarchs and black baseball. The different perspectives of these scholars on how to interpret often conflicting data suggest that the Won-Lost records of teams and pitchers are still open to question. For example, according to Holway's accounting, in the Won-Lost records of the 1923 Monarchs, pitchers totaled 127 games (78–49), while the team's record that year is reputed to have been only 57–33 (90 games). Other seasons with obvious contradictions are 1922, 1926, 1940, 1944, 1945, and 1948.

Key to Sources:
CL—Dick Clark and Larry Lester, ed. *The Negro League Book*. Cleveland: Society for American Baseball Research, 1994.
JB—Janet Bruce. *The Kansas City Monarchs: Champions of Black Baseball* (Lawrence: University of Kansas, 1985), 133–41.
JH—John B. Holway. *The Complete Book of Baseball's Negro Leagues: The Other Half of Baseball History*. Fern Park, FL: Hastings House, 2001.
LH—Leslie A. Heaphy. *Satchel Paige and Company: Essays on the Kansas City Monarchs, Their Greatest Star and the Negro Leagues* (Jefferson, NC: McFarland, 2007), Appendix C, 226–29.

1920 Negro National League (NNL) Season

Roster:
José Méndez, Manager (CL 76, JB 133–34, JH 141, LH 228)
Hugh Blackburn, first base (LH)
Lemuel "Hawk" Hawkins, first base (JB, LH)
Edgar "Blue" Washington, first base (CL)
Joaquin Arumis, second base (CL)
Frank Blukoi, second base (CL, JB, LH)
Bob Fagin/Fagan, second base (JB, LH)
Herman Gordon, second base (CL)
Roosevelt "Chappy" Gray, second base (CL, LH)
Roy "Bubba" Johnson, second base (CL, JB, LH)
Carroll "Dink" Mothell, second base (JB, LH)
Bartolo Portuando .319, second base (LH), third base (CL, JB, JH, LH)
Walter "Dobie" Moore .306, shortstop (CL, JB, JH, LH)
Bernardo Baro, outfield (CL, JB, LH)
Hurley McNair .332, outfield (CL, JB, JH, LH)
Charles Wilber "Bullet Joe" Rogan .273 (JB, CL, JH, LH)
Oscar "Heavy" Johnson, catcher (JB)
Otto "Jaybird" Ray, catcher (CL, JB, LH)
Vincente "José" Rodríguez .200, catcher (CL, JB, JH, LH)
John Donaldson .309, utility (CL, JH, LH)
Sylvester "Hooks" Foreman, utility (LH)

Méndez .205, utility (CL, JH)
George "Tank" Carr .336, utility (JB, JH, LH)

Pitchers:
Clifford Alsop (CL. LH)
Atame (CL)
Hugh Blackburn (CL, LH)
Sam Crawford 14–7 (CL, JB, JH, LH)
Rube Curry 12–13 (CL, JB, JH, LH)
John Donaldson 5–4 (JB, JH)
Bill "Plunk" Drake (JB)
Frank Evans (CL, LH)
Fern (CL)
Zack "Hooks" Foreman 2–1 (CL, JB, JH)
Charley Lightner 0–1 (CL, JB, JH)
José Méndez 2–1 (JH, LH)
Bullet Joe Rogan 10–4 (CL, JB, JH, LH)

Record (JH 139):
Chicago American Giants 31–15 (.674)
Detroit Stars 40–21 (.656)
Kansas City Monarchs 45–35 (.563)
Indianapolis A.B.C.'s 42–34 (.553)
St. Louis Giants 21–21 (.500)
Cuban Stars 22–28 (.440)
Dayton Marcos 10–18 (.357)
Chicago Giants 2–12 (.143)

The American Giants won the pennant. There were no playoffs.

1921 NNL Season

Roster:
José Méndez, Manager (CL 80, JB 134, JH 155, LH 228)
George "Tank" Carr .330, first base (CL, JB, JH), utility (LH)
Lemuel "Hawk" Hawkins, first base (CL, JB, LH)
Mike McAlister, first base (CL), outfield (JB)
Augustin Parpetti, first base (CL, JB, LH)
Frank Blattner, second base, first base (CL, JB, LH), outfield (LH)
Bob Fagan/Fagin .283, second base (LH), utility (JH)
Roy "Bubba" Johnson, second base (CL, JB, LH)
John Henry "Pop" Lloyd, shortstop (CL, LH)
"Dobie" Moore .372, shortstop (CL, JH, LH)
Barr, third base, shortstop (CL)
Cordova, third base (CL, JB, LH)
Frank Warfield (JB)
John Donaldson .285, outfield (LH, JH)
Leonard King, outfield (CL, LH)
Hurley McNair .236, outfield (JB, JH, LH)
Bartolo Portuando .280, outfield (JH), second base (JB, LH), third base (CL, JB, LH)
"Bullet Joe" Rogan .293, outfield (JB, JH, LH)
Wharton, outfield (CL)
Frank Duncan .237, catcher (CL, JH, LH)
Sylvester "Hooks" Foreman, catcher (CL, JB, LH), outfield (LH)
Méndez .278, utility (JH)
Carroll "Dink" Mothell, utility (CL, LH), second base (JB)
Otto "Jaybird" Ray, utility (CL), catcher (JB, LH)
George Sweatt, utility (CL, LH)

Pitchers:
Clifford "Cliff" or "Cherry" Bell (CL, JB, LH)
William Bell 5–3 (JH)
Coffee (CL)
Sam Crawford 8–3 (CL, JB, JH, LH)
Rube Curry 13–12 (CL, JB, JH, LH)
James Davis (CL, LH)
John Donaldson 2–0 (JB, JH, LH)
Zack "Hooks" Foreman, 4–5 (CL, JB, JH, LH)
Hamilton (JB, CL)
Harper (CL, LH)
Hoard (CL)
McNair 1–1 (JH, LH)
Méndez 1–0 (JB, JH)
Hurland Ragland (CL, LH)
Ed Rile (CL, JB, LH)
Rogan 20–11 (CL, JB, JH, LH)
Percy Segula (CL, LH)
"Lefty" Smith (CL, JB)
John "Red" or "Big" Taylor (CL, JB, LH)

Record (JH 153):
Chicago American Giants 50–27 (.649)
St. Louis Giants 54–30 (.643)
Kansas City Monarchs 73–43 (.629)
Detroit Stars 46–46 (.500)
Columbus Buckeyes 30–39 (.435)
Cincinnati Cubans 30–39 (.435)
Indianapolis A.B.C.'s 43–60 (.417)
Chicago Giants 7–37 (.159)

The American Giants won the pennant. There were no playoffs.

1922 NNL Season

Roster:
Sam Crawford, Manager (CL 82, JB 134, JH 167, LH 227)
George "Tank" Carr, first base (CL), utility (LH)

Lemuel "Hawk" Hawkins .298, first base (CL, JB, JH, LH)
Newton "Newt" or "Colt" Allen, second base, third base (CL, JB, LH)
Theodore "Bubbles" Anderson, second base (CL, JB, LH)
Bob Fagin/Fagan, second base (JB, LH)
Roy "Bubba" Johnson, second base (CL, JB, LH)
George Sweatt .135, second base (JH), utility (CL, JB, LH)
Dan Thomas, second base (CL, LH)
José Méndez, shortstop (CL, LH), second base (JB, LH)
Percy Miller, shortstop (CL, JB)
Carroll "Dink" Mothell, second base (JB)
"Dobie" Moore .406, shortstop (CL, JB, JH, LH)
Walter "Newt" Joseph .269, third base (CL, JB, JH, LH)
Bartolo Portuando, third base (CL, JB, LH)
Eugene Redd, third base (CL, JB, LH)
George Bennette, outfield (CL, LH)
John Donaldson .350, outfield (CL, JB, LH), Utility (JH)
Oscar "Heavy" Johnson .451, outfield (CL, LH), catcher (JB)
Hurley McNair .420, outfield (CL, JB, LH)
"Bullet Joe" Rogan .439, outfield (CL, LH)
William Carter, catcher (CL, JB, LH)
Fred Dewitt, catcher (CL, LH)
Frank Duncan .292, catcher (CL, JB, JH. LH)
Sylvester "Hooks" Foreman, catcher (CL, JB, LH), outfield (LH)
Charles O'Neill, catcher (LH)
C. Neil Pullen, catcher (JB)
Otto "Jaybird" Ray .287, catcher (CL, JB, JH, LH)
Henry Williams, catcher (CL, JB, LH)
Branch Russell, utility (CL, JB, LH)

Pitchers:
Clifford Alsop (CL, JB, LH)
Cliff Bell (CL, JB, LH)
Sam Crawford 11-6 (CL, JB, JH, LH)
Rube Currie 19-11 (CL, JH, LH)
Donaldson (CL, JB, LH)
Bill "Plunk" Drake 10-0 (CL, JB, JH, LH)
Sylvester Foreman 0-1 (JH)
Willie "Lefty" Gisentaner 8-5 (CL, JB, JH, LH)
"Big Bill" Gatewood 0-2 (JH)
Linder 1-0 (JH)
Charley Lightner (CL)
Jack Marshall (CL, JB, LH)

McNair 3-0 (JH)
Méndez 3-1 (CL, JB, JH, LH)
Percy Miller 0-1 (JH)
Murphy 1-0 (CL JB, JH)
Rogan 20-11 (CL, JB, JH, LH)
William Sheppard (CL, JB)
John "Red" or "Big" Taylor (CL, JB, LH)
Yokum (CL, JB)

Record (JH 165):
Chicago American Giants 36-23 (.610)
Indianapolis A.B.C.'s 46-33 (.582)
Detroit Stars 43-32 (.573)
Kansas City Monarchs 44-33 (.571)
St. Louis Stars 23-23 (.500)
Pittsburgh Keystones 16-21 (.432)
Cuban Stars 19-30 (.388)
Cleveland Tate Stars 17-29 (.370)

The American Giants won the pennant. There were no playoffs.

1923 NNL Season

Roster:
Sam Crawford, Manager (CL 85, JB 134-35, JH 177, LH 227)
José Méndez, Manager (JH, LH)
Lemuel "Hawk" Hawkins .220, first base (CL, JB, JH, LH)
"Newt" Allen, second base, shortstop (CL, JB, LH)
Theodore "Bubbles" Anderson, second base (CL, JB, LH)
George Sweatt .220, second base (JH), outfield (CL), utility (JB, LH)
"Dobie" Moore .319, shortstop (CL, JB, JH, LH)
"Newt" Joseph .167, third base (CL, JB, JH, LH)
John Donaldson, outfield (CL, JB, LH)
Oscar "Heavy" Johnson .367, outfield (CL, JB, JH, LH)
Wade Johnston, outfield (CL, JB, LH)
Hurley McNair .303, outfield (JB, JH, LH)
"Bullet Joe" Rogan .355, outfield (CL, JH, LH)
Wharton, outfield (CL)
Frank Duncan .196, catcher (CL, JB, JH, LH)
Sylvester "Hooks" Foreman, catcher (JB)
Henry Williams, catcher (JB, LH), utility (CL)

Pitchers:
Cliff Bell (JB)
William Bell 3-1 (CL, JH, LH)
Coley (CL, JB)
Alfred "Army" Cooper 0-1 (CL, JH, LH)

Crawford 0–1 (JH, LH)
Rube Currie 23–11 (CL, JB, JH, LH)
Donaldson (LH)
Bill "Plunk" Drake 15–9 (CL, JB, JH, LH)
Willie "Lefty" Gisentaner, 2–1 (CL, JB, JH, LH)
Lightner (CL)
Méndez 15–6 (CL, JH, LH)
Rogan 20–19 (CL, JB, JH, LH)

Record (JH 175):
Kansas City Monarchs 57–33 (.633)
Detroit Stars 40–27 (.597)
Chicago American Giants 41–29 (.586)
Indianapolis A.B.C.'s 45–34 (.570)
Cuban Stars 27–31 (.466)
St. Louis Stars 29–33, (.468)
Toledo Tigers/Cleveland Tate Stars 21–30 (.423)
Milwaukee Bears 14–32 (.304)

The Memphis Red Sox 17–8 (.680) were not in the league, but the team's games counted in the standings. The Monarchs won the pennant. There were no playoffs.

1924 NNL Season

Roster:
José Méndez, Manager (JH 186, LH 228)
William Bobo, first base (CL 88, JB 135, LH)
Lemuel "Hawk" Hawkins .295, first base (CL, JB, JH, LH)
Newt Allen .275, second base (CL, JH, LH)
Theodore "Bubbles" Anderson, second base (LH)
Ed Manese, second base (CL, JB, LH)
"Dobie" Moore .356, shortstop (CL, JB, JH, LH)
A. D. "Dewey" Creacy, third base (CL, JB, LH)
Newt Joseph .361, third base (CL, JB, JH, LH)
John Donaldson, outfield (CL, JB, LH)
Wade Johnston, outfield (JB, LH)
Hurley McNair .346, outfield (CL, JB, JH, LH)
Oscar "Heavy" Johnson .374, outfield (CL, JB, JH, LH)
"Bullet Joe" Rogan .409, outfield (CL, JH, LH)
Frank Duncan .273, catcher (CL, JB, JH, LH)
Carroll "Dink" Mothell .278, utility (CL, JB, JH, LH)
George Sweatt .267, utility (CL, JB, JH, LH)

Pitchers:
Howard or Homer "Hop" Bartley (CL, JB, LH)
Cliff Bell 5–2 (CL, JB, JH, LH)

William Bell, 10–2 (CL, JB, JH, LH)
Chet Brewer, 1–0 (JH)
Sam Crawford, 0–1 (JH, LH)
Donaldson (LH)
Bill "Plunk" Drake, 11–9 (CL, JB, JH, LH)
Jack Marshall, 1–1 (CL, JB, JH, LH)
William "Bill" McCall (CL, JB, LH)
McNair (CL)
Méndez, 5–2 (CL, JB, JH, LH)
Harold "Yellowhorse" Morris, 7–5 (CL, JB, JH, LH)
Rogan, 17–5 (CL, JB, JH, LH)

Record (JH 185):
Kansas City Monarchs 60–27 (.690)
Chicago American Giants 63–29 (.685)
St. Louis Stars 36–31 (.537)
Detroit Stars 38–37 (.507)
Cuban Stars 17–19 (.472)
Birmingham Black Barons 37–46 (.446)
Memphis Red Sox 26–36 (.419)
Cleveland Browns 17–34 (.333)

The Indianapolis A.B.C.'s 3–12 (.200) dropped out of the NNL in June and were replaced by the Memphis Red Sox.

The Monarchs won the pennant. There were no playoffs. They beat the Hilldale Daisies, champions of the Eastern Colored League (ECL), five games to four (with one tie) in the first Negro Leagues World Series.

1925 NNL Season

Roster:
José Méndez, Manager (JH 198, LH 228)
Fred Dewitt, first base (CL 91, JB 135), catcher (LH)
Lemuel "Hawk" Hawkins .273, first base (CL, JB, JH, LH)
Newt Allen .307, second base, third base (CL, JB, JH, LH)
"Bull" Barber, second base (CL)
"Dobie" Moore .333, shortstop (CL, JB, JH, LH)
Newt Joseph .335, third base (CL, JB, JH, LH)
John Donaldson, outfield (LH)
Oscar "Heavy" Johnson, outfield (CL, LH)
Wade Johnston .304, outfield (CL, JB, JH, LH)
Louis LaFlora, outfield (CL, LH)
Hurley McNair .365, outfield (CL, JB, JH, LH)
"Bullet Joe" Rogan .374, outfield (CL, JH, LH)
William "Simmy" Simms, outfield (JB)
Frank Duncan .222, catcher (CL, JB, JH, LH)
Sylvester "Hooks" Foreman, .241, catcher (CL, JH, LH), outfield (LH)

Henry Williams, catcher (CL, JB, LH)
T. J. "Tom" Young," catcher (CL, JB. LH)
Carroll "Dink" Mothell .282, utility (CL, JB, JH, LH)
George Sweatt, utility (CL, JB, LH)

Pitchers:
Barnes (CL)
Howard or Homer "Hop" Bartley (CL, LH)
Cliff Bell 5-7 (CL, JB, JH, LH)
William Bell 10-3 (CL, JB, JH, LH)
Chet Brewer 4-1 (CL, JB, JH, LH)
Sol Butler 1-0 (CL, JH)
Nelson Dean 11-3 (CL, JB, JH, LH)
John Donaldson (LH)
Bill "Plunk" Drake 10-3 (CL, JH, LH)
Méndez 1-0 (CL, JB, JH, LH)
Rogan 20-2 (CL, JB, JH, LH)

Record (JH 197):
Kansas City Monarchs 62-20 (.756)
St. Louis Stars 69-26 (.726)
Chicago American Giants 54-40 (.574)
Detroit Stars 53-40 (.570)
Cuban Stars 22-35 (.468)
Memphis Red Sox 30-48 (.385)
Birmingham Black Barons 24-49 (.329)
Indianapolis A.B.C.'s 17-57 (.230)

Kansas City won the first half; St. Louis won the second half. Kansas City beat St. Louis in a playoff, five games to three. Hilldale beat the Monarchs in the Negro Leagues World Series, five games to one.

1926 NNL Season

Roster:
"Bullet Joe" Rogan, Manager (CL 93, JB 135, LH 229)
José Méndez, Manager (JH 208)
Lemuel "Hawk" Hawkins .278, first base (CL, JB, JH, LH)
Newt Allen .232, second base (CL, JB, JH, LH)
Grady Orange, second base (JB, LH)
Walter "Dobie" Moore .390, shortstop (CL, JB, JH, LH)
Newt Joseph .277, third base (CL, JB, JH, LH)
Wade Johnston .292, outfield (CL, JB, JH, LH)
Hurley McNair, .289, outfield (CL, LB, JH, LH)
Cristóbal Torriente .371, outfield (CL, JB, JH, LH)
Harold Vaughn, outfield (CL, JB, LH)
Frank Duncan .247, catcher (CL, JB, JH, LH)

T. J. "Tom" Young .394, catcher (CL, JH, LH)
Carroll "Dink" Mothell .289, utility (CL, JB, JH, LH)
Rogan .329, utility (JH, LH)
William Bell .320, utility (JH)

Pitchers:
Cliff Bell 5-3 (CL, JB, JH, LH)
William Bell 19-4 (CL, JB, JH, LH)
Chet Brewer 14-1 (CL, JH, LH)
Nelson Dean 7-5 (CL, JB, JH, LH)
Wade Johnston 0-1 (CL, JH)
José Méndez (CL, JH, LH)
Dempsey "Dimp" Miller (CL, JB, LH)
Squire "Square" Moore (JB)
Randolph Prim 10-0 (CL, JB, JH, LH)
Rogan 24-4 (JH, LH)
Bob Saunders 2-0 (CL, JB, JH, LH)

Record (JH 206):
Kansas City Monarchs 56-19 (.747)
Chicago American Giants 57-23 (.713)
St. Louis Stars 49-29 (.628)
Detroit Stars 46-40 (.535)
Indianapolis A.B.C.'s 43-43 (.500)
Cuban Stars 16-47 (.254)
Dayton Marcos 7-32 (.179)
Cleveland Elite Giants 5-32 (.135)

Kansas City won the first-half pennant; Chicago won the second half. Chicago beat Kansas City, five games to four in a playoff. Chicago beat the Atlantic City Bacharach Giants in the Negro Leagues World Series, five games to four (with two ties).

1927 NNL Season

Roster:
"Bullet Joe" Rogan, Manager (CL 96, JB 136, JH 223, LH 229)
Fred Dewitt, first base (CL, JB), catcher (LH)
George Giles .287, first base (CL, JB, JH, LH)
Carl "Lefty" Glass, first base (LH)
Lemuel "Hawk" Hawkins, first base (JB, LH)
Grady Orange, second base, third base (CL, LH)
Newt Allen .330, shortstop (CL, JB, JH, LH)
Newt Joseph .293, third base (CL, JB, JH, LH)
A. Hughes, outfield (CL, JB)
Wade Johnston .316, outfield (CL, JB, JH, LH)
Rogan .330, outfield (CL, JH, LH)
Hurley McNair .275, outfield (CL, JB, JH, LH)
T. J. "Tom" Young .290, catcher (CL, JB, JH, LH
Frank Duncan .395, catcher (CL, JB, JH, LH)

Evans, catcher (CL)
Sylvester "Hooks" Foreman, catcher (CL, JB, LH), outfield (LH)
Chet Brewer .413, utility (JH)
William Bell .333, utility (CL, JH)
Clarence Everett, utility (CL, LH)
Grady Orange, utility (JB)
Lem "Hawk" Hawkins, utility (CL)
Clarence "Dink" Mothell .289, utility (CL, JB, JH, LH)

Pitchers:
Cliff Bell (JB, JH, LH)
William Bell 14–6 (CL, JB, JH, LH)
Brewer 9–6 (CL, JB, JH, LH)
G. Brown (CL, JB)
Glass 1–2 (JH, LH)
George Mitchell 9–6 (CL, JB, JH, LH)
Rogan 15–6 (CL, JB, JH, LH)
Owen Smaulding 2–1 (CL, JB, JH, LH)
William "Steel Arm" Tyler 2–1 (CL, JH, LH)
Harold Vaughn (CL, LH)
Admiral "Deacon" Walker 3–2 (CL, JB, JH)
Maurice "Doolittle" Young 3–3 (CL, JB, JH, LH)
William Young (CL, JB, LH)

Record (JH 222):
Chicago American Giants 54–28 (.659)
Kansas City Monarchs 58–33 (.637)
St. Louis Stars 60–35 (.632)
Detroit Stars 70–53 (.569)
Birmingham Black Barons 53–41 (.564)
Cuban Stars 21–40 (.344)
Cleveland Hornets 17–42 (.288)
Memphis Red Sox 28–74 (.275)

Chicago won the first half; Birmingham won the second half. Chicago beat Birmingham four games to zero in a playoff. Chicago beat the Atlantic City Bacharach Giants in the Negro Leagues World Series five games to three (with one tie).

1928 NNL Season

Roster:
"Bullet Joe" Rogan, Manager (JB 136, JH 234, LH 229)
George Giles .292, first base (CL 98, JB, JH, LH)
"Dink" Mothell .279, second base (JH)
Newt Allen .280, shortstop (CL, JB, JH, LH)
Newt Joseph .258, third base (CL, JH, LH)
Eddie "Pee Wee" Dwight .282, outfield (CL, JB, JH, LH)

Reginald Hopwood, outfield (CL, LH)
L. D. "Goo Goo" Livingston .276, outfield (CL, JB, JH, LH)
Leroy "Ben" Taylor .134, outfield (CL, JB, JH, LH)
T. J. "Tom" Young .254, catcher (CL, JB, JH, LH)
Frank Duncan .182, catcher (CL, JB, JH, LH)
Rogan .358, utility (CL, JH, LH
William Bell .300, utility (CL, JH)
Chet Brewer, utility (CL)
A. "Hallie" Harding .242, utility (CL, JB, JH, LH)
Carroll "Dink" Mothell, utility (CL, JB, LH)

Pitchers:
William Bell 11–7 (CL, JB, JH, LH)
Brewer 7–9 (CL, JB, JH, LH)
Ray Brown (CL, JB, LH)
Andy "Lefty" Cooper 13–7 (CL, JB, JH, LH)
Alfred "Army" Cooper 5–4 (CL, JB, JH, LH)
Harry Kenyon (CL, JB, LH)
Sam Streeter 0–1 (JH)
Rogan 11–3 (JB, JH, LH)
William "Steel Arm" Tyler (JB)
Herbert Wilson 2–1 (CL, JB, JH, LH)

Record (JH 233):
St. Louis Stars 68–25 (.731)
Kansas City Monarchs 49–31 (.613)
Detroit Stars 58–38 (.604)
Chicago American Giants 45–37 (.549)
Birmingham Black Barons 44–54 (.449)
Memphis Red Sox 30–52 (.366)
Cleveland Tigers 21–53 (.284)
Cuban Stars 14–44 (.241)

St. Louis won the first half; Chicago won the second half. St. Louis beat Chicago 5 games to 4 in a playoff. There was no Negro Leagues World Series. It did not resume until 1942.

1929 NNL Season

Roster:
"Bullet Joe" Rogan, Manager (CL 100, JB 136, JH 245, LH 229)
George Giles, first base (CL, JB, LH)
Carroll "Dink" Mothell .218, first base (CL, JB, JH, LH)
Newt Allen .284, second base (CL, JB, JH, LH)
Hallie Harding .292, shortstop (CL, JB, JH), outfield (LH)
Newt Joseph .257, third base (CL, JB, JH, LH)

Eddie "Pee Wee" Dwight, outfield (CL, JB, LH)
L. D. Livingston .320, outfield (CL, JB, JH, LH)
Rogan .325, outfield (JB, JH), utility (CL, LH)
Leroy Taylor .346, outfield (CL, JB, JH, LH)
T. J. "Tom" Young .361, catcher (CL, JB, JH, LH)
Frank Duncan .346, catcher (CL, JB, JH, LH)

Pitchers:
William Bell 17-4 (CL, JB, JH, LH)
Chet Brewer 17-3 (CL, JB, JH, LH)
"Army" Cooper 14-4 (CL, JB, JH, LH)
Andy "Lefty" Cooper 13-3 (CL, JB, JH, LH)
Rogan (JB, LH)
Herbert Wilson 2-0 (CL, JB, JH, LH)

Record (JH 243):
Kansas Monarchs 66-14 (.825)
St. Louis Stars 60-28 (.682)
Chicago American Giants, 44-25 (.638)
Detroit Stars 38-39 (.494)
Cuban Stars 15-34 (.306)
Birmingham Black Barons 24-41 (.369)
Memphis Red Sox 10-38 (.208)

The Nashville Elite Giants (5-14, .263) were not in the league but their games counted in the standings. The Monarchs won both the first half and second half of the pennant race.

1930 NNL Season

Roster:
"Bullet Joe" Rogan, Manager (CL 103, JB 136, JH 260, LH 229)
T. J. "Tom" Young .324, first base (JH), catcher (CL, JB, LH)
Newt Allen .333, second base (CL, JB, JH, LH), shortstop (CL)
Carroll "Dink" Mothell .260, first base (JB), shortstop (JH), utility (CL, LH)
Newt Joseph .270, third base (CL, JB, JH, LH)
Hallie Harding .288, shortstop (JB), outfield (JH, LH), utility (CL)
L. D. Livingston .303, outfield (CL, JH, LH), first base (JB)
Wilson "Frog" Redus, outfield (CL, LH)
Rogan .295, outfield (JB, JH, LH)
Frank Duncan .378, catcher (JB, JH, LH), utility (CL)
William Bell, utility (CL)
Chet Brewer, utility (CL)
Leroy Taylor .290, utility (CL, JB, JH, LH)

Pitchers:
Brewer 13-10 (CL, JH, LH)
William Bell 11-4 (CL, JB, JH, LH)
Alfred "Army" Cooper 15-1 (CL, JH, LH)
Andy "Lefty" Cooper (JB, LH)
Roosevelt "Rosey" Davis (CL)
Tomlini Harrison (CL, LH)
Henry McHenry 11-9 (CL, JB, JH, LH)
John Markham 4-8 (CL, JB, JH, LH)
Roosevelt Davis 0-1 (JH, LH)

Record (JH 258):
St. Louis Stars 69-29 (.742)
Kansas City Monarchs 54-33 (.621)
Detroit Stars 58-37 (.611)
Chicago American Giants 59-52 (.532)
Birmingham Black Barons 43-49 (.467)
Memphis Red Sox 27-31 (.466)
Nashville Elite Giants 39-47 (.453)
Cuban Stars 23-35 (.397) (JH)

The Louisville Redcaps (14-27, .341) were not in the league but the team's games counted in the standings. St. Louis won the first half; Detroit won the second half. St. Louis beat Detroit, four games to three in a playoff. The Monarchs withdrew from the NNL after the 1930 season. They would remain an independent team until 1937.

1931 Barnstorming Roster

"Bullet Joe" Rogan, Manager (CL 105, JB 136-37, JH 274, LH 229)
Chick "Popsickle" Harris .215, first base (JH), outfield (LH), utility (CL)
L. D. Livingston, first base (CL, JB), outfield (LH)
Carroll "Dink" Mothell .283, second base (CL, JH), first base (CL, JB), utility (LH)
Newt Allen .300, second base (CL, LH), shortstop (CL, JH, LH)
Hallie Harding, shortstop (CL, JB), outfield (LH)
Grady Orange, shortstop (JB, LH), utility (CL)
Newt Joseph .281, third base (CL, JB, JH, LH)
Roy Brown, outfield (CL, JB)
Richard "Subby" Byas, outfield (CL, LH)
John Donaldson .313, outfield (CL, JB, JH, LH)
Wesley Hicks, outfield (CL, LH)
William "Nat" Rogers, outfield (CL, JB, LH)
Ray Sheppard, outfield (CL, JB)
Norman "Turkey" Stearnes .095, outfield (CL, JB, JH, LH)

Nat Rogers .277, outfield (JH)
Frank Duncan .297, catcher (CL, JB, JH, LH)
T. J. "Tom" Young .296, utility (JH), catcher (CL, JB, LH)
Rogan .200, utility (JH, LH)

Pitchers:
Charles "Lefty" Beverly 6–1 (CL, JB, JH, LH)
Chet Brewer 2–2 (CL, JH, LH)
Ray Brown 1–0 (CL, JH, LH)
Alfred "Army" Cooper 6–1 (CL, JH, LH)
Andy "Lefty" Cooper 0–1 (JB, JH)
Donaldson (LH)
Bill "Willie" Foster 2–0 (CL, JB, JH, LH)
Harris (JB, LH)
Alto Lane 0–1 (CL, JH, LH)
Henry McHenry 4–0 (CL, JH, LH)
Rogan (JB, LH)
Samuel "Sad Sam" Thompson (CL, JB, LH)

1932 Barnstorming Roster

Newt Allen .364, captain (JB), second base (CL, JB, JH, LH)
George Giles .311, first base (CL 109, JB 137, JH 294, LH 227)
Willie Wells .255, shortstop (CL, JB, JH, LH)
Newt Joseph, third base (CL, JB, LH)
Carroll "Dink" Mothell .237, third base (JH), utility (CL, JB, LH)
Leroy Taylor .313, outfield (CL, JH, LH)
James "Cool Papa" Bell .396, outfield (CL, JB, JH, LH)
Chick "Popsickle" Harris .211, outfield (CL, JB, JH, LH)
Norman "Turkey" Stearnes, outfield (LH)
Quincy Trouppe .333, outfield (CL, JB, JH, LH)
Frank Duncan, catcher (CL, LH)
T. J. "Tom" Young .250, catcher (CL, JB, JH, LH)

Pitchers:
Cliff Bell (CL, JB, LH)
William Bell (CL, JB, LH)
Charles "Lefty" Beverly 2–1 (CL, JB, JH, LH)
Chet Brewer 3–0 (CL, JB, JH, LH)
Maceo Broadnax (CL, LH)
William "Lefty" Clay (CL, JB, JH, LH)
Andy "Lefty" Cooper (CL, JB, LH)
Rube Currie 1–0 (CL, JH, LH)
Nelson Dean 1–0 (CL, JB, JH, LH)
Harris (LH)
Bertram Hunter 2–2 (CL, JB, JH, LH)
Samuel "Sad Sam" Thompson (CL, JB, LH)
Ted Trent (CL, JB)
Trouppe 0–1 (CL, JH, LH)

1933 Barnstorming Roster

"Bullet Joe" Rogan, Manager (JB 137, LH 229)
George Giles, first base (CL 112, JB, LH)
Newt Allen, shortstop (CL, JB, LH)
Newt Joseph, third base (CL, JB, LH)
Ollie "Turk" Boyd, outfield (CL, JB, LH)
Dooley, outfield (CL)
Eddie "Pee Wee" Dwight, outfield (CL, JB, LH)
Garrett Norman, outfield (CL, LH)
Rogan, outfield (CL, JB, LH)
Leslie Starks, outfield (CL, LH)
Norman "Turkey" Stearnes, outfield (LH)
Frank Duncan, catcher (CL, JB, LH)
Sylvester "Hooks" Foreman, catcher (CL, JB, LH), outfield (LH)
Carroll "Dink" Mothell, utility (CL, LH), second base (JB)
T. J. "Tom" Young, utility (CL, JB), catcher (LH)

Pitchers:
Charles "Lefty" Beverly (CL, JB, LH)
Chet Brewer (CL, JB, LH)
Andy "Lefty" Cooper (CL, JB, LH)

1934 Barnstorming Roster

Sam Crawford, Manager (CL 114, JB 137, LH 226)
"Bullet Joe" Rogan, Manager (CL)
George Giles, first base (CL, JB, LH)
Newt Allen, second base, shortstop (CL, JB, LH)
Willie Wells, shortstop (CL, JB, LH)
Sam Bankhead, second base, third base (CL, JB, LH)
Newt Joseph, third base (CL, JB, LH)
James "Cool Papa" Bell, outfield (CL, JB, LH)
Eddie "Pee Wee" Dwight, outfield (CL, JB, LH)
John Donaldson, outfield (LH)
Chick "Popsickle" Harris, outfield (CL, JB, LH)
Hurley McNair, outfield (CL, JB, LH)
"Bullet Joe" Rogan, outfield (JB)
Norman "Turkey" Stearnes, outfield (CL, JB, LH)
Leroy Taylor, outfield (CL, JB, LH)
Quincy Trouppe, outfield (CL, JB, LH)
Frank Duncan, catcher (CL, JB, LH)
T. J. "Tom" Young, catcher (CL, JB, LH)
Carroll "Dink" Mothell, utility (CL, JB, LH)

Pitchers:
Charles "Lefty" Beverly (CL, JB, LH)

Chet Brewer (CL, JB, LH)
Andy "Lefty" Cooper (CL, JB, LH)
Harris (LH)
John Donaldson (CL, JB)
Bill "Willie" Foster (CL, LH)
Bertram Hunter (CL, JB, LH)

1935 Barnstorming Roster

Sam Crawford, Manager (CL, 116, JB 137-38, JH 319, LH 226)
Eldridge "Ed"/"Chill" Mayweather, first base (CL, JB, JH, LH)
Newt Allen, captain (JB), second base (CL, JB, JH, LH), shortstop (CL, LH)
Willard Brown, shortstop (CL, JB, JH), third base (CL, JB), outfield (LH)
Robert Madison, shortstop (LH)
Newt Joseph, third base (CL, JB, JH)
"Bullet Joe" Rogan, outfield (CL, JH, LH)
Eddie "Pee Wee" Dwight, outfield (CL, JB, JH, LH)
Leroy Taylor, outfield (CL, JB, JH, LH)
Quincy Trouppe, catcher (JH), outfield (CL, JB, LH)
T. J. "Tom" Young, catcher (CL, JB, LH)
Henry Milton, utility (CL, JB, LH)

Pitchers:
John Paul Berry (CL, JB, LH)
Charles "Lefty" Beverly (CL, JB, LH)
Eugene Bremer (LH)
Chet Brewer (CL, JB, JH, LH)
Andy "Lefty" Cooper (CL, JB, JH, LH)
Floyd Kranson (or Cranson) (CL, JB, JH, LH)
Robert Madison (CL, JB, JH, LH)
Leroy "Satchel" Paige (CL, JH, LH)

1936 Barnstorming Roster

Andy Cooper, Manager (CL 118, JB 138, JH 326, LH 226)
"Bullet Joe" Rogan, Manager (CL, JB, LH)
Curtis "Popeye" Harris .276, first base (CL, JH, LH)
Eldridge "Ed" Mayweather, first base (CL, JB, LH), third base (JB)
Newt Allen .385, second base (CL, JB, JH, LH)
Willard Brown .367, shortstop (CL, JB, JH), outfield (LH)
Robert Madison, shortstop (LH)
Andrew "Pat" Patterson, third base (CL, JB, LH)
Eddie "Pee Wee" Dwight .476, outfield (CL, JB, JH, LH)
Chick "Popsicle" Harris, outfield (CL, JB, LH)

Henry Milton .333, outfield (CL, JB, JH, LH)
Leroy Taylor .407, outfield (CL, JB, JH, LH)
Harry "Speedy" Else, catcher (CL, JB, LH)
Quincy Trouppe .545, catcher (CL, JH), outfield (CL, JB, LH)
Jim "Double Duty" Webster, catcher, pitcher (CL, LH)
"Bullet Joe" Rogan .600, utility (JH, LH)

Pitchers:
John Paul Berry (CL, JB, LH)
E. Brooks (CL, JB)
Andy "Lefty" Cooper (CL, JB, JH, LH)
Floyd Kranson (or Cranson) 2-0 (CL, JB, JH, LH)
Robert Madison (CL, JB, LH)
Harold "Yellowhorse" Morris (CL, JB, LH)
Leroy "Satchel" Paige (CL, JB, LH)
Rogan 1-0 (JB, JH, LH)
Walter Thomas (CL, LH)
Ted Trent (CL, LH)
Woodrow "Lefty" Wilson 2-0 (CL, JB, JH, LH)

1937 Negro American League (NAL) Season

Roster:
Andy Cooper, Manager (CL 120, JB 138, JH 339, LH 226)
Eldridge "Ed" Mayweather .281, first base (CL, JB, JH, LH)
Newt Allen .389, second base (CL, JB, LH)
Jesse Douglas, second base (LH), outfield (CL)
Theodore Stockard, second base (CL, LH)
Jesse Brooks .395, third base (CL, JB, JH, LH)
Willard Brown .361, outfield (CL, JB, LH), shortstop (CL, JB, JH)
Byron "Mex" Johnson, shortstop (CL, JB, LH)
Eddie "Pee Wee" Dwight .238, outfield (CL, JB, JH, LH)
Dave Mays, outfield (LH)
Henry Milton .151, outfield (CL, JB, JH, LH)
Bill Simms .318, outfield (CL, JB, JH, LH)
Frank Duncan .183, catcher (CL, JB, JH, LH)
Harry Else, catcher (CL, JB, LH)
"Bullet Joe" Rogan .410, utility (CL, JB, JH, LH)
Hilton Smith .281, utility (JH)
T. R. "Ted" Strong, utility (CL, LH)

Pitchers:
Ed Barnes, 2-0 (CL, JB, JH, LH)
Frank Bradley (CL, LH)
Eugene Bremer (CL, LH)

Chet Brewer (CL, LH)
Andy "Lefty" Cooper, 2-0 (CL, JB, JH, LH)
Floyd Kranson (or Cranson), 0-1 (CL, JB, JH, LH)
John Markham, 1-0 (CL, JB, JH, LH)
Henry McHenry, 1-3 (CL, JB, JH, LH)
Hilton Smith, 6-4 (CL, JB, JH, LH)
Woodrow "Lefty" Wilson, 1-0 (CL, JB, JH, LH)

Record (JH 338):
Cincinnati Tigers 19-10 (.655)
Chicago American Giants 25-14 (.641)
Kansas City Monarchs 13-8 (.619)
Memphis Red Sox 12-10 (.545)
Birmingham Black Barons 17-21 (.447)
Indianapolis Athletics 16-20 (.444)
St. Louis Stars 9-27 (.250)
Detroit Stars 4-12 (.250)

The Monarchs were awarded the first-half championship, but the American Giants had a better record and disputed it. No second half of the season was recorded, and Kansas City was awarded the pennant.

1938 NAL Season

Roster:
Andy Cooper, Manager (CL 122-23, JH 352, LH 226)
Eldridge "Ed" Mayweather, first base (CL, JB, LH)
John "Buck" O'Neil .260, first base, outfield (CL, JB, JH, LH)
Newt Allen .267, second base (CL, JB, JH, LH)
William Marshall, second base (CL, LH)
Byron "Mex" Johnson .212, shortstop (CL, JB, JH, LH)
T. R. "Ted" Strong, shortstop (CL, JB, LH)
"Packinghouse "Adams, third base (CL, JB, LH)
Junius "Rainey" Bibbs .343, third base (CL, JB, JH, LH)
Roosevelt "Indian Joe" Cox, third base, catcher (CL, JB, LH)
Willard Brown .362, outfield (CL, JB, LH)
Luther Gillard, outfield (LH), catcher (CL)
Henry Milton .325, outfield (CL, JB, JH, LH)
Bill Simms, outfield (CL, JB, LH)
Norman "Turkey" Stearnes .292, outfield (CL, JB, JH, LH)
Johnny Dawson, catcher (CL, LH)
Frank Duncan .247, catcher (CL, JB, LH), utility (JH)
Harry Else .308, catcher (CL, JH, LH)
Raymond Taylor, catcher (CL, LH)
"Bullet Joe" Rogan .263, utility (JH)

Pitchers:
Ed Barnes (CL, LH)
Randolph "Bob" Bowe (CL, JB, LH)
Frank Bradley 8-2 (CL, JB, JH, LH)
Andy "Lefty" Cooper 2-0 (CL, JB, JH, LH)
W. "Big Train" Jackson 1-4 (CL, JB, JH, LH)
Floyd Kranson (or Cranson) 3-2 (CL, JB, JH, LH)
John Markham 1-3 (CL, JB, JH, LH)
Alfred Marvin 1-0 (CL, JB, JH, LH)
C. Moses 1-0 (CL, JB, JH, LH)
C. D. Mosley 3-0 (CL, JH, LH)
Rogan (CL, JB, LH)
Hilton Smith 12-2 (CL, JB, JH, LH)

Record (JH 351):
Kansas City Monarchs 32-15 (.681)
Memphis Red Sox 29-19 (.604)
Atlanta Black Crackers 21-14 (.600)
Chicago American Giants 25-20 (.556)
Indianapolis A.B.C.'s 4-19 (.424)
Jacksonville Red Caps 3-4 (.429)
Birmingham Black Barons 8-23 (.258)

Memphis won the first half of the pennant race; Atlanta won the second half. The playoff series ended with Memphis leading 2-0 in games.

1939 NAL Season

Roster:
Andy Cooper, Manager (CL 125, JB 138-39, JH 360, LH 226)
John "Buck" O'Neil .240, first base (CL, JB, JH, LH)
Newt Allen .265, second base (CL, JB, JH, LH)
Byron "Mex" Johnson, shortstop (CL, LH)
T. R. "Ted" Strong .296, shortstop (CL, JB, JH, LH)
Rainey Bibbs .219, third base (CL. JB, JH, LH)
Herbert Cyrus, third base (LH)
Jesse Williams, second base, shortstop (LH), third base (CL, JB), outfield (CL)
Willard Brown .336, outfield (CL, JB, JH, LH)
Henry Milton .236, outfield (CL, JB, JH, LH)
Neil Robinson, outfield (LH)
Norman "Turkey" Stearnes .453, outfield (CL, JB, JH, LH)
Lionel DeCuir, catcher (CL, JB, LH)
James "Joe" Greene .259, catcher (CL, JB, JH, LH)

Paul Hardy, catcher (CL, JB, LH)
Everett Marcell, catcher (CL, LH)
Henry "Frazier" Robinson, catcher (LH)

Pitchers:
Randolph "Bob" Bowe (CL, JB, LH)
Frank Bradley 5-5 (CL, JB, JH, LH)
Andy "Lefty" Cooper (CL, JB, LH)
Willie "Ace" Hutchinson 1-3 (CL, JB, JH, LH)
W. "Big Train" Jackson (CL, JB, LH)
Floyd Kranson (or Cranson) 1-1 (CL, JB, JH, LH)
Marcell (CL, LH)
John Markham (CL, LH)
Jack Matchett (LH)
C. Moses 3-2 (CL, JB, JH, LH)
Leroy "Satchel" Paige (CL, LH)
"Bullet Joe" Rogan (CL)
Hilton Smith 8-2 (CL, JB, JH, LH)
Elbert Treadway (CL, JB, LH)
George Walker 6-0 (CL, JB, JH, LH)

Record (JH 359):
Cleveland Bears 22-4 (.846)
Kansas City Monarchs 25-13 (.658)
Memphis Red Sox 12-13 (.480)
Chicago American Giants 16-20 (.444)
St. Louis Stars 8-11 (.421)
Toledo Crawfords 8-11 (.421)
Indianapolis A.B.C.'s 2-10 (.167)

Despite having the second-best record, Kansas City was awarded the pennant.

1940 NAL Season

Roster:
Andy Cooper, Manager (CL 127-28, JB 139, JH 376, LH 226)
John "Buck" O'Neil .342, first base (CL, JB, JH, LH)
Newt Allen .323, outfield (JH), second base (CL, JB, LH)
Rainey Bibbs .324, second base (CL, JB, JH), third base (LH)
Jesse Douglas, second base (CL, JB, LH)
Byron "Mex" Johnson, shortstop (CL, LH)
Jesse Williams .430, shortstop (CL, JB, JH, LH)
Herbert Cyrus, third base (JB)
Herb "Baldy" Souell, third base (CL, JB, LH)
V. Barnes, outfield (CL, JB), second base (LH)
Willard Brown, outfield (LH)
Booker McDaniels, outfield (CL, JB, LH)
Henry Milton .265, outfield (CL, JB, LH)
Norman "Turkey" Stearnes .287, outfield (CL, JB, JH, LH)
Leandy Young, outfield (CL, LH)

Lionel DeCuir, catcher (CL, JB, LH)
James "Joe" Greene .253, catcher (CL, JB, JH, LH)

Pitchers:
Frank Bradley 6-1 (CL, JB, JH, LH)
Chet Brewer (CL, LH)
Allen "Lefty" Bryant 0-1 (JB, JH, LH)
Clifford "Connie" Johnson (CL, LH)
Floyd Kranson (or Cranson) (CL, JB, JH, LH)
John Markham (CL, LH)
Jack Matchett 5-0 (CL, JB, JH, LH)
C. Moses (CL, LH)
Leroy "Satchel" Paige 2-0 (CL, JH, LH)
Hilton Smith 6-4 (CL, JB, JH, LH)
Elbert Treadway (CL, LH)
George Walker 4-0 (CL, JB, JH, LH)

Record (JH 375):
Kansas City Monarchs 28-7 (.800)
Memphis Red Sox 12-4 (.750)
St. Louis/New Orleans Stars 3-2 (.600)
Chicago American Giants 11-11 (.500)
Birmingham Black Barons 9-11 (.450)
Indianapolis Crawfords 3-5 (.375)
Cleveland Bears 6-16 (.273)

Kansas City won the pennant.

1941 NAL Season

Roster:
Newt Allen, Manager (CL 129, JB 139, JH 384, LH 226)
William "Dizzy" Dismukes, Manager (LH)
John "Buck" O'Neil .269, first base (CL, JB, JH, LH)
Jesse Douglas, second base (CL, LH)
Andrew "Pat" Patterson, second base, third base (JB, LH)
Jesse Williams .222, second base (JH, LH), utility (CL, JB)
Rainey Bibbs .245, third base (CL, JH, LH), second base (JB)
Herb "Baldy" Souell, third base (CL, LH)
Bill Simms .179, outfielder (JH, LH)
Willard Brown .333, outfield (CL, JB, JH, LH)
Sylvester Snead, outfield (CL)
Ted Strong .333, outfield (CL, JB, JH), third base (CL, JB), utility (LH)
Johnny Dawson, catcher (LH)
Frank Duncan, catcher (CL, JB, LH)
James "Joe" Greene .313, catcher (CL, JB, JH. LH)
T. J. "Tom" Young, catcher (CL, JB, LH)
Allen, .245, utility (CL, JB, JH)
Hilton Smith .571, utility (JH)

Pitchers:
Frank Bradley 3-1 (CL, JB, JH, LH)
Chet Brewer 0-1 (CL, JB, JH, LH)
Allen "Lefty" Bryant 1-1 (CL, JH, LH)
Andy "Lefty" Cooper (LH)
Frank Duncan III (CL, LH)
Willie "Ace" Hutchinson (CL, LH)
Clifford "Connie" Johnson 2-2 (CL, JB, JH, LH)
Jack Matchett (CL, LH)
Booker McDaniels 2-2 (CL, JB, JH, LH)
Leroy "Satchel" Paige 7-0 (CL, JB, JH, LH)
Bill Simms (JB, LH)
Eugene Smith (CL, LH)
Hilton Smith 10-1 (CL, JB, JH, LH)
John Ford Smith (CL, LH)
Sylvester Snead (JB)
Samuel "Sad Sam" Thompson (CL, LH)
George Walker (CL, JB, LH)

Record (JH 383):
Kansas City Monarchs 24-6 (.800)
New Orleans/St. Louis Stars 20-12 (.625)
Birmingham Black Barons 14-10 (.583)
Memphis Red Sox 8-8 (.500)
Jacksonville Red Caps 8-10 (.444)
Chicago American Giants 7-13 (.350)

Kansas City won the pennant.

1942 NAL Season

Roster:
William "Dizzy" Dismukes, Manager (CL. 131, JB 139, JH 393, LH 227)
Frank Duncan, Manager (CL, JB, JH, LH)
John "Buck" O'Neil .255, first base (CL, JB, JH, LH)
Newt Allen .318, second base (JB), outfield (JH), utility (CL, LH 226)
William "Barney"/"Bonnie" Serrell .406, second base (CL, JB, JH, LH)
Jesse Williams .325, shortstop (CL, JB, JH, LH)
Herb Souell .286, third base (CL, JH, LH)
Herb Cyrus, third base (JB)
Willard Brown .310, outfield (CL, JB, JH, LH)
Bill Simms, outfield (CL, JB, LH)
Ted Strong .322, outfield (CL, JB, JH, LH)
Johnny Dawson, catcher (CL, JB, LH)
James "Joe" Greene .366, catcher (CL, JB, JH, LH)
Duncan, catcher (LH), utility (CL, JB)
Paul Hardy, catcher (LH), utility (CL, JB)
Henry "Frazier" Robinson, catcher (LH)
Hilton Smith .375, utility (JH)

Pitchers:
Ted Alexander 0-1 (JH)
Frank Bradley (CL, JB, LH)
Clifford "Connie" Johnson 4-0 (CL, JB, JH, LH)
Booker "Cannonball" McDaniels 6-0 (CL, JB, JH, LH)
Greg McInnis (LH)
James "Jim"/"Lefty" LaMarque (CL, JB LH, LH)
Jack Matchett 6-1 (CL, JB, JH, LH)
Leroy "Satchel" Paige 7-5 (CL, JB, JH, LH)
Norris Phillips 1-0 (CL, JB, JH, LH)
Hilton Smith 4-3 (CL, JB, JH, LH)
George Walker (CL, JB, LH)

Record (JH 392):
Kansas City Monarchs 28-10 (.667)
Cincinnati/Cleveland Buckeyes 12-8 (.600)
Birmingham Black Barons 14-10 (.583)
Memphis Red Sox 16-18 (.471)
Jacksonville Red Caps 2-6 (.250)
Chicago American Giants 2-16 (.111)

Kansas City won the pennant and the Negro Leagues World Series championship over the Homestead Grays, five games to none (with one game thrown out).

1943 NAL Season

Roster:
Frank Duncan, Manager (CL 133, JB 139-40, JH 406, LH 227)
John "Buck" O'Neil .222, first base (JB, JH, LH)
William "Barney"/"Bonnie" Serrell .267, second base (CL, JB, JH, LH)
Jesse Williams .287, shortstop (CL, JB, JH, LH)
Herb Cyrus, third base (JB)
Herb Souell .229, third base (CL, JB, JH, LH)
Bill Simms .167, outfield (JH)
Willard Brown .309, outfield (CL, JB, JH, LH)
Bill Hoskins, outfield (CL, JB, LH)
Bill Simms, outfield (CL, JB, LH)
Hilton Smith, outfield (CL)
R. Smith, outfield (CL)
Henry "Hank" Thompson .317, outfield (CL, JB, JH), second base (LH)
Herbert Barnhill, catcher (CL, LH)
Duncan, catcher (CL, JH, LH)
James "Joe" Greene, catcher (CL, JB, LH)
Sammy Haynes, catcher (CL, JB, LH)
Newt Allen, utility (CL, JB, LH 226)
Henry "Frazier" Robinson, utility (CL), catcher (LH)
Eugene Tyler, utility (CL, LH)

Pitchers:
Ted Alexander 0–2 (CL, JB, JH, LH)
Dave Barnhill (JB)
Allen "Lefty" Bryant (CL, JB, LH)
Jack Matchett (CL, JB, JH, LH)
Booker McDaniels 10–1 (CL, JB, JH, LH)
Leroy "Satchel" Paige 9–15 (CL, JB, JH, LH)
"Sonny" Parker (CL)
Norris Philips 1–1 (CL, JH, LH)
Hilton Smith 4–2 (CL, JB, JH, LH)
George Walker (CL, JB, JH, LH)

Record (JH 404):
Birmingham Black Barons 20–14 (.588)
Memphis Red Sox 15–11 (.577)
Cleveland Buckeyes 25–20 (.556)
Kansas City Monarchs 29–29 (.500)
Chicago American Giants 20–23 (.465)
Cincinnati Clowns 15–18 (.455)

Birmingham won the pennant and played in the Negro Leagues World Series, losing to the Homestead Grays, four games to three, with one tie.

1944 NAL Season

Roster:
Frank Duncan, Manager (CL 135, JB 140, JH 415, LH 227)
Lee Moody .251, first base (CL, JB, JH, LH), third base (LH), outfield (JB)
Newt Allen .247, first base (JB, LH 226), second base (CL, LH), outfield (JB, JH)
William "Barney" Serrell .410, second base (CL, JB, JH, LH)
Jesse Williams .259, shortstop (CL, JB, JH, LH)
Herb Souell .244, third base (CL, JB, JH, LH)
Earl Bumpus, outfield (JB, LH), pitcher (CL, LH)
Dave "Chick" Harper .211, outfield (CL, JB, JH, LH)
Bill Rivers, outfield (CL, JB, LH)
Monroe "Mance" Smith, outfield (CL, JB, JH, LH)
Walter Thomas, outfield (JB, LH)
Ollie Waldon, outfield (CL, LH)
Sammy Haynes .177, catcher (JH, LH, CL, JB)
Duncan .132, catcher (JH, LH)
Raymond Taylor, catcher (CL, LH)
Britt Ward, catcher (CL, LH)
Edward "Pep" Young, catcher (CL, LH)
Julio Arnago "Bill" Ortiz, utility (CL)
Hilton Smith .333, utility (JH)
Jim LaMarque .316, utility (JH)
Bobby Vanever, utility (CL, LH)

Pitchers:
Ted Alexander (CL, JB, LH)
William Edwards (CL, LH)
Robert Johnson (CL, LH)
James "Jim"/"Lefty" LaMarque (CL, JB, LH)
Eddie Locke 3–3 (CL, JB, JH, LH)
Jim Matchett 5–3 (CL, JB, JH, LH)
Booker McDaniels 2–5 (CL, JB, JH, LH)
Fred McDaniels (CL, LH)
Leroy "Satchel" Paige 5–6 (CL, JB, JH, LH)
Clarence Rochelle (CL, JB, LH)
Hilton Smith 2–4 (CL, JB, JH, LH)
Thomas (CL, LH)
Enloe Wylie (CL, JB, LH)
Edward "Pep" Young (JB)

Record (JH 413):
Birmingham Black Barons 48–22 (.686)
Indianapolis/Cincinnati Clowns 40–31 (.563)
Cleveland Buckeyes 40–41 (.494)
Memphis Red Sox 44–51 (.463)
Chicago American Giants 32–39 (.451)
Kansas City Monarchs 23–42 (.354)

Birmingham won the pennant and played in the Negro Leagues World Series, losing to the Homestead Grays, four games to one.

1945 NAL Season

Roster:
Frank Duncan, Manager (CL 137–38, JB 140, JH 423, LH 227)
John Paul Berry, first base (CL, JB, LH)
Lee Moody .325, first base (CL, JB, JH, LH), third base (LH)
William "Barney"/"Bonnie" Serrell, first base (CL, JB, LH)
Matthew Carlisle, second base (JB)
Jesse Williams .253, second base (JH, LH), utility (JB)
Jackie Robinson .345, shortstop (CL, JB, JH, LH)
Herb "Baldy" Souell .277, third base (JB, JH, LH), utility (CL)
James Abernathy, outfield (CL) (LH)
Dave "Chick" Harper, outfield (CL, JB, LH)
Emory "Bang" Long, outfield (CL, LH)
Clarence McMufin, outfield (CL, JB, LH)
John Ray .375, outfield (CL, JH, LH)
John Scott, outfield (CL, JB, LH)
Walter Thomas .385, outfield (CL, JB, JH, LH)
Eddie Williams .270, outfield (JB, JH)
Leandy Young, outfield (JB, JH, LH)

Chelsley "Chester" Gray, catcher (CL, JB, LH)
Sammy Haynes, catcher (CL, JB, LH)
Dozier Hood, catcher (CL, LH)
Ted "Double Duty" Radcliffe, catcher (CL, JB, LH)
Othello "Chico" Renfroe .351, catcher (JH), utility (CL, JB, LH)
Sylvestar "Junius" Carlyle, utility (CL, LH)
John Williams .300, utility (JH)

Pitchers:
Lee Davis (CL, LH)
James "Jim"/"Lefty" LaMarque 8-2 (CL, JB, JH, LH)
Eddie Locke (CL, JB, LH)
John Mack (CL, JB, LH)
Jim Matchett 1-2 (CL, JB, JH, LH)
Booker McDaniels 6-4 (CL, JB, JH, LH)
Nate Moreland (CL, JB, LH)
Leroy "Satchel" Paige 5-9 (CL, JB, JH, LH)
Hilton Smith 5-2 (CL, JB, JH, LH)
Theolic "Fireball" Smith (CL, JB, LH)
George Walker (CL, JB, LH)
Lafayette "Fay" Washington (JB, LH)
Thomas (LH)
Enloe Wylie 0-2 (CL, JB, JH, LH)

Record (JH 422):
Cleveland Buckeyes 53-16 (.768)
Birmingham Black Barons 39-30 (.565)
Chicago American Giants 39-35 (.527)
Kansas City Monarchs 32-30 (.516)
Cincinnati Clowns 30-39 (.435)
Memphis Red Sox 17-61 (.218)

Cleveland won the pennant and played in the Negro Leagues World Series, beating the Homestead Grays, four games to none.

1946 NAL Season

Roster:
Frank Duncan, Manager (CL 141, JB 140-41, JH 433, LH 227)
John "Buck" O'Neil .350, first base (CL, JB, JH, LH)
Henry "Hank" Thompson .226, second base (CL, JB, JH, LH)
Jim Hamilton .204, shortstop (CL, JH, LH)
Jesse Williams, shortstop (CL, JB, JH, LH
Herb Souell .316, third base (CL, JB, JH, LH)
Willard Brown .286, outfield (CL, JB, JH, LH)
Clarence McMullin, outfield (CL, JB, LH)
Ted Strong .278, outfield (CL, JB, JH, LH)
John Scott .306, outfield (CL, JB, JH, LH)
James "Joe" Greene .300, catcher (CL, JB, JH, LH)

Fred Smith, catcher (JB, LH)
Earl Taborn, catcher (CL JB, LH)
Bob Turner, catcher (CL, JB, LH)
Larry Hubbard, utility (CL, JB, LH)
Lee Moody, utility (CL, JB, LH)
Othello "Chico" Renfroe, utility (CL, JB, LH)
Hilton Smith .431, utility (JH)

Pitchers:
Ted Alexander 4-1 (CL, JB, JH, LH)
Allen "Lefty" Bryant (CL, JB, LH)
Frank Duncan III (CL, LH)
Clifford "Connie" Johnson 9-3 (CL, JB, JH, LH)
James "Jim"/"Lefty" LaMarque 15-5 (CL, JB, JH, LH)
Larry Napoleon (CL, JB, LH)
Leroy "Satchel" Paige 5-1 (CL, JB, JH, LH)
John Ford Smith 3-1 (CL, JH, LH)
Hilton Smith 5-2 (CL, JB, JH, LH)
Amos Watson (CL, JB, LH)
Enloe Wylie (CL, JB, LH)

Record (JH 432):
Kansas City Monarchs 43-14 (.755)
Birmingham Black Barons 35-25 (.583)
Cleveland Buckeyes 26-27 (.491)
Indianapolis Clowns 27-35 (.435)
Memphis Red Sox 24-36 (.400)
Chicago American Giants 27-45 (.375)

Kansas City won the pennant and played in the Negro Leagues World Series, losing to the Newark Eagles, four games to three.

1947 NAL Season

Roster:
Frank Duncan, Manager (CL, 143, JB 141, JH 447, LH 227)
John "Buck" O'Neil .358, first base (CL, JB, JH, LH)
Curt Roberts, second base (CL, JH, LH)
Lee Moody, shortstop (JB)
Curtis Roberts, shortstop (JB)
Johnny Sanderson, shortstop (CL, LH)
Herb Souell, third base (CL, JB, JH, LH)
Willard Brown .336, outfield (CL, JB, JH, LH)
Tom Cooper, outfield (JB)
John Scott, outfield (CL, JB, JH, LH)
Ted Strong, outfield (CL, JB, JH, LH)
Bill Duffy, catcher (CL, JB, LH)
James "Joe" Greene .324, catcher (CL, JB, JH, LH)
Earl Taborn, catcher (CL, JB, LH)
Tom Cooper, utility (CL, LH)
Thomas "Monk" Favor, utility (CL, CL)

Lee Moody, utility (CL, LH)
Othello "Chico" Renfroe, utility (CL, JB, JH, LH)
Henry "Hank" Thompson .344, utility (CL, JB, JH, LH)

Pitchers:
Ted Alexander 1–0 (CL, JB, JH, LH)
Mike "Red" Berry (CL, JB, LH)
Allen "Lefty" Bryant (CL, LH)
Gene Collins 0–1 (CL, JB, JH, LH)
Clifford "Connie" Johnson 1–1 (CL, JB, JH, LH)
James "Jim"/"Lefty" LaMarque 12–2 (CL, JB, JH, LH)
Booker McDaniels (CL, LH)
Larry Napoleon 0–1 (CL, JB, JH, LH)
Leroy "Satchel" Paige 1–1 (CL, JB, JH, LH)
Gene Richardson (CL, JB, LH)
John Scroggins (CL, JB, LH)
John Ford Smith 1–0 (CL, JB, JH, LH)
Hilton Smith 7–0 (CL, JB, JH, LH)
Enloe Wylie 1–0 (CL, JB, JH, LH)

No NAL standings were published in 1947, though the Cleveland Buckeyes won the pennant and played in the Negro Leagues World Series, losing to the New York Cubans, four games to one, with one tie.

1948 NAL Season

Roster:
John "Buck" O'Neil .253, Manager/first base (CL 145, JB 141, JH 456, LH 228)
Tom Cooper, first base (JB)
Curt Roberts .265, second base (CL, JB, JH, LH)
Gene Baker .293, shortstop (CL, JB, JH, LH)
Herb "Baldy" Souell .302, third base (CL, JB, JH, LH)
Hank Thompson .348, outfield (JB, JH), utility (CL, LH)
Willard Brown .374, outfield (CL, JB, JH, LH)
John Scott, outfield (CL, JB, JH, LH)
Bill Wright, outfield (CL, LH)
Elston Howard .283, catcher (CL, JB, JH, LH), outfield (CL)
Earl Taborn .301, catcher (JB, JH, LH)
Tom Cooper, utility (CL, LH)
Charley Hall, utility (CL, LH)

Pitchers:
Gene Collins 9–3 (CL, JB, JH, LH)
Herb Howard (CL, LH)
Clifford "Connie" Johnson 2–2 (JB, JH, LH)
Leonard Johnson (CL, JB, LH)
James "Jim"/"Lefty" LaMarque 15–5 (CL, JB, JH, LH)
Gene Richardson (CL, JB, LH)
Hilton Smith (CL, JB, LH)
John Ford Smith 10–5 (CL, JB, JH, LH)
Mickey Stubblefield (LH)

Record (JH 455):
Birmingham Black Barons 55–21 (.724)
Kansas City Monarchs 43–25 (.632)
Cleveland Buckeyes 41–42 (.494)
Memphis Red Sox 33–44 (.429)
Indianapolis Clowns 27–46 (.370)
Chicago American Giants 27–48 (.360)

Birmingham won the first half, Kansas City the second half. Birmingham beat Kansas City three games to one in a playoff and played in the Negro Leagues World Series, losing to the Homestead Grays, four games to one.

Chapter Notes

Preface and Acknowledgments

1. Buck O'Neil, with Steve Wolf and David Conrads, *I Was Right on Time* (New York: Simon & Schuster, 1996).
2. Janet Bruce, *The Kansas City Monarchs: Champions of Black Baseball* (Lawrence: University of Kansas, 1985). Note: The author later married and took the name Janet Bruce Vaughn.

Prologue

1. Cited by Larry Lester and Sammy Miller, *Black Baseball in Kansas City* (Charleston, SC: Arcadia, 2000), 128; Larry Lester, "J. L. Wilkinson: Only the Stars Come Out at Night," *Satchel Paige and Company: Essays on the Kansas City Monarchs, Their Greatest Star and the Negro Leagues*, ed. Leslie A. Heaphy (Jefferson, NC: McFarland, 2007), 141.
2. http://baseballhall.org/hof/wilkinson-jl (accessed 1/22/15).
3. Thomas Fredrick, "KC Connection Began Baseball's Globalization," *The Kansas City Star* (October 16, 2004), C5. J. L. Wilkinson File, National Baseball Hall of Fame, Cooperstown, NY.
4. Buck O'Neil, with Steve Wolf and David Conrads, *I Was Right on Time* (New York: Simon & Schuster, 1996), 83, 67.
5. Interview with Connie Johnson conducted on February 25, 1991 (Lester, "J.L. Wilkinson" 138).
6. Leslie A. Heaphy, *The Negro Leagues, 1869–1960* (Jefferson, NC: McFarland, 2003), 75.
7. Jerry Crasnick, "Sharing Memories of the Negro Leagues," *Denver Post* (July 22, 1996), 6D (cited by Heaphy, *Negro Leagues* 81).
8. Interview with Dick Wilkinson conducted by Larry Lester on December 30, 1990 (Lester, "J.L. Wilkinson" 125). See also Jeff Passan, "Monarchs Owner Elected," *The Kansas City Star* (February 28, 2006), C-7; and personal interviews conducted by the author with Sharon Brescian (October 11, 2014), Ed Catron (June 25, July 15, and October 11, 2014), Diane Pond (August 4 and October 11, 2014).
9. Lester, "J.L. Wilkinson" 139–41.
10. *Kansas City Call*, May 28, 1948.
11. Bill James, *The New Bill James Historical Baseball Abstract* (New York: Free Press, 2001), 69; see also Lawrence Hogan, *Shades of Glory: The Negro Leagues and the Story of African-American Baseball* (Washington, D.C.: National Geographic, 2006), 307.
12. *Philadelphia Tribune*, October 15, 1936 (cited by Neil Lanctot, *Negro League Baseball: The Rise and Ruin of a Black Institution* [Philadelphia: University of Pennsylvania Press, 2004], 31).
13. *Kansas City Call*, October 27, 1922.
14. Bruce Chadwick, *When the Game Was Black and White: The Illustrated History of the Negro Leagues* (New York: Abbeville Press, 1992), 113.

Chapter One

1. Donn Rogosin, et. al., *Invisible Men: Life in Baseball's Negro Leagues* (New York: Athenuem, 1983).
2. John Naughton, "'Invisible Man Among Invisible Men," *Des Moines Sunday Register* (July 10, 2005), 1C.
3. *Kansas City Call*, January 21, 1922.
4. James A. Riley, *The Biographical Encyclopedia of the Negro Baseball Leagues* (New York: Carroll and Graf, 1994), 842.
5. Jim Overmyer, "J. L. Wilkinson: Negro Leagues Ballot Candidate," *Baseball Hall of Fame News*, February 24, 2006. J. L. Wilkinson File, National Baseball Hall of Fame, Cooperstown, NY See also Naughton, "Invisible Man" 1C.
6. Cited by Ralph J. Christian, "Wilkie: James Leslie Wilkinson and the Iowa Years," *Iowa Heritage Illustrated* (Spring 2006), 38.
7. Janet Bruce, *The Kansas City Monarchs: Champions of Black Baseball* (Lawrence: University of Kansas, 1985), 14; Larry Tye, *Satchel: The Life and Times of an American Legend* (New York: Random House, 2009), 138.
8. Lawrence Hogan, *Shades of Glory: The Negro Leagues and the Story of African-American Baseball* (Washington, D.C.: National Geographic, 2006), 136.
9. Overmyer, "J.L. Wilkinson" 1.
10. Ty, *Satchel* 139.
11. Christian, "Wilkie" 38.
12. Benjamin F. Reed, *History of Kossuth County, Iowa, Vol. 1* (http://books.google.com/books?id=wKAy AQAAMAAJ&pg=PA439&lpg=PA439&dq; accessed 5/18/14). See also Riley 1994: 843.
13. William H. Young and Nathan B. Young, Jr.,

"The Story of the Kansas City Monarchs," *Your Kansas City and Mine* (Kansas City: Midwest Afro-American Genealogy Interest Coalition, 1950), 69. Despite this author's attempts to track down additional information on Wilkinson's parents, their values and associations, nothing of substance was found. Even the owner's grandchildren have little information to share on this topic as Wilkinson only infrequently spoke about himself, and his personal files were discarded after his death.

14. Christian, "Wilkie" 38–41. On Wilkinson's early life, see also Bruce, *Kansas City Monarchs* 14; Naughton, "Invisible Man" 2C; Henry Metcalfe, *A Game for All Races: An Illustrated History of the Negro Leagues* (New York: Metro Books, 2000), 41; Mark Ribowsky, *A Complete History of the Negro Leagues* (New York: Birch Lane Press, 1995), 85.

15. Charles Faber, "J L. Wilkinson," SABR Baseball Biography Project. http://sabr.org/ bioproj/person/ db4ae51d (accessed 5/18/14).

16. Doug Cook, "Son of Legendary Executive Heads Off to Hall of Fame," *The Daily Courier* (July 30, 2006). J. L. Wilkinson File, National Baseball Hall of Fame, Cooperstown, NY.

17. Buck O'Neil, with Steve Wolf and David Conrads, *I Was Right on Time* (New York: Simon & Schuster, 1996), 77.

18. Hogan, *Shades of Glory* 136.

19. Maury White, "A Forgotten Chapter of Baseball History: Remarkable Iowan Pioneered Black Teams, Women Players," *Des Moines Sunday Register* (August 21, 1994), 12D. J. L. Wilkinson File, National Baseball Hall of Fame, Cooperstown, NY.

20. Tye, *Satchel* 139.

21. http://www.exploratorium.edu/baseball/girlsofsummer.html (accessed 9/20/14).

22. Naughton, "Invisible Man" 2C.

23. See http://www.exploratorium.edu/baseball/murphy.html (accessed 9/20/14).

24. 1910 census (accessed via ancestry.com on 9/21/14).

25. Interview with Gladys Wilkinson Catron conducted by Janet Bruce (11/17/80). Kansas City Monarchs Oral History Collection (K0047), Tape No. A0022-23. State Historical Society of Missouri Research Center—Kansas City.

26. White, "A Forgotten Chapter" 12D.

Chapter Two

1. The following profile is based on Ralph J. Christian, "Wilkie: James Leslie Wilkinson and the Iowa Years," *Iowa Heritage Illustrated* (Spring 2006), 41–42.

2. Larry Lester, "J. L. Wilkinson: Only the Stars Come Out at Night," *Satchel Paige and Company: Essays on the Kansas City Monarchs, Their Greatest Star and the Negro Leagues*, ed. Leslie A. Heaphy (Jefferson, NC: McFarland, 2007), 113.

3. Buck O'Neil, with Steve Wolf and David Conrads, *I Was Right on Time* (New York: Simon & Schuster, 1996), 78.

4. Bill Clark, "It's Time John Donaldson Got His Due," *The Columbia [Missouri] Daily Tribune*, November 13, 2009.

5. Maury White, "A Forgotten Chapter of Baseball History: Remarkable Iowan Pioneered Black Teams, Women Players," *Des Moines Sunday Register* (August 21, 1994), 12D. J. L. Wilkinson File, National Baseball Hall of Fame, Cooperstown, NY.

6. Peter Gorton, "John Donaldson: A Great Mound Artist," 4. This chapter in the book *Swinging for the Fences*, ed. Stephen R. Hoffbeck may be downloaded at http://johndonaldson.bravehost.com/h.html.

7. Interview with Gladys Wilkinson Catron conducted by Janet Bruce (11/17/80). Kansas City Monarchs Oral History Collection (K0047), Tape No. A0022-23. State Historical Society of Missouri Research Center—Kansas City.

8. Interview with Richard (Dick) Wilkinson conducted by Janet Bruce (10/1/79). Kansas City Monarchs Oral History Collection (K0047), Tape No. A0016-17. State Historical Society of Missouri Research Center—Kansas City.

9. *Chicago Defender,* May 22, 1926.

10. Phil S. Dixon, *Wilber "Bullet" Rogan and the Kansas City Monarchs* (Jefferson, NC: McFarland, 2010), 26–27, 29.

11. "All Nations Tackle the American Giants," *Chicago Defender,* September 23, 1916.

12. Dixon, *Wilber* 29.

13. *Kansas City Call*, September 18, 1925.

14. Gorton maintains an exhaustive website (johndonaldson.bravehost. com/index.html), which is the definitive source on Donaldson.

15. *Los Angeles Times,* February 16, 1917; Leslie A. Heaphy, *Satchel Paige and Company: Essays on the Kansas City Monarchs, Their Greatest Star and the Negro Leagues* (Jefferson, NC: McFarland, 2007), 237–38.

16. Mark Ribowsky, *A Complete History of the Negro Leagues* (New York: Birch Lane Press, 1995), 187.

17. http://baseballhall.org/hof/mendez-jose (accessed 5/14/14).

18. Heaphy, *Satchel* 246. See also John B. Holway, *Black Ball Stars, Negro League Pioneers* (Westport, CT: Meckler, 1988), 50–59; Henry Metcalfe, *A Game for All Races: An Illustrated History of the Negro Leagues* (New York: Metro Books, 2000), 41.

19. Lester, "J.L. Wilkinson" 113.

20. Thomas Fredrick, "KC Connection Began Baseball's Globalization," *The Kansas City Star* (October 16, 2004), C5-6. J. L. Wilkinson File, National Baseball Hall of Fame, Cooperstown, NY.

21. John B. Holway, *Voices from the Great Black Baseball Leagues* (New York: Dover, 2010 [originally published 1975]), 25–26.

22. Interview with Bill "Plunk" Drake conducted by Dr. Charles Korr and Dr. Steven Hause (12/8/71), Negro Baseball League Project, http://shs.umsystem. edu/stlouis/manuscripts/ transcripts/s0829/t0067.pdf (accessed 5/20/14).

23. For a brief overview of Torriente's life and career, see John B. Holway, *Black Ball Stars, Negro League Pioneers* (Westport, CT: Meckler, 1988), 125–34.

24. William H. Young and Nathan B. Young, Jr., "The Story of the Kansas City Monarchs," *Your Kansas*

City and Mine (Kansas City: Midwest Afro-American Genealogy Interest Coalition, 1950), 69.
25. Heaphy, *Satchel* 225; Bruce, *Kansas City Monarchs* 14; Lester, "J.L. Wilkinson" 113.
26. Larry Lester and Sammy Miller, *Black Baseball in Kansas City* (Charleston, SC: Arcadia, 2000), 14; see also Lester, "J.L. Wilkinson" 113–14.
27. White, "A Forgotten Chapter" 12D; interview with Richard (Dick) Wilkinson conducted by Janet Bruce on October 1, 1979.
28. Ribowsky, *A Complete History* 86.
29. *Austin [Minnesota] Daily Herald,* August 24, 1914; cited by Dixon, *Wilbur* 96.
30. Larry Tye, *Satchel: The Life and Times of an American Legend* (New York: Random House, 2009), 138–39.
31. Bruce, *Kansas City Monarchs* 15.
32. Dixon, *Wilbur* 28.
33. Lester, "J.L. Wilkinson" 113.
34. Cited by Ribowsky, *A Complete History* 86; John B. Holway, *Black Ball Stars, Negro League Pioneers* (Westport, CT: Meckler, 1988), 329.
35. Young and Young, "The Story of the Kansas City Monarchs" 69–70.
36. Dixon, *Wilbur* 28.
37. 1918 Wilkinson draft registration (accessed via ancestry.com, 9/20/14).
38. Lawrence Hogan, *Shades of Glory: The Negro Leagues and the Story of African-American Baseball* (Washington, D.C.: National Geographic, 2006), 16.
39. *Kansas City Call,* March 25 and July 1, 1922; March 21, 1924.
40. *Kansas City Call,* July 6, 1923.
41. Bruce, *Kansas City Monarchs* 17.
42. John B. Holway, *Black Diamonds: Life in the Negro Leagues from the Men Who Lived It* (Westport, CT: Meckler Books, 1989), 24.
43. *Bismarck Tribune,* June 8, 1928.
44. Timothy M. Gay, *Satchel, Dizzy and Rapid Robert: The Wild Saga of Interracial Baseball Before Jackie Robinson* (New York: Simon & Schuster, 2010), 25–26. See also Heaphy, *Satchel* 113; John B. Holway, *The Complete Book of Baseball's Negro Leagues: The Other Half of Baseball History* (Fern Park, NJ: Hastings House, 2001), 104.

Chapter Three

1. Sol White, *Sol White's History of Colored Baseball: With Other Documents on the Early Black Gam* (Lincoln: University of Nebraska, 1995. Originally published in 1907. Compiled and introduced by Jerry Malloy), xvi–xvii. See also James A. Riley, *Of Monarchs and Black Barons: Essays on Baseball's Negro Leagues* (Jefferson, NC: McFarland, 2012), 19–24; Roger Kahn, *Rickey and Robinson: The True, Untold Story of the Integration of Baseball* (New York: Rodale, 2014), 17–18.
2. John B. Holway, *Black Ball Stars, Negro League Pioneers* (Westport, CT: Meckler, 1988), 1.
3. White, *Sol White's History* 76.
4. Cited by White, *Sol White's History* 137.
5. Leslie A. Heaphy, *The Negro Leagues, 1869–1960* (Jefferson, NC: McFarland, 2003), 15.

6. September 1919, 2, 10; cited by Heaphy, *The Negro Leagues* 36.
7. Janet Bruce, *The Kansas City Monarchs: Champions of Black Baseball* (Lawrence: University of Kansas, 1985), 17; Phil S. Dixon, *Wilber "Bullet" Rogan and the Kansas City Monarchs* (Jefferson, NC: McFarland, 2010), 8–9; Larry Lester and Sammy Miller, *Black Baseball in Kansas City* (Charleston, SC: Arcadia, 2000), 6; Larry Lester, "J. L. Wilkinson: Only the Stars Come Out at Night," *Satchel Paige and Company: Essays on the Kansas City Monarchs, Their Greatest Star and the Negro Leagues,* ed. Leslie A. Heaphy (Jefferson, NC: McFarland, 2007), 118–19.
8. Geoffrey C. Ward and Ken Burns, *Baseball: An Illustrated History* (New York: Alfred A. Knopf, 2010 [first published 1994]), 157.
9. Heaphy, *Negro Leagues* 33.
10. Ward and Burns, *Baseball: An Illustrated History* 156–57.
11. Robert C. Cottrell, *The Best Pitcher of Baseball: The Life of Rube Foster, Negro League Giant* (New York: New York University Press, 2001), 137–38, 142.
12. Ward and Burns, *Baseball: An Illustrated History* 157.
13. William H. Young and Nathan B. Young, Jr., "The Story of the Kansas City Monarchs," *Your Kansas City and Mine* (Kansas City: Midwest Afro-American Genealogy Interest Coalition, 1950), 12–13, 130–31.
14. Sources on the formation of the Negro National League (NNL): *Kansas City Call,* February 20 and 27, 1920; Cottrell, *The Life of Rube Foster* 149–54; Heaphy, *Negro Leagues* 41–42; James A. Riley, *Of Monarchs and Black Barons: Essays on Baseball's Negro Leagues* (Jefferson, NC: McFarland, 2012), 57–61, 114, 118–20, 122–23, 177; Larry Lester, *Rube Foster in His Time* (Jefferson, NC: McFarland, 2012), 114, 118–20, 122–23, 177; Larry Lester, *Baseball's First Colored World Series: The 1924 Meeting of the Hilldale Giants and Kansas City Monarchs* (Jefferson, NC: McFarland, 2006, 2014), 11, 18–21; Robert Peterson, *Only the Ball Was White* (New York: Oxford University Press, 1970), 82–84; Henry Metcalfe, *A Game for All Races: An Illustrated History of the Negro Leagues* (New York: Metro Books, 2000), 50, 52–53; Bruce, *Kansas City Monarchs* 13–14; Michael Harkness-Roberto and Leslie A. Heaphy, "The Monarchs: A Brief History of the Franchise," *Satchel Paige and Company: Essays on the Kansas City Monarchs, Their Greatest Star and the Negro Leagues,* ed. Leslie Heaphy (Jefferson, NC: McFarland, 2007), 100–101.
15. *Kansas City Call,* June 17, 1922.
16. Harkness-Roberto and Heaphy, "A Brief History" 100; Bruce, *Kansas City Monarchs* 18.
17. Buck O'Neil, with Steve Wolf and David Conrads, *I Was Right on Time* (New York: Simon & Schuster, 1996), 76.
18. Bruce, *Kansas City Monarchs* 18.
19. Interview with Richard (Dick) Wilkinson conducted by Larry Tye, published in *Satchel: The Life and Times of an American Legend* (New York: Random House, 2009), 141.
20. Interview with Richard (Dick) Wilkinson conducted by Larry Lester on December 30, 1990 (Lester, "J.L. Wilkinson" 125).

21. Interview with Richard (Dick) Wilkinson conducted by Janet Bruce (10/1/79). Kansas City Monarchs Oral History Collection (K0047), Tape No. A0016–17. State Historical Society of Missouri Research Center—Kansas City.
22. Dixon, *Wilbur* 136.
23. Bruce, *Kansas City Monarchs* 23.
24. The T. Y. Baird Collection at the Kenneth Spencer Research Library at the University of Kansas in Lawrence includes a Rock Island Employee Pass dated August 7, 1917. RH MS 414, Box 5, Folder 9.
25. Martha Ackmann, *Curveball: The Remarkable Story of Toni Stone, the First Woman to Play Professional Baseball in the Negro League* (Chicago: Lawrence Hill Books, 2010), 170.
26. Young and Young, "The Story of the Kansas City Monarchs" 70.
27. Interview with Harriett Baird Wickstrom, conducted by Janet Bruce (10/2/79). Kansas City Monarchs Oral History Collection (K0047), Tape No. A0018. State Historical Society of Missouri Research Center—Kansas City. She also told a reporter in 1983 that it was her father who named the Monarchs (*Kansas City Kansan*, March 19, 1983).
28. Dixon, *Wilbur* 28–29.
29. Interview with Richard (Dick) Wilkinson conducted by Janet Bruce (10/1/1979).
30. Tim Rives, "Tom Baird: A Challenge to the Modern Memory of the Kansas City Monarchs," *Satchel Paige and Company: Essays on the Kansas City Monarchs, Their Greatest Star and the Negro Leagues*, ed. Leslie Heaphy (Jefferson, NC: McFarland, 2007), 144–55. In the same article Rives makes the controversial claim, based largely on circumstantial evidence, that Baird was associated with the Ku Klux Klan in the Kansas City area. Baird's family strongly rejects that assertion.
31. Interview with Alberta (Mrs. Quincy) Jordan Penn (Gilmore), Janet Bruce (9/18/79). Kansas City Monarchs Oral History Collection (K0047), Tape No. A0013 (but listed on index as 14). State Historical Society of Missouri Research Center—Kansas City.
32. Interview with Alberta (Mrs. Quincy) Jordan Penn conducted by Janet Bruce (9/18/79). See also Bruce, *Kansas City Monarchs* 22, 58; Heaphy, *Negro Leagues* 95; Dixon, *Wilbur* 56.
33. Interview with Roy Johnson conducted by Janet Bruce (1/12/81). Kansas City Monarchs Oral History Collection (K0047), Tape No. A0024. State Historical Society of Missouri Research Center—Kansas City.
34. Ribowsky, *A Complete History* 104; Bruce, *Kansas City Monarchs* 20–21.
35. Bruce, *Kansas City Monarchs* 27.
36. *Kansas City Call*, May 28, 1948.
37. *Kansas City Call*, July 27, 1928.
38. *Chicago Defender*, July 10, 1920 (cited by Dixon, *Wilbur* 65).
39. Dixon, *Wilbur* 33.
40. Holway, *Black Ball Stars* 167. For fuller of overviews of Rogan's life and career see Holway, *Black Ball Stars* 167–87; Dixon, *Wilbur*.
41. Undated article. T. Y. Baird Collection, Kansas Collection, RH MS 414, Box 3, Folder 23, Kenneth Spencer Research Library, University of Kansas Libraries.
42. Dixon, *Wilbur* 31–34. Note: rosters and records are difficult to compile. Not all sources agree. For reconstructions of records and rosters for the Wilkinson era [1920–48], see the Appendix.
43. Metcalfe, *A Game for All Races* 53.
44. Lester, *Rube Foster in His Time* 121–22; Cottrell, *The Life of Rube Foster* 156–57.
45. Lester, *Rube Foster in His Time* 124–26.
46. Metcalfe, *A Game for All Races* 55–57.
47. Dixon, *Wilbur* 85, 36–40.
48. Dixon, *Wilbur* 39.
49. Cottrell, *The Life of Rube Foster* 160–61; Lester, *Rube Foster in His Time* 128–38.
50. Metcalfe, *A Game for All Races* 55–57.
51. *Kansas City Call*, January 21, 1922.
52. *Kansas City Call*, February 11, 1922.
53. John B. Holway, *Voices from the Great Black Baseball Leagues* (New York: Dover, 2010 [originally published 1975]), 22–23, 31–32.
54. Bruce, *Kansas City Monarchs* 24–25.
55. Holway, *Black Ball Stars* 342.
56. Interview with Newt Allen, conducted by John Holway (1970) University of Missouri–St. Louis, Archive & Manuscript Division (T208). See also Holway, *Voices* 90–103.
57. Interview with Newt Allen conducted by Janet Bruce (11/7/78). Kansas City Monarchs Oral History Collection (K0047), Tape No. A0005. State Historical Society of Missouri Research Center—Kansas City. See also Holway, *Voices* 90–103.
58. Dixon, *Wilbur* 58.
59. *Kansas City Call*, April 29, 1922.
60. *Kansas City Call*, May 13, 1922.
61. *Kansas City Call*, April 29 and May 13, 1922.
62. Interview with Alberta (Mrs. Quincy) Jordan Penn conducted by Janet Bruce (9/18/79).
63. *Kansas City Call*, June 3, 1922.
64. *Kansas City Call*, July 1, 1922.
65. *Kansas City Call*, September 9, 1922.
66. Cited by Lester, *Rube Foster in His Time* 139.
67. Sources for the Monarchs-Blues 1922 Series: Interview with Bill "Plunk" Drake conducted by Dr. Charles Korr and Dr. Steven Hause (12/8/71), Negro Baseball League Project, http://shs.umsystem.edu/stlouis/manuscripts/ transcripts/s0829/t0067.pdf (accessed 5/20/14); Dixon, *Wilbur* 44–48; Lester and Miller, *Black Baseball* 6; Lester, "J.L. Wilkinson" 118–19; Holway, *Black Ball Stars* 331.
68. *Kansas City Call*, October 20, 1922.
69. Holway, *Black Ball Stars* 331, *Voices* 32–33.
70. Cited by Lester and Miller, *Black Baseball* 6.
71. *Kansas City Call*, October 22, 1922.
72. *Kansas City Call*, November 3, 1922.
73. John B. Holway, *The Complete Book of Baseball's Negro Leagues: The Other Half of Baseball History* (Fern Park, NJ: Hastings House, 2001), 173.
74. Lloyd Johnson, Steve Garlick, Jeff Magaliff, eds. *Unions to Royals: The Story of Professional Baseball in Kansas* City (Kansas City Society for American Baseball Research, 1996), 3; Lester and Miller, *Black Base-*

ball 6; Holway, *Complete Book of Baseball's Negro Leagues* 11, 173).

75. Metcalfe, *A Game for All Races* 57.
76. O'Neil, *Right on Time* 78.
77. *Kansas City Call,* November 3, 1922.
78. Dixon, *Wilbur* 86–87, Bruce, *Kansas City Monarchs* 52.
79. Johnson, et al., *Unions to Royals* 2; Lester, "J.L. Wilkinson" 119.
80. The letter was reprinted in the *Kansas City Call* on January 19, 1923.
81. The letter was reprinted in the *Kansas City Call,* December 22, 1922. On the formation of the ECL, see Larry Lester. *Baseball's First Colored World Series: The 1924 Meeting of the Hilldale Giants and Kansas City Monarchs* (Jefferson, NC: McFarland, 2006, 2014), 25–29; Peterson, *Only the Ball Was White* 87; Heaphy, *Negro Leagues* 56–68, 92; Lester, *Rube Foster in His Time* 144, 150; Riley, *Monarchs and Black Barons* 61–63; Metcalfe, *A Game for All Races* 59; Bruce, *Kansas City Monarchs* 31.
82. *Kansas City Call,* February 9, 1923.
83. Lester, *Rube Foster in His Time* 142.
84. *Kansas City Call,* March 30, 1923.
85. *Kansas City Call,* April 20, 1923.
86. Interview with Newt Allen conducted by Janet Bruce (11/7/78).
87. Dixon, *Wilbur* 85.
88. Holway, *Voices* 84, *Black Ball Stars* 331.
89. *Kansas City Call,* December 14, 1923.
90. *Kansas City Call,* October 5, 1923.
91. *Kansas City Call,* October 19, 1923.
92. Lester, *First Colored World Series* 19; Cottrell, *The Life of Rube Foster* 166.
93. Heaphy, *Negro Leagues* 48; Lester, *First Colored World Series* 21; Peterson, *Only the Ball Was White* 89; Lester, *Rube Foster in His Time* 147.
94. *Kansas City Call,* July 20, 1923.

Chapter Four

1. Larry Lester, *Baseball's First Colored World Series: The 1924 Meeting of the Hilldale Giants and Kansas City Monarchs* (Jefferson, NC: McFarland, 2006, 2014), 188.
2. Phil S. Dixon, *Wilber "Bullet" Rogan and the Kansas City Monarchs* (Jefferson, NC: McFarland, 2010), 49, 53, 71.
3. *Kansas City Call,* January 25, 1924.
4. *Kansas City Call,* May 9, 1924.
5. *Kansas City Call,* July 11, 1924.
6. *Kansas City Call,* January 16, 1925.
7. Larry Lester, *Rube Foster in His Time* (Jefferson, NC: McFarland, 2012), 153–54; Lester, *First Colored World Series* 29–33; Robert C. Cottrell, *The Best Pitcher of Baseball: The Life of Rube Foster, Negro League Giant* (New York: New York University Press, 2001), 167.
8. Cited by Lester, *First Colored World Series* 29–31.
9. Cited by Lester, *Rube Foster in His Time* 154–55.
10. *Kansas City Call,* September 19, 1924.
11. Sources for the 1924 Negro Leagues World Series: *Kansas City Call,* October 17, 24, 31, 1924; Lester, *First Colored World Series* 44–45, 104–89; James A. Riley, *Of Monarchs and Black Barons: Essays on Baseball's Negro Leagues* (Jefferson, NC: McFarland, 2012), 76–80; Lester, *Rube Foster in His Time* 158; John B. Holway, *Voices from the Great Black Baseball Leagues* (New York: Dover, 2010 [originally published 1975]), 7, 35; Leslie A. Heaphy, *The Negro Leagues, 1869–1960* (Jefferson, NC: McFarland, 2003), 65; Cottrell, *The Best Pitcher* 167–68; Buck O'Neil, with Steve Wolf and David Conrads, *I Was Right on Time* (New York: Simon & Schuster, 1996), 81–82; Henry Metcalfe, *A Game for All Races: An Illustrated History of the Negro Leagues* (New York: Metro Books, 2000), 64–69; Mark Ribowsky, *A Complete History of the Negro Leagues* (New York: Birch Lane Press, 1995), 125–27; Janet Bruce, *The Kansas City Monarchs: Champions of Black Baseball* (Lawrence: University of Kansas, 1985), 55–57; Robert Peterson, *Only the Ball Was White* (New York: Oxford University Press, 1970), 99; Dixon, *Wilbur* 54–55; John B. Holway, *The Complete Book of Baseball's Negro Leagues: The Other Half of Baseball History* (Fern Park, NJ: Hastings House, 2001), 191–95; Thomas Fredrick, "KC Connection Began Baseball's Globalization," *The Kansas City Star* (October 16, 2004), C5; Sam Mellinger, "J. L. Wilkinson: He Was a Man Apart," *Kansas City Star,* July 30, 2006, C1.
12. Lester, *First Colored World Series* 44–45; Kyle McNary, *Black Baseball: A History of African-Americans and the National Game* (London: PRC Publishing, 2003), 107–09. The *Kansas City Call* (October 3, 1924) ran a comparison of the two teams by Ollie Mack of the Associated Negro Press.
13. O'Neil, *Right on Time* 81.
14. Metcalfe, *A Game for All Races* 65.
15. William A. Young, *John Tortes "Chief" Meyers: A Baseball Biography* (Jefferson, NC: McFarland, 2012), 128–29.
16. Lester, *First Colored World Series* 181.
17. Lester, *First Colored World Series* 189.
18. Lester, *Rube Foster in His Time* 120–21; Lester, *First Colored World Series* 22.
19. Cited in Lester, *Rube Foster in His Time* 159–60.
20. Lester, *Rube Foster in His Time* 166–67.
21. *Kansas City Call,* February 6, 1925; Lester, *Rube Foster in His Time* 161–65.
22. *Kansas City Call,* May 15, 1925.
23. John B. Holway, *Black Ball Stars, Negro League Pioneers* (Westport, CT: Meckler, 1988), 332.
24. *Kansas City Call,* September 25, 1925, October 2, 1925; John B. Holway, *The Complete Book of Baseball's Negro Leagues: The Other Half of Baseball History* (Fern Park, NJ: Hastings House, 2001), 199–201; Metcalfe, *A Game for All Races* 71.
25. Sources for the 1925 Negro Leagues World Series: *Kansas City Call,* October 2, 9, and 10 [special edition], 16, 1925; McNary, *Black Baseball* 110; Riley, *Monarchs and Black Barons* 64; Bruce, *Kansas City Monarchs* 57; Peterson, *Only the Ball Was White* 100; Holway, *Complete Book of Baseball's Negro Leagues* 204; Metcalfe, *A Game for All Races* 73–77; Dixon, *Wilbur* 58–61.
26. *Kansas City Call,* January 15, 1926.
27. Interview with Robert Sweeney conducted by

Janet Bruce (1/12/81). Kansas City Monarchs Oral History Collection (K0047), Tape No. A0025. State Historical Society of Missouri Research Center—Kansas City.

28. Bruce, *Kansas City Monarchs* 44–50.
29. *Kansas City Call*, April 30, 1926.
30. *Kansas City Call*, March 12, 1926.
31. O'Neil, *Right on Time* 83. See also Bruce, *Kansas City Monarchs* 61 and an interview with Richard (Dick) Wilkinson conducted by Janet Bruce (10/1/79). Kansas City Monarchs Oral History Collection (K0047), Tape No. A0016-17. State Historical Society of Missouri Research Center—Kansas City.
32. Geoffrey C. Ward and Ken Burns *Baseball: An Illustrated History* (New York: Alfred A. Knopf, 2010 [first published 1994]), 156. 244; Heaphy, *Negro Leagues* 81; Ribowsky, *A Complete History* 142–43.
33. *Kansas City Call*, March 12, 1926.
34. *Kansas City Call*, April 9, 1926.
35. *Kansas City Call*, November 9, 1928.
36. *Kansas City Call*, April 23, 1926.
37. *Kansas City Call*, May 21, 1926; Metcalfe, *A Game for All Races* 80; Dixon, *Wilbur* 57, 62; Holway, *Black Ball Stars* 191, 198. For an overview of Dobie Moore's career see Holway, *Black Ball Stars* 191–99.
38. *Kansas City Call*, July 23, 1926.
39. *Kansas City Call*, September 10, 1926.
40. Sources for the 1926 NNL Playoffs: *Kansas City Call*, September 24, October 1 and 8, 1926; Riley, *Monarchs and Black Barons* 82–86, Holway, *Book of Baseball's Negro Leagues* 210–11; Metcalfe, *A Game for All Races* 79–81, Dixon, *Wilbur* 57–58. 63–64.
41. *Kansas City Call*, October 29 and November 5, 1926.
42. Holway, *Book of Baseball's Negro Leagues* 211; Lawrence Hogan, *Shades of Glory: The Negro Leagues and the Story of African-American Baseball* (Washington, D.C.: National Geographic, 2006), 246.
43. *Kansas City Call*, December 3, 1926.
44. *Kansas City Call*, January 21, 1927.
45. *Kansas City Call*, February 4, 1927.
46. *Kansas City Call*, March 11, 1927.
47. Interview with Maurice Young conducted by Janet Bruce (11/8/78). Kansas City Monarchs Oral History Collection (K0047), Tape No. A0008. State Historical Society of Missouri Research Center—Kansas City.
48. *Kansas City Call*, February 24, 1928.
49. *Kansas City Call*, June 22, 1928.
50. Dixon, *Wilbur* 70–74.
51. Interview with Georgia (Mrs. Eddie) Dwight conducted by Janet Bruce (11/1/78). Kansas City Monarchs Oral History Collection (K0047), Tape No. A0001-3. State Historical Society of Missouri Research Center—Kansas City.
52. *Kansas City Call*, March 30, 1928.
53. *Kansas City Call*, April 27, 1928.
54. *Kansas City Call*, June 22, 1928.
55. *Kansas City Call*, August 10, 1928.
56. *Kansas City Call*, January 4 and 18, 1929.
57. *Kansas City Call*, January 4 and 11, February 3, 1929.
58. *Kansas City Call*, March 1, 1929.
59. *Kansas City Call*, March 8, 1929.
60. *Kansas City Call*, May 24 and June 28, 1929.
61. Hogan, *Shades of Glory* 235–36.
62. *Kansas City Call*, August 16, 1929.
63. *Kansas City Call*, July 26, 1929.
64. *Kansas City Call*, August 30, 1929.
65. *Kansas City Call*, September 20 and 27; October 4, 11 1929; Dixon, *Wilbur* 82–83.
66. Thomas Barthel, *Baseball Barnstorming and Exhibition Games, 1901-1962: A History of Off-Season Major League Play* (Jefferson, NC: McFarland, 2007), 110; Holway, *Book of Baseball's Negro Leagues* 253–54; Bruce, *Kansas City Monarchs* 64; Ribowsky, *A Complete History* 170.
67. *Kansas City Call*, July 27, 1929.
68. *Wichita Eagle* (June 9, 1928), p 6; cited by Dixon, *Wilbur*, 91.
69. *Kansas City Call*, September 7, 1928.
70. Charles Faber, "J L. Wilkinson," SABR Baseball Biography Project. http://sabr.org/ bioproj/person/db4ae51d (accessed 5/18/14); Dixon 2010: 8.

Chapter Five

1. Charles C. Alexander, *Breaking the Slump: Baseball in the Depression Era* (New York: Columbia University Press, 2002), 206.
2. Neil Lanctot, *Negro League Baseball: The Rise and Ruin of a Black Institution* (Philadelphia: University of Pennsylvania Press, 2004), 14.
3. *Kansas City Call*, January 10, 1930.
4. Cited by Lawrence Hogan, *Shades of Glory: The Negro Leagues and the Story of African-American Baseball* (Washington, D.C.: National Geographic, 2006), 254.
5. *Kansas City Call*, January 24, 1930.
6. *Kansas City Call*, February 14, 1930.
7. *Kansas City Call*, February 14, 1930.
8. *Kansas City Call*, March 28, 1930.
9. *Kansas City Call*, April 25, 1930.
10. John Naughton, "Invisible Man Among Invisible Men," *Des Moines Sunday Register* (July 10, 2005), 2C; Mark Ribowsky, *A Complete History of the Negro Leagues* (New York: Birch Lane Press, 1995), 144; Larry Lester, "J. L. Wilkinson: Only the Stars Come Out at Night," *Satchel Paige and Company: Essays on the Kansas City Monarchs, Their Greatest Star and the Negro Leagues*, ed. Leslie A. Heaphy (Jefferson, NC: McFarland, 2007), 20; Buck O'Neil, with Steve Wolf and David Conrads, *I Was Right on Time* (New York: Simon & Schuster, 1996), 67.
11. Interview with Gladys Wilkinson Catron conducted by Janet Bruce (11/17/80). Kansas City Monarchs Oral History Collection (K0047), Tape No. A0022-23. State Historical Society of Missouri Research Center—Kansas City.
12. Janet Bruce, *The Kansas City Monarchs: Champions of Black Baseball* (Lawrence: University of Kansas, 1985), 70.
13. John B. Holway, *The Complete Book of Baseball's Negro Leagues: The Other Half of Baseball History* (Fern Park, NJ: Hastings House, 2001), 257; *Black Ball Stars, Negro League Pioneers* (Westport, CT: Meckler, 1988),

333–34; *Voices from the Great Black Baseball Leagues* (New York: Dover, 2010 [originally published 1975]), 27.

14. *Kansas City Call*, March 24, 1930.

15. Leighton Housh, "Fair Play," *Des Moines Sunday Register*, May 20, 1973. J. L. Wilkinson File, National Baseball Hall of Fame, Cooperstown, NY.

16. *Kansas City Call*, April 25, 1930.

17. *Kansas City Call*, April 18, 1930.

18. *Kansas City Star*, June 12, 1930.

19. Undated, unattributed article. T. Y. Baird Collection, Kansas Collection, RH MS 414, Box 5, Folder 6, Kenneth Spencer Research Library, University of Kansas Libraries.

20. Larry Lester and Sammy Miller, *Black Baseball in Kansas City* (Charleston, SC: Arcadia, 2000), 31.

21. Interview with Richard (Dick) Wilkinson conducted by Janet Bruce (10/1/79). Kansas City Monarchs Oral History Collection (K0047), Tape No. A0016-17. State Historical Society of Missouri Research Center—Kansas City.

22. *Kansas City Call*, April 25, 1930.

23. *Kansas City Call*, May 2, 1930. Note: In an earlier version of the story, Holway (*Voices* 85) said the first night game was in Arkansas City, Kansas, on Saturday April 26, 1930, followed by a game the next night in Okmulgee, Oklahoma, then Enid on Monday.

24. *Kansas City Call*, May 16, 1930.

25. Holway, *Book of Baseball's Negro Leagues* 257.

26. Ribowsky, *A Complete History* 145.

27. *Sports Illustrated*, April 1970, 114.

28. *Kansas City Call*, May 2, 1930.

29. Undated, unattributed article. Baird Collection, RH MS 414, Box 5, Folder 6.

30. *Kansas City Call*, May 9, 1930.

31. Holway, *Voices* 86.

32. *Kansas City Call*, May 30 and June 13, 1930.

33. Undated article. Baird Collection, RH MS 414, Box 5, Folder 6.

34. *Kansas City Star*, June 12, 1930; cited by Lester 2007: 125.

35. *Kansas City Call*, July 18, 1930.

36. Interview with Richard (Dick) Wilkinson conducted by Janet Bruce (10/1/79).

37. *Kansas City Call*, August 1, 1930.

38. James, *Historical Baseball Abstract* 17; Hogan, *Shades of Glory* 256.

39. Henry Metcalfe, *A Game for All Races: An Illustrated History of the Negro Leagues* (New York: Metro Books, 2000), 91.

40. Larry Lester, "J. L. Wilkinson: Only the Stars Come Out at Night," *Unions to Royals: The Story of Professional Baseball in Kansas City*, ed. Lloyd Johnson, Steve Garlick, Jeff Magaliff (Kansas City Society for American Baseball Research, 1996), 10.

41. O'Neil, *Right on Time* 67.

42. Undated, unattributed article, Baird Collection, RH MS 414, Box 3, Folder 23.

43. *Kansas City Call*, August 29, 1930 and January 2, 1931.

44. Sources for the Monarchs and night baseball in addition to *Kansas City Call* and *Kansas City Star* articles cited: Holway, *Black Ball Stars* 74, 333–37, *Book of Baseball's Negro Leagues* 257–258, 264, *Voices* 84–87; Leslie A. Heaphy, *The Negro Leagues, 1869-1960* (Jefferson, NC: McFarland, 2003), 117; Ribowsky, *A Complete History* 144–46; Lester and Miller, *Black Baseball* 31; Lester, "J.L. Wilkinson" 120–21; Lester, "Leroy Robert 'Satchel' Paige" 9–10; Metcalfe, *A Game for All Races* 91; O'Neil, *Right on Time* 67; Bruce, *Kansas City Monarchs* 68–72; William H. Young and Nathan B. Young, Jr., "The Story of the Kansas City Monarchs," *Your Kansas City and Mine* (Kansas City: Midwest Afro-American Genealogy Interest Coalition, 1950), 71; Robert Peterson, *Only the Ball Was White* (New York: Oxford University Press, 1970), 124–25; Phil S. Dixon, *Wilber "Bullet" Rogan and the Kansas City Monarchs* (Jefferson, NC: McFarland, 2010), 105; Hogan, *Shades of Glory* 254–56; Alexander, *Breaking the Slump* 210.

45. Larry Lester, *Rube Foster in His Time* (Jefferson, NC: McFarland, 2012), 171.

46. Peterson, *Only the Ball Was White* 103.

47. Robert C. Cottrell, *The Best Pitcher of Baseball: The Life of Rube Foster, Negro League Giant* (New York: New York University Press, 2001), 5, 176–77. For brief overviews of Foster's life and influence, see Holway, *Black Ball Stars* 8–35 and the SABR biographies (http://sabr.org/bioproj/person/fcf322f7 and http://sabr.org/bioproj/person/1b44e1da).

48. *Kansas City Call*, December 19, 1930.

49. Heaphy, *Negro Leagues* 7, 154.

50. Thomas Barthel, *Baseball Barnstorming and Exhibition Games, 1901-1962: A History of Off-Season Major League Play* (Jefferson, NC: McFarland, 2007), 4.

51. Ribowsky, *A Complete History* 143–44; Bruce, *Kansas City Monarchs* 59–61.

52. *Kansas City Call*, July 27, 1934.

53. Interview with Bill "Plunk" Drake conducted by Dr. Charles Korr and Dr. Steven Hause (12/8/71), Negro Baseball League Project, http://shs.umsystem.edu/stlouis/manuscripts/transcripts/s0829/t0067.pdf (accessed 5/20/14).

54. Tom Dunkel, *Color Blind: The Forgotten Team That Broke Baseball's Color Line* (New York: Atlantic Monthly Press, 2013), 34–35.

55. Interview of Richard (Dick) Wilkinson conducted by Janet Bruce (10/1/79).

56. Lanctot, *Negro League Baseball* 138.

57. Tom Fredrick, "First There Was Baseball: Following the Globetrotters on a Path Back to Kansas City," *Kansas City Star Magazine* (January 4, 2004), 25–29. J. L. Wilkinson File, National Baseball Hall of Fame Library, Cooperstown, NY. The cards are treasured by Wilkinson's grandson Ed Catron. One from Rome says, "The Females All Say, 'You Have a Fine Grecian Figure, but I Can't Love Your Roman Hands.'" To be sure, the two men had very different personalities!

58. Ribowsky, *A Complete History* 194.

59. Alexander, *Breaking the Slump* 208–209.

60. *Kansas City Call*, April 3, 1931.

61. *Kansas City Call*, May 22, 1931.

62. *Kansas City Call*, July 10 and 17, 1931.

63. *Kansas City Call*, July 31, August 7 and 21, 1931.

64. *Kansas City Call*, September 4 and 18, 1931; Holway, *Book of Baseball's Negro Leagues* 280–81.
65. *Kansas City Call*, September 25 and October 2, 1931; Barthel, *Baseball Barnstorming* 133; Metcalfe *A Game for All Races* 90; Dixon, *Wilbur* 101–03; Holway, *Book of Baseball's Negro Leagues* 284.
66. *Kansas City Call*, October 31, 1931.
67. O'Neil, *Right on Time* 84.
68. Holway, *Voices* 87, *Black Ball Stars* 338, *Book of Baseball's Negro Leagues* 288.
69. *Springfield News Leader*, May 3, 1936.
70. Lester, "J.L. Wilkinson" 138–39.
71. *Kansas City Call*, October 9, 1931.
72. *Chicago Defender*, August 22, 1932.
73. Joel Hawkins, and Terry Bertolino, *Images of America: The House of David Baseball Team* (Chicago: Arcadia Publishing, 2000), 8–9, 29–39, 102; Michael Harkness-Roberto and Leslie A. Heaphy, "The Monarchs: A Brief History of the Franchise," *Satchel Paige and Company: Essays on the Kansas City Monarchs, Their Greatest Star and the Negro Leagues*, ed. Leslie Heaphy (Jefferson, NC: McFarland, 2007), 103; Dunkel, *Color Blind* 38; Ribowsky, *A Complete History* 169; Bruce, *Kansas City Monarchs* 77.
74. *Kansas City Call*, January 9, 1931 and September 4, 1931.
75. *Kansas City Call*, February 13, 1931.
76. Dunkel, *Color Blind* 106; Hawkins and Bertolino, *Images of America* 33–34, 76.
77. Ben Green, *Spinning the Globe: The Rise, Fall, and Return to Greatness of the Harlem Globetrotters* (New York: Amistad, 2006), 279.
78. Lester, "J.L. Wilkinson" 127.
79. *Kansas City Call*, June 3, 1932. Note: The E-W League folded in early July (*Kansas City Call*, July 8, 1932).
80. *Kansas City Call*, July 8 and 15, 1932.
81. Dixon, *Wilbur* 108–9.
82. *Kansas City Call*, August 12 and 19; September 2, 16, 23, and 30; October 7, 1932.
83. *Wichita Beacon*, October 10, 1932, 10.
84. *Kansas City Call*, October 28, November 11, 18, 1932.
85. *Kansas City Call*, July 5, 1940.
86. Lester, "J.L. Wilkinson" 127; Harkness-Roberto and Heaphy, "The Monarchs" 102, 104; Dixon, *Wilbur* 107–109.
87. On Posey and Greenlee, see Holway, *Black Ball Stars* 299–326; Lester, *National Showcase* 9–19.
88. Peterson, *Only the Ball Was White* 91–93; Alexander, *Breaking the Slump* 212, 214–16; Lanctot, *Negro League Baseball* 17.
89. *Kansas City Call*, November 23, 1933; January 12 and 26, February 9, March 9, 1934; Bruce, *Kansas City Monarchs* 84.
90. *Kansas City Call*, June 2, 1933.
91. *Kansas City Call*, July 14, 1933.
92. *Kansas City Call*, July 28, 1933.
93. *Kansas City Call*, August 11, 1933.
94. Bruce, *Kansas City Monarchs* 83.
95. *Kansas City Call*, September 8, 1933.
96. *Kansas City Call*, September 15 and 22, 1933. The *Call* may have conflated the seventeen-year-old Mitchell's strikeouts of Babe Ruth and Lou Gehrig in a pre-season exhibition game between the New York Yankees and the Chattanooga Lookouts, a Washington Senators farm team. The Lookouts' General Manager Joe Engel, who shared J.L. Wilkinson's flair for crowd-pleasing promotions, staged the contest.
97. *Kansas City Call*, September 29 and October 6, 1933.
98. *Wichita Eagle*, October 11, 1934, 8.
99. *Kansas City Call*, October 13, 1933.
100. Dixon, *Wilbur* 113–21; Timothy M. Gay, *Satchel, Dizzy and Rapid Robert: The Wild Saga of Interracial Baseball Before Jackie Robinson* (New York: Simon & Schuster, 2010), 50–52, 64–65, 70.
101. *Kansas City Call*, December 1, 1933.
102. Lanctot, *Negro League Baseball* 54.
103. The definitive study of the East-West games is Larry Lester's *Black Baseball's National Showcase* (Lincoln: University of Nebraska Press, 2001). See also Bruce, *Kansas City Monarchs* 87–88; Heaphy, *Negro Leagues* 119–22; Lanctot, *Negro League Baseball* 22–23, 188–190; Riley, *Monarchs and Black Barons* 15–16, 87–9; Hogan, *Shades of Glory* 284–8.
104. *Kansas City Call*, January 26, 1934.
105. *Kansas City Call*, April 20, 1934.
106. *Kansas City Call*, June 20, 1934.
107. *Kansas City Call*, July 20, 1934.
108. *Kansas City Call*, August 3, 1934.
109. Dixon, *Wilbur* 139–41, 50–51.
110. Sources for the 1934 *Denver Post* tournament: *Kansas City Call*, July 27, August 3, 10, 17, and 24; Bruce, *Kansas City Monarchs* 75; Metcalfe, *A Game for All Races* 106; Dunkel, *Color Blind* 124; Holway, *Voices* 87; Dixon, *Wilbur* 142–45; Heaphy, *Negro Leagues* 148; Gay, *Satchel* 74–79; Holway, *Book of Baseball's Negro Leagues* 309.
111. *Wichita Beacon*, August 26, 1934, 8b; cited by Dixon, *Wilbur* 146–47.
112. *Kansas City Call*, September 7, 1934.
113. *Kansas City Call*, October 5, 1934.
114. *Kansas City Call*, October 12, 1934.
115. Sources for the "Dizzy and Daffy" tour: *Kansas City Call*, October 19, 1934; Holway, *Book of Baseball's Negro Leagues* 315; Barthel, *Baseball Barnstorming* 139; Lester, "J.L. Wilkinson" 127; Bruce, *Kansas City Monarchs* 7, 18; Gay, *Satchel* 76–88; Lester, *National Showcase* 44–45; Vince Staten, *Ol' Diz: A Biography of Dizzy Dean* (New York: HarperCollins, 1992), 152–53; Leroy "Satchel" Paige, as told to David L. Lipman. *Maybe I'll Pitch Forever; a Great Baseball Player Tells the Hilarious Story Behind the Legend* (Lincoln: University of Nebraska Press, 1993), 91–93.
116. Lanctot, *Negro League Baseball* 107.
117. http://www.footballgeography.com/nfl-exhibition-games-played-at-neutral-sites/ (accessed 2/11/15).
118. Interview of Richard (Dick) Wilkinson conducted by Janet Bruce (10/1/79).
119. Letter to John Antonello dated April 1, 1952. Baird Collection. RH MS 414, Box 1, Folder 9.
120. Dixon, *Wilbur* 151–54.
121. *Kansas City Call*, April 5, 1935.
122. *Kansas City Call*, May 3, 10, 17, and 24, 1935.
123. Dixon, *Wilbur* 155.

124. *Springfield News Leader,* May 3, 1936.
125. Bruce, *Kansas City Monarchs* 78–80.
126. *Kansas City Call,* June 7, 1935.
127. Interview conducted with Hilton Smith by Janet Bruce (11/10/78). Kansas City Monarchs Oral History Collection (K0047), Tape No. A0009. State Historical Society of Missouri Research Center—Kansas City.
128. *Kansas City Call,* June 21, 1935.
129. *Kansas City Call,* September 6, 1935.
130. *Kansas City Call,* October 4, 1935.
131. *Kansas City Call,* August 16, 1935.
132. *Kansas City Call,* August 30, 1935.
133. *Kansas City Call,* October 11, 1935.
134. *Kansas City Call,* October 18, 1935.
135. *Kansas City Call,* October 25, 1935.
136. Sources for the 1935 season in addition to *Kansas City Call* articles cited: Holway, *Book of Baseball's Negro Leagues* 322; Dixon, *Wilbur* 151–60; Gay, *Satchel* 108–110.
137. *Springfield News Leader,* May 3, 1936.
138. Joe Posnanski, *The Soul of Baseball: A Road Trip Through Buck O'Neil's America* (New York: William Morrow, 2006), 158, 175.
139. Interview of Hilton Smith conducted by Janet Bruce (11/10/78); Holway, *Voices* 287 (see complete interview, 280–89).
140. *Kansas City Call,* April 10 and 17, 1936.
141. *Kansas City Call,* May 15, 22, 29.
142. *Kansas City Call,* May 29, 1936.
143. *Kansas City Call,* July 10 and August 7, 1936.
144. *Kansas City Call,* September 4 and 11, 1936.
145. *Kansas City Call,* September 25, 1936.
146. *Kansas City Call,* October 2 and 9, 1936.
147. Bruce, *Kansas City Call* 59–61.
148. Interviews with Georgia (Mrs. Eddie) Dwight, conducted by Janet Bruce (1–11/1/78 and 7/13/80). Kansas City Monarchs Oral History Collection (K0047), Tape No. A0001–3. State Historical Society of Missouri Research Center—Kansas City; Bruce, *Kansas City Monarchs* 59–61.

Chapter Six

1. Janet Bruce, *The Kansas City Monarchs: Champions of Black Baseball* (Lawrence: University of Kansas, 1985), 90.
2. The story was frequently told by Satchel Paige, as, for example, in an interview published in the *Kansas City Call* on March 26, 1943.
3. Leroy "Satchel" Paige, as told to David L. Lipman, *Maybe I'll Pitch Forever; a Great Baseball Player Tells the Hilarious Story Behind the Legend* (Lincoln: University of Nebraska Press, 1993), 117–20.
4. Larry Lester, *Black Baseball's National Showcase* (Lincoln: University of Nebraska Press, 2001), 97–99.
5. *Kansas City Call,* April 30, 1937.
6. *Kansas City Call,* August 13, 1937.
7. *Kansas City Call,* September 3, 1937.
8. *Kansas City Call,* April 30, 1937.
9. Joe Posnanski, *The Soul of Baseball: A Road Trip Through Buck O'Neil's America* (New York: William Morrow, 2006), 104–10.

10. *Kansas City Call,* May 7, 14; John B. Holway, *Black Ball Stars, Negro League Pioneers* (Westport, CT: Meckler, 1988), 338.
11. *Kansas City Call,* May 21, 1937.
12. *Kansas City Call,* May 28, 1937.
13. *Kansas City Call,* June 4, 1937.
14. *Kansas City Call,* June 25, 1937.
15. *Kansas City Call,* June 11, 1937.
16. *Kansas City Call,* July 9, 1937.
17. *Kansas City Call,* July 30, August 6, and 13, 1937.
18. Brent P. Kelly, *The Negro Leagues Revisited: Conversations with 66 More Baseball Heroes* (Jefferson, NC: McFarland, 2000), 61.
19. *Kansas City Call,* September 17 and 24, 1937.
20. *Kansas City Call,* September 24 and October 1, 1937.
21. *Wichita Eagle,* October 10, 1937.
22. Sources for the October 1937 series with the major leaguers: *Kansas City Call,* October 8 and 15, 1937; Michael Harkness-Roberto and Leslie A. Heaphy, "The Monarchs: A Brief History of the Franchise," *Satchel Paige and Company: Essays on the Kansas City Monarchs, Their Greatest Star and the Negro Leagues,* ed. Leslie Heaphy (Jefferson, NC: McFarland, 2007), 105; Phil S. Dixon, *Wilber "Bullet" Rogan and the Kansas City Monarchs* (Jefferson, NC: McFarland, 2010), 170, 173–77; John B. Holway, *The Complete Book of Baseball's Negro Leagues: The Other Half of Baseball History* (Fern Park, NJ: Hastings House, 2001), 341–342, 346, 349; Timothy M. Gay, *Satchel, Dizzy, and Rapid Robert: The Wild Saga of Interracial Baseball Before Jackie Robinson* (New York: Simon & Schuster, 2010), 170–75.
23. Neil Lanctot, *Negro League Baseball: The Rise and Ruin of a Black Institution* (Philadelphia: University of Pennsylvania Press, 2004), 59–67; Charles C. Alexander, *Breaking the Slump: Baseball in the Depression Era* (New York: Columbia University Press, 2002), 223–36.
24. *Chicago Defender,* September 11, 1937.
25. Lanctot, *Negro League Baseball* 68–70.
26. Leslie A. Heaphy, *The Negro Leagues, 1869–1960* (Jefferson, NC: McFarland, 2003), 86.
27. *Kansas City Call,* January 21; February 18, 25; March 4, 11, 18; April 1; June 3, 1938.
28. O'Neil's nickname "Buck" came from the co-owner of the black Miami Giants, a man named Buck O'Neal.
29. Interview with Buck O'Neil conducted by Fay Vincent, recorded in Fay Vincent, *The Only Game in Town: Baseball Stars of the 1930s and 1940s Talk About the Game They Loved* (New York: Simon & Schuster, 2006), 87; Joe Klima, *Willie's Boys: The 1948 Birmingham Black Barons, the Last Negro League World Series, and the Making of a Baseball Legend* (Hoboken, NJ: John Wiley & Sons, 2009), 29–31.
30. Buck O'Neil, with Steve Wolf and David Conrads, *I Was Right on Time* (New York: Simon & Schuster, 1996), 68.
31. O'Neil, *Right on Time* 85–93, 95–98; Dixon, *Wilbur* 177.
32. *Kansas City Times,* February 9, 1983.
33. *Kansas City Call,* May 20, 1938.

34. *Chicago Defender,* August 6, 1938; see also *Kansas City Call,* August 5 and 19, 1938; Roger Kahn, *Rickey and Robinson: The True, Untold Story of the Integration of* Baseball (New York: Rodale, 2014), 61–62; Alexander, *Breaking the Slump* 228; Lester, *National Showcase* 107–09.

35. Cited in Alexander, *Breaking the Slump* 228–29.

Chapter Seven

1. *Chicago Defender,* September 28, 1935; cited by Larry Tye, *Satchel: The Life and Times of an American Legend* (New York: Random House, 2009), 143.

2. Janet Bruce, *The Kansas City Monarchs: Champions of Black Baseball* (Lawrence: University of Kansas, 1985), 148; Larry Lester, "J. L. Wilkinson: Only the Stars Come Out at Night," *Unions to Royals: The Story of Professional Baseball in Kansas* City, eds. Lloyd Johnson, Steve Garlick, Jeff Magaliff (Kansas City Society for American Baseball Research, 1996), 22; Tom Dunkel, *Color Blind: The Forgotten Team That Broke Baseball's Color Line* (New York: Atlantic Monthly Press, 2013), 69.

3. Sources for Paige's early life and career: Bruce, *Kansas City Monarchs* 95; Dunkel, *Color Blind* 70–77, 240, 262; Leroy "Satchel" Paige, as told to David L. Lipman, *Maybe I'll Pitch Forever; a Great Baseball Player Tells the Hilarious Story Behind the Legend* (Lincoln: University of Nebraska Press, 1993), 87–88, 91–93, 97–98, 117–20; Buck O'Neil, with Steve Wolf and David Conrads, *I Was Right on Time* (New York: Simon & Schuster, 1996), 103–04, 118–19; Geoffrey C. Ward and Ken Burns, *Baseball: An Illustrated History* (New York: Alfred A. Knopf, 2010 [first published 1994]), 201–07; Kyle McNary, *Black Baseball: A History of African-Americans and the National Game* (London: PRC Publishing, 2003), 152–54, 29; Larry Lester, *Black Baseball's National Showcase* (Lincoln: University of Nebraska Press, 2001), 65, 68; Charles C. Alexander, *Breaking the Slump: Baseball in the Depression Era* (New York: Columbia University Press, 2002), 219–222; Roger Kahn, *Rickey and Robinson: The True, Untold Story of the Integration of Baseball* (New York: Rodale, 2014), 59; Robert Peterson, *Only the Ball Was White* (New York: Oxford University Press, 1970), 131–37; Lawrence Hogan, *Shades of Glory: The Negro Leagues and the Story of African-American Baseball* (Washington, D.C.: National Geographic, 2006), 252–53, 289, 308; Neil Lanctot, *Negro League Baseball: The Rise and Ruin of a Black Institution* (Philadelphia: University of Pennsylvania Press, 2004), 73–74.

4. *Kansas City Call,* March 11, 1949.

5. Sources for Wilkinson's signing of Paige: Paige, *Maybe I'll Pitch Forever* 123–31; O'Neil, *I Was Right* 105–08; Peterson, *Only the Ball Was White* 137–38; Dunkel, *Color Blind* 262, 276; Hogan, *Shades* 135–38; Donald. Spivey, *"If You Were Only White": The Life of Leroy "Satchel" Paige* (Columbia: University of Missouri Press, 2012), 167–69; John B. Holway, *Voices from the Great Black Baseball Leagues* (New York: Dover, 2010 [originally published 1975], 2010: 103; John B. Holway, *Black Ball Stars, Negro League Pioneers* (Westport, CT: Meckler, 1988), 33. Note: Henry Metcalfe claims Abe Saperstein convinced Wilkinson to put the injured Paige on the Monarchs traveling squad (Henry Metcalfe, *A Game for All Races: An Illustrated History of the Negro Leagues* [New York: Metro Books, 2000]), 112.

6. Holway, *Voices* 87; *Black Ball Stars* 339–40.

7. Bruce, *Kansas City Monarchs* 93; Tye, *Satchel* 144–45: Alexander, *Breaking the Slump* 233; Spivey, *"If You Were Only White"* 175–78, 84–85; Lanctot, *Negro League Baseball* 91–92: Bob Luke, *The Most Famous Woman in Baseball: Effa Manley and the Negro Leagues* (Washington, D.C.: Potomac Books, 2011), 62–63, 76.

8. John B. Holway, *Black Diamonds: Life in the Negro Leagues from the Men Who Lived It* (Westport, CT: Meckler Books, 1989), 21.

9. Interview with Bill "Plunk" conducted by Dr. Charles Korr and Dr. Steven Hause (12/8/71), Negro Baseball League Project, http://shs.umsystem.edu/stlouis/manuscripts/ transcripts/s0829/t0067.pdf (accessed 5/20/14).

10. Paige, *Maybe I'll Pitch Forever* 132.

11. Spivey, *"If You Were Only White"* 168–69.

12. Bruce, *Kansas City Monarchs* 93–94.

13. Paige, *Maybe I'll Pitch Forever* 133–36, Tye, *Satchel* 123–24, Spivey, *"If You Were Only White"* 169; Interview with Buck O'Neil conducted by Fay Vincent, recorded in Fay Vincent, *The Only Game in Town: Baseball Stars of the 1930s and 1940s Talk About the Game They Loved* (New York: Simon & Schuster, 2006), 88–89.

14. *Kansas City Call,* June 16, 23, July 7, 1939.

15. *Kansas City Call,* July 28, August 4, and August 11, 1939.

16. Bruce, *Kansas City Monarchs* 78–80; Holway, *Black Ball Stars* 338.

17. *Kansas City Call,* September 29, 1939.

18. Spivey, *"If You Were Only White"* 176.

19. Tye, *Satchel* 145; Mark Ribowsky, *A Complete History of the Negro Leagues* (New York: Birch Lane Press, 1995), 231–32.

20. Neil Lanctot records the date as May 11, 1939 (Lanctot, *Negro League Baseball* 105).

21. Tye, *Satchel* 146–47, Alexander, *Breaking the Slump* 235.

22. Holway, *Black Ball Stars* 339.

23. Ribowsky, *History of the Negro Leagues* 237.

24. Lanctot, *Negro League Baseball* 105–06.

25. Lester, *National Showcase* 153–71.

26. Holway, *Black Ball Stars* 339.

27. Holway, *Voices* 302.

28. *Time Magazine,* June 30, 1940 edition (p. 44); *Saturday Evening Post,* July 27, 1940 (pp. 79–81). Cited in Alexander, *Breaking the Slump* 233–34; Lanctot, *Negro League Baseball* 227.

29. Frazier "Slow" Robinson, with Paul Bauer, *Catching Dreams: My Life in the Negro Baseball Leagues* (Syracuse: Syracuse University Press, 1999), 37–38.

30. Paige, *Maybe I'll Pitch Forever* 175–78.

31. Cited in Tye, *Satchel* 136–38.

32. Robinson, *Catching Dreams* 50.

33. Tye, *Satchel* 165–66; Paige, *Maybe I'll Pitch Forever* 138–39, 142, 168–69; Interview with Richard (Dick) Wilkinson conducted by Janet Bruce (10/1/79). Kansas City Monarchs Oral History Collection (K0047),

Tape No. A0016-17. State Historical Society of Missouri Research Center—Kansas City; Larry Lester and Sammy Miller, *Black Baseball in Kansas City* (Charleston, SC: Arcadia, 2000), 103.

34. Paige, *Maybe I'll Pitch Forever* 138-39.

35. Jim Reisler, *Black Writers, Black Baseball: An Anthology of Articles from Black Sportswriters Who Covered the Negro Leagues*, revised edition (Jefferson, NC: McFarland, 2007), 128.

36. *Kansas City Call*, July 5, 1946; Spivey, "If You Were Only White" 199, 209-11; Thomas Fredrick, "KC Connection Began Baseball's Globalization," *The Kansas City Star* (October 16, 2004), C6. J. L. Wilkinson File, National Baseball Hall of Fame, Cooperstown, NY.

37. Tye, *Satchel* 205.

38. Paige, *Maybe I'll Pitch Forever* 195-98; Tye, *Satchel* 217-18; Robinson, *Catching Dreams* 50; Lanctot, *Negro League Baseball* 335-36; Timothy M. Gay, *Satchel, Dizzy and Rapid Robert: The Wild Saga of Interracial Baseball Before Jackie Robinson* (New York: Simon & Schuster, 2010), 263-66.

39. For Paige's vivid description of his major league debut, see Paige, *Maybe I'll Pitch Forever* 200-25.

40. baseballhall.org/hof/paige-satchel (accessed 1/24/15).

41. Interview with Drake conducted by Dr. Charles Korr and Dr. Steven Hause (12/8/71).

42. Interview with Bob Feller conducted by Fay Vincent, recorded in Fay, *The Only Game in Town: Baseball Stars of the 1930s and 1940s Talk About the Game They Loved* (New York: Simon & Schuster, 2006), 51.

43. Paige, *Maybe I'll Pitch Forever* 233-35; Spivey, "If You Were Only White" 246; Tye, *Satchel* 264.

44. Spivey, "If You Were Only White" 250.

45. *Kansas City Star*, March 9, 1971.

46. *Kansas City Times*, August 9, 1971.

47. *Kansas City Times*, October 4, 1971.

48. Peterson, *Only the Ball Was White* 120-21.

49. Tye, *Satchel* 288-89.

50. Spivey, "If You Were Only White" xix-xx.

51. O'Neil, *Right on Time* 100-101; Joe Posnanski, *The Soul of Baseball: A Road Trip Through Buck O'Neil's America* (New York: William Morrow, 2006), 144.

52. Tom Dunkel, *Color Blind: The Forgotten Team That Broke Baseball's Color Line* (New York: Atlantic Monthly Press, 2013), 277.

53. Paige, *Maybe I'll Pitch Forever* 227; Ward and Burns, *An Illustrated History* 206.

Chapter Eight

1. Rachel Robinson and Lee Daniels, *Jackie Robinson: An Intimate Portrait* (New York: Harry N. Abrams, 1996), 33.

2. For example, interview conducted with Jesse Williams by Janet Bruce 1/16/79. Kansas City Monarchs Oral History Collection (K0047), Tape No. 12. State Historical Society of Missouri Research Center—Kansas City.

3. Charles C. Alexander, *Breaking the Slump: Baseball in the Depression Era* (New York: Columbia University Press, 2002), 238; Neil Lanctot, *Negro League Baseball: The Rise and Ruin of a Black Institution* (Philadelphia: University of Pennsylvania Press, 2004), 97-98, x; Robert Peterson, *Only the Ball Was White* (New York: Oxford University Press, 1970), 93; Janet Bruce, *The Kansas City Monarchs: Champions of Black Baseball* (Lawrence: University of Kansas, 1985), 98.

4. *Kansas City Call*, March 22, 1940.

5. *Kansas City Call*, May 17, 1940; July 19, 1940; October 18, 1940.

6. Unidentified article dated May 23, 1940. T. Y. Baird Collection, Kansas Collection, RH MS 414, Box 5. Kenneth Spencer Research Library, University of Kansas Libraries.

7. *Kansas City Call*, June 7, 1940.

8. *Kansas City Call*, June 21, 1940.

9. *Kansas City Call*, August 30 and September 6, 1940.

10. *Kansas City Call*, September 27, 1940.

11. *Kansas City Call*, September 22, 1940. Actually, by 1940 he had been involved in baseball as a player, manager, and owner for four decades.

12. Lanctot, *Negro League Baseball* 97-98; Kyle McNary, *Black Baseball: A History of African-Americans and the National Game* (London: PRC Publishing, 2003), 113.

13. *Kansas City Call*, June 21 and 28, 1940.

14. *Kansas City Call*, August 30 and September 6, 1940.

15. *Kansas City Call*, July 26, 1940.

16. Interview with Jessie Williams conducted by Janet Bruice (10/1/79).

17. Bruce, *Kansas City Monarchs* 102.

18. Frazier "Slow" Robinson, with Paul Bauer, *Catching Dreams: My Life in the Negro Baseball Leagues* (Syracuse: Syracuse University Press, 1999), 58-59.

19. *Kansas City Call*, November 1, 1940.

20. *Kansas City Call*, February 28, 1941; Larry Lester, *Black Baseball's National Showcase* (Lincoln: University of Nebraska Press, 2001), 154.

21. Interview with Clifford "Connie" Johnson conducted by Janet Bruce (11/15/78). Kansas City Monarchs Oral History Collection (K0047), Tape No. A0010. State Historical Society of Missouri Research Center—Kansas City.

22. *Kansas City Call, Call*, May 30, 1941.

23. *Kansas City Call*, June 6 and 20, 1941.

24. *Kansas City Call*, June 13 and 27, 1941.

25. John B. Holway, *The Complete Book of Baseball's Negro Leagues: The Other Half of Baseball History* (Fern Park, NJ: Hastings House, 2001), 383-84.

26. *Kansas City Call*, June 13 and 20, 1941.

27. *Kansas City Call*, July 18 and August 15, 1941.

28. *Chicago Defender*, August 2, 1941; *Kansas City Call*, August 1, 1941; Lester, *National Showcase* 168-70.

29. *Kansas City Call*, July 25; August 1, 15, 22, and 29, 1941.

30. *Kansas City Call*, September 5, 1941.

31. Holway, *Book of Baseball's Negro Leagues* 383.

32. Ribowsky, *A Complete History* 244; Holway, *Book of Baseball's Negro Leagues* 390.

33. Lanctot, *Negro League Baseball* 118-19.

34. *Kansas City Call*, December 12, 1941.

35. *Kansas City Call,* April 4, 11 and 25, 1941.
36. Lanctot, *Negro League Baseball* 109.
37. Alan J. Pollock, *Barnstorming to Heaven: Syd Pollock and His Great Black Teams* (Tuscaloosa: University of Alabama Press, 2006), 156–57.
38. Pollock, *Barnstorming to Heaven* 96–98.
39. *Kansas City Call,* July 4, 1941.
40. John B. Holway, *Voices from the Great Black Baseball Leagues* (New York: Dover, 2010 [originally published 1975]), 341.
41. Pollock, *Barnstorming to Heaven* 14–18, 21, 22, 30.
42. *Kansas City Call,* January 2, 1942.
43. *Kansas City Call,* February 27, 1942.
44. Buck O'Neil, with Steve Wolf and David Conrads, *I Was Right on Time* (New York: Simon & Schuster, 1996), 119–20; Brent P. Kelly, *The Negro Leagues Revisited: Conversations with 66 More Baseball Heroes* (Jefferson, NC: McFarland, 2000), 164, 166, 168; Bruce, *Kansas City Monarchs* 101.
45. *Kansas City Call,* June 5, 1942.
46. Holway, *Voices* 304.
47. *Kansas City Call,* April 19, 1942.
48. *Kansas City Call,* May 15, 22 and June 12, 1942.
49. *Kansas City Call,* May 29, 1942; Lester, *National Showcase* 174–75; Holway, *Voices* 11–12; Lanctot, *Negro League Baseball* 126–27; Holway, *Book of Baseball's Negro Leagues* 401–02.
50. *Kansas City Call,* June 26, 1942.
51. *Kansas City Call,* July 24 and 31, 1942.
52. Lanctot, *Negro League Baseball* 126.
53. *Kansas City Call,* July 31, 1942; Donald Spivey, *"If You Were Only White": The Life of Leroy "Satchel" Paige* (Columbia: University of Missouri Press, 2012), 186.
54. Lester, *National Showcase* 198–99; Holway, *Book of Baseball's Negro Leagues* 397; Lanctot, *Negro League Baseball* 123; 2012: 188.
55. Interview with Newt Allen conducted by John Holway (1970). University of Missouri–St. Louis, Archive & Manuscript Division (T208).
56. Geoffrey C. Ward and Ken Burns, *Baseball: An Illustrated History* (New York: Alfred A. Knopf, 2010 [first published 1994]), 219–20, 244.
57. *Kansas City Star,* August 14, 1942.
58. Sources for the 1942 Negro Leagues World Series: *Kansas City Call,* September 18 and 25, 1942; January 8, 1943; Holway, *Book of Baseball's Negro Leagues* 398–99; Lawrence Hogan, *Shades of Glory: The Negro Leagues and the Story of African-American Baseball* (Washington, D.C.: National Geographic, 2006), 311–12; Mark Ribowsky, *A Complete History of the Negro Leagues* (New York: Birch Lane Press, 1995), 258–62; Robinson, *Catching Dreams* 93, 95; Bruce, *Kansas City Monarchs* 103–04; Bob Luke, *The Most Famous Woman in Baseball: Effa Manley and the Negro Leagues* (Washington, D.C.: Potomac Books, 2011), 91–92; Leroy "Satchel" Paige, as told to David L. Lipman. *Maybe I'll Pitch Forever; a Great Baseball Player Tells the Hilarious Story Behind the Legend* (Lincoln: University of Nebraska Press, 1993), 146–4); O'Neil, *Right on Time* 126–38; James A. Riley, *Of Monarchs and Black Barons: Essays on Baseball's Negro Leagues* (Jefferson, NC: McFarland, 2012), 153.
59. *Kansas City Call,* February 26, 1943.
60. *Kansas City Call,* March 12, 19, and 26, 1943; Lanctot, *Negro League Baseball* 129–34; Bruce, *Kansas City Monarchs* 99–100; John Beer, "Order Banning Use of Own Buses Worries Negro League," *The Sunday Call* (Newark, NJ), March 14, 1943.
61. *Kansas City Star,* March 3, 1943.
62. *Kansas City Call,* March 26, 1943.
63. *Kansas City Star,* August 14, 1943. The actual date of the raid was August 1, 1943. See also http://www.eyewitnesstohistory.com/ploesti.htm (accessed 12/2/15).
64. *Kansas City Call,* April 9, 1943.
65. *Kansas City Call,* April 16, 1943.
66. *Kansas City Call,* May 21, 1943.
67. *Kansas City Call,* June 25 and July 2.
68. Lanctot, *Negro League Baseball* 128.
69. *Kansas City Call,* February 18 and 25, 1944.
70. *Chicago Defender,* July 24, 1943.
71. *Kansas City Call,* July 23 and August 6, 1943; Peterson, *Only the Ball Was White* 100; Lester, *National Showcase* 220; Lanctot, *Negro League Baseball* 139; Paige, *Maybe I'll Pitch Forever* 159–61; Jim Reisler, *Black Writers, Black Baseball: An Anthology of Articles from Black Sportswriters Who Covered the Negro Leagues,* revised edition (Jefferson, NC: McFarland, 2007), 89.
72. *Kansas City Call,* October 1, 1943.
73. *Pittsburgh Courier,* December 28, 1943.
74. O'Neil, *Right on Time* 162, 194.
75. Bruce, *Kansas City Monarchs* 98–101; Spivey, *"If You Were Only White"* 186; Hogan, *Shades of Glory* 315; Michael Harkness-Roberto and Leslie A. Heaphy, "The Monarchs: A Brief History of the Franchise," *Satchel Paige and Company: Essays on the Kansas City Monarchs, Their Greatest Star and the Negro Leagues,* ed. Leslie Heaphy (Jefferson, NC: McFarland, 2007), 105.
76. *Kansas City Call,* December 3, 1943.
77. *Kansas City Call,* April 16, 1943.
78. *Kansas City Call,* December 24 and 31, 1943.
79. *Kansas City Call,* March 17, 24, and 31, 1944.
80. *Philadelphia Tribune,* March 25, 1944.
81. Lanctot, *Negro League Baseball* 116, 147.
82. Lanctot, *Negro League Baseball* 143.
83. *Kansas City Call,* August 4, 1944.
84. *Kansas City Call,* May 5, 12,19, 26, 1944.
85. *Kansas City Call,* June 9, 1944; Lester, *National Showcase* 225.
86. *Kansas City Call,* July 7, 1944.
87. *Kansas City Call,* July 14, 1944.
88. *Kansas City Call,* July 28, August 11 and 18, 1944; Holway, *Book of Baseball's Negro Leagues* 418; Ribowsky, *A Complete History* 262; Paige, *Maybe I'll Pitch Forever* 163–66; Reisler, *Black Baseball* 89–90; Lanctot, *Negro League Baseball* vii–viii; Bruce, *Kansas City Monarchs* 106; Hogan, *Shades of Grey* 315.
89. *Kansas City Call,* September 8 and 15, 1944; Lanctot, *Negro League Baseball* 142–43.
90. *Kansas City Call,* December 22, 1944.
91. *Kansas City Call,* January 26, 1945.
92. *Kansas City Call,* February 16, 1945.
93. *Kansas City Call,* March 9 and April 20, 1945.
94. *Kansas City Star,* January 23, 1945.
95. Holway, *Voices* 87, *Black Ball Stars* 340–41.

96. Interview with Othello "Chic" Renfroe conducted by Janet Bruce (1/29/80). Kansas City Monarchs Oral History Collection (K0047), Tape No. A0019. State Historical Society of Missouri Research Center—Kansas City.
97. Robinson, *Catching Dreams* 54.
98. *Kansas City Call*, May 25 and June 8, 1945.
99. *Kansas City Call*, July 13, 1945.
100. *Kansas City Call*, July 27, 1945.
101. *Kansas City Call*, August 31, 1945.

Chapter Nine

1. Robert Peterson, *Only the Ball Was White* (New York: Oxford University Press, 1970), 174–75.
2. Jules Tygiel, *Baseball's Greatest Experiment: Jackie Robinson and His Legacy* (New York: Oxford University Press, 1983). 35; for excerpts of Smith's columns over the years see Jim Reisler, *Black Writers, Black Baseball: An Anthology of Articles from Black Sportswriters Who Covered the Negro Leagues*, revised edition (Jefferson, NC: McFarland, 2007), 41–60.
3. Reisler, *Black Baseball* 41–42.
4. *Kansas City Call*, July 14, 1939; Larry Lester, *Black Baseball's National Showcase* (Lincoln: University of Nebraska Press, 2001), 109–11; Neil Lanctot, *Negro League Baseball: The Rise and Ruin of a Black Institution* (Philadelphia: University of Pennsylvania Press, 2004), 223; Charles C. Alexander, *Breaking the Slump: Baseball in the Depression Era* (New York: Columbia University Press, 2002), 232; John B. Holway, *The Complete Book of Baseball's Negro Leagues: The Other Half of Baseball History* (Fern Park, NJ: Hastings House, 2001), 371–72; Lawrence Hogan, *Shades of Glory: The Negro Leagues and the Story of African-American Baseball* (Washington, D.C.: National Geographic, 2006), 325–28.
5. Reisler, *Black Baseball* 14–15.
6. Reisler, *Black Baseball* 19–21; for a sampling of Lacy's articles over the years, see Reisler, *Black Baseball* 19–36.
7. *Kansas City Call*, August 14, 1942; Holway, *Voices* 11–12; Lee Lowenfish, *Branch Rickey: Baseball's Ferocious Gentleman* (Lincoln: University of Nebraska Press, 2007), 351; Holway, *Book of Baseball's Negro Leagues* 402; Lester, *National Showcase* 180, 185; Lanctot, *Negro League Baseball* 233–34, 238–39.
8. *Kansas City Call*, December 10, 1943.
9. Lanctot, *Negro League Baseball* 260–61; Leslie A. Heaphy, *The Negro Leagues, 1869–1960* (Jefferson, NC: McFarland, 2003), 183; Roger Kahn, *Rickey and Robinson: The True, Untold Story of the Integration of Baseball* (New York: Rodale, 2014), 97–98.
10. David Falkner, *Great Time Coming: The Life of Jackie Robinson from Baseball to Birmingham* (New York: Simon & Schuster, 1995), 88; Tom Dunkel, *Color Blind: The Forgotten Team That Broke Baseball's Color Line* (New York: Atlantic Monthly Press, 2013), 275; Arnold Rampersad, *Jackie Robinson: A Biography* (New York: Alfred A. Knopf, 1997), 115.
11. Rachel Robinson and Lee Daniels, *Jackie Robinson: An Intimate Portrait* (New York: Harry N. Abrams, 1996), 33–34.
12. Falkner, *Great Time Coming* 87–88; Rampersad, *Jackie Robinson* 113; Jackie Robinson with Alfred Duckett, *I Never Had It Made: An Autobiography* (Hopewell, NJ: Ecco Press, 1995 [first published 1972]), 23–24; Mark Ribowsky, *A Complete History of the Negro Leagues* (New York: Birch Lane Press, 1995), 275.
13. *Kansas City Call*, December 29, 1939; November 22, 1940; September 5, 1941; October 27, 1944.
14. *Kansas City Call*, March 2, 1945.
15. *Kansas City Call*, April 13, 1945.
16. *Kansas City Call*, April 27, 1945.
17. *Kansas City Call*, May 4, 1945.
18. *Kansas City Call*, June 1, 1945.
19. *Kansas City Call*, June 8, 1945.
20. *Kansas City Call*, June 15, 1945.
21. *Kansas City Call*, June 22, 1945.
22. *Kansas City Call*, July 6, 1945.
23. *Kansas City Call*, July 13, 1945.
24. *Kansas City Call*, July 27, 1945.
25. Ribowsky, *A Complete History* 275.
26. Robinson, *I Never Had It Made* 23.
27. Interview with Richard (Dick) Wilkinson conducted by Janet Bruce (10/1/79). Kansas City Monarchs Oral History Collection (K0047), Tape No. A0016–17. State Historical Society of Missouri Research Center—Kansas City. In point of fact, the Monarchs actually purchased the bus in 1941 and slept on the bus more often than Dick recalled.
28. Interview with Hilton Smith conducted by Janet Bruce (11/10/78). Kansas City Monarchs Oral History Collection (K0047), Tape No. A0009. State Historical Society of Missouri Research Center—Kansas City.
29. Robinson, *Jackie Robinson* 34–35; see also an interview with Jackie Robinson in the October 31, 1947, edition of the *Kansas City Call*.
30. Rampersad, *Jackie Robinson* 118.
31. Alan J. Pollock, *Barnstorming to Heaven: Syd Pollock and His Great Black Teams* (Tuscaloosa: University of Alabama Press, 2006), 145.
32. Interview with Hilton Smith conducted by Fay Vincent, recorded in Fay Vincent, *The Only Game in Town: Baseball Stars of the 1930s and 1940s Talk About the Game They Loved* (New York: Simon & Schuster, 2006), 95–96; Geoffrey C. Ward and Ken Burns, *Baseball: An Illustrated History* (New York: Alfred A. Knopf, 2010 [first published 1994]), 285–86; Buck O'Neil, with Steve Wolf and David Conrads, *I Was Right on Time* (New York: Simon & Schuster, 1996), 163–64; for a slightly different version of the story, see Falkner, *Great Time Coming* 63–64.
33. Rampersad, *Jackie Robinson* 117.
34. Ribowsky, *A Complete History* 275.
35. Janet Bruce, *The Kansas City Monarchs: Champions of Black Baseball* (Lawrence: University of Kansas, 1985), 105.
36. John Holway, *Voices from the Great Black Baseball Leagues* (New York: Dover, 2010 [originally published 1975]), 103.
37. John B. Holway, *Black Ball Stars, Negro League Pioneers* (Westport, CT: Meckler, 1988), 342.
38. Falkner, *Great Time Coming* 91.

39. Hogan, *Shades of Glory* 355; Holway, *Voices* 316–17; Falkner, *Great Time Coming* 93; William C. Kashatus, *Jackie and Campy: The Untold Story of Their Rocky Relationship and the Breaking of Baseball's Color Line* (Lincoln: University of Nebraska Press, 2014), 113.
40. Interview with Hilton Smith conducted by Janet Bruce (11/10/78).
41. Rampersad, *Jackie Robinson* 123.
42. Kahn, *Rickey and Robinson* 2.
43. Kahn, *Rickey and Robinson* 156–57.
44. Ward and Burns, *An Illustrated History* 284.
45. Lanctot, *Negro League Baseball* 255–56; Kahn, *Rickey and Robinson* 24.
46. Robinson, *I Never Had It Made* 25–27; Kahn, *Rickey and Robinson* ix–x, 48; Lowenfish, *Branch Rickey* 22–24; Falkner, *Great Time Coming* 104–5; Jimmy Breslin, *Branch Rickey* (New York: Penguin, 2011), 27–28. According to Falkner's source, when Arthur Mann sent Charley Thomas a copy of a book he had written with the story in it, Thomas replied that the story was exaggerated. Roger Kahn (*Rickey and Robinson*, 42) thinks that in the final analysis Rickey's was "overwhelmingly, a moral decision," as powerful as the revelation that knocked St. Paul off his horse. On Rickey's moral foundations, see Kashatus, *Jackie and Campy* 31–34.
47. Lowenfish, *Branch Rickey* 349–51.
48. Robinson, *I Never Had It Made* 29; Robinson, *Jackie Robinson* 36.
49. *Kansas City Call*, April 13, 20, 27 1945. On the Boston Red Sox tryout, see Lanctot, *Negro League Baseball* 254–58; Lester, *National Showcase* 240–42; Reisler, *Black Baseball* 8–81; Kahn, *Rickey and Robinson* 64–67; Holway, *Book of Baseball's Negro Leagues* 42; Holway, *Black Ball Stars* 341; Lowenfish, *Branch Rickey* 361–3; Reisler, *Black Baseball* 91–93; Falkner, *Great Time Coming* 101–103; Rampersad, *Jackie Robinson* 119–20.
50. Lester, *National Showcase* 243–44; Lowenfish, *Branch Rickey* 368; Kashatus, *Jackie and Campy* 44–48; Falkner, *Great Time Coming* 109; Kyle McNary, *Black Baseball: A History of African-Americans and the National Game* (London: PRC Publishing, 2003), 157.
51. Kashatus, *Jackie and Campy* 49–53; Falkner, *Great Time Coming* 106–07; Lowenfish, *Branch Rickey* 373–77; Kahn, *Rickey and Robinson* 104–08; Ward and Burns, *An Illustrated History* 286–87; Breslin, *Branch Rickey* 64–68.
52. Robinson, *Jackie Robinson* 35–38.
53. Rampersad, *Jackie Robinson* 128.
54. *Kansas City Call*, September 14, 1945.
55. *Kansas City Call*, September 21, 1945.
56. Ribowsky, *A Complete History* 276.
57. *New York Times*, October 24, 1945; *Kansas City Call*, October 26, 1945.
58. Rampersad, *Jackie Robinson* 125–29, Lowenfish, *Branch Rickey* 379.
59. *Kansas City Call*, October 26, 1945.
60. *New York Times*, October 24, 1945; see also, for example, the Daytona Beach *Evening Gazette*, October 24, 1945.
61. Bruce, *Kansas City Monarchs* 112.
62. Bruce, *Kansas City Monarchs* 114–15; Ribowsky, *A Complete History* 283; Holway, *Black Ball Stars* 341–42; Peterson, *Only the Ball Was White* 192; Hogan, *Shades of Glory* 343.
63. *Chicago Defender*, March 6, 1948.
64. *Philadelphia Independent*, February 5, 1949; cited by Lanctot, *Negro League Baseball* 280–81.
65. *Pittsburgh Courier*, November 3, 1945.
66. Bruce, *Kansas City Monarchs* 112.
67. *Des Moines Sunday Register*, May 20, 1973; cited by Lester Larry Lester, "J. L. Wilkinson: Only the Stars Come Out at Night," *Satchel Paige and Company: Essays on the Kansas City Monarchs, Their Greatest Star and the Negro Leagues*, ed. Leslie A. Heaphy (Jefferson, NC: McFarland, 2007), 20, 131.
68. *New York Times*, October 25, 1945.
69. Tygiel, *Baseball's Greatest Experiment* 86; Lowenfish, *Branch Rickey* 383; Metcalfe, *A Game for All Races* 13.
70. *New York Times*, February 21, 1948; Joe Klima, *Willie's Boys: The 1948 Birmingham Black Barons, the Last Negro League World Series, and the Making of a Baseball Legend* (Hoboken, NJ: John Wiley & Sons, 2009), 52.
71. *New York Amsterdam News* and *Baltimore Afro-American*, March 6, 1948; cited by Lester, *National Showcase* 324–25.
72. *Kansas City Call*, October 26, 1945; Hogan, *Shades of Glory* 354–55.
73. Cited by Lester, "J.L. Wilkinson" 131.
74. Cited by Kahn, *Rickey and Robinson* 179–85.
75. *Sporting News*, February 12, 1948.
76. Cited in Tygiel, *Baseball's Greatest Experiment* 86; Ribowsky, *A Complete History* 285.
77. Leroy "Satchel" Paige, as told to David L. Lipman. *Maybe I'll Pitch Forever; a Great Baseball Player Tells the Hilarious Story Behind the Legend* (Lincoln: University of Nebraska Press, 1993), 171–74; Tygiel, *Baseball's Greatest Experiment* 78; Dunkel, *Color Blind* 276.
78. Ward and Burns, *An Illustrated History* 230; O'Neil, *Right on Time* 172; Timothy M. Gay, *Satchel, Dizzy and Rapid Robert: The Wild Saga of Interracial Baseball Before Jackie Robinson* (New York: Simon & Schuster, 2010), 200.
79. James A. Riley, *Of Monarchs and Black Barons: Essays on Baseball's Negro Leagues* (Jefferson, NC: McFarland, 2012), 214–15.
80. Holway, *Voices* 15.
81. Donn Rogosin, et. al., *Invisible Men: Life in Baseball's Negro Leagues* (New York: Athenuem, 1983), 214. For other responses by Negro Leaguers, see Falkner, *Great Time Coming* 120–23.
82. Hank Aaron with Lonnie Wheeler, *I Had a Hammer: The Hank Aaron Story* (New York: HarperCollins, 1991), 14.
83. *Kansas City Call*, November 2, 1945; *Montreal Gazette*, October 27, 1945.
84. Chris Lamb, *Conspiracy of Silence: Sportswriters and the Long Campaign to Desegregate Baseball* (Lincoln: University of Nebraska Press, 2012), 299; Kahn, *Rickey and Robinson* 195; Lowenfish, *Branch Rickey* 382; Heaphy, *Negro Leagues* 182; Lanctot, *Negro League Baseball* 281; Rampersad, *Jackie Robinson* 131; Tygiel,

Baseball's Greatest Experiment 89–90; Holway, *Book of Baseball's Negro Leagues* 430.

85. Joe Posnanski, *The Soul of Baseball: A Road Trip Through Buck O'Neil's America* (New York: William Morrow, 2006), 187.
86. *Kansas City Call*, January 25 and February 1, 1946; Heaphy, *Negro Leagues* 206–07; Hogan, *Shades of Glory* 344–45.
87. *Sporting News*, February 25, 1948.
88. Kahn, *Rickey and Robinson* 21.
89. *Kansas City Call*, February 27, 1948; Lanctot, *Negro League Baseball* 297; Kahn, *Rickey and Robinson* 43, 111; Lester, *National Showcase* 258–59; Breslin, *Branch Rickey* 85–89.
90. *Kansas City Call*, October 26, 1945.
91. *Chicago Defender*, November 3, 1945.
92. *Kansas City Call*, November 2, 1945.
93. Hogan, *Shades of Glory* 339, 342, 345–46; Lester, *National Showcase* 244, 280; Kahn, *Rickey and Robinson* 44.
94. *Kansas City Call*, October 26, 1945.
95. Kashatus, *Jackie and Campy* 1.
96. *Kansas City Call*, October 26, 1945.
97. Holway, *Book of Baseball's Negro Leagues* 431.

Chapter Ten

1. *Kansas City Call*, April 12, 1946.
2. T. Y. Baird Collection, Kansas Collection, RH MS 414, Box 2, Folder 13. Kenneth Spencer Research Library, University of Kansas Libraries.
3. Neil Lanctot, *Negro League Baseball: The Rise and Ruin of a Black Institution* (Philadelphia: University of Pennsylvania Press, 2004), 200.
4. Baird Collection, Box 2, Folder 13.
5. Baird Collection, Box 1, Folder 9.
6. Baird Collection, Box 3, Folder 22.
7. Leslie A. Heaphy, *The Negro Leagues, 1869–1960* (Jefferson, NC: McFarland, 2003), 125–27.
8. *Kansas City Call*, March 5 and March 29, 1946.
9. *Kansas City Call*, May 17, 1946.
10. *Kansas City Call*, May 31 and June 7, 1946.
11. *Kansas City Call*, July 5 and August 2, 1946.
12. *Kansas City Call*, July 19, 1946.
13. *Kansas City Call*, August 16, 1946.
14. *Kansas City Call*, September 23, 1946; June 20 and 27, 1947.
15. *Kansas City Call*, September 6, 1946; Leroy "Satchel" Paige, as told to David L. Lipman, *Maybe I'll Pitch Forever; a Great Baseball Player Tells the Hilarious Story Behind the Legend* (Lincoln: University of Nebraska Press, 1993), 179.
16. *Kansas City Call*, May 17 and July 26, 1946.
17. Sources for the 1946 World Series: *Kansas City Call*, September 13, 20, 27 and October 4, 11 1946; Larry Lester, "J. L. Wilkinson: Only the Stars Come Out at Night," *Satchel Paige and Company: Essays on the Kansas City Monarchs, Their Greatest Star and the Negro Leagues*, ed. Leslie A. Heaphy (Jefferson, NC: McFarland, 2007), 129; Lawrence Hogan, *Shades of Glory: The Negro Leagues and the Story of African-American Baseball* (Washington, D.C.: National Geographic, 2006), 320; John B. Holway, *The Complete Book of Baseball's Negro Leagues: The Other Half of Baseball History* (Fern Park, NJ: Hastings House, 2001), 438–440; James A. Riley, *Of Monarchs and Black Barons: Essays on Baseball's Negro Leagues* (Jefferson, NC: McFarland, 2012), 162–63; Buck O'Neil, with Steve Wolf and David Conrads, *I Was Right on Time* (New York: Simon & Schuster, 1996), 175–78; Kyle McNary, *Black Baseball: A History of African-Americans and the National Game* (London: PRC Publishing, 2003), 120, 122–23; Frazier "Slow" Robinson, with Paul Bauer, *Catching Dreams: My Life in the Negro Baseball Leagues* (Syracuse: Syracuse University Press, 1999), 146–47.
18. Sources for the Feller and Paige All-Stars Tour: *Kansas City Call*, July 19, September 27, October 4 and 18, November 1 and 15, 1946; Fay Vincent, *The Only Game in Town: Baseball Stars of the 1930s and 1940s Talk About the Game They Loved* (New York: Simon & Schuster, 2006), 46–49; William H. and Nathan B. Young, Jr., "The Story of the Kansas City Monarchs," *Your Kansas City and Mine* (Kansas City: Midwest Afro-American Genealogy Interest Coalition, 1950), 70–71; Janet Bruce, *The Kansas City Monarchs: Champions of Black Baseball* (Lawrence: University of Kansas, 1985), 105; Thomas Barthel, *Baseball Barnstorming and Exhibition Games, 1901–1962: A History of Off-Season Major League Play* (Jefferson, NC: McFarland, 2007), 147–52; Timothy M. Gay, *Satchel, Dizzy and Rapid Robert: The Wild Saga of Interracial Baseball Before Jackie Robinson* (New York: Simon & Schuster, 2010), 220–44; O'Neil, *Right on Time* 155–56.
19. *Kansas City Call*, March 14, 1947.
20. Reprinted in the *Kansas City Call*, May 30, 1947.
21. *Kansas City Call*, April 18, 1947.
22. *Kansas City Call*, July 13, 1962.
23. *Kansas City Call*, January 31, 1947.
24. *Kansas City Call*, January 10, 1947.
25. *Kansas City Call*, August 1 and 8, 1947.
26. *Kansas City Call*, June 13, 1947.
27. Interview with Richard (Dick) Wilkinson conducted by Janet Bruce (10/1/79). Kansas City Monarchs Oral History Collection (K0047), Tape No. A0016-17. State Historical Society of Missouri Research Center—Kansas City.
28. Hogan, *Shades of Glory* 346; Lanctot, *Negro League Baseball* 313–18.
29. *Kansas City Call*, July 11, 1947.
30. *New York Amsterdam News*, July 26, 1947.
31. *Kansas City Call*, August 1, 1947.
32. *Kansas City Call*, August 22, 1947.
33. *Kansas City Call*, August 29 and September 5, 1947; Joe Posnanski, *The Soul of Baseball: A Road Trip Through Buck O'Neil's America* (New York: William Morrow, 2006), 110–14.
34. Lanctot, *Negro League Baseball* 325–26.
35. Lanctot, *Negro League Baseball* 327–28.
36. Interview with Richard (Dick) Wilkinson conducted by Janet Bruce (10/1/79).
37. Baird Collection, Box 3, Folder 24.
38. *Kansas City Star*, February 12, 1948.
39. Baird Collection, Box 2, Folder 13. Baird apparently ignored the $6,000 monthly cap for players' salaries approved by NNL and NAL owners before the 1948 season.

40. *Kansas City Kansan,* February 12, 1948.
41. Interview with James "Cool Papa" Bell conducted by Arthur Shaffer and Charles Korr (9/8/71). University of Missouri–St. Louis, Archive & Manuscript Division (T015).
42. Holway, *Voices* 129.
43. Interview with Richard (Dick) Wilkinson (10/1/79).
44. Alan J. Pollock, *Barnstorming to Heaven: Syd Pollock and His Great Black Teams* (Tuscaloosa: University of Alabama Press, 2006), 62–63.
45. Young and Young, "The Story of the Kansas City Monarchs" 129.
46. Undated article, Baird Collection.
47. O'Neil, *Right on Time* 181–84.
48. Arlene Howard, with Ralph Wimbish, *Elston and Me: The Story of the First Black Yankee* (Columbia: University of Missouri Press, 2001), 18, 20.
49. Undated article, Baird Collection.
50. Howard, *Elston and Me* 21.
51. Baird Collection, Box 1, Folder 24; Joe Klima, *Willie's Boys: The 1948 Birmingham Black Barons, the Last Negro League World Series, and the Making of a Baseball Legend* (Hoboken, NJ: John Wiley & Sons, 2009), 274.
52. Baird Collection, Box 1, Folder 15.
53. Baird Collection, Box 1, Folder 24.
54. Howard, *Elston and Me* 22; Klima, *Willie's Boys* 274–75.
55. Howard, *Elston and Me* 36.
56. Young and Young, "The Story of the Kansas City Monarchs" 129.
57. Klima, *Willie's Boys* 121–25.
58. Klima, *Willie's Boys* 149; Holway, *Book of Baseball's Negro Leagues* 457–58.
59. Hogan, *Shades of Glory* 346.
60. *Kansas City Call,* January 14, 1949.
61. Baird Collection, Box 1, Folder 9.
62. Baird Collection, Box 1, Folder 9.
63. Baird Collection, Box 1, Folder 10.
64. Lanctot, *Negro League Baseball* 343–44, 348; Klima, *Willie's Boys* 166.
65. Baird Collection, Box 1, Folder 24.
66. Baird Collection, Box 1, Folder 15.
67. *Kansas City Star,* May 20, 1949.
68. Michael Harkness-Roberto and Leslie A. Heaphy, "The Monarchs: A Brief History of the Franchise," *Satchel Paige and Company: Essays on the Kansas City Monarchs, Their Greatest Star and the Negro Leagues,* ed. Leslie Heaphy (Jefferson, NC: McFarland, 2007), 106–07.
69. Hogan, *Shades of Glory* 359.
70. Klima, *Willie's Boys* 201–03, 279.
71. *Sporting News,* April 19 and May 10, 1950.
72. Young and Young, "The Story of the Kansas City Monarchs" 129.
73. Baird Collection, Box 1, Folders 24 and 17.
74. Baird Collection, Box 2, Folders 13 and 14.
75. Heaphy, *The Negro Leagues* 216.
76. Baird Collection, Box 1, Folder 24.
77. Baird Collection, Box 2, Folders 13 and 14.
78. *Kansas City Call,* March 10, 1950.
79. Hogan, *Shades of Glory* 363.
80. Baird Collection, Box 1, Folder 10.
81. Baird Collection, Box 1, Folder 11.
82. Hogan, *Shades of Glory* 363.
83. Lanctot, *Negro League Baseball* 376–77.
84. Baird Collection, Box 1, Folder 16.
85. Pollock, *Barnstorming to Heaven* 225, 228; Klima, *Willie's Boys* 275, 278. Hank Aaron with Lonnie Wheeler, *I Had a Hammer: The Hank Aaron Story* (New York: HarperCollins, 1991), 37; Lanctot, *Negro League Baseball* 376–80.
86. Baird Collection, Box 1, Folder 15; http://www.baseball-reference.com/bullpen/ Jim_LaMarque (accessed 11/29/15).
87. Heaphy, *The Negro Leagues* 216–17.
88. Baird Collection, Box 1, Folder 9.
89. Lanctot, *Negro League Baseball* 381–82; Riley, *Of Monarchs and Black Barons* 224–26.
90. Baird Collection, Box 1, Folder 53.
91. *Kansas City Call,* June 12, 1953.
92. O'Neil, *Right on Time* 190.
93. Baird Collection, Box 1, Folder 24.
94. Baird Collection, Box 1, Folder 24; Klima, *Willie's Boys* 274.
95. O'Neil, *Right on Time* 191; Holway, *Voices* 129; Bruce, *Kansas City Monarchs* 11; Vincent, *The Only Game in Town* 98–99; Klima, *Willie's Boys* 274–75.
96. Lanctot, *Negro League Baseball* 382–84.
97. Riley, *Of Monarchs and Black Barons* 226; Ackmann, *Curveball* 168, 172–82; Lester and Miller, *Black Baseball in Kansas City* 78.
98. Ackman, *Curveball* 187.
99. Bob Gibson and Phil Pope, *From Ghetto to Glory: The Story of Bob Gibson* (Englewood Cliffs, NJ: Prentice Hall, 1996), 21–22; O'Neil, *Right on Time* 194.
100. Ackman, *Curveball* 188.
101. Baird Collection, Box 1, Folder 3.
102. Ackmann, *Curveball* 189–90. Note: O'Neil says, "There wasn't much resentment against her, because the other players knew the team was fighting for survival and she helped at the gate" (O'Neil, *Right on Time* 195).
103. Baird Collection, Box 3, Folder 26.
104. Baird Collection, Box 1, Folder 3; Heaphy, *The Negro Leagues* 104.
105. Lanctot, *Negro League Baseball* 382.
106. Lester, "J.L. Wilkinson" 136.
107. Hogan, *Shades of Glory* 370.
108. Baird Collection, Box 3, Folder 26.
109. Baird Collection, Box 1, Folder 9.
110. Lanctot, *Negro League Baseball* 384–85.
111. Baird Collection. Box 4, Folder 28.
112. Baird Collection, Box 1, Folder 3.
113. Hogan, *Shades of Glory* 370.
114. Lanctot, *Negro League Baseball* 386.
115. Interview with Ted Rasberry conducted by Janet Bruce (10/2/79). Kansas City Monarchs Oral History Collection (K0047), Tape No. A0020-21. State Historical Society of Missouri Research Center—Kansas City; Brent P. Kelly, *The Negro Leagues Revisited: Conversations with 66 More Baseball Heroes* (Jefferson, NC: McFarland, 2000), 336–41.
116. Bruce, *Kansas City Monarchs* 126.
117. Baird Collection, Box 1, Folder 3.

118. Pollock, *Barnstorming to Heaven* 320.
119. Harkness-Roberto and Heaphy, "The Monarchs" 106.
120. Bruce, *Kansas City Monarchs* 126; O'Neil, *Right on Time* 195.
121. Lanctot, *Negro League Baseball* 386; Hogan, *Shades of Glory* 371.
122. Klima, *Willie's Boys* 276.
123. *Kansas City Call,* July 13, 1962.
124. *Kansas City Star,* July 2, 1962.
125. Steve Penn, "No Buck, but Hall to Induct a KC Man," *Kansas City Star,* June 13, 2006.
126. Doug Cook, "Son of Legendary Executive Heads Off to Hall of Fame," *The Daily Courier,* July 30, 2006. J.L. Wilkinson File, National Baseball Hall of Fame, Cooperstown, NY.
127. Interview with Richard (Dick) Wilkinson, conducted by Janet Bruce (10/1/79). Kansas City Monarchs Oral History Collection (K0047), Tape No. 16–17. State Historical Society of Missouri Research Center—Kansas City.
128. Personal interviews conducted by the author with Diane Pond, Sharon Brescian, and Ed Catron (6/25/14, 7/14/14, 8/4/14, 10/11/14).
129. *Kansas City Call,* July 4, 1947.
130. Interview with Alberta (Mrs. Quincy) Jordan Penn (Filmore), conducted by Janet Bruce (9/18/79). Kansas City Monarchs Oral History Collection (K0047), Tape No. A0013 (but listed on index as 14). State Historical Society of Missouri Research Center—Kansas City.
131. Personal interviews conducted by the author with Ed Catron (6/25/14, 7/14/14, 10/11/14).
132. *Kansas City Call,* September 4, 1964.
133. Holway, *Black Ball Stars* 342.
134. Holway, *Voices* 87.
135. Lester, "J.L. Wilkinson" 136.
136. Cited by Sharon Rice, "Duo Hopes Relative Will Be Named to Baseball Hall of Fame," *The Friday Flyer* (January 20, 2006). J. L. Wilkinson File, National Baseball Hall of Fame, Cooperstown, New York.
137. Young and Young, "The Story of the Kansas City Monarchs" 128–29.

Epilogue

1. William McNeil, *Cool Papas and Double Duties: The All-Time Greats of the Negro Leagues* (Jefferson, NC: McFarland, 2001), 3–5.
2. Buck O'Neil, with Steve Wolf and David Conrads, *I Was Right on Time* (New York: Simon & Schuster, 1996), 222.
3. John B. Holway, *The Complete Book of Baseball's Negro Leagues: The Other Half of Baseball History* (Fern Park, NJ: Hastings House, 2001), 463–64.
4. Sharon Rice, "Duo Hopes Relative Will Be Named to Baseball Hall of Fame," *The Friday Flyer* (January 20, 2006). J. L. Wilkinson File, National Baseball Hall of Fame, Cooperstown, New York.
5. See *Kansas City Call,* February 24, March 3, July 28, 2006.
6. Jeff Passan, "Monarchs Owner Elected," *The Kansas City Star,* February 28, 2006, C-7.
7. Sam Mellinger, "J. L. Wilkinson: He Was a Man Apart," *Kansas City Star,* July 30, 2006, C1, 12.
8. Geoffrey C. Ward and Ken Burns, *Baseball: An Illustrated History* (New York: Alfred A. Knopf, 2010 [first published 1994]), 231.
9. Joe Posnanski, *The Soul of Baseball: A Road Trip Through Buck O'Neil's America* (New York: William Morrow, 2006), 164–65.

Bibliography

Aaron, Hank, with Lonnie Wheeler. *I Had a Hammer: The Hank Aaron Story.* New York: HarperCollins, 1991.

Ackmann, Martha. *Curveball: The Remarkable Story of Toni Stone, the First Woman to Play Professional Baseball in the Negro League.* Chicago: Lawrence Hill Books, 2010.

Alexander, Charles C. *Breaking the Slump: Baseball in the Depression Era.* New York: Columbia University Press, 2002.

"All Nations Team Plays in Duluth," *St. Paul (MN) Northwestern Bulletin,* June 23, 1923, C6.

Allen, Newt. Interview conducted by Janet Bruce, November 7, 1978. Kansas City Monarchs Oral History Collection (K0047), Tape No. A0005. State Historical Society of Missouri Research Center—Kansas City.

———. Interview conducted by John Holway, [no month or day specified] 1970. University of Missouri–St. Louis, Archive & Manuscript Division (T208).

Baird, T. Y., Papers, 1913–1992. Kansas Collection. Kenneth Spencer Research Library, University of Kansas Libraries.

Barthel, Thomas. *Baseball Barnstorming and Exhibition Games, 1901–1962: A History of Off-Season Major League Play.* Jefferson, NC: McFarland, 2007.

Baylis, Hank. Interview conducted by Janet Bruce, November 7, 1978. Kansas City Monarchs Oral History Collection (K0047), Tape No. A0004. State Historical Society of Missouri Research Center—Kansas City.

Beer, John. "Order Banning Use of Own Buses Worries Negro League." *Newark Sunday Call,* March 14, 1943.

Bell, James "Cool Papa." Interview conducted by Arthur Shaffer and Charles Korr, September 8, 1971. University of Missouri–St. Louis, Archives and Manuscript Division (T015).

"Bismarck Loses to All-Nations in Cold Game Here Last Night." *Bismarck Tribune,* June 9, 1928.

Breslin, Jimmy. *Branch Rickey.* New York: Penguin, 2011.

Brescian, Sharon. Interview conducted by author, October 11, 2014.

Bruce, Janet. *The Kansas City Monarchs: Champions of Black Baseball.* Lawrence: University of Kansas, 1985.

Catron, Ed. Personal interviews conducted by author, June 25 and October 11, 2014.

Catron, Gladys Wilkinson. Interview conducted by Janet Bruce, November 17, 1980. Kansas City Monarchs Oral History Collection (K0047), Tape No. A0022–23. State Historical Society of Missouri Research Center—Kansas City.

Chadwick, Bruce. *When the Game Was Black and White: The Illustrated History of the Negro Leagues.* New York: Abbeville Press, 1992.

Christian, Ralph J. "Wilkie: James Leslie Wilkinson and the Iowa Years." *Iowa Heritage Illustrated,* Spring 2006, 38–42.

Clark, Dick, and Larry Lester, eds. *The Negro League Book.* Cleveland: Society for American Baseball Research, 1994.

"Colorful All-Nations Nine Will Play Bismarck Club Here Tonight." *Bismarck Tribune,* July 20, 1933.

Cook, Doug, "Son of Legendary Executive Heads Off to Hall of Fame." *Daily Courier,* July 30, 2006. J. L. Wilkinson File, National Baseball Hall of Fame, Cooperstown, NY.

Cottrell, Robert C. *The Best Pitcher in Baseball: The Life of Rube Foster, Negro League Giant.* New York: New York University Press, 2001.

Craft, David. *The Negro Leagues: 40 Years of Black Professional Baseball in Words and Pictures.* New York: Crescent Books, 1993.

Crasnick, Jerry. "Sharing Memories of the Negro Leagues." *Denver Post,* July 22, 1996, 6D.

Dixon, Phil S.. *Wilber "Bullet" Rogan and the Kansas City Monarchs.* Jefferson, NC: McFarland, 2010.

Drake, Bill ("Plunk"). Interview conducted by Dr. Charles Korr and Dr. Steven Hause, December

8, 1971. Negro Baseball League Project, http://shs.umsystem.edu/stlouis/manuscripts/transcripts/s0829/t0067.pdf. Accessed May 20, 2014.

Dunkel, Tom. *Color Blind: The Forgotten Team That Broke Baseball's Color Line.* New York: Atlantic Monthly Press, 2013.

Dwight, Georgia (Mrs. Eddie). Interviews conducted by Janet Bruce, November 1, 1978, and July 13, 1980. Kansas City Monarchs Oral History Collection (K0047), Tape No. A0001–3. State Historical Society of Missouri Research Center—Kansas City.

Faber, Charles, "J L. Wilkinson," SABR Baseball Biography Project. http://sabr.org/bioproj/person/db4ae51d. Accessed May 18, 2014.

Falkner, David. *Great Time Coming: The Life of Jackie Robinson from Baseball to Birmingham.* New York: Simon & Schuster, 1995.

Fredrick, Thomas. "KC Connection Began Baseball's Globalization." *Kansas City Star,* October 16, 2004, C5. J. L. Wilkinson File, National Baseball Hall of Fame, Cooperstown, NY.

Fredrick, Tom. "First There Was Baseball: Following the Globetrotters on a Path Back to Kansas City." *Kansas City Star Magazine,* January 4, 2004, 25–29. J. L. Wilkinson File, National Baseball Hall of Fame Library, Cooperstown, NY.

Gay, Timothy M. *Satchel, Dizzy and Rapid Robert: The Wild Saga of Interracial Baseball Before Jackie Robinson.* New York: Simon & Schuster, 2010.

Gibson, Bob, and Phil Pope. *From Ghetto to Glory: The Story of Bob Gibson.* Englewood Cliffs, NJ: Prentice Hall, 1996.

Green, Ben. *Spinning the Globe: The Rise, Fall, and Return to Greatness of the Harlem Globetrotters.* New York: Amistad, 2006.

Harkness-Roberto, Michael, and Leslie A. Heaphy. "The Monarchs: A Brief History of the Franchise." In *Satchel Paige and Company,* edited by Leslie A. Heaphy, 99–109. Jefferson, NC: McFarland, 2007.

Hawkins, Joel, and Terry Bertolino, *Images of America: The House of David Baseball Team.* Chicago: Arcadia, 2000.

Heaphy, Leslie A. *The Negro Leagues, 1869–1960.* Jefferson, NC: McFarland, 2003.

_____. *Satchel Paige and Company: Essays on the Kansas City Monarchs, Their Greatest Star and the Negro Leagues.* Jefferson, NC: McFarland, 2007.

Hogan, Lawrence. *Shades of Glory: The Negro Leagues and the Story of African-American Baseball.* Washington, D.C.: National Geographic, 2006.

Holway, John B. *Black Ball Stars, Negro League Pioneers.* Westport, CT: Meckler, 1988.

_____. *Black Diamonds: Life in the Negro Leagues from the Men Who Lived It.* Westport, CT: Meckler Books, 1989.

_____. "Bullet Joe and the Monarchs: Will Cooperstown Let Them?" In *Unions to Royals,* edited by Lloyd Johnson et al., 34–36. Cleveland: Society for American Baseball Research, 1996.

_____. *The Complete Book of Baseball's Negro Leagues: The Other Half of Baseball History.* Fern Park, NJ: Hastings House, 2001.

_____. *Voices from the Great Black Baseball Leagues.* New York: Dodd, Mead, 1975. (New York: De Capo, 1992; Mineola, NY: Dover, 2010 [reprinting 1992 edition]).

Housh, Leighton, "Fair Play," *Des Moines Sunday Register,* May 20, 1973. J. L. Wilkinson File, National Baseball Hall of Fame, Cooperstown, NY.

Howard, Arlene, with Ralph Wimbish. *Elston and Me: The Story of the First Black Yankee.* Columbia: University of Missouri Press, 2001.

James, Bill. *The New Bill James Historical Baseball Abstract.* New York: Free Press, 2001.

Jasper, Michael. *The All Nations Team.* N.p.: Un-Wrecked Press, 2010.

Johnson, Clifford ("Connie"). Interview conducted by Janet Bruce, November 15, 1978. Kansas City Monarchs Oral History Collection (K0047), Tape No. A0010. State Historical Society of Missouri Research Center—Kansas City.

Johnson, Lloyd, Steve Garlick, Jeff Magaliff, eds. *Unions to Royals: The Story of Professional Baseball in Kansas City.* Cleveland: Society for American Baseball Research, 1996.

Johnson, Roy. Interview conducted by Janet Bruce, January 12, 1981. Kansas City Monarchs Oral History Collection (K0047), Tape No. A0024. State Historical Society of Missouri Research Center—Kansas City.

Kahn, Roger. *Rickey and Robinson: The True, Untold Story of the Integration of Baseball.* New York: Rodale, 2014.

Kashatus, William C. *Jackie and Campy: The Untold Story of Their Rocky Relationship and the Breaking of Baseball's Color Line.* Lincoln: University of Nebraska Press, 2014.

Kelly, Brent P. *The Negro Leagues Revisited: Conversations with 66 More Baseball Heroes.* Jefferson, NC: McFarland, 2000.

Klima, Joe. *Willie's Boys: The 1948 Birmingham Black Barons, the Last Negro League World Series, and the Making of a Baseball Legend.* Hoboken, NJ: John Wiley & Sons, 2009.

Lamb, Chris. *Conspiracy of Silence: Sportswriters and the Long Campaign to Desegregate Baseball.* Lincoln: University of Nebraska Press, 2012.

Lanctot, Neil. *Negro League Baseball: The Rise and Ruin of a Black Institution.* Philadelphia: University of Pennsylvania Press, 2004.

Lester, Larry. *Baseball's First Colored World Series: The 1924 Meeting of the Hilldale Giants and Kansas City Monarchs.* Jefferson, NC: McFarland, 2006.

_____. *Black Baseball's National Showcase.* Lincoln: University of Nebraska Press, 2001.

_____. "Leroy Robert 'Satchel' Paige." *Unions to Royals*, edited by Lloyd Johnson et al., 22–23. Cleveland: Society for American Baseball Research, 1996.

_____. *Rube Foster in His Time: On the Field and in the Papers with Black Baseball's Greatest Visionary.* Jefferson, NC: McFarland, 2012.

Lester, Larry, and Sammy Miller. *Black Baseball in Kansas City.* Charleston, SC: Arcadia, 2000.

Lowenfish, Lee. *Branch Rickey: Baseball's Ferocious Gentleman.* Lincoln: University of Nebraska Press, 2007.

Luke, Bob. *The Most Famous Woman in Baseball: Effa Manley and the Negro Leagues.* Washington, D.C.: Potomac, 2011.

McNary, Kyle. *Black Baseball: A History of African-Americans and the National Game.* London: PRC, 2003.

McNeil, William. *Cool Papas and Double Duties: The All-Time Greats of the Negro Leagues.* Jefferson, NC: McFarland, 2001.

Mellinger, Sam. "J. L. Wilkinson: He Was a Man Apart." *Kansas City Star*, July 30, 2006, C1, 12.

Metcalfe, Henry. *A Game for All Races: An Illustrated History of the Negro Leagues.* New York: Metro Books, 2000.

Naughton, John. "Invisible Man Among Invisible Men." *Des Moines Sunday Register*, July 10, 2005, 1–2C.

O'Neil, Buck, with Steve Wolf and David Conrads. *I Was Right on Time.* New York: Simon & Schuster, 1996.

Overmyer, Jim. "J. L. Wilkinson: Negro Leagues Ballot Candidate." *Baseball Hall of Fame News*, February 24, 2006. J. L. Wilkinson File, National Baseball Hall of Fame, Cooperstown, New York.

Paige, Leroy ("Satchel"), as told to David L. Lipman. *Maybe I'll Pitch Forever; A Great Baseball Player Tells the Hilarious Story Behind the Legend.* Lincoln: University of Nebraska Press, 1993. First published 1962 by Doubleday.

Passan, Jeff. "Monarchs Owner Elected." *Kansas City Star*, February 28, 2006, C-1, 7.

Penn, Alberta (Mrs. Quincy Jordan Gilmore). Interview conducted by Janet Bruce, September 18, 1979. Kansas City Monarchs Oral History Collection (K0047). Tape No. A0013 (but listed on index as 14). State Historical Society of Missouri Research Center—Kansas City.

Penn, Steve. "No Buck, but Hall to Induct a KC Man." *Kansas City Star*, June 13, 2006.

Peterson, Robert. *Only the Ball Was White.* New York: Oxford University Press, 1970.

Pollock, Alan J. *Barnstorming to Heaven: Syd Pollock and His Great Black Teams.* Tuscaloosa: University of Alabama Press, 2006.

Pond, Diane. Personal interviews conducted by the author, August 4 and October 11, 2014.

Posnanski, Joe. *The Soul of Baseball: A Road Trip Through Buck O'Neil's America.* New York: William Morrow, 2006.

Rampersad, Arnold. *Jackie Robinson: A Biography.* New York: Alfred A. Knopf, 1997.

Rasberry, Ted. Interview conducted by Janet Bruce, October 2, 1979. Kansas City Monarchs Oral History Collection (K0047), Tape No. A0020–21. State Historical Society of Missouri Research Center—Kansas City.

Reisler, Jim. *Black Writers, Black Baseball: An Anthology of Articles from Black Sportswriters Who Covered the Negro Leagues.* Revised edition. Jefferson, NC: McFarland, 2007.

Renfroe, Othello "Chico." Interview conducted by Janet Bruce, January 29, 1980. Kansas City Monarchs Oral History Collection (K0047), Tape No. A0019. State Historical Society of Missouri Research Center—Kansas City.

Ribowsky, Mark. *A Complete History of the Negro Leagues.* New York: Birch Lane Press, 1995.

Rice, Sharon. "Duo Hopes Relative Will Be Named to Baseball Hall of Fame." *Canyon Lake (Ca.) Friday Flyer*, January 20, 2006. J. L. Wilkinson File, National Baseball Hall of Fame, Cooperstown, New York.

Riley, James A. *The Biographical Encyclopedia of the Negro Baseball Leagues.* New York: Carroll and Graf, 1994.

_____. *Of Monarchs and Black Barons: Essays on Baseball's Negro Leagues.* Jefferson, NC: McFarland, 2012.

Rives, Tim. "Tom Baird: A Challenge to the Modern Memory of the Kansas City Monarchs." In *Satchel Paige and Company*, edited by Leslie Heaphy, 144–156. Jefferson, NC: McFarland, 2007.

Robinson, Frazier ("Slow"), with Paul Bauer. *Catching Dreams: My Life in the Negro Baseball Leagues.* Syracuse: Syracuse University Press, 1999.

Robinson, Jackie, with Alfred Duckett. *I Never Had It Made: An Autobiography.* New York: G. P. Putnam's Sons, 1972. Reprint: Hopewell, NJ: Ecco Press, 1995.

Robinson, Rachel, and Lee Daniels. *Jackie Robinson: An Intimate Portrait.* New York: Harry N. Abrams, 1996.

Rogosin, Donn. *Invisible Men: Life in Baseball's Negro Leagues.* New York: Athenuem, 1983.

Smith, Hilton. Interview conducted by Janet Bruce, November 10, 1978. Kansas City Monarchs Oral History Collection (K0047), Tape No. A0009. State Historical Society of Missouri Research Center—Kansas City.

Spivey, Donald. *"If You Were Only White": The Life of Leroy "Satchel" Paige.* Columbia: University of Missouri Press, 2012.

Staten, Vince. *Ol' Diz: A Biography of Dizzy Dean.* New York: HarperCollins, 1992.

Sweeney, Robert. Interview conducted by Janet Bruce, January 12, 1981. Kansas City Monarchs Oral History Collection (K0047), Tape No. A0025. State Historical Society of Missouri Research Center—Kansas City.

Trouppe, Quincy. *20 Years Too Soon: Prelude to Major-League Integrated Baseball.* Los Angeles: S & S, 1977.

Tye, Larry. *Satchel: The Life and Times of an American Legend.* New York: Random House, 2009.

Tygiel, Jules. *Baseball's Greatest Experiment: Jackie Robinson and His Legacy.* New York: Oxford University Press, 1983.

Vincent, Fay. *The Only Game in Town: Baseball Stars of the 1930s and 1940s Talk About the Game They Loved.* New York: Simon & Schuster, 2006.

Ward, Geoffrey C., and Ken Burns. *Baseball: An Illustrated History.* New York: Alfred A. Knopf, 2010. First published 1994.

White, Maury. "A Forgotten Chapter of Baseball History: Remarkable Iowan Pioneered Black Teams, Women Players." *Des Moines Sunday Register,* August 21, 1994, 11D–12D. J. L. Wilkinson File, National Baseball Hall of Fame, Cooperstown, NY.

White, Sol. *Sol White's History of Colored Baseball: With Other Documents on the Early Black Game.* Compiled and introduced by Jerry Malloy. Lincoln: University of Nebraska Press, 1995. White's *Official Baseball Guide* first published 1907 by H. Walter Schlichter.

Wickstrom, Harriett Baird. Interview conducted by Janet Bruce, October 2, 1979. Kansas City Monarchs Oral History Collection (K0047), Tape No. A0018. State Historical Society of Missouri Research Center—Kansas City.

Wilkinson, Richard (Dick). Interview conducted by Janet Bruce, October 1, 1979. Kansas City Monarchs Oral History Collection (K0047), Tape No. A0016–17. State Historical Society of Missouri Research Center—Kansas City.

Williams, Jessie. Interview conducted by Janet Bruce, January 16, 1979. Kansas City Monarchs Oral History Collection (K0047), Tape No. 12. State Historical Society of Missouri Research Center—Kansas City.

Young, Maurice. Interview by Janet Bruce, November 8, 1978. Kansas City Monarchs Oral History Collection (K0047), Tape No. A0008. State Historical Society of Missouri Research Center—Kansas City.

Young, William A. *John Tortes "Chief" Meyers: A Baseball Biography.* Jefferson, NC: McFarland, 2012.

Young, William H., and Nathan B. Young, Jr. "The Story of the Kansas City Monarchs," *Your Kansas City and Mine.* Kansas City: Midwest Afro-American Genealogy Interest Coalition, 1950.

Index

Numbers in **_bold italics_** indicate pages with photographs.

Aaron, Hank 152, 167, 176, 182
Adams, "Packinghouse" 103, 200
admission prices 6, 20, 28, 56–7, 94, 100, 102, 122, 134, 137, 168
Alexander, Grover Cleveland 17, 41, 81–2, **_83_**, 85, 87, 90–1, 94–5, 125
Alexander, Ted 142–3, 202–5
Algona, Iowa 7, 8
Algona Brownies 10, 24
All-Nations Team 4, 13, **_14_**, 15, **_16_**, **_17_**, 18–22, 28–29, 31–2, **_33_**, 36, 38, 49, 55, 59, 79, 80, **_85_**, 95, 108, 115, 178, 184, 187
All-Star Game, East-West *see* East-West All Star Game
All-star team, Babe Ruth 39
All-star teams: Major League 25, 29, 39, 42, 81, 87–8, 92, **_93_**, 95, 97, 101, 107, 116, 122, 140, **_162_**, 163, 174, 178; Negro Leagues 60, 91, 97, 99, 105
All-Stars: Bob Feller 160–1, **_162_**, 163; Dean Brothers 92–3, 95, 106, 107; Satchel Paige 111–2, 114, 121, 137, **_162_**
Allen, Newt 21, 33, 36–7, 42, 45, **_46_**, 48, 50–52, 55, 58, 60–1, 73–5, 80, 84, 86, **_89_**, 92, 100–1, 122, 125, 127, 145, 181, 188, 193–205
Allen, Touissant "Tommy" 48, 51
American Association 23, 35, 75, 86, 101, 105, 138
American Giants, Chicago *see* Chicago American Giants
Anson, Cap 23
Antique Shop 113, 183
Articles of Confederation, Negro National League 53–4
Associated Negro Press (ANP) 39, 47, 89, 120, 129, 141, 163
Association Park 6, 33, 38–40, 44
Atlanta Black Crackers 98, 116, 200
Atlanta Braves 116
Atlantic City Bacharach Giants 28, 34, 40, 54, 59, 61, 195–6
Austin, Minnesota 20

Baird, T.Y. "Tom" 2, 30–2, 34, 37, 71, 77, **_82_**, **_85_**, 86, 90, **_93_**, 94, 98, 101, 109, 112, 114, 115, 116, 119–21, 123–4, 127, 129, **_130_**, 131–2, 134, 136–8, 142, 148, 150–2, 155, 157–8, 161, 165–82, 184, 209n30
Baltimore Afro-American 6, 152
Baltimore Black Sox 24, 40, 48, 53, 107
Baltimore Orioles 5, 121
Bankhead, Sammy 90, 99, 141, 188, 198
Banks, Ernie 167, 171, 174, 178, 182, 188
Barnes, Frank 171, 174
Barnes, Virgil 19
Barnhill, Dave 141, 203
barnstorming 4, 5–6, 11, **_14_**, 20, 28, 35, 39, 40, 58, 66, 68–70, 76, 78–80, 85–7, 89, 90, **_93_**, 95, 97, 98, 101, 104, 109, 111, 114, 116, 120, 122, 124, 126–7, 146, 157, 161, **_162_**, 163, 165, 172, 175, **_177_**, 179, 181, 197, 198, 199
Barrow, Ed 8
Bartley, Homer "Hop" 45, 194–5
beauty contests 6, 111, 120
Beckwith, Carl 38–9, 45
Bell, Clifford "Cliff"/"Cherry" **_46_**, 48, 50–51, 59, 61, 192–6, 198
Bell, James "Cool Papa" 45, 55, 84, 86, **_89_**, 99, 107, 111–2, 140, 167, **_168_**, 171–2, 178, 186, 188, 198
Bell, William **_46_**, 48, 50–2, 56, 73, 188, 192–8
Bender, Albert "Chief" 20
Benswanger, William E. 141
Beverly, Charles 80, 86, **_89_**, 94, 198–9
Bibbs, Junius "Rainey" 103, 200–201
Birmingham, Alabama Black Barons 41, 44, 49, 56, 60–1, 98, 100, 107, 127, 132, 136, 137, 158, 171–2, 178, 180, 194–7, 200–5
Bismarck Churchills 94–6, 107–8, 162
Blackburn, Hugh 29, 191–2

Blattner, Frank 19, 192; *see also* Blukoi, Frank
Bloomer girls teams 10–11
Blount, John "Tenny" 27–9
Blues Stadium 94, **_162_**, 165, 175
Blukoi, Frank 16, 19, 21, 29, 191; *see also* Blattner, Frank
Bolden, Ed 6, 40, 41, 45, 47–49, 175
booking agents 28, 31, 40, 78–79, **_82_**, 98, 109, 124, 127, 135, 142, 172
Boosters, Monarch 6, 56–8, 100, 103, 122, 135
Boston All Stars 12
Boston Bloomer Girls 11
Boston Braves 147–8, 173, 171, 176
Boston Red Sox 147, 162–3, 171
Boudreau, Lou 114, 116
Bowe, Randolph 103, 200–1
Bradley, Frank 103, 199–202
Breadon, Sam 74
Brescian, Sharon 2, 4, 182
Brewer, Chet 22, 33, 39, 64, 73, 76, 80, 86–7, **_89_**, 91–2, 94, 96, 99, 108, 110, 112–3, 188, 194–202
Briggs, Otto 48, 50, 52
Briggs Stadium 143, 176–7
Brooklyn, Iowa 8
Brooklyn Brown Dodgers 142, 149
Brooklyn Dodgers 2, 8, 10, 14, 23, 25, 87, 97, 136, 139, 141–2, 146–52, 154–5, 158, 163–6, 172, 175, 178–80
Brooklyn Royal Giants 40, 61
Brown, Elsie 58
Brown, Mordecai "Three Finger" 82
Brown, Stirling 102
Brown, Willard "*Ese Hombre*" 94, 100–3, 125, 128, 132, **_133_**, 134, 145, 159–60, 162–3, 188 196–202, 204–5
Bruce, Janet 2, 21, 31, 56, 71, 97, 121, 191
Bryant, Allen "Lefty" 81, 120, 201–5
Burley, Dan 89, 106, 136
Burns, Ken 1, **_104_**, 187

227

Index

Buses, Monarchs 37, 57–58, 62, 71, 73, 78, 81, 97, 103, 119, 127, 129–32, 144–5, 161, *177*, 181
businesses, African American 24–6, 32, 53, 102
Buxton, Iowa Wonders 9, 10

Call, Kansas City see *Kansas City Call*
Campanella, Roy 141, 151, 163, 187
Canada 6, 12, 15, 45, 68, 78, 85–6, 89–91, 95, 97, 104, 110–1, 119, 124, 127
Carr, George "Tank" 29, *30*, 34–5, 37, 51, 192
Catron, Ed 2, 4, 9, 182, 183, 212n57
Catron, Gladys Wilkinson 2, 12, 14, 71, 184
Cee Bee, Jay 181, 184
Chadwick, Bruce 6
Chandler, Happy 150, 154, 162–3
Charleston, Oscar 28, 76, 107, 140, 142, 186
Chase Brothers Grocery 8
Chattanooga Lookouts 107, 213n96
Chicago American Giants 24–5, 27, 33–40, 42–45, 49, 53–4, 57–9, 61, 83, 85–6, 88, 90, 96, 98, 100, 103–4, 111–2, 120–2, 125–6, 132, 136, 143, 158, 174, 176, 181, 192–4, 197, 200–5
Chicago Cubs 40, 83, 96, 157, 173–5, 178
Chicago Defender 6, 15, *17*, 25, 27–8, 33, 35, 38, 45, 47, 51, 54, 81, 87, 101, 152
Chicago Giants 27, 32
Chicago Mills 80, 85
Chicago Union Giants 15, 57
Chicago White Sox 5, 15, 19, 88, 121, 174
Chicago White Stockings 23
Chinese All-Stars 94
Christian, Ralph 8
Churchill, Neil 95, 107–8
Cincinnati Clowns 98, 129, 132, 134–5, 203–4
Cincinnati Cubans 35
Cincinnati Tigers 98, 100, 200
Ciudad Trujillo 99, 108
civil rights 27, 120, 155, 165
Clark, Bill 14
Clark, Dick 2, 187
Clark, Jane Forbes *188*
Cleveland Bears/Buckeyes 98, 147, 162, 201, 202–5
Cleveland Cubs 107
Cleveland Indians 114–6
Cleveland Tate Stars 35
Cleveland Tigers 63
Clowns *see* Cincinnati Clowns; Ethiopian Clowns; Indianapolis Clowns
Cobb, Ty 16, 105
Cochrane, Mickey 65
Cockrell, Phil 48–50, 56
Coleman, Clarence "Pops" 19
Comiskey Field 88, 121, 125–6, 132, 136, 159

constitutions, Negro Leagues 26, 28, 32, 34, 151
contracts 23, 25, 28, 31, 34–5, 45, 47, 54, 60, 63–4, 69, 79, 107–9, 113, 115–6, 121–3, 137, 140, 141–2, 146–52, 164, 167–8, 170–1, 173–4, 176, 178–80
Cooper, Alfred "Army" 63, 181, 193, 196–8
Cooper, Andy "Lefty" 29, 63, 75, 94–96, 99, 100–3, 120, 125, 188, 196–202
Cooperstown, New York *see* Hall of Fame, National Baseball
Cornelius, Slug 79, 101
Cottrell, Robert 77
Cox, "Indian Joe" 103, 200
Crawford, Sam 16, 22, *30*, 34, 37, 42, 90, 94, 192–4, 198–9
Crawfords, Pittsburgh 81, 86, 88, 90, 92, 106–9, 141
Crosley Field 121, 129
Crow, Sam 19
"Cuban," meaning of 24
Cuban baseball players 13, 15–17, 18–19, 22, 24, 49, 52, 57. 59, 108, 124
Cuban Giants 23–4, 121, 179
Cuban House of David 82, 86
Cuban Stars 27–8, 38, 42, 61, 192–97
Currie, Rube 29, *30*, 34, 39, 45, 48, 50–1, 52, 56, 58, 193–4, 198
curveball 13–15, 36, 48–9, 73, 96, 100, 103, 108, 112, 121, 128

Dandridge, Ray 186
Daniel Boone Regional Library 3
Darby, Pennsylvania 28, 40, 47
Davis, Johnny 160, 163
Day, Leon 129, 159, 187
Dayton, Ohio Marcos 27, 34, 192, 195
Dean, Jay Hanna/Jerome "Dizzy" 87, 92, *93*, *95*, 106–7, 125, 136, 138, 140
Dean, Nelson 56, 61, 195, 198
Dean, Paul "Daffy" 92, *93*, 95, 106–7
Denver Post tournament 89–91, 97, 99, 107–8, 122–3
Depression, Great 6, 22, 40, 67–8, 76–8, 80–1, 83, 88, 92, 98
Des Moines 8, 9, 11–14, 18–22, 40, 66, 69, 71, 87, 92, 101
Des Moines Demons 69–71, 87
Des Moines Register 18
Des Moines Register and Leader 9–12
Des Moines Stars 8
Detroit Stars 27–9, 33, 35, 38–9, 42, 53, 55, 60, 63, 75, 86, 98, 112, 178, 180–1, 192–7, 200
Detroit Tigers 16, 92, 95
Detroit Wolves 83
Didrikson, Mildred "Babe" 81, *84*, 90, 92
Dihigo, Martín 99, 186
DiMaggio, Joe 117, 167

DiMaggio, Vince 191, 162
Dismukes, William "Dizzy" 28, 125, 136, 151, 158, 163, 169 174, 181, 201–2
Dixon, Phil 2
Doan, Ray *82*, 90–2, 99, 101
Doby, Larry 159, 166
Dodgers, Brooklyn *see* Brooklyn Dodgers
Dominican Republic 99, 104
Donaldson, Billy 42
Donaldson, John 13, *14*, 15, *18*, 20–2, 28, 29, *30*, 32–4, 38, 42, 45, 49, 80, 85, 90, 91, 140, 145, 174, 184, 188, 191–5, 197–9
donkey ball *83*, 92
Drake, Bill "Plunk" 18–19, 21, 36, 39, 42, 45, *46*, 48–9, 51–2, 56, 69, 71, 78, 110, 115, 137, 192–5
Dubois, W.E.B. 26
Dunbar, Art 19
Duncan, Frank 34, 41, 45, *46*, 48, 50–2, 55, 60–61, 80, 86, *89*, 91, 100–1, 103, 125, 128–9, 143, *145*, 146, 151, 161, 169, 181, 192–3, 204
Durocher, Leo 5, 120, 164
Dwight, Eddie "Pee Wee" 61, *62*, 63, 94, 97, 101, 181, 196–9
Dwight, Georgia 63, 97

East-West All Star Game 6, 36, 88, 100, 105, 108, 112–3, 122, 125–7, 132, 134, 136, 145, 165, 167, 174, 178, 180–1
East-West League 83
Eastern Colored League (ECL) 1, 40–2, 44–8, 53–7, 59–61
Ebbets Field 136, 139, 142, 155, 164
Emery ball 18–19, 61, 76, 94
Enid, Oklahoma 73–74, 91, 212n23
Ethiopian Clowns 79, 91, 93, 119, 121–4, 129
Evans, Frank 19, 192
exhibition games 15, 21, 31–2, 34, 39–40, 44, 55–6, 58, 60–1, 63–4, 69–75, 78, 81, 92, 93–4, 101, 106–7, 112, 118, 126, 135–7, 142, 152, 163, 175

fastball 13, 49, 103, 106–7, 111–2, 121, 128, 163
Feller, Bob "Rapid Robert" 101, 116, 122, 125–6, 160–1, *162*, 163
Fette, Lou 101
Field of Dreams 6
Finley, Charlie 5
Flood, Curt 112
Floyd, Frank "Jew Baby" 30, *46*, 59, 111, 119, 128, 135
Foreman, Sylvester "Hooks" *30*, 120, 191–4, 196, 198
Foster, Rube 6, 20, *24*, 25–9, 33–7, 40–3, 45, 47–50, 53–4, 58–9, 77, 80, 86, 129, 186
Foster, Willie 53–4, 58–9, 80. 90–1, 100, 186–8, 198–9
Fowler, John W. "Bud" 23
Franklin, Chester Arthur "C.A." 26–7, 122, *130*, 131–2, 154

Index

Fredrick, Tom 79
Frick, Ford 154

Garner, Eddie 63
"Gashouse Gang" 87, 92,-3, 107
gate receipts 10, 2, 35, 39, 42, 43, 53, 56, 78–9, 88, 112, 135, 146, 157, 165, 167, 175, 177
Gatto, "Pops" Steno 19
Gaul, J.E. *16*, 20
Gay, Timothy 22, 90
Gehrig, Lou 65, 213*n*96
"Gentleman's Agreement" 1, 23
Gholston, Bert 42
Giant Manufacturing Company of Omaha 71
"Giants," meaning of 24
Giants, New York *see* New York Giants
Gibson, Bob 179
Gibson, Josh 1, 77, 99, 107, 117, 127–9, 132, 134, 140–1, 147, 179, 186–7
Giles, George 61, 64, 83–4, 86, *89*, 111, 195–6, 198
Gilkerson Union Giants 29, 60, 63, 64
Gilmore, Quincy "Q.J." 6, 31–2, 35, 37–8, 41, 44, 47, 49, 55–6, 59–60, 64–5, 75, *85*, 86, *89*, 102, 119, 125, 138, 158, 169, 183
Glass, Carl "Lefty" 60, 195–6
Goldsmith Hardware Store (Des Moines, Iowa) Baseball Team 13, *14*, *17*
Gorton, Peter 15
Gottlieb, Eddie 79, 110, 113, 116
Graves, Joe 20
Gray, Chester *145*, *204*
Green, Joe 27, 77
Greenberg, Hank 116
Greene, Joe 113, 121, 125, 127, 134, 161, 200–2, 204
Greenlee, Gus "Big Red" 6, 86, 88, 90, 99, 107–8, 128, 141
Griffith, Clark 140, 154
Griffith Stadium 126–7, 132, 140, 143
Grinnell College 10

Hall of Fame, National Baseball (Cooperstown, New York) 2, 4, 7, 8, 11, 15, 17–21, 24, 28, 33, 40, 46, 59, 65, 81, 82–3, 86, 92, 96, 98–9, 104, 110, 115–6, 132, 145, 148, 153, 159, 162–3, 165, 168, 178, 179, 182, 184, 186–9
Harding, "Hallie"/"Halley" 63, 174, 196–7
Harlem Globetrotters 78–9, 124, 179, 188
Harmon, W. Bea 131, 134–5, 138, 147
Harris, Leroy 86
Harris, Moocha *89*
Haskell Institute 71, 73
Hawkins, Lemuel "Lem"/"Hawk" 29, 34, 45, *46*, 48–9, 52, 61, 90, 191–6

Haynes, Sammy 127, *145*, 202–4
Heaphy, Leslie 2, 78, 191
Hernández, Ricardo "Chico" 19
Hershey, Pennsylvania 75
Hickey, Thomas 75
Highland Park Normal College 8
Hill, Pete 188
Hilldale Daisies 1, 6, 28, 34, 40, 45–53, 55–6, 61, 194
Hogan, Larry 2, 187
Holway, John 2, 36, 39, 92, 109, 127, 145, 156, 167, 184, 186, 191
Homestead Grays 64, 75, 80, 83–4, 91, 99, 124, 126–7, 132, 136, 141, 143, 147, 154, 172
Hood, Dozier *145*
Hopkins Brothers Champion Ladies Baseball Club 10
Hopkins Brothers Sporting Goods (Des Moines, Iowa) Baseball Team 8, *9*, 10, 13
Hopwood, Reginald 61, 196
Hornsby, Rogers 11, 154
Hoskins, Dave 147
House of David 69, 80–1, *82*, *83*, *84*, 85, 93, 107, 120, 127; Colored 82; Cuban 80; Eastern 87; Israelite 81, 97; original 80, 85, 87, 9–92, 94–5, 168; reorganized by Mary Purcell 82
Howard, Elston 167, 169, *170*, 141, 174, 182, 205
Hueston, William C. 60, 63, 65, 83
Hunter, Bertram 86, 198–9

Indian baseball players, American 2, 13, 19–20, 22, 51, 71, 74, 93
Indianapolis 34, 54, 68, 126
Indianapolis A.B.C.'s 17, 21, 27–33, 38, 61, 63, 85–6, 192–5, 200–1
Indianapolis Athletics 98, 200
Indianapolis Clowns 135–3, 143, 149, 158, 165, 168–9, 175–9, 181, 203–5
Indianapolis Crawfords 121, 201
Indianapolis Freeman 25, 27, 29
Indianapolis Ledger 27
integration, racial 4, 6, 27, 90, 118, 121–2, 139–41, 146–7, 155–6, 159, 165, 179, 184, 186
interracial games 22, 39, 65, 184
Interurban League 9–10
Iowa Heritage Illustrated 8
Irvin, Monte 96, 159–60, 162–3, 179, 186

Jackson, Jess "Cannonball" 20
Jackson, Robert R. 98, 100
Jacksonville Red Caps 98, 122, 200, 202
James, Bill 6
Jamestown, North Dakota 85, 92
Japan 13, 18, 44, 60
Japanese baseball players 14, 18, 22, 187
Jazz District (Kansas City) 27, 103, 188
Jenkins, Harry 173–4, 176
Jethroe, Sam 147

Jim Crow laws 19, 24, 68, 92, 108, 123, 126, 131–2, 140, 161
Johnson, Arnold 180
Johnson, Ban 77
Johnson, Byron "Mex" 5, 100, 199–201
Johnson, Clifford "Connie" 5, 121, 125, 134, 158, 174–5, 182, 201–2, 204–5
Johnson, George 48, 51
Johnson, James Weldon 102
Johnson, John L. 155, 157–8, 166, 175
Johnson, Judy 48, 502, 186
Johnson, Oscar "Heavy" 29, 38, 39, *46*, 48, 51–3, 188, 191, 193–4
Johnson, Roy "Bubba" 31–2, 191–3
Johnson, Walter 17, 140
Johnston, Wade 61, 193–5
Joseph, Walter "Newt" 45, *46*, 48, 50–2, 59, 73, *89*, 111, 193–8
jumping contracts 25, 45, 47–8, 64, 94, 99, 107–9, 112–3, 121, 137

Kansas City Athletics 116, 181
Kansas City Blues 19, 29, 33, 35, 38–40, 44, 55, 75, 86, 94, 101, 104, 120, 122, 125–6, 134, 138, 165, 174–5, 180
Kansas City Call 3, 6, 7, 22, 28, 31, 32, 40, 43–4, 49, 50, 53, 61, 64, 65, 66, 69, 71, 73–4, 77–9, 81, 86, 88–9, 91–2, 94–5, 100, 108, 118–20, 122, 125–6, *130*, 13–32, 134, 141, 143–4, 147, 149–50, 154, 157–8, *160*, *162*, *164*, 165, 172, 175, 179, 181–4
Kansas City Giants 24
Kansas City Journal 33, 51
Kansas City Monarchs *see* Monarchs, Kansas City
The Kansas City Monarchs Baseball and Entertainment Company 35
Kansas City Royals 53
Kansas City Star 39, 73–5, 129–31, 174, 177, 182, 184
Kansas State Historical Society 3, *85*, *89*
Kaysees 33, 39, 58, 86, 88, 90–1, 94, 121, 125, 132, 135, 174
Kelly, W.A. 27
Kenyon, Harry 60, 196
Keyser, E. Lee 40, 69–71, 87
Kiner, Ralph 146, 162
King, Martin Luther, Jr. 156–7
Kling, Johnny 40
Knox, Elwood C. 27
Knox College 18
knuckleball 50, 103, 112
Kranson, Floyd 94, 96, 103, 199–201
Ku Klux Klan 22, 95, 184, 209*n*30
Kuhn, Bowie 186

Lacy, Sam 136, 139–40, 142, 152, 155, 218*n*6
Ladies Day 5, 57, 58, 97, 100, 102
Lafferty, Kathy A. 2–3

Index

LaMarque, Jim "Lefty" 125, *145*, 176, 202–5
Lanctot, Neil 2
Landis, Kenesaw Mountain 39, 47, 77, 105, 126, 141
Lane, Alto 80, 198
Lazzeri, Tony 65
Leavenworth, Kansas Federal Penitentiary 37, 50
Lee, Scrip 48, 50–2, 74
Leland Giants 24–5
Leonard, Buck 77, 128, 152, 163, 186
Lester, Larry 2, 3, 5, 77, 187, 191
Lewis, Cary B. 27
lighting system, portable 4, 5, 11, 12, 68–9, *70*, 71, *72*, *76*, 77, 82–3, 101, 114, 184
Lincoln Giants 40, 53
Livingston, Larry "Goo Goo" 61, 65, 75, 196-7
Lloyd, John Henry "Pop" 186, 188, 192
Locke, Eddie 176, 203–4
Los Angeles Stars/White Sox 65
Louis, Joe 121, 159
lynchings 27, 64, 68, 120, 143, 160, 164

Mack, Connie 20
Mackey, Biz 48, 50–2, 159, 188
MacPhail, Larry 142, 154
MacPhail, Lee 172, 175, 178
Madison, Bob 94, 199
Malarcher, Dave 36, 58
Manley, Abe 6, 108–9, 159, 166
Manley, Effa 6, 108–9, 146, 159, 166, 175, 188
Markham, John 74, 103, 197, 200–1
Marshall, Charles 27–28
Marshall, Jack 45, 193–4
Martin, J.B. 88, 121–2, 134–5, 152–54, 165, 179–80
Matchett, Jack 125, 128–9, 141, *145*, 201–4
Mathewson, Christy 2, 15, 17–8, 77, 83, 125, 186
Matthews, John 27
Matthews, Wid 178
Mays, Carl 39, 41
Mays, Willie 167, 171, 174, 179, 183
Mayweather, Eldridge "Chili" 94, 99, 102–3, 199–200
McCall, Bill 45, *46*, 49, 194
McDaniels, Booker "Cannonball" 125, *145*, 158, 173, 201–5
McGraw, John 2, 17, 43, 77, 105
McHenry, Henry 80, 197–8, 200
McKibben, Sam 122, 125–6
McNair, Hurley 19, 21, 29, *30*, 41, 45, *46*, 48, 50–2, 63, 94, 126, 158, 188, 191–5, 198
Memphis Red Sox 44, 56, 60, 74, 87, 98, 102, 119, 121, 125, 144, 180, 195–7, 200–5
Méndez, José *14*, 15, *16*, 17–8, 20–1, 28–9, *30*, 32, 42, 45, *46*, 48–9, 51–2, 56–7, 59, 140, 145, 188, 191–5
Metcalfe, Henry 76
Methodism 12, 15, 146, 149

Meusel, Bob 39, 41
Mexico 6, 65, 68, 78, 80, 86, 89, 99, 108–9, 119, 137, 176
Meyers, John Tortes "Chief" 2, 51
Mikami, Goro "Jap Mikado"/"Jap Jacobs" *14*, 18
Miller, Dempsey 36, 195
Mills, Charlie 27
Milton, Henry "Streak" 94, 96, 99, 101, 103, 199–201
Milwaukee Bears 41, 44, 194
Ministers Days 6, 56, 120, 122
Mitchell, George 60, 63, 196
Mitchell, Jackie 87
Mobile Tigers 107
Monarchs Billiard Room 31
Monarchs, Kansas City: formation 29–32; name selection 32; sale 167; seasons: (1920) 29–34, 191–2; (1921) 34–5, 192; (1922) 35–40, 192–93; (1923) 40–3, 193–4; (1924) 44–54, 194; (1925) 54–6, 194–5; (1926) 56–60, 195; (1927) 60–6, 195–6; (1928) 61–64, 196; (1929) 64–67, 196–97; (1930) 68–77, 197; (1931) 77–78, 79–83, 197–8; (1932) 83–6, 198; (1933) 86–8, 198; (1934) 88, *89*, 90–4, 198–9; (1935) 94–6, 199; (1936) 96–7, 199; (1937) 98–103, 199–200; (1938) 103–5, 110–1, 200; (1939) 111–2, 200–1; (1940) 112, 119–20, 201; (1941) 112–3, 121–4, 201–2; (1942) 124–9, 202; (1943) 129–35, 202–3; (1944) 135–7; (1945) 137–8, 143–4, 149, 203–4; (1946) 114, 157–61, 204; (1947) 165–6 , 204–5; (1948) 114, 167–72, 205; (1949) 172–4; (1950) 174–5; (1951) 175; (1952) 175–6; (1953) 177–8; (1954) 178–80; (1955) 180; (1956) 181; (1957–60) 181
Monarchs traveling team 109–111, 114, 120, 123, 167, *168*, 169, 172, 178, 215n5
Montreal Royals 150, 155, 157, 164
Moody, Lee 143, *145*, 203–5
Moore, Walter "Dobie" 29, *30*, 32, 34, 37, 41, 45, *46*, 48, 50–3, 58–9, 145, 188, 191–5, 211n37
Morris, Harold "Yellowhorse" *46*, 48–9, 194, 199
Moses, Al 120, 129
Mothell, Carroll "Dink" 29–30, 45, *46*, 48, 52, 61, 73, 80, 84, *85*, 86, *89*, 94, 181, 191–8
Muehlebach, George 40
Muehlebach Field 40, 42, 44, 50–1, 55–6, 58, 63, 70, 74–5, 79, 80, 85–7, 95, 97, 99–101
Murakami, Masanori 18
Musial, Stan 122, 162–3

Nashville Elite Giants 75, 87–8, 90, 107, 146, 197
National Association for the Advancement of Colored People (NAACP) 32, 56, 95, 102, 119, 155, 158, 165

National Baseball Congress 108, 176
Native American baseball players *see* Indian baseball players, American
Nebraska Indians 21
Negro American League (NAL) 79, 88, 98–99, 101–2, 104–5, 110 112, 119, 121–7, 129, 134–5, 137–8, 142, 151, 154, 157–8, 165–6, 172, 174–81, 187, 199–205
Negro Leagues 1–2, 4–7, 10, 18, 23–26, 29, 35–6, 44–9, 51–6, 59, 60–1, 69, 76–9, 81, 88–9, 92, 94, 98–9, 101–2, *104*, 105–6, 108–9, 112–3, 116, 118–21, 123–4, 127–30, 132, 134–7, 140–4, 146–4, 150–7, 159–161, 163, 165–6, 168, 169, 173–6, 178–9, 181, 184, 186–9, 191
Negro Leagues Baseball Museum (Kansas City, Missouri) 1, *104*
Negro National League (NNL) 1, *24*, 27–2, 30, 32, 34–6, 38–48, 50, 53–6, 58, 60–1, 63–66, 6, 74, 75, 77, 79–83, 86–88, 90–1, 97–100, 108, 110, 112–3, 121, 124, 126–7, 129, 136–7, 142, 152, 154, 157, 162, 165–6, 172, 187, 191–7
New Orleans Pelicans 107, 124
New York Black Yankees 108, 112, 118
New York Cubans 98, 126, 136, 141, 158, 172, 175
New York Giants 2, 19, 51, 53, 101, 159, 172–3, 176
New York Yankees 39–40, 79, 101, 104–5, 125, 134, 142, 154, 163, 169–74, 178, 213n96
Newark Eagles 98, 108–10, 112, 129, 141, 159–62, 165–6
Newcombe, Don 151, 179
newspapers, African American 3, 6, 24, 26, 27, 47, 57, 134–3, 141, 152, 157
night baseball games 4, 5–6, 12, 20, 68–78, 82, 87, 109, 130, 131, 157, 187
Noir-Tech Research, Inc. 3, *14*, *30*, *115*

Office of Defense Transportation (ODT) 129, *130*
Ogle, Floyd 73
Oklahoma City 92, 101, 132
Olympic Games (1936) 96, 11–12, 142
Omaha 8, 21, 38, 71, 80, 91, 95, 177, 179
Omaha Enterprise 26
Omaha Packers 91
Omaha Robin Hoods 97
O'Neil, John "Buck" 1–2, 5, 13, 24, 29, 40, 48, 53, 77, 80, 88, 96, 102–204, 110–1, 117, 123, 125–8, 132, 134, 152, 160, 162, 169, 171, 174, 178–9, 181, 183, 187–9, 200–5
Opening Day festivities 32, 37, 41–2, 56–8, 63, 100, 104, 119, 135, 174
Orange, Grady 63, 80, 195–7

Orioles, Baltimore *see* Baltimore Orioles
Owens, Jesse 6, 111-2, 121, 136
owners: Major League Baseball 1, 5, 25, 47, 77, 79, 139-42, 172, 184; Negro Leagues 2, 6, 25-29, 32, 34, 36, 40-1, 43, 47, 53-54, 56, 60-1, 71, 75, 86, 88, 98-100, 102-3, 108, 112-3, 119, 121, 124, 129, 132, 135-7, 141-2, 146, 154-5, 157, 165-66, 172, 180, 189

Pacific Coast League 77, 173, 175
Paige, Lahoma 113, 116
Paige, Leroy "Satchel" 1, 13-14, 33, 77, 88, 90-2, 95-96, 99, **104**, 106-9, **110**, 111-4, **115**, 116-29, 132, 134-3, 140-1, 144, 145, 147, 152, **153**, 158-60, 162-3, 165, 167-68, 180-4, 186-8, 199-205
Paige All-Stars, Satchel *see* All-Stars, Satchel Paige
Paseo 26-27, 32, 36, 131, 159, 189
Patterson, Andrew "Pat" 96-7, 199, 201
Peanuts Davis/Nyassas 124
Penn, Alberta Gilmore 31, 37, 183-4
pepper games 81, 110, 123
Peterson, Robert 2, 77, 139
Petroskey, Dale **188**
Philadelphia Athletics 20, 92, 180
Philadelphia Pythinas 23
Philadelphia Royal Giants 65
Philadelphia Stars 98, 112-13, 129, 141, 143, 172
Philadelphia Tribune 108, 114
Pirrone, Joe 65-66
Pittsburgh Courier 4, 6, 40, 47, 56, 113, 123, 140, 152, 172
Pittsburgh Keystones 35, 193
Pittsburgh Pirates 25, 80, 87, 140-1
Polk, H.H. 9
Pollack, Syd 82, 86, 123, 129, 132, 168-9, 176, 179
Pollock, Alan 123-4
Polo Grounds 79, 108, 158, 159, 165
Pompez, Alejandro "Alex" 61, 124, 188
Ponca City, Oklahoma 74
Pond, Diane 2, 4, 111, 182-83, 187
portable grandstands 11, 14, 22
portable lighting system *see* lighting system, portable
Portuando, Bartolo **20**, 191-3
Posey, Cum 6, 86, 119, 121, 123, 129, 137, 154, 175, 188
Posnanski, Joe 96
Powell, Jake 104-5
Powell, "Wee Willie" 54
prejudice, racial 5, 6, 8, 23, 31, 37, 39, 97, 118, 134, 140, 144-4, 149, 154, 184, 189
pride, racial 24, 43, 79, 88, 102
profit 11-12, 38, 34, 40-1, 59, 87, 92, 119, 127, 134-6, 154-55, 157, 167-8, 175-76, 182
Pullman Railroad Cars 11, 12, 14, 19, 22, 57, 59

Purnell, Benjamin Franklin 81-2
Purnell, Mary 81-2

Quinn, Jack 39

race relations 38-40, 43, 77, 8-81, 97, 104-5, 122, 125-6, 139-40, 158, 169, 176
Radcliffe, Alex 136
Radcliffe, Ted "Double Duty" 36, 79, 95, 137, 204
Rasberry, Ted 178, 181
Ray, Otto "Jaybird" 29, **30**, 34, 192-3
Reeves, Ben 11, 12
Renfroe, Othello "Chico" 124, 137, **145**, 162, 204-5
reserve clause 26, 34, 112, 151
revenue sharing 128
Ribowsky, Mark 79
Rickey, Branch 4, 10, 23, 139, 142, 146-7, **148**, 156, 163-6, 172, 180, 184
riots 25, 33, 66, 126, 139
Robeson, Paul 142
Robinson, Frank 187
Robinson, Frazier "Slow" 113, 120, 128, 159, 201-2
Robinson, Jackie 1, 4, 6, 7, 10, 23, 36, 58, 77, 104, 118, 137, 139, 141-7, **148**, 149-52, **153**, 154-9, 161, 163-5, 167, 169, 171-2, 174, 176, 178, 179, 183, 186-8, 203
Robinson, Mack 142
Robinson, Mallie 142
Robinson, Rachel Isum 118, 142, 144, 146-7, 149, 155, 165
Rodríguez, Vicente "José" **30**
Rogan, Charles Wilber "Bullet Joe" 21, 29, **30**, 31-2, **33**, 34, 39, 41-3, 45, **46**, 48-52, 55, 57, **58**, 59, 65, 80, 83, 86-7, **89**, 99-101, 103, 120, 140, 145, 181, 186, 187, 188, 191-201
Roosevelt, Franklin D. 120, 143
Roussey, Ken 2
rowdyism at games 38, 126, 146
Rowe, "Schoolboy" 95
Rules for Living ("How to Stay Young"), Satchel Paige's 117
Ruppert, Jacob 40, 79, 104
Ruppert Stadium 104, 119, 122, 126, 129, 132, 137-8, 143, 158-9, 169, 174, 180
Russell, Branch 36, 193
Ruth, Babe 39, 41, 51, 65, 79-80, 85, 87, 186
Ryan, Red 48, 50

St. Clair, Harry 34
St. Louis Browns 110, 116, 125, 132, 159, 166, 172
St. Louis Cardinals 36, 82, 87, 92-93, 107, 129, 140, 146, 154, 163-5, 171, 175, 179
St. Louis Cubans 65
St. Louis Giants 27, 35-6, 38
St. Louis Stars 37, 42-3, 45, 55, 58, 63, 74, 98, 100, 112, 122, 193-97, 200-202

salaries 5, 26, 28-29, 36, 39, 43, 47, 56, 60-1, 64, 81, 84, 88, 94, 96, 99, 107, 116-7, 119-20, 128, 131, 142, 146, 149, 167, 174, 220n39
San Francisco Giants 18, 175
Santop, Lewis 48, 50-52, 188
Saperstein, Abe 78-79, 98, 103, 110, 114-7, 124-5, 135, 137, 157, 184, 188, 216n5
Saunders, Bob 57, 195
Sayama, Kazuo 18
Schang, Wallie 39
Schoolcraft, Cindy 3
Schorling, John M. 54
Schorling Park 42, 51-2, 58
Scott, Elisha 27-28
Scott, John **145**
Scottsboro Boys 118
segregation, racial 1, 24, 27, 40, 92, 105, 118, 126, 139, 142, 155
Selig, Bud **188**
semi-pro teams 8-12, 22, 24, 28-32, 65, 69, 78-79, 92, 95-7, 102, 107-8, 111, 119, 121, 137, 140-2, 169, 181
Serrell, William "Bonnie" 125-6, 136-37, 175, 202-3
shadow ball 110-1, 123
Sherbert, Nancy 3
Shibe Park 128, 132
Shreveport, Louisiana 64, 94, 99, 102, 104, 135
Simms, Bill 103, 125, 194, 199-202
Sioux Indians 108
slavery 112, 117
Smaulding, Owen "Buzz" 60, 196
Smith, Art 19
Smith, Earl 15
Smith, Ford 173
Smith, Hilton 92, 95-96, 99-101, 103, 108, 113, 121-22, 125-6, 142, 144, **145**, 146, 151-2, 158, 162, 165, 169, 181, 184, 187-8, 199-205
Smith, Dr. Howard 28, 32
Smith, Wendell 4, 123, 134-6, 139, 140-41, 147-8, 155, 178
Souell, Herb "Baldy" 125, **145**, 201-5
Southern League 60, 80, 87, 89, 107, 137
Speaker, Tris 40-1, 167
Spencer Research Library (University of Kansas) 2, 62, 70, 72, 76, 82-4, 93, 130, 170, 177
spitball 48-9, 56, 76, 94
Spivey, Donald 112, 117
Sporting News 23, 69, 152, 163
Sportsman Park 74, 79, 82, 121-2, 166
sportswriters 7, 8, 27, 45, 47, 49, 57, 66, 88, 105, 124-6, 136, 139, 141, 157, 166, 180
spring training 20, 41, 60, 63, 64, 73, 83, 94, 99, 102, 104, 118, 124, 130-1, 142-4, 155, 158, 167, 171, 179, 189
Starks, Charles A. 39, 43

Index

State Historical Society of Missouri 2, 3
Stearnes, Norman "Turkey" 86, **89**, 90, 103, 186-8, 197-98, 200-1
Stengel, Charles Dillon "Casey" 25, 29, 33, 140
Stephens, Helen 136
Stewart, Donna 3
Stone, Marcenia "Toni" 177-9
Street Hotel 31, 169
Strong, Nat 40-1, 79
Strong, Ted 101, 103, 122, 125, 128, 132, **133**, 134, 160-1, 199-203, 204
Sukeforth, Clyde 148
Suttle, "Mules" 186, 188
Sweatt, George **46**, 48, 50-1, 192-5
Sweeney, Robert 32, 56

Taborn, Earl **173**, 204-5
Tatum, Goose 83, 124
Taylor, Ben 188
Taylor, C.I. 21, 27-8
Taylor, Leroy "Ben"/"Popsicle" 61-2, 84, 96, 196-9
Taylor, Olan "Jelly" 181
Tennessee Rats 13, 19, 63
Texas-Oklahoma-Louisiana (T.O.L.) League 31, 64-5
Thomas, Charley 147, 219*n*46
Thomas, Cliff "The Best of the East" 48, 50, 52
Thomas, Walter **145**
Thompson, Fresco 172
Thompson, Hank 132, 134, 159, 162, 166, 198, 202, 204-5
Thorpe, Jim 86, 93, 148
Thurman, Bob 173-4
Toledo Blue Stockings 23
Toledo Crawfords 111, 201
Toledo Tigers 41, 44, 194
Topeka Giants 29
Torriente, Cristóbal 19, 21, 34, 49, 57, **59**, 60, 188, 195
travel conditions 8, 19, 31-2, 41, 57, 66, 78, 81, 92, 94, 97, 121, 123, 127, 129-32, 134, 139, 144, 246, 158, 163, 189
traveling teams 6, 18, 27, 35-6, 39, 68, 77, 79-97, 102, 109-11, 114, 119-21, 167-9, 172, 178-9
Trouppe, Quincy 84, 92, 94-6, 108, 162, 198-9
Truman, Harry 63, 92, 120, 129, 143, **160**
Tut, King 123-4
Twenty-fifth (25th) Infantry Baseball Team 21, 32, 57, 63, 75
Tye, Larry 113, 117
Tygiel, Jules 140
Tyler, William "Steel Arm" 60, 196
Tyree, Rube 29

umpires 25, 28, 35, 37-38, 41-2, 45, 53, 60, 64, 94, 101, 159
United States Baseball League (USL) 142
University of California at Los Angeles (U.C.L.A.) 142-4
University of Missouri (Columbia) 2, 119

Vancouver, British Columbia 88-9, 163, 176
Vaughn, Janet Bruce *see* Bruce, Janet
Veeck, Bill 5, 114-7, 166-7
Vincent, Fay 161, 163, 187

Waco Cardinals 74
Waddell, Rube 24
Walker, Admiral "Deacon" 60, 196
Walker, Moses Fleetwood 23
Walker, Welday 23
Waner, Lloyd 80, 86
Waner, Paul 80, 86, 167
Warfield, Frank 48, 50-2, 192
Warneke, Lou 101
Washington, Edgar "Blue" 29, 191
Washington Senators 53, 85, 97, 132, 140, 213*n*96
Weiss, George 154
Welch, Winfield 102
Wells, Willie 84, 86, **89**, 186-8, 198
Western League 69, 87, 91, 97
Westminster College (Fulton, Missouri) 3
Wheat, Zack 25
White, Maury 18
White, Sol 23-4, 34
White Sox, Chicago *see* Chicago White Sox
Wichita, Kansas 63, 65-6, 85, 87, 91-2, 95, 101, 108, 137
Wichita Henry Clothiers 63, 65
Wickstrom, Harriett Baird 31
Wickstrom, M.L. 182
Wiley College 61, 63, 94, 96, 100, 118
"Wilkerson," J.L. 7, 31, 35, 41, 63, 78, 89, 108, 127, 137, 166
Wilkins, Wesley 19
Wilkinson, Bessie 2, 12, 19, 71, 113, 131, 183-4
Wilkinson, J.J. 7, 8
Wilkinson, J.L. (Leslie): attitudes of family toward 5, 182-3, 187-9; attitudes of historians toward 6; attitdues of owners toward 6; baseball manager 9-10; baseball player 8-**9**, 12, 19, 96; birth 7; businessman 5, 29, 35, 74-5, 96, 111, 114, 135; confusion about name 7; death 183-4; early life 7-8; entrepreneur 10, 12, 20, 68, 161; "Father of Night Baseball" 74, 77; Hall of Fame Induction (2006) 4, 7, 19, 59, 99, 182, 187-9; innovator 1, 5, 11, 22, 68-97, 175, 184, 187; integration of baseball, role in 4, 6, 139; Monarchs owner 6, 4-7, 20, 27, 29, 31-2, 35-7, 41, 44, **46**, 49, 53-4, 58, 60-1, 63-4, 66, 69, 71, 74-5, 77, 80, 82, **85**, 86, 89-90, 92, **93**, 96-8, 101-3, 106, 108-14, 119-20, 122, 124, **130**, 131-2, 137, 143, 145-46, 149-52, 156-8, 165-7, 172, 181, **182**, 184-5, 187, 189, 207*n*13, 216*n*11; Negro Leagues Museum exhibit 1; nicknames 7; owner of ladies baseball club, 10-13, 49,

80; promoter 5, 10-11, 20, 22, 56-7, 63, 66, 80-81, 91-2, 100-2, 111-2, 114, 117, 120, 134, 136, 184; pseudonym 8; racial reformer 40, 44; relations with players 5, 11, 13, 15, 31-32, 36-7, 42, 61, 66, 78-81, 96, 103-4, 109-10, 113-16, 120, 127-8, 135, 137, 159, 161, 169, 182, 184; religion 6
Wilkinson, Lee 12, 73, 125
Wilkinson Myrta ("Mertie," "Myrtel") 7, 8
Wilkinson, Richard ("Dick") 2, 4, 5, 14, 19, 29, 31, 58, 71, 73, 75, 79, 92, 93, 109, 114-5, 131, 137, 144, 145, 149, 151, 165, 167-69, 182, **188**, 189
Williams, A.D. 27, 60-1, 64-66, 69, 77
Williams, Eddie **145**
Williams, H.M. 37
Williams, Jesse 120, 125, 132, 134, **145**, 158, 176, 181, 199-204
Williams, "Smoky Joe" 76, 186-7
Williams, Ted 117, 162, 186
Wilson, Jud 141, 188
Winnipeg, Manitoba 81, 86-7, 89, 95, 119, 124
winter baseball 24, 65-6, 111-2
winter meetings 35, 42, 54, 56, 64, 69, 77, 135, 136, 165
Winters, Nip "Eastern Assassin" 48-52
Winterset, Iowa 8
Womack, Ollie 47
women's teams 10-11, 187
World Series: Major Leagues 2, 39, 43, 53, 92-3, 101, 107, 162-64, 171; Negro Leagues 44-5, 61, 65, 119, 181, 187, 136; (1924) 1-2, 18, 44-45, **46**, 47-53, 194; (1925) 55-6, 132, 195; (1926) 54, 59, 195; (1927) 61, 196; (1942) 98, 124, 127-9, 202; (1943) 203; (1944) 203; (1945) 204; (1946) 159-61, 204; (1947) 165-66, 205 ; (1948) 172, 205
World War I 21, 37, 53, 123
World War II 6, 114-15, 118, 130-2, 134-44, 147, 164
wrestlers 11-12, 20, 178
Wright, Bill 188, 205
Wright, Johnny 155
Wrigley Field 79, 83, 125-6, 136, 178
Wyatt, David 27-8
Wylie, Ensloe **145**, **203-5**

Yankee Stadium 79, 113, 128, 143, 154, 163, 175, 179, 181
"Yankees, Black" 118
Yendez, Rollo 19
Y.M.C.A. 26-7, 34, 159
Young, Frank A. 38, 78, 81, 101-2, 105, 132, 136
Young, Maurice "Doolittle" 60-1, 196
Young, Thomas Jefferson "T.J." 57, 73, 84, **89**, 96, 195, 197-9, 201

www.ingramcontent.com/pod-product-compliance
Lightning Source LLC
Chambersburg PA
CBHW060259240426
43661CB00060B/2840